THE HISTORY

OF

The Knights Templars

BY CHARLES G. ADDISON

Skyhorse Publishing

The Red Cross Knights

"And on his brest a bloodie crosse he bore
The deare remembrance of his dying Lord
For whose sweete sake that glorious badge he bore
And dead (as living) ever him ador'd
Upon his shield the like was also scor'd
For sovereign hope which in his helpe he had;
Right faithful true he was in deed and word;
But of his cheer did seem to solemn sad
Yet nothing did he dread but ever was ydrad.
                                        Faerie Queen

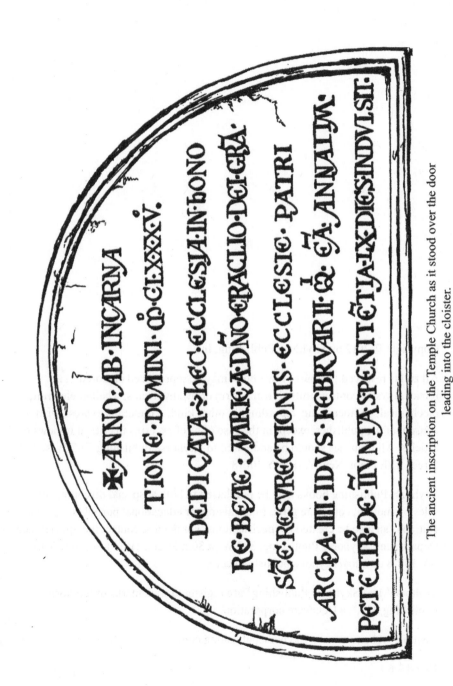

✠·ANNO·AB·INCARNA
TIONE·DOMINI·Ⓜ·CLXXXV·

DEDICATA·hec·ecclesia·in·bono
Re·Beae·Marie·A·DNO·ERACLIO·DEI·GRA·

Sce·Resurectionis·ecclesie·Patri

ARC·EA·IIII·IDVS·FEBRVARII·Ⓠ·EA·ANNALYM·

PETETIB·De·IVNTA·SPENITETIA·LX·DIES·INDVLSIT·

The ancient inscription on the Temple Church as it stood over the door
leading into the cloister.

Visit our website at www.skyhorsepublishing.com.

10 9 8 7 6

Print ISBN: 978-1-61608-846-0

Printed in the United States of America

TO THE

MASTERS OF THE BENCH OF THE HONOURABLE SOCIETIES

OF THE

Inner and Middle Temple,

THE RESTORERS
OF

The Ancient Church of the Knights Templars,

THIS WORK

IS

RESPECTFULLY DEDICATED

BY

THE AUTHOR.

PREFACE

The extraordinary and romantic career of the Knights Templars, their exploits and their misfortunes, render their history a subject of peculiar interest.

Born during the first fervour of the Crusades, they were flattered and aggrandized as long as their great military power and religious fanaticism could be made available for the support of the Eastern church and the retention of the Holy Land, but when the crescent had ultimately triumphed over the cross, and the religio-military enthusiasm of Christendom had died away, they encountered the basest ingratitude in return for the services they had rendered to the Christian faith, and were plundered, persecuted, and condemned to a cruel death, by those who ought in justice to have been their defenders and supporters. The memory of these holy warriors is embalmed in all our recollections of the wars of the cross; they were the bulwarks of the Latin kingdom of Jerusalem during the short period of its existence, and were the last band of Europe's host that contended for the possession of Palestine.

To the vows of the monk and the austere life of the convent, the Templars added the discipline of the camp, and the stern duties of the military life, joining

> "The fine vocation of the sword and lance,
> With the gross aims, and body-bending toil
> Of a poor brotherhood, who walk the
> earth Pitied."

The vulgar notion that the Templars were as wicked as they were fearless and brave, has not yet been entirely exploded; but it is hoped that the copious account of the proceedings against the Order in this country, given in the ninth and tenth chapters of the ensuing volume, will tend to dispel many unfounded prejudices still entertained against the fraternity, and excite emotions of admiration for their constancy and courage, and of pity for their unmerited and cruel fate.

Matthew Paris, who wrote at *St. Albans*, concerning events in *Palestine*, tells us that the emulation between the Templars and Hospitallers frequently broke out into open warfare to the great scandal and prejudice of Christendom, and that, in a pitched battle fought between them, the Templars were slain to a man. The solitary testimony of Matthew Paris, who was no friend to the two orders, is invalidated by the silence of contemporary historians, who wrote on the spot; and it is quite evident from the letters of the pope, addressed to the Hospitallers, the year after the date of the alleged battle, that such an occurrence never could have taken place.

The accounts, even of the best of the ancient writers, should not be adopted without examination, and a careful comparison with other sources of information. William of Tyre, for instance, tells us that *Nassr-ed-deen,* son of sultan *Abbas,* was taken prisoner by the Templars, and whilst in their hands became a convert to the Christian religion; that he had learned the rudiments of the Latin language, and earnestly sought to be baptized, but that the Templars were bribed with sixty thousand pieces of gold to surrender him to his enemies in Egypt, where certain death awaited him; and that they stood by to see him bound hand and foot with chains, and placed in an iron cage, to be conducted across the desert to Cairo. Now the Arabian historians of that period tell us that *Nassr-ed-deen* and his father murdered the caliph and threw his body into a well, and then fled with their retainers and treasure into Palestine; that the sister of the murdered caliph wrote immediately to the commandant at Gaza, which place was garrisoned by the Knights Templars, offering a handsome reward for the capture of the fugitives; that they were accordingly intercepted, and *Nassr-ed-deen was* sent to Cairo, where the female relations of the caliph caused his body to be cut into small pieces in the seraglio. The above act has constantly been made a matter of grave accusation against the Templars; but what a different complexion does the case assume on the testimony of the Arabian authorities!

It must be remembered that William archbishop of Tyre was hostile to the Order on account of its vast powers and privileges, and carried his complaints to a general council of the church at Rome. He is abandoned, in everything that he says to the prejudice of the fraternity, by James of Vitry, bishop of Acre, a learned and most talented prelate, who wrote in Palestine sub-sequently to William of Tyre, and has copied largely from the history of the latter. The bishop of Acre speaks of the Templars in the highest terms, and declares that they were universally loved by all men for their piety and humility. *"Nulli molesti erant!"* says he, *"sed ab omnibus propter humilitatem et religionem amabantur?"*

The celebrated orientalist *Von Hammer* has recently brought forward various extraordinary and unfounded charges, destitute of all authority, against the Templars; and *Wilcke*, who has written a German history of the Order, seems to have imbibed all the vulgar prejudices against the fraternity. I might have added to the interest of the ensuing work, by making the Templars horrible and atrocious villains; but I have endeavoured to write a fair and impartial account of the Order, not slavishly adopting everything I find detailed in ancient writers, but such matters only as I believe, after a careful examination of the best authorities, to be *true*.

It is a subject of congratulation to us that we possess, in the Temple Church at London, the most beautiful and perfect memorial of the Order of the Knights Templars now in existence. No one who has seen that building in its late dress of plaster and whitewash will recognize it when restored to its ancient magnificence. This venerable structure was one of the chief ecclesiastical edifices of the Knights Templars in Europe, and stood next in rank to the Temple at Jerusalem. As I have performed the pilgrimage to the Holy City, and wandered amid the courts of the ancient Temple of the Knights Templars on Mount Moriah, I could not but regard with more than ordinary interest the restoration by the societies of the Inner and the Middle Temple of their beautiful Temple Church.

The greatest zeal and energy have been displayed by them in that praiseworthy undertaking, and no expense has been spared to repair the ravages of time, and to bring back the structure to *what it was* in the time of the Templars.

In the summer I had the pleasure of accompanying one of the chief and most enthusiastic promoters of the restoration of the church (Mr. Burge, Q.C.) over the interesting fabric, and at his suggestion the present work was commenced. I am, afraid that it will hardly answer his expectations, and am sorry that the interesting task has not been undertaken by an abler hand.

Temple, Nov. 17, 1841.

P.S. Mr. Willement, who is preparing some exquisitely stained glass windows for the Temple Church, has just drawn my attention to the nineteenth volume of the "MÉMOIRES DE LA SOCIÉTÉ ROYALE DES ANTIQUAIRES DE FRANCE," published last year. It contains a most curious and interesting account of the church of Brelevennez, in the department des Cotes-du-Nord, supposed to have formerly belonged to the Order of the Temple, written by the Chevalier du FREMANVILLE. Amongst various curious devices, crosses, and symbols found upon the windows and the tombs of the church, is a copper medallion, which appears to have been suspended from the neck by a chain. This decoration consists of a small circle, within which are inscribed two equilateral triangles placed one upon the other, so as to form a six-pointed star. In the midst of the star is a second circle, containing within it the LAMB of the Order of the Temple holding the banner in its fore-paw, similar to what we see on the ancient seal of the Order delineated in the title-page of this work. Mr. Willement has informed me that he has received an offer from a gentleman in Brittany to send over casts of the decorations and devices lately discovered in that church. He has kindly referred the letter to me for consideration, but I have not thought it advisable to delay the publication of the present work for the purpose of procuring them.

Mr. Willement has also drawn my attention to a very distinct impression of the reverse of the seal of the Temple described in page 106, whereon I read very plainly the interesting motto, "TESTIS SVM AGNI."

CONTENTS

CHAPTER I.

CHAPTER II.

Regula Pauperum Commilitonum Christi et Cempli Salomonis.

CHAPTER III.

CHAPTER IV.

CHAPTER V.

CHAPTER VI.

CHAPTER VII.

CHAPTER VIII.

CHAPTER IX.

CHAPTER X.

CHAPTER XI.

THE TEMPLE CHURCH.

CHAPTER XII.

THE TEMPLE CHURCH.

CHAPTER XIII.

THE TEMPLE.

CHAPTER XIV.

THE TEMPLE.

ERRATA.

In note, page 6, *for* infinitus *read* infinitis.
29, *for* carissime, *read* carissime.
42, *for* Angli, *read* Anglia.
79, *for* promptia, *read* promptior.
79 *for* principos, *read* principes.
80 *for* Patriarcha, *read* patriarcham.

THE

KNIGHTS TEMPLARS

CHAPTER I.

> "Yet 'midst her towering fanes in ruin laid,
> The pilgrim saint his murmuring vespers paid;
> 'Twas his to mount the tufted rocks, and rove
> The chequer'd twilight of the olive-grove:
> 'Twas his to bend beneath the sacred gloom,
> And wear with many a kiss Messiah's tomb."

THE extraordinary and romantic institution of the Knights Templars, those military friars who so strangely blended the character of the monk with that of the soldier, took its origin in the following manner:—

On the miraculous discovery of the Holy sepulchre by the Empress Helena, the mother of Constantine, about 298 years after the death of Christ, and the consequent erection, by command of the first Christian emperor, of the magnificent church of the Resurrection, or, as it is now called, the Church of the Holy Sepulchre, over the sacred monument, the tide of pilgrimage set in towards Jerusalem, and went on increasing in strength as Christianity gradually spread throughout Europe. On the surrender of the Holy City to the victorious Arabians, (A.D. 637), the privileges and the security of the Christian population were provided for in the following guarantee, given under the hand and seal of the Caliph Omar to Sophronius the Patriarch.

"From OMAR EBNO 'L ALCHITAB to the inhabitants of ÆLIA."

"They shall be protected and secured both in their lives and fortunes, and their churches shall neither be pulled down nor made use of by any but themselves."*

Under the government of the Arabians, the pilgrimages continued steadily to increase; the old and the young, women and children, flocked in crowds to Jerusalem, and in the year 1064 the Holy Sepulchre was visited by an enthusiastic band of seven thousand pilgrims, headed by the Archbishop of Mentz and the Bishops of Utrecht, Bamberg, and Ratisbon.† The year following, however, Jerusalem was conquered by the wild Turcomans. Three thousand of the citizens were indiscriminately massacred, and the hereditary command over the Holy City and territory was confided to the Emir Ortok, the chief of a savage pastoral tribe.

Under the iron yoke of these fierce Northern strangers, the Christians were fearfully oppressed; they were driven from their churches; divine worship was ridiculed and interrupted; and the patriarch of the Holy City was dragged by the hair of his head over the sacred pavement of the church of the Resurrection, and cast into a dungeon, to extort a ransom from the sympathy of his flock. The pilgrims who, through innumerable perils, had reached the gates of the Holy City, were plundered, imprisoned, and frequently massacred; an *aureus*, or piece of gold, was exacted as the price of admission to the holy sepulchre, and many, unable to pay the tax, were driven by the swords of the Turcomans from the very threshold of the object of all their hopes, the bourne of their long pilgrimage, and were compelled to retrace their weary steps in sorrow and anguish to their distant homes.‡ The melancholy intelligence of the profanation of the holy places, and of the oppression and cruelty of the Turcomans, aroused the religious chivalry of Christendom; "a nerve was touched of exquisite feeling, and the sensation vibrated to the heart of Europe."

Then arose the wild enthusiasm of the crusades; men of all ranks, and even monks and priests, animated by the exhortations of the pope and the preachings of Peter the Hermit, flew to arms, and enthusiastically undertook "the pious and glorious enterprize" of rescuing the holy sepulchre of Christ from the foul abominations of the heathen.

When intelligence of the capture of Jerusalem by the Crusaders (A.D. 1099) had been conveyed to Europe, the zeal of pilgrimage blazed forth with increased fierceness; it had gathered intensity from the

---

* Elmacin, Hist. Saracen. Eutychius.

† Ingulphus, the secretary of William the Conqueror, one of the number, states that he sallied forth from Normandy with *thirty* companions, all stout and well-appointed horsemen, and that they returned *twenty* miserable palmers, with the staff in their hand and the wallet at their back—*Baronius ad ann.* 1064, No. 43, 56.

‡ *Will. Tyr.,* lib. i. cap. 10, ed. 1564.

interval of its suppression by the wild Turcomans, and promiscuous crowds of both sexes, old men and children, virgins and matrons, thinking the road then open and the journey practicable, successively pressed forwards towards the Holy City, with the passionate desire of contemplating the original monuments of the Redemption.* The infidels had indeed been driven out of Jerusalem, but not out of Palestine. The lofty mountains bordering the sea-coast were infested by bold and warlike bands of fugitive Mussulmen, who maintained themselves in various impregnable castles and strongholds, from whence they issued forth upon the highroads, cut off the communication between Jerusalem and the sea-ports, and revenged themselves for the loss of their habitations and property by the indiscriminate pillage of all travellers. The Bedouin horsemen, moreover, making rapid incursions from beyond the Jordan, frequently kept up a desultory and irregular warfare in the plains; and the pilgrims, consequently, whether they approached the Holy City by land or by sea, were alike exposed to almost daily hostility, to plunder, and to death.

To alleviate the dangers and distresses to which these pious enthusiasts were exposed, to guard the honour of the saintly virgins and matrons,† and to protect the gray hairs of the venerable palmer, nine noble knights formed a holy brotherhood in arms, and entered into a solemn compact to aid one another in clearing the highways of infidels, and of robbers, and in protecting the pilgrims through the passes and defiles of the mountains to the Holy City. Warmed with the religious and military fervour of the day, and animated by the sacredness of the cause to which they had devoted their swords, they called themselves the *Poor Fellow-soldiers of Jesus Christ*. They renounced the world and its pleasures, and in the holy church of the Resurrection, in the presence of the patriarch of Jerusalem, they embraced vows of perpetual chastity, obedience, and poverty, after the manner of monks.‡ Uniting in themselves the two most popular qualities of the age, devotion and valour, and exercising them in

---

* Omnibus mundi partibus divites et pauperes, juvenes et virgines, senes cum junioribus, loca sancta visitaturi Hierosolymam pergerent.—Jac. de Vitriaco. *Hist. Hierosol*. cap. Lxv

† "To kiss the holy monuments," says William of Tyre, "came sacred and chaste widows, forgetful of feminine fear, and the multiplicity of dangers that beset their path." —Lib. xviii. cap. 5.

‡ Quidam autem Deo amabiles et devoti milites, charitate ferventes, mundo renuntiantes, et Christi se servitio mancipantes in manu Patriarchæ Hierosolymitani professione et voto solemni sese astrinxerunt, ut a prædictis latronibus, et viris sanguinum, defenderent peregrinos, et stratas publicas custodirent, more canonicorum regularium in *obedientia et castitiate et sine proprio* militaturi summon regi. *Jac. De Vitr. Hist. Hierosol. apud Gesta Dei per Francos*, cap. lxv. p. 1083.—*Will. Tyr.* lib. xii. cap.7. There were three kinds of poverty. The first and strictest (*altissima*) admitted not of the possession of any description of property whatever. The second (*media*) forbade the possession of individual property, but sanctioned any amount of wealth when shared by a fraternity in common. The lowest was where a separate property in some few things was allowed, such as food and clothing, whilst everything else was shared in common. The second kind of poverty (*media*) was adopted by the Templars.

the most popular of all enterprises, the protection of the pilgrims and of the road to the holy sepulchre, they speedily acquired a vast reputation and a splendid renown.

At first, we are told, they had no church and no particular place of abode, but in the year of our Lord 1118, (nineteen years after the conquest of Jerusalem by the Crusaders), they had rendered such good and acceptable service to the Christians, that Baldwin the Second, king of Jerusalem, granted them a place of habitation within the sacred inclosure of the Temple on Mount Moriah, amid those holy and magnificent structures, partly erected by the Christian Emperor Justinian, and partly built by the Caliph Omar, which were then exhibited by the monks and priests of Jerusalem, whose restless zeal led them to practise on the credulity of the pilgrims, and to multiply relics and all objects likely to be sacred in their eyes, as the *Temple of Solomon*, whence the Poor Fellow-soldiers of Jesus Christ came thenceforth to be known by the name of "*the Knighthood of the Temple of Solomon.*"*

A few remarks in elucidation of the name Templars, or Knights of the Temple, may not be altogether unacceptable.

By the Mussulmen, the site of the great Jewish temple on Mount Moriah has always been regarded with peculiar veneration. Mahomet, in the first year of the publication of the Koran, directed his followers, when at prayer, to turn their faces towards it, and pilgrimages have constantly been made to the holy spot by devout Moslems. On the conquest of Jerusalem by the Arabians, it was the first care of the Caliph Omar to rebuild "the Temple of the Lord." Assisted by the principal chieftains of his army, the Commander of the Faithful undertook the pious office of clearing the ground with his own hands, and of tracing out the foundations of the magnificent mosque which now crowns with its dark and swelling dome the elevated summit of Mount Moriah.†

This great house of prayer, the most holy Mussulman Temple in the world after that of Mecca, is erected over the spot where "Solomon began to build the house of the Lord at Jerusalem on Mount Moriah, where the Lord appeared unto David his father, in the place that David had prepared in the threshing-floor of Ornan the Jebusite." It remains to this day in a state of perfect preservation, and is one of the finest

---

* *Pantaleon*, lib. iii. p. 82.

† *D'Herbelot Bib. Orient*. p. 270, 687, ed. 1697. William of Tyre, who lived at Jerusalem shortly after the conquest of the city by the Crusaders, tells us that the Caliph Omar required the Patriarch Sophronius to point out to him the site of the temple destroyed by Titus, which being done, the caliph immediately commenced the erection of a fresh temple thereon, "Quo postea infra modicum tempus juxta conceptum mentis suæ feliciter consummato, *quale hodie Hierosolymis esse dinoscitur*, multis et infinites ditavit possessionibus." —*Will. Tyr.* lib. i. cap. 2.

specimens of Saracenic architecture in existence. It is entered by four spacious doorways, each door facing one of the cardinal points; the *Bab el D'jannat*, or gate of the garden, on the north; the *Bab el Kebla*, or gate of prayer, on the south; the *Bab ib'n el Daoud*, or the gate of the son of David, on the east; and the *Bab el Garbi*, on the west. By the Arabian geographers it is called *Beit Allah*, the house of God, also *Beit Almokaddas,* or *Beit Almacdes*, the holy house. From it Jerusalem derives its Arabic name, *el Kods*, the holy, *el Schereef,* the noble, and *el Mobarek*, the blessed; while the governors of the city, instead of the customary high-sounding titles of sovereignty and dominion, take the simple title of *Hami*, or protectors.

On the conquest of Jerusalem by the crusaders, the crescent was torn down from the summit of this famous Mussulman Temple, and was replaced by an immense golden cross, and the edifice was then consecrated to the services of the Christian religion, but retained its simple appellation of "The Temple of the Lord." William, Archbishop of Tyre and Chancellor of the Kingdom of Jerusalem, gives an interesting account of this famous edifice as it existed in his time, during the Latin dominion. He speaks of the splendid mosaic work, of the Arabic characters setting forth the name of the founder, and the cost of the undertaking, and of the famous rock under the centre of the dome, which is to this day shown by the Moslems as the spot whereon the destroying angel stood, "with his drawn sword in his hand stretched out over Jerusalem."* This rock he informs us was left exposed and uncovered for the space of fifteen years after the conquest of the Holy City by the crusaders, but was, after that period, cased with a handsome altar of white marble, upon which the priests daily said mass.

To the south of this holy Mussulman temple, on the extreme edge of the summit of Mount Moriah, and resting against the modern walls of the town of Jerusalem, stands the venerable Christian church of the Virgin, erected by the Emperor Justinian, whose stupendous foundations, remaining to this day, fully justify the astonishing description given of the building by Procopius. That writer informs us that in order to get

---

* Erant porro in eodem Templi ædificio, intus et extra ex opere musaico, Arabici idiomatis literarum vetustissima monimenta, quibus et auctor et impensarum quantitas et quo tempore opus inceptum quodque consummatum fiierit evidenter declaratur. . . In hujus superioris areæ medio Templum ædificatum est, forma quidem *octogonum* et laterum totidem, tectum habens sphericum plumbo artificiose copertum. ... Intus vero in medio Templi, infra interiorem columnarum ordinem *rupes* est, &c.—*Will. Tyr.* lib. i. cap 2, lib. viii. cap. 3. In hoc loco, supra *rupem* quæ adhuc in eodem Templo consistit, dicitur stetisse et apparuisse David exterminator Angelus. ... Templum Dominicum in tanta veneratione habent Saraceni, ut nullus eorum ipsum audeat aliquibus sordibus maculare; sed a remotis et longinquis regionibus, a temporibus Salomonis usque ad tempora præsentia, veniunt adorare.—*Jac. de Vitr. Hist. Hicrosol.* cap. lxii. p 1080.

a level surface for the erection of the edifice, it was necessary, on the east and south sides of the hill, to raise up a wall of masonry from the valley below, and to construct a vast foundation, partly composed of solid stone and partly of arches and pillars. The stones were of such magnitude, that each block required to be transported in a truck drawn by forty of the emperor's strongest oxen; and to admit of the passage of these trucks it was necessary to widen the roads leading to Jerusalem. The forests of Lebanon yielded their choicest cedars for the timbers of the roof, and a quarry of variegated marble, seasonably discovered in the adjoining mountains, furnished the edifice with superb marble columns.* The interior of this interesting structure, which still remains at Jerusalem, after a lapse of more than thirteen centuries, in an excellent state of preservation, is adorned with six rows of columns, from whence spring arches supporting the cedar beams and timbers of the roof; and at the end of the building is a round tower, surmounted by a dome. The vast stones, the walls of masonry, and the subterranean colonnade raised to support the south-east angle of the platform whereon the church is erected, are truly wonderful, and may still be seen by penetrating through a small door, and descending several flights of steps at the south-east corner of the inclosure. Adjoining the sacred edifice, the emperor erected hospitals, or houses of refuge, for travellers, sick people, and mendicants of all nations; the foundations whereof, composed of handsome Roman masonry, are still visible on either side of the southern end of the building.

On the conquest of Jerusalem by the Moslems, this venerable church was converted into a mosque, and was called *D'jamé al Acsa*; it was enclosed, together with the great Mussulman Temple of the Lord erected by the Caliph Omar, within a large area by a high stone wall, which runs around the edge of the summit of Mount Moriah, and guards from the profane tread of the unbeliever the whole of that sacred ground whereon once stood the gorgeous temple of the wisest of kings.†

When the Holy City was taken by the crusaders, the *D'jamé* al Acsa, with the various buildings constructed around it, became the property of the kings of Jerusalem; and is denominated by William of Tyre "the palace," or "royal house to the south of the Temple of the Lord, vulgarly called *the Temple of Solomon*."‡ It was this edifice or temple on Mount

---

* *Procopius de œdificiis Justiniani*, lib. 5.

† Phocas believes the whole space around these buildings to be the area of the ancient temple. Ἐν τῷ ἀρχαίῳ δαπεδῳ τοῦ περιώνῦμου ναοῦ ἐκείνου τοῦΣολομῶντος Θεωρυμενος... Ἐξωσεν του δὲ τοῦ ναοῦ ἐστι περιαύλιον μεγα λιθόστωτον τὺ παλαιδν, ὡς οἶμαι, τού μεγαλου ναου δπεδον.—*Phocæ descript. Terr. Sanc.* cap. xiv. Colon. 1653.

‡ Quibus quoniam neque ecclesia erat, neque certum habebant domicilium, Rex in Palatio suo, quod secus Templum Domini ad *australem* habet partem, eis concessit habitaculum.—*Will. Tyr.* lib. xii. cap. 7. And in another place, speaking of the Temple of the Lord, he says, Ab *Austro* vero domum habet Regiam, quæ vulgari appellatione *Templum Salomonw* dicitur.—*Ib.* lib. viii. cap. 3.

Moriah which was appropriated to the use of the poor fellow-soldiers of Jesus Christ, as they had no *church* and no particular place of abode, and from it they derived their name of Knights Templars.*

James of Vitry, Bishop of Acre, who gives an interesting account of the holy places, thus speaks of the Temple of the Knights Templars. "There is, moreover, at Jerusalem another temple of immense spaciousness and extent, from which the brethren of the knighthood of the Temple derive their name of Templars, which is called the Temple of Solomon, perhaps to distinguish it from the one above described, which is specially called the Temple of the Lord."† He moreover informs us in his oriental history, that "in the Temple of the Lord there is an abbot and canons regular; and be it known that the one is the Temple of the *Lord*, and the other the Temple of the *Chivalry*. These are *clerks*, the others are *knights*."‡

The canons of the Temple of the Lord conceded to the poor fellow-soldiers of Jesus Christ the large court extending between that building and the Temple of Solomon; the king, the patriarch, and the prelates of Jerusalem, and the barons of the Latin kingdom, assigned them various gifts and revenues for their maintenance and support,§ and the Order being now settled in a regular place of abode, the knights soon began to entertain more extended views, and to seek a larger theatre for the exercise of their holy profession.

Their first aim and object had been, as before mentioned, simply to protect the poor pilgrims, on their journey backwards and forwards, from the sea-coast to Jerusalem;** but as the hostile tribes of Mussulmen, which everywhere surrounded the Latin kingdom, were gradually recovering from the stupifying terror into which they had been plunged by the successful and exterminating warfare of the first crusaders, and were assuming an aggressive and threatening attitude, it was determined that the holy warriors of the Temple should, in addition to the protection of pilgrims, make the defence of the Christian kingdom of Jerusalem, of the eastern church, and of all the holy places, a part of their particular profession.

The two most distinguished members of the fraternity were Hugh de

---

* Qui quoniam juxta Templum Domini, ut prædiximu in Palatio regio mansionem habent, fraters militiæ Templi dicuntur.—*Will. Tyr.* lib. xii. cap. 7.

† Est praterea Hierosolymis Templum aliud immense quantitatis et amplitudinis, *a quo fratres militiæ Templi, Templarii nominantur,* quod Templum Salomonis nuncupatur, forsitan ad distinctionem alterius quod specialiter Templum Domini appellatur.—*Jac. de Vitr.* cap. 62.

‡ In Templo Domini abbas est et canonici regulares, et sciendum est quod aliud est Templum Domini, aliud Templum militia. Isti *clerici,* illi *milites.*—*Hist. Orient. Jac de Vitr. apud Thesaur. Nov. Anecd. Mariene,* tom. iii. col. 277.

§ *Will. Tyr.* lib. xii. cap. 7.

** Prima autem eorum profession quodque eis a domino Patriarcha et reliquis episcopis in remissionem peccatorum injunctum est, ut vias et itiners, ad salutem peregrinorum contra latronum et incursantium insidias, pro viribus conservarent.—*Will. Tyr.* lib. xii. Cap. 7.

Payens and Geoffrey de St. Aldemar, or St. Omer, two valiant soldiers of the cross, who had fought with great credit and renown at the siege of Jerusalem. Hugh de Payens was chosen by the knights to be the superior of the new religious and military society, by the title of "The Master of the Temple and he has, consequently, generally been called the founder of the Order.

The name and reputation of the Knights *Templars* speedily spread throughout Europe, and various illustrious pilgrims from the far west aspired to become members of the holy fraternity. Among these was Fulk, Count of Anjou, who joined the society as a married brother, (A.D. 1120), and annually remitted the Order thirty pounds of silver. Baldwin, king of Jerusalem, foreseeing that great advantages would accrue to the Latin kingdom by the increase of the power and numbers of these holy warriors, exerted himself to extend the Order throughout all Christendom, so that he might, by means of so politic an institution, keep alive the holy enthusiasm of the west, and draw a constant succour from the bold and warlike races of Europe for the support of his Christian throne and kingdom.

St. Bernard, the holy abbot of Clairvaux, had been a great admirer of the Templars. He wrote a letter to the Count of Champagne, on his entering the Order, (A.D. 1123), praising the act as one of eminent merit in the sight of God; and it was determined to enlist the all-powerful influence of this great ecclesiastic in favour of the fraternity. "By a vow of poverty and penance, by closing his eyes against the visible world, by the refusal of all ecclesiastical dignities, the Abbot of Clairvaux became the oracle of Europe, and the founder of one hundred and sixty convents. Princes and pontiffs trembled at the freedom of his apostolical censures: France, England, and Milan, consulted and obeyed his judgment in a schism of the church: the debt was repaid by the gratitude of Innocent the Second; and his successor, Eugenius the Third, was the friend and disciple of the holy St. Bernard."*

To this learned and devout prelate two knights templars were despatched with the following letter:

"Baldwin, by the grace of the Lord JESUS CHRIST, King of Jerusalem, and Prince of Antioch, to the venerable Father Bernard, Abbot of Clairvaux, health and regard.

"The Brothers of the Temple, whom the Lord hath deigned to raise up, and whom by an especial Providence he preserves for the defence of this kingdom, desiring to obtain from the Holy See the confirmation of their institution, and a rule for their particular guidance, we have determined to send to you the two knights, Andrew and Gondemar, men as much distinguished by their military exploits as by the splendour of

---

* *Gibbon.*

their birth, to obtain from the Pope the approbation of their order, and to dispose his holiness to send succour and subsidies against the enemies of the faith, reunited in their design to destroy us, and to invade our Christianterritories.

"Well knowing the weight of your mediation with God and his vicar upon earth, as well as with the princes and powers of Europe, we have thought fit to confide to you these two important matters, whose successful issue cannot be otherwise than most agreeable to ourselves. The statutes we ask of you should be so ordered and arranged as to be reconcilable with the tumult of the camp and the profession of arms; they must, in fact, be of such a nature as to obtain favour and popularity with the Christian princes.

"Do you then so manage, that we may, through you, have the happiness of seeing this important affair brought to a successful issue, and address for us to heaven the incense of your prayers." *

Soon after the above letter had been despatched to St. Bernard, Hugh de Payens himself proceeded to Rome, accompanied by Geoffrey de St. Aldemar, and four other brothers of the Order, viz. Brother Payen de Montdidier, Brother Gorall, Brother Geoffrey Bisol, and Brother Archambauld de St. Amand. They were received with great honour and distinction by Pope Honorius, who warmly approved of the objects and designs of the holy fraternity. St. Bernard had, in the mean time, taken the affair greatly to heart; he negotiated with the Pope, the legate, and the bishops of France, and obtained the convocation of a great ecclesiastical council at Troyes, (A.D. 1128), which Hugh de Payens and his brethren were invited to attend. This council consisted of several archbishops, bishops, and abbots, among which last was St. Bernard himself. The rules to which the Templars had subjected themselves were there described by the master, and to the holy Abbot of Clairvaux was confided the task of revising and correcting these rules, and of framing a code of statutes fit and proper for the governance of the great religious and military fraternity of the Temple.

* *Reg. Constil et Privileg. Ordinis Cisterc.* p. 447.

CHAPTER II.

Regula Pauperum Commilitonum Christi et Cempli Salomonis.*

The most curious parts of the rule displayed—The confirmation of the rule by the Pope—The visit of Hugh de Payens, the Master of the Temple, to England—His cordial reception—The foundation of the Order in this country—Lands and money granted to the Templars—Their popularity in Europe—The rapid increase of their fraternity —St. Bernard takes up the pen in their behalf—He displays their valour and piety.

"Parmi les contradictions qui entrent dans le gouvernement de ce monde ce n'en est pas un petite que cette institution de *moines armées* qui font vœu de vivre là a fois en *anachoretes* et en *soldats.*"— *Voltaire sur les Maurs et l'Esprit des Nations.*

"THE RULE OF THE POOR FELLOW-SOLDIERS OF JESUS CHRIST AND OF THE TEMPLE OF SOLOMON," arranged by St. Bernard, and sanctioned by the Holy Fathers of the Council of Troyes, for the government and regulation of the monastic and military society of the Temple, is principally of a religious character, and of an austere and gloomy cast. It is divided into seventy-two heads or chapters, and is preceded by a short prologue, addressed "to all who disdain to follow after their own wills, and desire with purity of mind to fight for the most high and true king," exhorting them to put on the armour of obedience, and to associate themselves together with piety and humility for the defence of the holy catholic church; and to employ a pure diligence, and a steady perseverance in the exercise of their sacred profession, so that they might share in the happy destiny reserved for the holy warriors who had given up their lives for Christ.

---

* *Chron. Cisterc. Albertus Mirœus.* Brux. 1641. *Manricus ad ann.* 1128, cap. ii. *Act. Syn. Tree.* tom. x. edit. Labb.

The rule enjoins severe devotional exercises, self-mortification, fasting, and prayer, and a constant attendance at matins, vespers, and on all the services of the church, "that being refreshed and satisfied with heavenly food, instructed and stablished with heavenly precepts, after the consummation of the divine mysteries," none might be afraid of the *fight*, but be prepared for the *crown*. If unable to attend the regular service of God, the absent brother is for matins to say over thirteen pater-nosters, for every hour *seven*, and for vespers *nine*. When any templar draweth nigh unto death, the chaplains and clerk are to assemble and offer up a solemn mass for his soul; the surrounding brethren are to spend the night in prayer, and a hundred pater-nosters are to be repeated for the dead brother. "Moreover," say the holy Fathers, "we do strictly enjoin you, that with divine and most tender charity ye do daily bestow as much meat and drink as was given to that brother when alive, unto some poor man for forty days." The brethren are, on all occasions, to speak sparingly, and to wear a grave and serious deportment. They are to be constant in the exercise of charity and almsgiving, to have a watchful care over all sick brethren, and to support and sustain all old men. They are not to receive letters from their parents, relations, or friends, without the license of the master, and all gifts are immediately to be taken to the latter, or to the treasurer, to be disposed of as he may direct. They are, moreover, to receive no service or attendance from a woman, and are commanded, above all things, to shun *feminine kisses.*

There is much that is highly praiseworthy in this rule, and some extracts therefrom will be read with interest.

"VIII. In one common hall, or refectory, we will that you take meat together, where, if your wants cannot be made known by signs, ye are softly and privately to ask for what you want. If at any time the thing you require is not to be found, you must seek it with all gentleness, and with submission and reverence to the board, in remembrance of the words of the apostle: *Eat thy bread in silence,* and in emulation of the psalmist, who says, *I have set a watch upon my mouth;* that is, I have communed with myself that I may not offend, that is, with my tongue; that is, I have guarded my mouth, that I may not speak evil.

"IX. At dinner and at supper, let there be always some sacred reading. If we love the Lord, we ought anxiously to long for, and we ought to hear with most earnest attention, his wholesome words and precepts...

"X. Let a repast of flesh three times a week suffice you, excepting at Christmas, or Easter, or the feast of the Blessed Mary, or of All Saints. ... On Sunday we think it clearly fitting and expedient that two messes of flesh should be served up to the knights and the chaplains. But let the rest, to wit, the esquires and retainers, remain contented with one, and be thankful therefor.

"XI. Two and two ought in general to eat together, that one may have an eye upon another...

"XII. On the second and fourth days of the week, and upon Saturday, we think two or three dishes of pulse, or other vegetables, will be sufficient for all of you, and so we enjoin it to be observed; and whosoever cannot eat of the one may feed upon the other.

"XIII. But on the sixth day (Friday) we recommend the Lenten food, in reverence of the Passion, to all of you, excepting such as be sick; and from the feast of All Saints until Easter, it must be eaten but once a day, unless it happen to be Christmas-day, or the feast of Saint Mary, or of the Apostles, when they may eat thereof twice; and so at other times, unless a general fast should take place.

"XIV. After dinner and supper, we peremptorily command thanks to be given to Christ, the great Provider of all things, with a humble heart, as it becomes you, in the church, if it be near at hand, and if it be not, in the place where food has been eaten. The fragments (the whole loaves being reserved) should be given with brotherly charity to the domestics, or to poor people. And so we order it.

"XV. Although the reward of poverty, which is the kingdom of heaven, be doubtless due unto the poor, yet we command you to give daily unto the almoner the tenth of your bread for distribution, a thing which the Christian religion assuredly recommends as regards the poor.

"XVI. When the sun leaveth the eastern region, and descends into the west, at the ringing of the bell, or other customary signal, ye must all go to compline (evening prayer;) but we wish you beforehand to take a general repast. But this repast we leave to the regulation and judgment of the Master, that when he pleaseth you may have water, and when he commandeth you may receive it kindly tempered with wine: but this must not be done too plentifully, but sparingly, because we see even wise men fall away through wine.

"XVII. The compline being ended, you must go to bed. After the brothers have once departed from the hall, it must not be permitted any one to speak in public, except it be upon urgent necessity. But whatever is spoken must be said in an under tone by the knight to his esquire. Perchance, however, in the interval between prayers and sleep, it may behove you, from urgent necessity, no opportunity having occurred during the day, to speak on some military matter, or concerning the state of your house, with some portion of the brethren, or with the Master, or with him to whom the government of the house has been confided: this, then, we order to be done in conformity with that which hath been written: *In many words thou shalt not avoid sin*; and in another place, *Life and death are in the hands of the tongue.* In that discourse, therefore, we utterly prohibit scurrility and idle words moving unto laughter, and on going to bed, if any one amongst you hath uttered a foolish saying, we enjoin him, in all humility, and with purity of devotion, to repeat the Lord's Prayer.

"XVIII. We do not require the wearied soldiers to rise to matins, as it is plain the others must, but with the assent of the Master, or of him who hath been put in authority by the Master, they may take their rest; they must, nevertheless, sing thirteen appointed prayers, so that their minds be in unison with their voices, in accordance with that of the prophet: *Sing wisely unto the Lord,* and again, *I will sing unto thee in the sight of the angels.* This, however, should always be left to the judgment of the Master...

"XX. To all the professed knights, both in winter and summer, we give, if they can be procured, white garments, that those who have cast behind them a dark life may know that they are to commend themselves to their Creator by a pure and white life. For what is whiteness but perfect chastity, and chastity is the security of the soul and the health of the body. And unless every knight shall continue chaste, he shall not come to perpetual rest, nor see God, as the apostle Paul witnesseth: *Follow after peace with all men, and chastity, without which no man shall see God. ...*

"XXI. Let all the esquires and retainers be clothed in black garments; but if such cannot be found, let them have what can be procured in the province where they live, so that they be of one colour, and such as is of a meaner character, viz. brown.

"XXII. It is granted to none to wear white habits, or to have white mantles, excepting the above-named knights of Christ.

"XXIII. We have decreed in common council, that no brother shall wear skins or cloaks, or anything serving as a covering for the body in the winter, even the cassock made of skins, except they be the *skins of lambs or of rams...*

"XXV. If any brother wisheth as a matter of right, or from motives of pride, to have the fairest or best habit, for such presumption without doubt he merits the very worst. ...

"XXX. To each one of the knights let there be allotted three horses. The noted poverty of the House of God, and of the Temple of Solomon, does not at present permit an increase of the number, unless it be with the license of the Master...

"XXXI. For the same reason we grant unto each knight only one esquire; but if that esquire serve any knight gratis, and for charity, it is not lawful to chide him, nor to strike him for any fault.

"XXXII. We order you to purchase for all the knights desiring to serve Christ in purity of spirit, horses fit for their daily occasions, and whatever is necessary for the due discharge of their profession. And we judge it fitting and expedient to have the horses valued by either party equally, and let the price be kept in writing, that it may not be forgotten. And whatsoever shall be necessary for the knight, or his horses, or his esquire, adding the furniture requisite for the horses, let it be bestowed out of the same house, according to the ability of that house. If, in the meanwhile, by some mischance it should happen that the knight has lost his horses in the service, it is the duty of the Master and of the house to find him others; but, on this being done, the knight himself, through the love of God, should pay half the price, the remainder, if it so please him, he may receive from the community of the brethren.

"XXXIII. It is to be holden, that when anything shall have been enjoined by the Master, or by him to whom the Master hath given authority, there must be no hesitation, but the thing must be done without delay, as though it had been enjoined from heaven: as the truth itself says, *In the hearing of the ear he hath obeyed me.*

"XXXV. When in the field, after they shall have been sent to their quarters, no knight, or esquire, or servant, shall go to the quarters of other knights to see them, or to speak to them, without the Order of the superior before mentioned. We, moreover, in council, strictly command, that in this house, ordained of God, no man shall make war or make peace of his own free will, but shall wholly incline himself to the will of the Master, so that he may follow the saying of the Lord, *I came not to do mine own will, but the will of him that sent me.*

"XXXVII. We will not that gold or silver, which is the mark of private wealth, should ever be seen on your bridles, breastplates, or spurs, nor should it be permitted to any brother to buy such. If, indeed, such like furniture shall have been charitably bestowed upon you, the gold and silver must be so coloured, that its splendour and beauty may not impart to the wearer an appearance of arrogance beyond his fellows.

"XL. Bags and trunks, with locks and keys, are not granted, nor can any one have them without the license of the Master, or of him to whom the business of the house is intrusted after the Master. In this regulation, however, the procurators (preceptors) governing in the different provinces are not understood to be included, nor the Master himself.

"XLI. It is in nowise lawful for any of the brothers to receive letters from his parents, or from any man, or to send letters, without the license of the Master, or of the procurator. After the brother shall have had leave, they must be read in the presence of the Master, if it so pleaseth him. If, indeed, anything whatever shall have been directed to him from his parents, let him not presume to receive it until information has been first given to the Master. But in this regulation the Master and the procurators of the houses are not included.

"XLII. Since every idle word is known to beget sin, what can those who boast of their own faults say before the strict Judge? The prophet showeth wisely, that if we ought sometimes to be silent, and to refrain from good discourse for the sake of silence, how much the rather should we refrain from evil words, on account of the punishment of sin. We forbid therefore, and we resolutely condemn, all tales related by any brother, of the follies and irregularities of which he hath been guilty in the world, or in military matters, either with his brother or with any other man. It shall not be permitted him to speak with his brother of the irregularities of other men, nor of the delights of the flesh with miserable women; and if by chance he should hear another discoursing of such things, he shall make him silent, or with the swift foot of obedience he shall depart from him as soon as he is able, and shall lend not the ear of the heart to the vender of idle tales.

"XLIII. If any gift shall be made to a brother, let it be taken to the Master or the treasurer. If, indeed, his friend or his parent will consent to make the gift only on condition that he useth it himself, he must not receive it until permission hath been obtained from the Master. And whosoever shall have received a present, let it not grieve him if it be given to another. Yea, let him know assuredly, that if he be angry at it, he striveth against God.

"XLVI. We are all of opinion that none of you should dare to follow the sport of catching one bird with another: for it is not agreeable unto religion for you to be addicted unto worldly delights, but rather willingly to hear the precepts of the Lord, constantly to kneel down to prayer, and daily to confess your sins before God with sighs and tears. Let no brother, for the above especial reason, presume to go forth with a man following such diversions with a hawk, or with any other bird.

"XLVII. Forasmuch as it becometh all religion to behave decently and humbly without laughter, and to speak sparingly but sensibly, and not in a loud tone, we specially command and direct every professed brother that he venture not to shoot in the woods either with a long-bow or a cross-bow; and for the same reason, that he venture not to accompany another who shall do the like, except it be for the purpose of protecting him from the perfidious infidel; neither shall he dare to halloo, or to talk to a dog, nor shall he spur his horse with a desire of securing the game.

"LI. Under Divine Providence, as we do believe, this new kind of religion was introduced by you in the holy places, that is to say, the union of warfare with religion, so that religion, being armed, maketh her way by the sword, and smiteth the enemy without sin. Therefore we do rightly adjudge, since ye are called Knights of the Temple, that for your renowned merit, and especial gift of godliness, ye ought to have lands and men, and possess husbandmen and justly govern them, and the customary services ought to be specially rendered unto you.

"LII. Above all things, a most watchful care is to be bestowed upon sick brothers, and let their wants be attended to as though Christ himself was the sufferer, bearing in mind the blessed words of the Gospel, *I was sick, and ye visited me.* These are indeed carefully and patiently to be fostered, for by such is acquired a heavenly reward.

"LIII. We direct the attendants of those who are sick, with every attention, and with the most watchful care, diligently and faithfully to administer to them whatever is necessary for their several infirmities, according to the ability of the houses, for example, flesh and fowls and other things, until they are restored to health.

"LV. We permit you to have married brothers in this manner, if such should seek to participate in the benefit of your fraternity; let both the man and his wife grant, from and after their death, their respective portions of property, and whatever more they acquire in after life, to the unity of the common chapter; and, in the interim, let them exercise an honest life, and labour to do good to the brethren: but they are not permitted to appear in the white habit and white mantle. If the husband dies first, he must leave his portion of the patrimony to the brethren, and the wife shall have her maintenance out of the residue, and let her depart forthwith; for we consider it most improper that such women should remain in one and the same house with the brethren who have promised chastity unto God.

"LVI. It is moreover exceedingly dangerous to join sisters with you in your holy profession, for the ancient enemy hath drawn many away from the right path to paradise through the society of women: therefore, dear brothers, that the flower of righteousness may always flourish amongst you, let this custom from henceforth be utterly done away with.

"LVIII. If any knight out of the mass of perdition, or any secularman, wisheth to renounce the world and to choose your life and communion, he shall not be immediately received, but, according to the saying of Paul, *Prove the spirits, whether they be of God*; and if so, let him be admitted. Let the rule, therefore, be read in his presence; and if he shall have undertaken diligently to obey the precepts thereof, then, if it please the Master and the brothers to receive him, let the brothers be called together, and let him make known with sincerity of mind his desire and petition unto all. Then, indeed, the term of probation should altogether rest in the consideration and forethought of the Master, according to the honesty of life of the petitioner.

"LIX. We do not order all the brothers to be called, in every instance, to the council, but those only whom the Master shall know to be circumspect, and fit to give advice; when, however, important matters are to be treated of, such as the granting of the land of the fraternity, or when the thing debated immediately affects the Order itself, or when a brother is to be received, then it is fit that the whole society should be called together, if it please the Master, and the advice of the common chapter having been heard, the thing which the Master considereth the best and the most useful, that let him do. ...

"LXII. Although the rule of the holy fathers sanctions the dedication of children to a religious life, yet we will not suffer you to be burdened with them, but he who kindly desireth to give his own son or his kinsman to the military religion, let him bring him up until he arrives at an age when he can, with an armed hand, manfully root out the enemies of Christ from the Holy Land. Then, in accordance with our rule, let the father or the parents place him in the midst of the brothers, and lay open his petition to them all. For it is better not to vow in childhood, lest afterwards the grown man should foully fall away.

"LXIII. It behoves you to support, with pious consideration, all old men, according to their feebleness and weakness, and dutifully to honour them, and let them in nowise be restricted from the enjoyment of such things as may be necessary for the body; the authority of the rule, however, being preserved.

"LXIV. The brothers who are journeying through different provinces should observe the rule, so far as they are able, in their meat and drink, and let them attend to it in other matters, and live irreproachably, that they may get a good name out of doors. Let them not tarnish their religious purpose either by word or deed; let them afford to all with whom they may be associated, an example of wisdom, and a perseverance in all good works. Let him with whom they lodge be a man of the best repute, and, if it be possible, let not the house of the host on that night be without a light, lest the dark enemy (from whom God preserve us) should find some opportunity. But where they shall hear of knights not excommunicated meeting together, we order them to hasten thither, not considering so much their temporal profit as the eternal safety of their souls. ...

"LXVII. If any brother shall transgress in speaking, or fighting, or in any other light matter, let him voluntarily show his fault unto the Master by way of satisfaction. If there be no customary punishment for light faults, let there be a light penance; but if, he remaining silent, the fault should come to be known through the medium of another, he must be subjected to greater and more severe discipline and correction. If indeed the offence shall be grave, let him be withdrawn from the companionship of his fellows, let him not eat with them at the same table, but take his repast alone. The whole matter is left to the judgment and discretion of the Master, that his soul may be saved at the day of judgment.

"LXVIII. But, above all things, care must be taken that no brother, powerful or weak, strong or feeble, desirous of exalting himself, becoming proud by degrees, or defending his own fault, remain unchastened. If he showeth a disposition to amend, let a stricter system of correction be added: but if by godly admonition and earnest reasoning he will not be amended, but will go on more and more lifting himself up with pride, then let him be cast out of the holy flock in obedience to the apostle, *Take away evil from among you.* It is necessary that from the society of the Faithful Brothers the dying sheep be removed. But let the Master, who *ought to hold the staff and the rod in his hand*, that is to say, the staff that he may support the infirmities of the weak, and the rod that he may with the zeal of rectitude strike down the vices of delinquents; let him study, with the counsel of the patriarch and with spiritual circumspection, to act so that, as blessed Maximus saith, The sinner be not encouraged by easy lenity, nor the sinner hardened in his iniquity by immoderate severity. ...

"LXXI. Contentions, envyings, spite, murmurings, backbiting, slander, we command you, with godly admonition, to avoid, and do ye flee therefrom as from the plague. Let every one of you, therefore, dear brothers, study with a watchful mind that he do not secretly slander his brother, nor accuse him, but let him studiously ponder upon the saying of the apostle, *Be not thou an accuser or a whisperer among the people*. But when he knoweth clearly that his brother hath offended, let him gently and with brotherly kindness reprove him in private, according to the commandment of the Lord; and if he will not hear him, let him take to him another brother, and if he shall take no heed of both, let him be publicly reproved in the assembly before all. For they have indeed much blindness who take little pains to guard against spite, and thence become swallowed up in the ancient wickedness of the subtle adversary.

"LASTLY. We hold it dangerous to all religion to gaze too much on the countenance of women; and therefore no brother shall presume to kiss neither widow, nor virgin, nor mother, nor sister, nor aunt, nor any other woman. Let the knighthood of Christ shun *feminine kisses*, through which men have very often been drawn into danger, so that each, with a pure conscience and secure life, may be able to walk everlastingly in the sight of God."*

The above rule having been confirmed by a Papal bull, Hugh de Payens proceeded to France, and from thence he came to England, and the following account is given of his arrival, in the Saxon chronicle.

"This same year, (A.D. 1128), Hugh of the Temple came from Jerusalem to the king in Normandy, and the king received him with much honour, and gave him much treasure in gold and silver, and afterwards he sent him into England, and there he was well received by all good men, and all gave him treasure, and in Scotland also, and they sent in all a great sum in gold and silver by him to Jerusalem, and there went with him and after him so great a number as never before since the days of Pope Urban."† Grants of land, as well as of money, were at the same time made to Hugh de Payens and his brethren, some of which were shortly afterwards confirmed by King Stephen on his accession to the throne, (A.D. 1135). Among these is a grant of the manor of Bistelesham made to the Templars by Count Robert de Ferrara, and a grant of the church of

---

* Ego Joannes Michaelensis, Præsentis paginæ, jussu consilii ac venerabilis abbatis Clarævallensis, cui creditum ac debitum hoc fuit, humilis scriba esse, divinâ gratiâ merui.
—*Chron. Cisterc.* ut sup.

† See also Hoveden apud X script. page 479. Hen. Hunting. ib. page 384.

Langeforde in Bedfordshire made by Simon de Wahull, and Sibylla his wife, and Walter their son.

Hugh de Payens, before his departure, placed a Knight Templar at the head of the Order in this country, who was called the Prior of the Temple, and was the procurator and vicegerent of the Master. It was his duty to manage the estates granted to the fraternity, and to transmit the revenues to Jerusalem. He was also delegated with the power of admitting members into the Order, subject to the control and direction of the Master, and was to provide means of transport for such newly-admitted brethren to the far east, to enable them to fulfil the duties of their profession. As the houses of the Temple increased in number in England, sub-priors came to be appointed, and the superior of the Order in this country was then called the Grand Prior, and afterwards Master of the Temple.

Many illustrious knights of the best families in Europe aspired to the habit and the vows, but however exalted their rank, they were not received within the bosom of the fraternity until they had proved themselves by their conduct worthy of such a fellowship. Thus, when Hugh d'Amboise, who had harassed and oppressed the people of Marmontier by unjust exactions, and had refused to submit to the judicial decision of the Count of Anjou, desired to enter the Order, Hugh de Payens refused to admit him to the vows, until he had humbled himself, renounced his pretensions, and given perfect satisfaction to those whom he had injured.* The candidates, moreover, previous to their admission, were required to make reparation and satisfaction for all damage done by them at any time to churches, and to public or private property.

An astonishing enthusiasm was excited throughout Christendom in behalf of the Templars; princes and nobles, sovereigns and their subjects, vied with each other in heaping gifts and benefits upon them, and scarce a will of importance was made without an article in it in their favour. Many illustrious persons on their deathbeds took the vows, that they might be buried in the habit of the Order; and sovereigns, quitting the government of their kingdoms, enrolled themselves amongst the holy fraternity, and bequeathed even their dominions to the Master and the brethren of the Temple.

Thus, Raymond Berenger, Count of Barcelona and Provence, at a very advanced age, abdicating his throne, and shaking off the ensigns of royal authority, retired to the house of the Templars at Barcelona, and pronounced his vows (A.D. 1130) before brother Hugh de Rigauld, the Prior. His infirmities not allowing him to proceed in person to the chief house of the Order at Jerusalem, he sent vast sums of money thither, and immuring himself in a small cell in the Temple at Barcelona, he there remained in the constant exercise of the religious duties of his profession until the day of his death.* At the same period, the Emperor Lothaire

---

* *Annales Benedictini*, tom. vi. page 166.

bestowed on the Order a large portion of his patrimony of Supplinburg; and the year following, (A.D. 1131), Alphonso the First, king of Navarre and Arragon, also styled Emperor of Spain, one of the greatest warriors of the age, by his will declared the Knights of the Temple his heirs and successors in the crowns of Navarre and Arragon, and a few hours before his death he caused this will to be ratified and signed by most of the barons of both kingdoms. The validity of this document, however, was disputed, and the claims of the Templars were successfully resisted by the nobles of Navarre; but in Arragon they obtained, by way of compromise, lands, and castles, and considerable dependencies, a portion of the customs and duties levied throughout the kingdom, and of the contributions raised from the Moors.†

To increase the enthusiasm in favour of the Templars, and still further to swell their ranks with the best and bravest of the European chivalry, St. Bernard, at the request of Hugh de Payens,‡ took up his powerful pen in their behalf. In a famous discourse "In praise of the New Chivalry," the holy abbot sets forth, in eloquent and enthusiastic terms, the spiritual advantages and blessings enjoyed by the military friars of the Temple over all other warriors. He draws a curious picture of the relative situations and circumstances of the *secular* soldiery and the soldiery of *Christ*, and shows how different in the sight of God are the bloodshed and slaughter perpetrated by the one, from that committed by the other.

This extraordinary discourse is written with great spirit; it is addressed "To Hugh, Knight of Christ, and Master of the Knighthood of Christ," is divided into fourteen parts or chapters, and commences with a short prologue. It is curiously illustrative of the spirit of the times, and some of its most striking passages will be read with interest.

The holy abbot thus pursues his comparison between the soldier of the world and the soldier of Christ—the *secular* and the *religious* warrior.

"As often as thou who wagest a secular warfare marchest forth to battle, it is greatly to be feared lest when thou slayest thine enemy in the body, he should destroy thee in the spirit, or lest peradventure thou shouldst be at once slain by him both in body and soul. From the disposition of the heart, indeed, not by the event of the fight, is to be estimated either the jeopardy or the victory of the Christian. If, fighting with the desire of killing another, thou shouldest chance to get killed thyself, thou

---

* *Histoire de Languedoc*, lib. xvii. p. 407.

† *Hist, de l'eglise de Gandersheim. Mariana de rebus Hispanis, lib. x. cap. 15, 17, 18. Zurita anales de la corona de Aragon, tom.* i. lib. i. cap. 52. *Quarita, tom.* i lib. ii. cap. 4.

‡ Semel et secundo, et tertio, ni fallor, petiisti a me. Hugo carriaaime, ut tibi tuisque commilitonibus scriberem exhortationis sermonem, et adversus hostilem tyrannidem, quia lanceam non liceret, stilum vibrarem. *Exhortatio S. Bernardi ad Milites Templi, ed. Mabilom. Parisiis*, 1839, tom. i. col. 1253 to 1278.

diest a manslayer; if, on the other hand, thou prevailest, and through a desire of conquest or revenge killest a man, thou livest a manslayer. ... O unfortunate victory, when in overcoming thine adversary thou fallest into sin, and anger or pride having the mastery over thee, in vain thou gloriest over the vanquished ...

"What, therefore, is the fruit of this secular, I will not say '*militia*,' but '*malitia*,' if the slayer committeth a deadly sin, and the slain perisheth eternally? Verily, to use the words of the apostle, he that ploweth should plow in hope, and he that thresheth should be partaker of his hope. Whence, therefore, O soldiers, cometh this so stupendous error? What insufferable madness is this—to wage war with so great cost and labour, but with no pay except either death or crime? Ye cover your horses with silken trappings, and I know not how much fine cloth hangs pendent from your coats of mail. Ye paint your spears, shields, and saddles; your bridles and spurs are adorned on all sides with gold, and silver, and gems, and with all this pomp, with a shameful fury and a reckless insensibility, ye rush on to death. Are these military ensigns, or are they not rather the garnishments of women? Can it happen that the sharp-pointed sword of the enemy will respect gold, will it spare gems, will it be unable to penetrate the silken garment? Lastly, as ye yourselves have often experienced, three things are indispensably necessary to the success of the soldier; he must, for example, be bold, active, and circumspect; quick in running, prompt in striking; ye, however, to the disgust of the eye, nourish your hair after the manner of women, ye gather around your footsteps long and flowing vestures, ye bury up your delicate and tender hands in ample and wide-spreading sleeves. Among you indeed, nought provoketh war or awakeneth strife, but either an irrational impulse of anger, or an insane lust of glory, or the covetous desire of possessing another man's lands and possessions. In such causes it is neither safe to slay nor to be slain. ...

III. "But the soldiers of CHRIST indeed securely fight the battles of their Lord, in no wise fearing sin either from the slaughter of the enemy, or danger from their own death. When indeed death is to be given or received for Christ, it has nought of crime in it, but much of glory. ...

"And now for an example, or to the confusion of our soldiers fighting not manifestly for God but for the devil, we will briefly display the mode of life of the Knights of Christ, such as it is in the field and in the convent, by which means it will be made plainly manifest to what extent the soldiery of GOD and the soldiery of the WORLD differ from one another. ... The soldiers of Christ live together in common in an agreeable but frugal manner, without wives and without children; and that nothing may be wanting to evangelical perfection, they dwell together without property of any kind,* in one house, under one rule, careful to preserve the unity of the spirit in the bond of peace. You may say, that to the whole

multitude there is but one heart and one soul, as each one in no respect
followeth after his own will or desire, but is diligent to do the will of the
Master. They are never idle nor rambling abroad, but when they are
not in the field, that they may not eat their bread in idleness, they are
fitting and repairing their armour and their clothing, or employing
themselves in such occupations as the will of the Master requireth,
or their common necessities render expedient. Among them there is no
distinction of persons; respect is paid to the best and most virtuous, not
the most noble. They participate in each other's honour, they bear one
another's burthens, that they may fulfil the law of Christ. An insolent
expression, a useless undertaking, immoderate laughter, the least murmur or whispering, if found out, passeth not without severe rebuke.
They detest cards and dice, they shun the sports of the field, and take
no delight in that ludicrous catching of birds, (hawking), which men are
wont to indulge in. Jesters, and soothsayers, and storytellers, scurrilous
songs, shows and games, they contemptuously despise and abominate as
vanities and mad follies. They cut their hair, knowing that, according to
the apostle, it is not seemly in a man to have long hair. They are never
combed, seldom washed, but appear rather with rough neglected hair,
foul with dust, and with skins browned by the sun and their coats of mail.

"Moreover, on the approach of battle they fortify themselves with faith
within, and with steel without, and not with gold, so that, armed and not
adorned, they may strike terror into the enemy, rather than awaken his
lust of plunder. They strive earnestly to possess strong and swift horses,
but not garnished with ornaments or decked with trappings, thinking of
battle and of victory, and not of pomp and show, and studying to inspire
fear rather than admiration

"Such hath God chosen for his own, and hath collected together as his
ministers from the ends of the earth, from among the bravest of Israel,
who indeed vigilantly and faithfully guard the holy sepulchre, all armed
with the sword, and most learned in the art of war..."

"CONCERNING THE TEMPLE."

"There is indeed a Temple at Jerusalem in which they dwell together,
unequal, it is true, as a building, to that ancient and most famous one of
Solomon, but not inferior in glory. For truly, the entire magnificence of
that consisted in corrupt things, in gold and silver, in carved stone, and in
a variety of woods; but the whole beauty of this resteth in the adornment
of an agreeable conversation, in the godly devotion of its inmates, and
their beautifully-ordered mode of life. That was admired for its various
external beauties, this is venerated for its different virtues and sacred
actions, as becomes the sanctity of the house of God, who delighteth not

---

* i. e. Without any *separate* property.

so much in polished marbles as in well-ordered behaviour, and regardeth pure minds more than gilded walls. The face likewise of this Temple is adorned with arms, not with gems, and the wall, instead of the ancient golden chapiters, is covered around with pendent shields. Instead of the ancient candelabra, censers, and la vers, the house is on all sides furnished with bridles, saddles, and lances, all which plainly demonstrate that the soldiers burn with the same zeal for the house of God, as that which formerly animated their great leader, when, vehemently enraged, he entered into the Temple, and with that most sacred hand, armed not with steel, but with a scourge which he had made of small thongs, drove out the merchants, poured out the changers' money, and overthrew the tables of them that sold doves; most indignantly condemning the pollution of the house of prayer, by the making of it a place of merchandize."

"The devout army of Christ, therefore, earnestly incited by the example of its king, thinking indeed that the holy places are much more impiously and insufferably polluted by the infidels than when defiled by merchants, abide in the holy house with horses and with arms, so that from that, as well as all the other sacred places, all filthy and diabolical madness of infidelity being driven out, they may occupy themselves by day and by night in honourable and useful offices. They emulously honour the Temple of God with sedulous and sincere oblations, offering sacrifices therein with constant devotion, not indeed of the flesh of cattle after the manner of the ancients, but peaceful sacrifices, brotherly love, devout obedience, voluntary poverty."

"These things are done perpetually at Jerusalem, and the world is aroused, the islands hear, and the nations take heed from afar. . . ."

St. Bernard then congratulates Jerusalem on the advent of the soldiers of Christ, and declares that the Holy City will rejoice with a double joy in being rid of all her oppressors, the ungodly, the robbers, the blasphemers, murderers, perjurers, and adulterers; and in receiving her faithful defenders and sweet consolers, under the shadow of whose protection "Mount Zion shall rejoice, and the daughters of Judah sing for joy."

"Be joyful, O Jerusalem," says he, "in the words of the prophet Isaiah, "and know that the time of thy visitation hath arrived. Arise now, shake thyself from the dust, O virgin captive, daughter of Zion; arise, I say, and stand forth amongst the mighty, and see the pleasantness that cometh unto thee from thy God. Thou shalt no more be termed *forsaken*, neither shall thy land any more be termed *desolate*. ... Lift up thine eyes round about, and behold; all these gather themselves together, and come to thee. This is the assistance sent unto thee from on High. Now, now, indeed, through these is that ancient promise made to thee thoroughly to be performed. 'I will make thee an eternal joy, a glory from generation to generation.'

"HAIL, therefore, O holy city, hallowed by the tabernacle of the Most High! HAIL, city of the great King, wherein so many wonderful and welcome miracles have been perpetually displayed. HAIL, mistress of the nations, princess of provinces, possession of patriarchs, mother of the prophets and apostles, initiatress of the faith, glory of the Christian people, whom God hath on that account always from the beginning permitted to be visited with affliction, that thou mightest thus be the occasion of virtue as well as of salvation to brave men. HAIL, land of promise, which, formerly flowing only with milk and honey for thy possessors, now stretchest forth the food of life, and the means of salvation to the entire world. Most excellent and happy land, I say, which receiving the celestial grain from the recess of the paternal heart in that most fruitful bosom of thine, hast produced such rich harvests of martyrs from the heavenly seed, and whose fertile soil hast no less manifoldly engendered fruit a thirtieth, sixtieth, and a hundredfold in the remaining race of all the faithful throughout the entire world. Whence most agreeably satiated, and most abundantly crammed with the great store of thy pleasantness, those who have seen thee diffuse around them (*eructant*) in every place the remembrance of thy abundant sweetness, and tell of the magnificence of thy glory to the very end of the earth to those who have not seen thee, and relate the wonderful things that are done in thee."

"Glorious things are spoken concerning thee, CITY OF GOD!"

CHAPTER III.

Hugh de Payens returns to Palestine—His death—Robert de Craon made Master—Success of the Infidels—The second Crusade—The Templars assume the Red Cross—Their gallant actions and high discipline—Lands, manors, and churches granted them in England—Bernard de Tremelay made Master—He is slain by the Infidels—Bertrand de Blanquefort made Master—He is taken prisoner, and sent in chains to Aleppo—The Pope writes letters in praise of the Templars—Their religious and military enthusiasm—Their war banner called *Beauseant*—The rise of the rival religio-military order of the Hospital of St. John.

> "We heard the *tecbir*, so the Arabs call
> Their shouts of onset, when with loud appeal
> They challenge *heaven*, as if demanding conquest."

HUGH DE PAYENS.
A.D. 1129.

HUGH DE PAYENS, having now laid in Europe the foundations of the great monastic and military institution of the Temple, which was destined shortly to spread its ramifications to the remotest quarters of Christendom, returned to Palestine at the head of a valiant band of newly-elected Templars, drawn principally from England and France.

On their arrival at Jerusalem they were received with great distinction by the king, the clergy, and the barons of the Latin kingdom, a grand council was called together, at which Hugh de Payens assisted, and various warlike measures were undertaken for the extension and protection of the Christian territories.

ROBERT DE CRAON.
A.D. 1136.

Hugh de Payens died, however, shortly after his return, and was succeeded (A.D. 1136) by the Lord Robert, surnamed the Burgundian, (son-in-law of Anselm, Archbishop of Canterbury), who, after the death of his wife, had taken the vows and the habit of the Templars.* He was a valiant and skillful general;†

---

* *Will. Tyr.* lib. xiii. Cap. 26; *Anselmus,* lib. iii. epistolarum. Epist. 43, 63, 66, 67; *Duchesne in Hist. Burg.* lib. iv. cap. 37

† Miles eximius et in armis strenus, nobilis carne et morinus, dominus Robertus cognomine Burgundio Magister militiæ Templi. —*Will. Tyr.* lib. xv. cap. 6.

but the utmost exertions of himself and his military monks were found insufficient to sustain the tottering empire of the Latin Christians.

The fierce religious and military enthusiasm of the Mussulmen had been again aroused by the warlike Zinghis and his son Noureddin, two of the most famous chieftains of the age, who were regarded by the disciples of Mahomet as champions that could avenge the cause of the prophet, and recover to the civil and religious authority of the caliph the lost city of Jerusalem, and all the holy places so deeply venerated by the Moslems. The one was named *Emod-ed-deen*, "Pillar of religion;" and the other *Nour-ed-deen*, "Light of religion," vulgarly, Noureddin. The Templars were worsted by overpowering numbers in several battles; and in one of these the valiant Templar, Brother Odo de Montfaucon, was slain.* Emodeddeen took Tænza, Estarel, Hizam, Hesn-arruk, Hesn-Collis, &c. &c., and closed his victorious career by the capture of the important city of Edessa. Noureddin followed in the footsteps of the father: he obtained possession of the fortresses of Arlene, Mamoula, Basarfont, Kafarlatha; and overthrew with terrific slaughter the young Jocelyn de Courtenay, in a rash attempt to recover possession of his principality of Edessa.† The Latin kingdom of Jerusalem was shaken to its foundations, and the oriental clergy in trepidation and alarm sent urgent letters to the Pope for assistance. The holy pontiff accordingly commissioned St. Bernard to preach the second crusade.

The Lord Robert, Master of the Temple, was at this period Bark L. (A.D. 1146) succeeded by Everard des Barres, Prior of France, who convened a general chapter of the Order at Paris, which was attended by Pope Eugenius the Third, Louis the Seventh, king of France, and many prelates, princes, and nobles, from all parts of Christendom. The second crusade was there arranged, and the Templars, with the sanction of the Pope, assumed the blood-red cross, the symbol of martyrdom, as the distinguishing badge of the Order, which was appointed to be worn on their habits and mantles on the left side of the breast over the heart, whence they came afterwards to be known by the name of the *Red Friars* and the *Red Cross Knights*.‡

At this famous assembly various donations were made to the Templars, to enable them to provide more effectually for the defence of the Holy Land. Bernard Baliol, through love of God and for the good of his soul, granted them his estate of Wedelee, in Hertfordshire, which afterwards formed part of the preceptory of Temple Dynnesley. This grant is expressed to be made at the chapter held at Easter, in Paris, in the pres-

Marginal note: EVERARD DES BARRE A.D. 1146.

* Vir eximius frater militiæ Templi Otto de Monte Falconis, omnes de morte suâ mœrore et gemitu conficiens, occisus est.—*Will. Tyr.* lib. xv. cap. 6.

† *Abulfeda*, ad ann. Hegir. 534, 539. *Will. Tyr.* lib. xvi. cap. 4, 5, 7, 15, 16, who terras Zinghis, Sanguin. *Abulfaradge Chron. 'Syr.* p. 326, 328. *Will. Tyr.* lib. xvi. cap, 14.

‡ *Odo de Diogilo*, p. 33. *Will, Tyr.* lib. xii. cap. 7; *Jac. de Vitr.* cap. lxv.; *Paul. Æmil.* p. 254; Monast. Angl. vol. vii. p. 814.

ence of the Pope, the king of France, several archbishops, and one hundred and thirty Knights Templars clad in white mantles.* Shortly before
this, the Dukes of Brittany and Lorraine, and the Counts of Brabant and
Fourcalquier, had given to the Order various lands and estates; and the
possessions and power of the fraternity continued rapidly to increase in
every part of Europe.†

EVERARD
DES
BARRES.
A.D. 1147.

Brother Everard des Barres, the newly-elected Master of the Temple,
having collected together all the brethren from the western provinces,
joined the standard of Louis, the French king, and accompanied the crusaders to Palestine.

During the march through Asia Minor, the rear of the Christian army
was protected by the Templars, who greatly signalized themselves on
every occasion. Odo of Deuil or Diagolum, the chaplain of King Louis,
and his constant attendant upon this expedition, informs us that the king
loved to see the frugality and simplicity of the Templars, and to imitate it;
he praised their union and disinterestedness, admired above all things the
attention they paid to their accoutrements, and their care in husbanding
and preserving their equipage and munitions of war: he proposed them as
a model to the rest of the army, and in a council of war it was solemnly
ordered that all the soldiers and officers should bind themselves in confraternity with the Templars, and should march under their orders.‡

EVERARD
DES
BARRES.
A.D. 1148.

Conrad, emperor of Germany, had preceded King Louis at the head
of a powerful army, which was cut to pieces by the infidels in the north of
Asia; he fled to Constantinople, embarked on board some merchant vessels, and arrived with only a few attendants at Jerusalem, where he was
received and entertained by the Templars, and was lodged in the Temple
in the Holy City.§ Shortly afterwards King Louis arrived, accompanied
by the new Master of the Temple, Everard des Barres; and the Templars
now unfolded for the first time the red-cross banner in the field of battle.
This was a white standard made of woollen stuff, having in the centre
of it the blood-red cross granted by Pope Eugenius. The two monarchs,
Louis and Conrad, took the field, supported by the Templars, and laid

---

* In nomine sanctæ et individuæ Trinitatis omnibus dominis ct amicis suis, et Sanctæ
Dei ecclesiae filiis, Bernordus de Baliolo Salutem. Volo notum fieri omnibus tam futuris
quam presentibus, quod pro dilectione Dei et pro salute animae meae, antecesso-rumque
meorum fratribus militibus de Templo Salomonis dedi et concessi Wedelee, &c. . . . . Hoc
donum in capitulo, quod in Octavis Paschce Parisiis fuit feci, domino apostolico Eugenio
præsente, et ipso rege Franciæ et archicpiscopo Seuver, et Bardell et Rothomagi, et Fra-
scumme, et fratribus militibus Templi alba chlamide indutis cxxx præsentibus.—*Reg. Cart.
S. Joh. Jerus. in Bib. Cotton. Nero E. b.* No. xx. fo. 118.

† *Gallia Christiana nova,* tom. i. col. 486.

‡ *Odo de Diogiio de Ludov.* vii. *profectione in Orientem,* p. 67.

§ Rex per aliquot dies in Palatio Templariorum, ubi olim Regia Domus, quæ et Templum
Salomonis constructa fuit manens, et sancta ubique loca peragrans, per Samariam ad Galilæam
Ptolemaidam rediit . . . . . Convenerat enim cum rege militibusque Templi, circa proximum
Julium, in Syriam ad expugnationem Damasci exercitum ducere.—*Otto Frising,* car. 58.

siege to the magnificent city of Damascus, "the Queen of Syria," which was defended by the great Noureddin, "Light of religion," and his brother *Saif-eddin*, "Sword of the faith."

The services rendered by the Templars are thus gratefully recorded in the following letter sent by Louis, the French king, to his minister and vicegerent, the famous Suger, abbot of St. Denis.

"Louis, by the grace of God king of France and Aquitaine, to his beloved and most faithful friend Suger, the very reverend Abbot of St. Denis, health and good wishes.

". . . I cannot imagine how we could have subsisted for even the smallest space of time in these parts, had it not been for their (the Templars) support and assistance, which have never failed me from the first day I set foot in these lands up to the time of my despatching this letter— a succour ably afforded and generously persevered in. I therefore earnestlybeseech you, that as these brothers of the Temple have hitherto been blessed with the love of God, so now they may be gladdened and sustained by our love and favour.

"I have to inform you that they have lent me a considerable sum of money, which must be repaid to them quickly, that their house may not suffer, and that I may keep my word. ..."*

Among the English nobility who enlisted in the second crusade were the two renowned warriors, Roger de Mowbray and William de Warrenne.† Roger de Mowbray was one of the most powerful and warlike of the barons of England, and was one of the victorious leaders at the famous battle of the standard he marched with King Louis to Palestine; fought under the banners of the Temple against the infidels, and, smitten with admiration of the piety and valour of the holy warriors of the Order, he gave them, on his return to England, many valuable estates and possessions. Among these were the manors of Kileby and Witheley, divers lands in the isle of Axholme, the town of Balshall in the county of Warwick, and various places in Yorkshire; and so munificent were his donations, that the Templars conceded to him and to his heirs this special privilege, that as often as the said Roger or his heirs should find any brother of the Order of the Temple exposed to public penance, according to the rule and custom of the religion of the Templars, it should be lawful for the said Roger and his heirs to release such brother from the punishment of his public penance, without the interference or contradiction of any brother of the Order.*

About the same period, Stephen, king of England, for the health of

---

* Ludovici regis adabbatem Sugerium epist. 58.—*Duchesne hist. franc. scrip.* tom, iv. p. 512; see also epist. 59, ibid.

† *Simeonis Dunelmensis hist.* ad ann. 1148, *apud X script.*

EVERARD
DES
BARRES.
A.D. 1148.
his own soul and that of Queen Matilda his wife, and for the good of the souls of King Henry, his grandfather, and Eustace, his son, and all his other children, granted and confirmed to God and the blessed Virgin Mary, and to the brethren of the knighthood of the Temple of Solomon at Jerusalem, all the manor of Cressynge, with the advowson of the church of the same manor, and also the manors of Egle and Witham.† Queen Matilda, likewise, for the good of the souls of Earl Eustace, her father, the Lord Stephen, king of England, her husband, and of all her other children, granted "to the brethren of the Temple at Jerusalem" the manor of Covele or Cowley in Oxfordshire, two mills in the same county, common of pasture in Shotover forest, and the church of Stretton in Rutland.‡ Ralph de Hastings and William de Hastings also gave to the Templars, in the same reign, (A.D. 1152), lands at Hurst and Wyxham in Yorkshire, afterwards formed into the preceptory of Temple Hurst. William Asheby granted them the estate whereon the house and church of Temple Bruere were afterwards erected;§ and the Order continued rapidly to increase in power and wealth in England and in all parts of Europe, through the charitable donations of pious Christians.

After the miserable failure of the second crusade,** brother Everard des Barres, the Master of the Temple, returned to Paris, with his friend and patron Louis, the French king; and the Templars, deprived of their chief, were now left alone and unaided to withstand the victorious career of the fanatical Mussulmen. Their miserable situation is thus portrayed in
EVERARD
DES
BARRES.
A.D. 1149
a melancholy letter from the treasurer of the Order, written to the Master, Everard des Barres, during his sojourn at the court of the king of France.

"Since we have been deprived of your beloved presence, we have had the misfortune to lose in battle the prince of Antioch†† and all his nobility. To this catastrophe has succeeded another. The infidels invaded the territory of Antioch; they drove all before them, and threw garrisons into several strong places. On the first intelligence of this disaster, our brethren assembled in arms, and in concert with the king of Jerusalem went to the succour of the desolated province. We could only get together for this expedition one hundred and twenty knights and one thousand serv-

---

* *Dugdate Baronage*, tom. i. p. 122. *Dugd. Monast.* vol. 7, p. 838.

† Ex regist. Hosp. S. Joh. Jerusalem in Angli in *Bib. Cotton.* fol. 289, a-b. *Dugd. Monast. Angl.* Ed. 1830, vol. vii. p. 820.

‡ Ex. cod. Vet. M. S. penes Anton Wood, Oxon, fol. 14 a. Ib. p. 843.

§ *Liber Johannis Stillingflete*, M. S. in officio armorum (L. I7) fol. 141 a, Harleian M. S. No. 4937.

** *Geoffrey of Clairvaux* observes, however, that the second crusade could hardly be called *unfortunate*, since, though it did not at all help the Holy Land, it served to *people heaven with martyrs.*

†† His head and right hand were cut off by Noureddin, and sent to the caliph at Bagdad.— *Abulfarag. Chron. Syr.* p. 336.

ing brothers and hired soldiers, for whose equipment we expended seven thousand crowns at Acre, and one thousand at Jerusalem. Your paternity knows on what condition we assented to your departure, and our extreme want of money, of cavalry, and of infantry. We earnestly implore you to rejoin us as soon as possible, with all the necessary succours for the Eastern Church, our common mother.

". . . . Scarce had we arrived in the neighbourhood of Antioch, ere we were hemmed in by the Turcomans on the one side, and the sultan of Aleppo (Noureddin) on the other, who blockade us in the environs of the town, whilst our vineyards are destroyed, and our harvests laid waste. Overwhelmed with grief at the pitiable condition to which we are reduced, we conjure you to abandon everything, and embark without delay. Never was your presence more necessary to your brethren;— at no conjuncture could your return be more agreeable to God. ... The greater part of those whom we led to the succour of Antioch are dead. ... EVERARD

"We conjure you to bring with you from beyond sea all our knights and DES serving brothers capable of bearing arms. Perchance, alas! with all your BARRES. A.D. 1149. diligence, you may not find one of us alive. Use, therefore, all imaginable celerity; pray forget not the necessities of our house: they are such that no tongue can express them. It is also of the last importance to announce to the Pope, to the King of France, and to all the princes and prelates of Europe, the approaching desolation of the Holy Land, to the intent that they succour us in person, or send us subsidies. Whatever obstacles may be opposed to your departure, we trust to your zeal to surmount them, for now hath arrived the time for perfectly accomplishing our vows in sacrificing ourselves for our brethren, for the defence of the eastern church, and the holy sepulcher. ...

"For you, our dear brothers in Europe, whom the same engagements and the same vows ought to make keenly alive to our misfortunes, join yourselves to our chief, enter into his views, second his designs, fail not to sell everything; come to the rescue; it is from you we await liberty and life!"*

On the receipt of this letter, the Master of the Temple, instead of proceeding to Palestine, abdicated his authority, and entered into the monastery of Clairvaux, where he devoted the remainder of his days to the most rigorous penance and mortification.

He was succeeded (A.D. 1151) by Bernard de Tremelay, a nobleman of an illustrious family in Burgundy, in France, and a valiant and experienced soldier.*

The infidels made continual incursions into the Christian territories, BERNARD DE and shortly after his accession to power they crossed the Jordan, and advanced within sight of Jerusalem. Their yellow and green banners waved TREMELAY. A.D. 1152.

* *Spicilegii Dacheriani*, tom. ii. p. 511; see also *Will. Tyr.* lib. xvii. cap. 9.

on the summit of the Mount of Olives, and the warlike sound of their kettle-drums and trumpets was heard within the sacred precincts of the holy city. They encamped on the mount over against the Temple; and had the satisfaction of regarding from a distance the *Beit Allah*, or Temple of the Lord, their holy house of prayer. In a night attack, however, they were defeated with terrible slaughter, and were pursued all the way to the Jordan, five thousand of their number being left dead on the plain.†

Shortly after this affair the Templars lost their great patron, Saint Bernard, who died on the 20th of April, A.D. 1153, in the sixty-third year of his age. On his deathbed he wrote three letters in behalf of the Order. The first was addressed to the patriarch of Antioch, exhorting him to protect and encourage the Templars, a thing which the holy abbot assures him will prove most acceptable to God and man. The second was written to Melesinda, queen of Jerusalem, praising her majesty for the favour shown by her to the brethren of the Order; and the third, addressed to Brother Andre de Montbard, a Knight Templar, conveys the affectionate salutations of St. Bernard to the Master and brethren, to whose prayers he recommends himself.‡ The same year, at the siege of Ascalon, the Master of the Temple and his knights attempted alone and unaided to take that important city by storm. At the dawn of day they rushed through a breach made in the walls, and penetrated to the centre of the town. There they were surrounded by the infidels and overpowered, and, according to the testimony of an eye-witness, who was in the campaign from its commencement to its close, not a single Templar escaped: they were slain to a man, and the dead bodies of the Master and his ill-fated knights were exposed in triumph from the walls.§

TRAND DE
NQEFORT.
A.D. 1154. De Tremelay was succeeded (A.D. 1154) by Brother Bertrand de Blanquefort, a knight of a noble family of Guienne, called by William of Tyre a pious and God-fearing man.

The Templars continued to be the foremost in every encounter with the Mussulmen, and the Monkish writers exult in the number of infidels they sent to *hell*. A proportionate number of the fraternity must at the same time have ascended to *heaven*, for the slaughter amongst them was terrific. On Tuesday, June 19, A.D. 1156, they were drawn into an ambuscade whilst marching with Baldwin, king of Jerusalem, near Tiberias, three hundred of the brethren were slain on the field of battle, and eighty-seven fell into the hands of the enemy, among whom was Bertrand de Blanquefort himself, and Brother Odo, marshal of the kingdom.* Shortly afterwards, thirty Knights Templars put to flight, slaughtered, and captured, two

* *Will. Tyr.* lib. xvii. cap. 21. *L'art de verifier les dates*, p. 340. *Nobiliatre de Franche-Compté* par Dunod, p. 140.

† *Will. Tyr.* lib. xvii. cap. 20, ad ann. 1152.

‡ *S. Bernardi eptitoke*, 288, 289, 392, ed. Mabillon.

§ *Anselmi Gemblacensis Chron.* ad ann. 1153. *Will. Tyr.* lib. xvii. Cap. 27.

hundred infidels;† and in a night attack on the camp of Noureddin, they compelled that famous chieftain to fly, without arms and half-naked, from the field of battle. In this last affair the names of Robert Mansel, an Englishman, and Gilbert de Lacy, preceptor of the Temple of Tripoli, are honourably mentioned.‡ The services of the Templars were gratefully acknowledged in Europe, and the Pope, in a letter written in their behalf to the Archbishop of Rheims, his legate in France, characterizes them as "New Maccabees, far famed and most valiant champions of the Lord." "The assistance," says the Pope, "rendered by those holy warriors to all Christendom, their zeal and valour, and untiring exertions in defending from the persecution and subtilty of the filthy Pagans, those sacred places which have been enlightened by the corporal presence of our Saviour, we doubt not have been spread abroad throughout the world, and are known, not only to the neighbouring nations, but to all those who dwell at the remotest corners of the earth." The holy pontiff exhorts the archbishop to procure for them all the succour possible, both in men and horses, and to exert himself in their favour among all his suffragan bishops.§

BERTRAN DE BLANQE-FORT. A.D. 1154.

The fiery zeal and warlike enthusiasm of the Templars were equalled, if not surpassed, by the stern fanaticism and religious ardour of the followers of Mahomet. "Noureddin fought," says his oriental biographer, "like the meanest of his soldiers, saying, 'Alas! it is now a long time that I have been seeking martyrdom without being able to obtain it.' The Imaum Koteb-ed-din, hearing him on one occasion utter these words, exclaimed, 'In the name of God do not put your life in danger, do not thus expose Islam and the Moslems. Thou art their stay and support, and if (but God preserve us therefrom) thou shouldest be slain, it will be all up with us. 'Ah! Koteb-ed-deen,' said he, 'what hast thou said, who can save Islam** and our country, but that great God who has no equal?' 'What,' said he, on another occasion, 'do we not look to the security of our houses against robbers and plunderers, and shall we not defend religion?'"*

Like the Templars, Noureddin fought constantly with spiritual and with carnal weapons. He resisted the world and its temptations by fasting and prayer, and by the daily exercise of the moral and religious duties and virtues inculcated by the Koran. He fought with the sword against the foes

BERTRAND DE BLANQEFO A.D. 1154.

* Captus est inter cæteros ibi Bertrandus de Blanquefort, Magister Militiæ Templi, vir religious ac timens Deum. *Will. Tyr.* lib. xviii. cap. 14. *Registr. epist.* apud Martene vet. script. tom. ii. col. 647.

† Milites Templi circa triginta, ducentos Paganorum euntes ad nuphas verterent in fugam, et divino præsidio comitante, omnes partim ccperunt, partim gladio trucidarunt. *Registr. epist. ut sup.* col. 647.

‡ Will. *Tyr.* lib. xix. cap. 8.

§ *Epist.* xvi. S. Remensi archiepiscopo et ejus suffiraganeis pro ecclesia Jerosoly-mitana et militibus Templi, apud *Martene vet. Script.* tom. ii. col. 647.

** *Islam*, the name of the Mahometan religion. The word signifies literally, delivering oneself up to God

of Islam, and employed his whole energies, to the last hour of his life, in the enthusiastic and fanatic struggle for the recovery of Jerusalem.†

The close points of resemblance, indeed, between the religious fanaticism of the Templars and that of the Moslems are strikingly remarkable. In the Moslem camp, we are told by the Arabian writers, all profane and frivolous conversation was severely prohibited; the exercises of religion were assiduously practised, and the intervals of action were employed in prayer, meditation, and the study of the Koran.

The Templars style themselves "The Avengers of Jesus Christ," and the "instruments and ministers of God for the punishment of infidels," and the Pope and the holy fathers of the church proclaim that it is specially entrusted to them "to blot out from the earth all unbelievers," and they hold out the joys of paradise as the glorious reward for the dangers and difficulties of the task.‡ "In fighting for Christ," declares St. Bernard, in his address to the Templars, "the kingdom of Christ is acquired . . . Go forth, therefore, O soldiers, in nowise mistrusting, and with a fearless spirit cast down the enemies of the cross of Christ, in the certain assurance that neither in life nor in death can ye be separated from the love of God which is in Christ Jesus, repeating to yourselves in every danger,

BERTRAND
DE
BLANQE-
FORT.
A.D. 1156.

whether we live or whether we die we are the Lord's. How gloriously do the victors return from the fight, how happy do the martyrs die in battle! Rejoice, valiant champion, if thou livest and conquerest in the Lord, but rejoice rather and glory if thou shouldest die and be joined unto the Lord. ... If those are happy who die in the Lord, how much more so are those who die *for* the Lord! ... Precious in the sight of God will be the death of his holy soldiers."

"*The sword*," says the prophet Mahomet, on the other hand, "is the key of heaven and of hell; a drop of blood shed in the cause of God, a night spent in arms, is of more avail than two months of fasting and of prayer. Whosoever falls in battle, his sins are forgiven him at the day of judgment. His wounds will be resplendent as vermilion, and odoriferous as musk, and the loss of limbs shall be supplied by the wings of angels and of cherubims."

Thus writes the famous Caliph Abubeker, the successor of Mahomet, to the Arabian tribes:

"In the name of the most merciful God, *Abdollah Athich Ib'n Abi Kohapha*, to the rest of the true believers."... "This is to acquaint you, that I intend to send the true believers into Syria, to take it out of the hands of

---

** *Islam*, the name of the Mahometan religion. The word signifies literally, delivering oneself up to God.

* Keightley's Crusaders.

† The virtues of Noureddin are celebrated by the Arabic Historian Ben-Schunah, in his Raoudhat Almenadhir, by Azzeddin Ebn-al-ather, by Khondemir, and in the work entitled, "The flowers of the two gardens," by Omaddeddin Kateb. See also Will. Tyr. lib. xx. cap. 33.

‡ *Regula*, cap. xlviii.

the infidels, and I would have you to know, that *the fighting for religion is an act of obedience* to God."

"Remember," said the same successor of the prophet and commander of the faithful, to the holy warriors who had assembled in obedience to his mandate, "that you are always in the presence of God, on the verge of death, in the assurance of judgment, and the hope of paradise ... When you fight *the battles of the Lord*, acquit yourselves like men, and turn not your backs."

The prowess and warlike daring of the Templars in the field are thus described by St. Bernard.

"When the conflict has begun, then at length they throw aside their former meekness and gentleness, exclaiming, *Do not I hate them, O Lord, that hate thee, and am I not grieved with those who rise up against thee?* They rush in upon their adversaries, they scatter them like sheep, in nowise fearing, though few in number, the fierce barbarism or the immense multitude of the enemy. They have learned indeed to rely, not on their own strength, but to count on victory through the aid of the Lord God Sabaoth, to whom they believe it easy enough, accor ding to the words of Maccabees, to make an end of many by the hands of a few, for victory in battle dependeth not on the multitude of the army, but on the strength given from on high, which, indeed, they have very frequently experienced, since one of them will pursue a thousand, and two will put to flight ten thousand. Yea, and lastly, in a wonderful and remarkable manner, they are observed to be both more gentle than *lambs*, and more fierce than *lions* so that I almost doubt which I had better determine to call them, monks forsooth, or soldiers, unless perhaps, as more fitting, I should name them both the one and the other."

At a later period, Cardinal de Vitry, Bishop of Acre, the frequent companion of the Knights Templars on their military expeditions, thus describes the religious and military enthusiasm of the Templars: "When summoned to arms they never demand the number of the enemy, but where are they? Lions they are in war, gentle lambs in the convent; fierce soldiers in the field, hermits and monks in religion; to the enemies of Christ ferocious and inexorable, but to Christians kind and gracious. They carry before them," says he, "to battle, a banner, half black and white, which they call *Beauseant*, that is to say, in the Gallic tongue, *Bien-seant*, because they are fair and favourable to the friends of Christ, but black and terrible to his enemies."*

Among the many instances of the fanatical ardour of the Moslem warriors, are the following, extracted from the history of *Abu Abdollah Alwakidi*, Cadi of Bagdad. "Methinks," said a valiant Saracen youth, in the heat of battle against the Christians under the walls of Emesa — "me thinks I see the black-eyed girls looking upon me, one of whom, should she appear in this world, all mankind would die for love of her; and I see in the hand of one of them a handkerchief of green silk, and a cap made of precious stones, and she beckons me, and calls out, Come hither quickly, for I love thee." With these words, charging the infidels, he made havoc wherever he went, until he was at last struck down by a javelin. "It is not," said a dying Arabian warrior, when he embraced for the last time his sister and mother — "it is not the fading pleasure of this world that has prompted me to devote my life in the cause of religion, I seek the favour of God and his apostle, and I have heard from one of the companions of the prophet, that the spirits of the martyrs will be lodged in the crops of green birds who taste the fruits and drink of the waters of paradise. Farewell; we shall meet again among the groves and the fountains which God has prepared for his elect.†

The Master of the Temple, Brother Bertrand de Blanquefort, was liberated from captivity at the instance of Manuel Comnenus, Emperor of Constantinople.‡ After his release he wrote several letters to Louis VII., king of France, describing the condition and prospects of the Holy Land; the increasing power and boldness of the infidels; and the ruin and desolation caused by a dreadful earthquake, which had overthrown numerous castles, prostrated the walls and defences of several towns, and swallowed up the dwellings of the inhabitants. "The persecutors of the church," says he, "hasten to avail themselves of our misfortunes; they gather themselves together from the ends of the earth, and come forth as one man against the sanctuary of God."§

It was during his mastership, that Geoffrey, the Knight Templar, and Hugh of Caesarea, were sent on an embassy into Egypt, and had an interview with the Caliph. They were introduced into the palace of the Fatimites through a series of gloomy passages and glittering porticos, amid the warbling of birds and the murmur of fountains; the scene was enriched by a display of costly furniture and rare animals; and the long order of unfolding doors was guarded by black soldiers and domestic eunuchs. The sanctuary of the presence chamber was veiled with a curtain, and the vizier who conducted the ambassadors laid aside his scimetar, and prostrated himself three times on the ground; the veil was then removed, and they saw the Commander of the Faithful.*

Brother Bertrand de Blanquefort, in his letters to the king of France,

BERTRAND DE BLANQEFORT. A.D. 1159.

---

* Vexillum bipartitum ex Albo et Nigro quod nominant *Beau-seant* id est Gallicâ linguâ *Bien-seant*; eo quod Christi amicis candidi sunt et benigni, inimicis vero terribiles atque nigri, *Jac. de Vitr. Hist. Hierosol apud Gesta Dei*, cap. lxv. The idea is quite an oriental one, black and white being always used among the Arabs metaphorically, in the sense above described. Their customary salutation is, May your day be white, i. e. may you be happy.

† *Alwakidi Arab*. Hist. translated by Ockley. *Hist. Saracen*. It refers to a period antecedent to the crusades, but the same religio-military enthusiasm prevailed during the holy war for the recovery of Jerusalem.

‡ *Cinnamus*, lib. iv. num. 22.

§ *Gesta Dei*, inter regum et principum epistolas, tom. i. p. 1173, 6, 7. *Hist. Franc. Script.* tom. Iv. p. 692, 693.

gives an account of the military operations undertaken by the Order of Temple in Egypt, and of the capture of the populous and important city of Belbeis, the ancient Pelusium.† During the absence of the Master with the greater part of the fraternity on that expedition, the sultan Noureddin invaded Palestine; he defeated with terrible slaughter the serving brethren and Turcopoles, or light horse of the Order, who remained to defend the country, and sixty of the knights who commanded them were left dead on the plain.‡

BERTRAND DE BLANQEFORT. A.D. 1164.

The zeal and devotion of the Templars in the service of Christ continued to be the theme of praise and of admiration both in the east and in the west. Pope Alexander III., in his letters, characterizes them as the stout champions of Jesus Christ, who warred a divine warfare, and daily laid down their lives for their brethren, "We implore and we admonish your fraternity," says he, addressing the archbishops and bishops, "that out of love to God, and of reverence to the blessed Peter and ourselves, and also out of regard for the salvation of your own souls, ye do favour, and support, and honour them, and preserve all their rights entire and intact, and afford them the benefit of your patronage and protection."§

Amalric, king of Jerusalem, the successor of Baldwin the Third, in a letter "to his dear friend and father," Louis the Seventh, king of France, beseeches the good offices of that monarch in behalf of all the devout Christians of the Holy Land; "but above all," says he, "we earnestly entreat your Majesty constantly to extend to the utmost your favour and regard to the Brothers of the Temple, who continually render up their lives for God and the faith, and through whom we do the little that we are able to effect, for in them indeed, after God, is placed the entire reliance of all those in the eastern regions who tread in the right path."…*

The Master, Brother Bertrand de Blanquefort, was succeeded (A.D. 1167), by Philip of Naplous, the first Master of the Temple who had been born in Palestine. He had been Lord of the fortresses of Krak and Montreal in Arabia Petrea, and took the vows and the habit of the Order of the Temple after the death of his wife.†

PHILIP OF NAPLOUS. A.D. 1167.

We must now pause to take a glance at the rise of another great religio-military institution which, from henceforth, takes a leading part in the defence of the Latin kingdom.

In the eleventh century, when pilgrimages to Jerusalem had greatly increased, some Italian merchants of Amalfi, who carried on a lucrative

---

* Hist. de Saladin, par *M. Marin,* tom. i. p. 120, 1. *Gibbon,* cap. 59.

† *Gesta Dei,* epist. xiv. p. 1178, 9.

‡ De fratribus nostris ceciderunt LX. Milites fortissimo, præter fraters clients et Turcopulos, nec nisi *septem* tantum evasêre periculum. Epist. *Gauf Fulcherii* procuratoris Templi Ludovico regi Francorum. *Gesta Dei,* tom. i. p. 1182, 3, 4.

§ Registr. Epist. Apud *Mariene,* vel script. tom. ii. col. 846, 847, 883.

trade with Palestine, purchased of the Caliph *Monstasser-billah* a piece of ground in the Christian quarter of the Holy City, near the Church of the Resurrection, whereon two hospitals were constructed, the one being appropriated for the reception of male pilgrims, and the other for females. Several pious and charitable Christians, chiefly from Europe, devoted themselves in these hospitals to constant attendance upon the sick and destitute. Two chapels were erected, the one annexed to the female establishment being dedicated to St. Mary Magdalene, and the other to St. John the Eleemosynary, a canonized patriarch of Alexandria, remarkable for his exceeding charity. The pious and kind-hearted people who here attended upon the sick pilgrims, clothed the naked and fed the hungry, were called "The Hospitallers of Saint John."

On the conquest of Jerusalem by the Crusaders, these charitable persons were naturally regarded with the greatest esteem and reverence by their fellow-Christians from the west; many of the soldiers of the Cross, smitten with their piety and zeal, desired to participate in their good offices, and the Hospitallers, animated, by the religious enthusiasm of the day, determined to renounce the world, and devote the remainder of their lives to pious duties and constant attendance upon the sick. They took the customary monastic vows of obedience, chastity, and poverty, and assumed as their distinguishing habit a *black* mantle with a white *cross* on the breast. Various lands and possessions were granted them by the lords and princes of the Crusade, both in Palestine and in Europe, and the Order of the hospital of St. John speedily became a great and powerful institution.*

Gerard, a native of Provence, was at this period at the head of the society, with the title of "Guardian of the Poor." He was succeeded (A.D. 1118) by Raymond Dupuy, a knight of Dauphine, who drew up a series of rules for the direction and government of his brethren. In these rules no traces are discoverable of the military spirit which afterwards animated the Order of the Hospital of St. John. The Abbé de Vertot, from a desire perhaps to pay court to the Order of Malta, carries back the assumption of arms by the Hospitallers to the year 1119, and describes them as fiercely engaged under the command of Raymond Dupuy, in the battle fought between the Christians and Dol de Kuvin, Sultan of Damascus;

---

* "..... præcipue pro fratribus Templi, vestram exoramus Majestatem .... qui quotidie moriuntur pro Domino et servitio, et per quos possumus, si quid possumus. In illis enim tota summa post Deum conaistit omnium eorum, qui sano fiunt consilio in partibufl orientis .... "*Gesta Dei*, tom, i epist. xxi. p. 1181.

illis enim tota summa post Deum conaistit omnium eorum, qui sano fiunt consilio in partibufl orientis .... "*Gesta Dei,* tom, i epist. xxi. p. 1181.

† Dominus fuit Arabiæ secundæ, quæ eat Petracensis, qui locus hodie Crach dicitur, et Syria Sobal ... factus est Magister Militiae Templi.— *Will. Tyr.* lib. xxii. cap. 5.

but none of the historians of the period make any mention whatever of the Hospitallers in that action. De Vertot quotes no authority in support of his statement, and it appears to be a mere fiction.

The first authentic notice of an intention on the part of the Hospitallers to occupy themselves with military matters, occurs in the bull of Pope Innocent the Second, dated A.D. 1130. This bull is addressed to the archbishops, bishops, and clergy of the church universal, and informs them that the Hospitallers then retained, at their own expense, a body of horsemen and foot soldiers, to defend the pilgrims in going to and in returning from the holy places; the pope observes that the funds of the hospital were insufficient to enable them effectually to fulfill the pious and holy task, and he exhorts the archbishops, bishops, and clergy, to minister to the necessities of the Order out of their abundant property.† The Hospitallers consequently at this period had resolved to add the task of *protecting* to that of tending and relieving pilgrims.

After the accession (A.D. 1168) of Gilbert d'Assalit to the guardianship of the Hospital—a man described by De Yertot as "bold and enterprising, and of an extravagant genius"—a military spirit was infused into the Hospitallers, which speedily predominated over their pious and charitable zeal in attending upon the poor and the sick. Gilbert d'Assalit was the friend and confidant of Amalric, king of Jerusalem, and planned with that monarch a wicked invasion of Egypt in defiance of treaties. The Master of the Temple being consulted concerning the expedition, flatly refused to have anything to do with it, or to allow a single brother of the Order of theTemple to accompany the king in arms; "For it appeared a hard matter to the Templars," says William of Tyre, "to wage war without cause, in defiance of treaties, and against all honour and conscience, upon a friendly nation, preserving faith with us, and relying on our own faith."* Gilbert d'Assalit consequently determined to obtain for the king from his own brethren that aid which the Templars denied; and to tempt the Hospitallers to arm themselves generally as a great military society, in imitation of the Templars,† and join the expedition to Egypt, Gilbert d'Assalit was authorised to promise them, in the name of the king, the possession of the wealthy and important city of Belbeis, the ancient Pelusium, in perpetual sovereignty.‡

According to De Vertot, the senior Hospitallers were greatly averse to the military projects of their chief: "They urged," says he, "that they were

PHILIP OF
NAPLOUS.
A.D. 1167.

---

* *Will. Tyr.* lib. xviii. cap. 4, 5.

† Fratres ejusdem domus non formidantes pro fratribus suis animas ponere; cum servientibus et equitaturis *ad hoc officium specialiter depulatis et propriis sumptibus retentis*, tam in eundo, quam redeundo ab incursibus Paganorum defensant.— *De Veriot.* Hist. des chev. De Malte, liv. i. prevue 9.

PHILIP OF
NAPLOUS.
A.D. 1167.

a religious order, and that the church had not put arms into their hands to make conquests;"§ but the younger and more ardent of the brethren, burning to exchange the monotonous life of the cloister for the enterprize and activity of the camp, received the proposals of their superior with enthusiasm, and a majority of the chapter decided in favour of the plans and projects of their Guardian. They authorized him to borrow money of the Florentine and Genoese merchants, to take hired soldiers into the pay of the Order, and to organize the Hospitallers as a great military society.

PHILIP OF
NAPLOUS.
A.D. 1168.

Gilbert d'Assalit bestirred himself with great energy in the execution of these schemes; he wrote letters to the king of France for aid and assistance,** and borrowed money of the emperor of Constantinople. "Assalit," says De Vertot, "with this money levied a great body of troops, which he took into the pay of the Order; and as his fancy was entirely taken up with flattering hopes of conquest, he drew by his indiscreet liberalities a great number of volunteers into his service, who like him shared already in imagination all the riches of Egypt."

It was in the first year of the government of Philip of Naplous (A.D. 1168) that the king of Jerusalem and the Hospitallers marched forth upon their memorable and unfortunate expedition. The Egyptians were taken completely by surprise; the city of Belbeis was carried by assault, and the defenceless inhabitants were barbarously massacred; "they spared," says De Vertot "neither old men nor women, nor children at the breast," after which the desolated city was delivered up to the brethren of the Hospital of St. John. They held it, however, for a very brief period; the immorality, the cruelty, and the injustice of the Christians, speedily met with condign punishment. The king of Jerusalem was driven back into Palestine; Belbeis was abandoned with precipitation; and the Hospitallers fled before the infidels in sorrow and disappointment to Jerusalem. There they vented their indignation and chagrin upon the unfortunate Gilbert d'Assalit, their superior, who had got the Order into debt to the extent of 100,000 pieces of gold; they compelled him to resign his authority, and the unfortunate guardian of the hospital fled from Palestine to England, and was drowned in the Channel.*

From this period, however, the character of the Order of the Hospital

---

* *Will. Tyr.* lib. xx. cap. 5.

† Prædicti enim Hospitalis fraters ad *imitationem* fratrum militiæ Templi, armis materialibus utentes, milites cum servientibus in suo collegio receperunt.— *Jac. De Vit. cap. lxv.*

‡ *Will. Tyr.* lib. xx. cap. 5.

§ This assumption of arms by the Hospitallers was entirely at variance with the original end and object of their institution. Pope Anastasius, in a bull dated A.D. 1154, observes, "omnia vestra *sustentationibus peregrinorum et pauperum* debent cedere, ac per hoc nullatenus aliis usibus ea convenit applicari." — De Veriot, liv. i. preuve 13.

** *Gest. Dei per Francos,* p. 1177.

of St. John was entirely changed; the Hospitallers appear henceforth as a great military body; their superior styles himself Master, and leads in person the brethren into the field of battle. Attendance upon the poor and the sick still continued, indeed, one of the duties of the fraternity, but it must have been feebly exercised amid the clash of arms and the excitement of war.

---

* *Will. Tyr.* lib. xx. cap. 5. *Hoveden* in Hen. 2, p. 622. **De Vertot, Hist.** des Chevaliers de Malte, liv. Ii. p. 150 to 161, ed. 1726.

CHAPTER IV.

The contests between Saladin and the Templars—The vast privileges of the Templars—The publication of the bull, *omne datum optimum*—The Pope declares himself the immediate Bishop of the entire Order—The different classes of Templars—The knights—Priests—Serving brethren—The hired soldiers—The great officers of the Temple—Punishment of cowardice—The Master of the Temple is taken prisoner, and dies in a dungeon—Saladin's great successes—The Christians purchase a truce—The Master of the Temple and the Patriarch Heraclius proceed to England for succour—The consecration of the Temple Church at London.

"The firmest bulwark of Jerusalem was founded on the knights of the Hospital of St. John and of the Temple of Solomon; on the strange association of a monastic and military life, which fanaticism might suggest, but of which policy must approve. The flower of the nobility of Europe aspired to wear the cross and profess the vows of these respectable orders; their spirit and discipline were immortal; and the speedy donation of twenty-eight thousand farms or manors enabled them to support a regular force of cavalry and infantry for the defence of Palestine."—*Gibbon.*

ODO DE
ST. AMAND.
A.D. 1170.

THE Master, Philip of Naplous, resigned his authority after a short government of three years, and was succeeded by Brother Odo de St. Amand, a proud and fiery warrior, of undaunted courage and resolution; having, according to William, Archbishop of Tyre, the fear neither of God nor of man before his eyes.*

The Templars were now destined to meet with a more formidable opponent than any they had hitherto encountered in the field, one who was again to cause the crescent to triumph over the cross, and to plant the

ODO DE
ST. AMAND.
A.D. 1170.

standard of the prophet upon the walls of the holy city.

When the Fatimite caliph had received intelligence of Amalric's invasion of Egypt, he sent the hair of his women, one of the great-

* *Will. Tyr.* lib. xxi cap. 29.

est tokens of distress known in the East, to the pious Noureddin, who immediately dispatched a body of troops to his assistance, headed by Sheerkoh, and his nephew, *Youseef-Ben-Acoub-Ben-Schadi,* the famous Saladin. Sheerkoh died immediately after his arrival, and Youseef succeeded to his command, and was appointed vizier of the caliph. Youseef had passed his youth in pleasure and debauchery, sloth and indolence: he had quitted with regret the delights of Damascus for the dusty plains of Egypt; and but for the unjustifiable expedition of King Amalric and the Hospitallers against the infidels, the powerful talents and the latent energies of the young Courdish chieftain, which altogether changed the face of affairs in the East, would in all probability never have been developed.

As soon as Saladin grasped the power of the sword, and obtained the command of armies, he threw off the follies of his youth, and led a new life. He renounced the pleasures of the world, and assumed the character of a saint. His dress was a coarse woollen garment; water was his only drink; and he carefully abstained from everything disapproved of by the Mussulman religion. Five times each day he prostrated himself in public prayer, surrounded by his friends and followers, and his demeanour became grave, serious, and thoughtful. He fought vigorously with spiritual weapons against the temptations of the world; his nights were often spent in watching and meditation, and he was always diligent in fasting and in the study of the Koran. With the same zeal he combated with carnal weapons the foes of Islam, and his admiring brethren gave him the name of *Salah-ed-deen,* "Integrity of Religion," vulgarly called Saladin.

At the head of forty thousand horse and foot, he crossed the desert and ravaged the borders of Palestine; the wild Bedouins and the enthusiastic Arabians of the far south were gathered together under his standard, and hastened with holy zeal to obtain the crown of martyrdom in defence of the faith. The long remembered and greatly dreaded Arab shout of onset, *Allah achat,* God *is victorious,* again resounded through the plains and the mountains of Palestine, and the grand religious struggle for the possession of the Holy City of Jerusalem, equally reverenced by Mussulmen and by Christians, was once more vigorously commenced. Saladin besieged the fortified city of Gaza, which belonged to the Knights Templars, and was considered to be the key of Palestine towards Egypt. The luxuriant gardens, the palm and olive groves of this city of the wilderness, were destroyed by the wild cavalry of the desert, and the innumerable tents of the Arab host were thickly clustered on the neighbouring sand-hills. The warlike monks of the Temple fasted and prayed, and invoked the aid of the God of battles; the gates of the city were thrown open, and in an unexpected sally upon the enemy's camp they performed such prodigies of valour, that Saladin, despairing of being able to take the place, abandoned the siege, and retired into Egypt.*

The year following, Pope Alexander's famous bull, *omne datum opti-mum*, confirming the previous privileges of the Templars, and conferring upon them additional powers and immunities, was published in England. It commences in the following terms:

ODO DE
ST. AMAND.
A.D. 1172.

"Alexander, bishop, servant of the servants of God, to his beloved sons, Odo, Master of the religious chivalry of the Temple, which is situated at Jerusalem, and to his successors, and to all the regularly professed brethren.

"Every good gift and every perfect reward† cometh from above, descending from the Father of light, with whom there is no change nor shadow of variety. Therefore, O beloved children in the Lord, we praise the Almighty God, in respect of your holy fraternity, since your religion and venerated institution are celebrated throughout the entire world. For although by nature ye are children of wrath, and slaves to the pleasures of this life, yet by a favouring grace ye have not remained deaf hearers of the gospel, but, throwing aside all earthly pomps and enjoyments, and rejecting the broad road which leadeth unto death, ye have humbly chosen the arduous path to everlasting life. Faithfully fulfilling the character of soldiery of the Lord, ye constantly carry upon your breasts the sign of the life-giving cross. Moreover, like true Israelites, and most instructed fighters of the divine battle, inflamed with true charity, ye fulfil by your works the word of the gospel which saith, 'Greater love hath no man than this, that a man lay down his life for his friends;' so that, in obedienceto the voice of the great Shepherd, ye in nowise fear to lay down your lives for your brethren, and to defend them from the inroad of the pagans; and ye may well be termed holy warriors, since ye have been appointed by the Lord defenders of the catholic church and combatants of the enemies of Christ."

After this preamble, the pope earnestly exhorts the Templars to pursue with unceasing diligence their high vocation; to defend the eastern church with their whole hearts and souls, and to strike down the enemies of the cross of Christ. "By the authority of God, and the blessed Peter prince of apostles," says the holy pontiff, "we have ordained and do determine, that the Temple in

ODO DE
ST. AMAND.
A.D. 1172.

which ye are gathered together to the praise and glory of God, for the defence of the faithful, and the deliverance of the church, shall remain for evermore under the safeguard and protection of the holy apostolic see, together with all the goods and possessions which ye now lawfully enjoy, and all that ye may hereafter rightfully obtain, through the liberality of Christian kings and princes, and the alms and oblations of the faithful.

---

* *Will. Tyr.* lib. xx. xxi. xxii.

† *Omne datum optimum* et omne donum perfectum desursum est, descendens a Patre luminum, apud quem non est transmutatio, nee vicissitudinis obumbratio.

"We moreover by these presents decree, that the regular discipline, which, by divine favour, hath been instituted in your house, shall be inviolably observed, and that the brethren who have there dedicated themselves to the service of the omnipotent God, shall live together in chastity and without property and making good their profession both in word and deed, they shall remain subject and obedient in all things to the Master, or to him whom the Master shall have set in authority over them.

"Moreover, as the chief house at Jerusalem hath been the source and fountain of your sacred institution and order, the Master thereof shall always be considered the head and chief of all the houses and places appertaining thereunto. And we further decree, that at the decease of Odo, our beloved son in the Lord, and of each one of his successors, no man shall be set in authority over the brethren of the same house, except he be of the religious and military order; and has regularly professed your habit and fellowship; and has been chosen by all the brethren unanimously, or, at all events, by the greater part of them.

"And from henceforth it shall not be permitted to any ecclesiastical or secular person to infringe or diminish the customs and observances of your religion and profession, as instituted by the Master and brethren in common; and those rules which have been put into writing and observed by you for some time past, shall not be changed or altered except by the authority of the Master, with the consent of the majority of the chapter

". . . . . No ecclesiastic or secular person shall dare to exact from the Master and Brethren of the Temple, oaths, guarantees, or any such securities as are ordinarily required from the laity.

"Since your sacred institution and religious chivalry have been established by divine Providence, it is not fit that you should enter into any other order with the view of leading a more religious life, for God, who is immutable and eternal, approveth not the inconstant heart; but wisheth rather the good purpose, when once begun, to be persevered in to the end of life.

"How many and great persons have pleased the lord of an earthly empire, under the military girdle and habit! How many and distinguished men, gathered together in arms, have bravely fought, in these our times, in the cause of the gospel of God, and in defence of the laws of our Father; and, consecrating their hands in the blood of the unbelievers in the Lord, have, after their pains and toil in this world's warfare, obtained the reward of everlasting life! Do ye therefore, both knights and serving brethren, assiduously pay attention to your profession, and in accordance with the saying of the apostle, 'Let each one of you stedfastly remain in the vocation to which you have been called.' We therefore ordain, that when your brethren have once taken the vows, and have been received in your sacred college, and have taken upon themselves your warfare, and the habit of your religion, they shall no lon-

ODO DE
ST. AMAND,
A.D. 1172.

ger have the power of returning again to the world; nor can any, after they have once made profession, abjure the cross and habit of your religion, with the view of entering another convent or monastery of stricter or more lax discipline, without the consent of the brethren, or Master, or of him whom the Master hath set in authority over them; nor shall

ODO DE
ST. AMAND.
A.D. 1172.

any ecclesiastic or secular person be permitted to receive or retain them.

"And since those who are defenders of the church ought to be supported and maintained out of the good things of the church, we prohibit all manner of men from exacting tithes from you in respect of your moveables or immoveables, or any of the goods and possessions appertaining unto your venerable house.

"And that nothing may be wanting to the plenitude of your salvation, and the care of your souls; and that ye may more commodiously hear divine service, and receive the sacraments in your sacred college; we in like manner ordain, that it shall be lawful for you to admit within your fraternity, honest and godly clergymen and priests, as many as ye may conscientiously require; and to receive them from whatever parts they may come, as well in your chief house at Jerusalem, as in all the other houses and places depending upon it, so that they do not belong to any other religious profession or order, and so that ye ask them of the bishop, if they come from the neighbourhood; but if peradventure the bishop should refuse, yet nevertheless ye have permission to receive and retain them by the authority of the holy apostolic see.

"If any of these, after they have been professed, should turn out to be useless, or should become disturbers of your house and religion, it shall be lawful for you, with the consent of the major part of the chapter, to remove them, and give them leave to enter any other order where they may wish to live in the service of God, and to substitute others in their places who shall undergo a probation of one year in your society; which term being completed, if their morals render them worthy of your fellowship, and they shall be found fit and proper for your service, then let them make the regular profession of life according to your rule,

ODO DE
ST. AMAND.
A.D. 1172.

and of obedience to their Master, so that they have their food and clothing, and also their lodging, with the fraternity.

"But it shall not be lawful for them presumptuously to take part in the consultations of your chapter, or in the government of your house; they are permitted to do so, so far only as they are enjoined by yourselves. And as regards the cure of souls, they are to occupy themselves with that business so far only as they are required. Moreover, they shall be subject to no person, power, or authority, excepting that of your own chapter, but let them pay perfect obedience, in all matters and upon all occasions, to thee our beloved son in the Lord, Odo, and to thy successors, as their *Master* and *Bishop*.

"We moreover decree, that it shall be lawful for you to send your clerks, when they are to be admitted to holy orders, for ordination to whatever catholic bishop you may please, who, clothed with our apostolical power, will grant them what they require; but we forbid them to preach with a view of obtaining money, or for any temporal purpose whatever, unless perchance the Master of the Temple for the time being should cause it to be done for some special purpose. And whosoever of these are received into your college, they must make the promise of steadfastness of purpose, of reformation of morals, and that they will fight for the Lord all the days of their lives, and render strict obedience to the Master of the Temple; the book in which these things are contained being placed upon the altar.

"We moreover, without detracting from the rights of the bishops in respect of tithes, oblations, and buryings, concede to you the power of constructing oratories in the places bestowed upon the sacred house of the Temple, where you and your retainers and servants may dwell; so that both ye and they may be able to assist at the divine offices, and receive there the rite of sepulture; for it would be unbecoming and very dangerous to the souls of the religious brethren, if they were to be mixed lip with crowd of secular persons, and be brought into the company of women on the occasion of their going to church. But as to the tithes, which, by the advice and with the consent of the bishops, ye may be able by your zeal to draw out of the hands of the clergy or laity, and those which with the consent of the bishops ye may acquire from their own clergy, we confirm to you by our apostolical authority." ODO DE ST. AMAND. A.D. 1172.

The above bull further provides, in various ways, for the temporal and spiritual advantage of the Templars, and expressly extends the favours and indulgences, and the apostolical blessings, to all the serving brethren, as well as to the knights. It also confers upon the fraternity the important privilege of causing the churches of towns and villages lying under sentence of interdict to be opened once a year, and divine service to be celebrated within them.*

A bull exactly similar to the above appears to have been issued by Pope Alexander, on the seventh id. Jan. A.D. 1162, addressed to the Master Bertrand de Blanquefort.† Both the above instruments are to a great extent merely confirmatory of the privileges previously conceded to the Templars.

The exercise or the abuse of these powers and immunities speedily brought the Templars into collision with the ecclesiastics. At the general council of the church, held at Rome, (A.D. 1179), called the third of Lateran, a grave reprimand was addressed to them by the holy Fathers. "We find," say they, "by the frequent complaints of the bishops our col-

---

* Acta Hymen, tom. i. ad ann. 1172, p. 30, 31, 32.
† *Wilcke*, Geachichte des Tempelherrenordens, vol. ii. p. 230.

leagues, that the Templars and Hospitallers abuse the privileges granted them by the Holy See; that the chaplains and priests of their rule have caused parochial churches to be conveyed over to themselves without the ODO DE ordinaries' consent; that they administer the sacraments to excommuni- ST. AMAND. cated persons, and bury them with all the usual ceremonies of the church; A.D. 1172. that they likewise abuse the permission granted the brethren of having divine service said once a year in places under interdict, and that they admit seculars into their fraternity, pretending thereby to give them the same right to their privileges as if they were really professed." To provide a remedy for these irregularities, the council forbad the military orders to receive for the future any conveyances of churches and tithes without the ordinaries' consent; that with regard to churches not founded by them- selves, nor served by the chaplains of the Order, they should present the priests they designed for the cure of them to the bishop of the diocese, and reserve nothing to themselves but the cognizance of the temporals which belonged to them; that they should not cause service to be said, in churches under interdict, above once a year, nor give burial there to any person whatever; and that none of their fraternity or *associates* should be allowed to partake of their privileges, if not actually professed.*

Several bishops from Palestine were present at this council, together with the archbishop of Caesarea, and William archbishop of Tyre, the great historian of the Latin kingdom.

The order of the Temple was at this period divided into the three great classes of knights, priests, and serving brethren, all bound together by their vow of obedience to the Master of the Temple at Jerusalem, the chief of the entire fraternity. Every candidate for admission into the first class must have received the honour of knighthood in due form, accord- ing to the laws of chivalry, before he could be admitted to the vows; and as no person of low degree could be advanced to the honours of knight- hood, the brethren of the first class, i. e. the *Knights* Templars, were all men of noble birth and of high courage.

ODO DE Previous to the council of Troyes, the Order consisted of knights only, ST. AMAND. but the rule framed by the holy fathers enjoins the admission of esquires A.D. 1172. and retainers to the vows, in the following terms.

"LXI. We have known many out of divers provinces, as well retain- ers as esquires, fervently desiring for the salvation of their souls to be admitted for life into our house. It is expedient, therefore, that you admit them to the vows, lest perchance the old enemy should suggest something to them whilst in God's service by stealth or unbecomingly, and should suddenly drive them from the right path." Hence arose the great class of serving brethren, (*fratres servientes*), who attended the knights into the field both on foot and on horseback, and added vastly to the power and

* 3 Concil. Lat. cap. 9.

military reputation of the Order. The serving brethren were armed with bows, bills, and swords; it was their duty to be always near the person of the knight, to supply him with fresh weapons or a fresh horse in case of need, and to render him every succour in the affray. The esquires of the knights were generally serving brethren of the Order, but the services of secular persons might be accepted.

The order of the Temple always had in its pay a large number of retainers, and of mercenary troops, both cavalry and infantry, which were officered by the knights. These, were clothed in black or brown garments, that they might, in obedience to the rule,* be plainly distinguished from the professed soldiers of Christ, who were habited in white. The black or brown garment was directed to be worn by all connected with the Templars who had not been admitted to the vows, that the holy soldiers might not suffer, in character or reputation, from the irregularities of secular men their dependents.†

The white mantle of the Templars was a regular monastic habit, having the red cross on the left breast; it was worn over armour of chain mail, and could be looped up so as to leave the sword-arm at full liberty. On his head the Templar wore a white linen coif, and over that a small round cap made of red cloth. When in the field, an iron scull-cap was probably added. We must now take a glance at the military organization of the order of the Temple, and of the chief officers of the society.

ODO DE ST. AMAND. A.D. 1172.

Next in power and authority to the Master stood the Marshal, who was charged with the execution of the military arrangements on the field of battle. He was second in command, and in case of the death of the Master, the government of the Order devolved upon him until the new superior was elected. It was his duty to provide arms, tents, horses, and mules, and all the necessary appendages of war.

The Prior or Preceptor of the kingdom of Jerusalem, also styled "Grand Preceptor of the Temple," had the immediate superintendence over the chief house of the Order in the holy city. He was the treasurer general of the society, and had charge of all the receipts and expenditure. During the absence of the Master from Jerusalem, the entire government of the Temple devolved upon him.

The Draper was charged with the clothing department, and had to distribute garments "free from the suspicion of arrogance and superfluity" to all the brethren. He is directed to take especial care that the habits be "neither too long nor too short, but properly measured for the wearer, with equal measure, and with brotherly regard, that the eye of the whisperer or the accuser may not presume to notice anything."*

* Regula, cap. 20
† Cap 21, 22.

ODO DE
ST. AMAND.
A.D. 1172.
The Standard Bearer (*Balcanifer*) bore the glorious *Beauseant*, or war-banner, to the field; he was supported by a certain number of knights and esquires, who were sworn to protect the colours of the Order, and never to let them fall into the hands of the enemy.

The Turcopilar was the commander of a body of light horse called Turcopoles (*Turcopuli*). These were natives of Syria and Palestine, the offspring frequently of Turkish mothers and Christian fathers, brought up in the religion of Christ, and retained in the pay of the Order of the Temple. They were lightly armed, were clothed in the Asiatic style, and being inured to the climate, and well acquainted with the country, and with the Mussulman mode of warfare, they were found extremely serviceable as light cavalry and skirmishers, and were always attached to the war-battalions of the Templars.

The Guardian of the Chapel (*Custos Capellæ*) had charge of the portable chapel and the ornaments of the altar, which were always carried by the Templars into the field. This portable chapel was a round tent, which was pitched in the centre of the camp; the quarters of the brethren were disposed around it, so that they might, in the readiest and most convenient manner, participate in the divine offices, and fulfill the religious duties of their profession.

Besides the Grand Preceptor of the kingdom of Jerusalem, there were the Grand Preceptors of Antioch and Tripoli, and the Priors or Preceptors of the different houses of the Temple in Syria and in Palestine, all of whom commanded in the field, and had various military duties to perform under the eye of the Master.

The Templars and the Hospitallers were the constituted guardians of the true cross when it was brought forth from its sacred repository in the church of the Resurrection to be placed at the head of the Christian army.
ODO DE
ST. AMAND
A.D. 1172.
The Templars marched on the right of the sacred emblem, and the Hospitallers on the left; and the same position was taken up by the two orders in the line of battle.†

An eye-witness of the conduct of the Templars in the field tells us that they were always foremost in the fight and the last in the retreat; that they proceeded to battle with the greatest order, silence, and circumspection, and carefully attended to the commands of their Master. When the signal to engage had been given by their chief, and the trumpets of the Order sounded to the charge; "then," says he, "they humbly sing the psalm of David, *Non nobis, non nobis, Domine, sed nomini tuo da gloriam*, 'Not unto us, not unto us, O Lord, but unto thy name give the praise;' and placing their lances in rest, they either break the enemy's line or die. If any

* Cap. 20, 27, of the rule.
† *Jac. De Vitr.* Hist. Orient. Apud *Martene* thesaur. nov. anecdot. tom. iii. col. 276, 277.

one of them should by chance turn back, or bear himself less manfully than he ought, the white mantle, the emblem of their order, is ignominiously stripped off his shoulders, the cross worn by the fraternity is taken away from him, and he is cast out from the fellowship of the brethren; he is compelled to eat on the ground without a napkin or a table-cloth for the space of one year; and the dogs who gather around him and torment him he is not permitted to drive away. At the expiration of the year, if he be truly penitent, the Master and the brethren restore to him the military girdle and his pristine habit and cross, and receive him again into the fellowship and community of the brethren. The Templars do indeed practise the observance of a stern religion, living in humble obedience to their Master, without property, and spending nearly all the days of their lives under tents in the open fields."* Such is the picture of the Templars drawn by one of the leading dignitaries of the Latin kingdom.

We must now resume our narrative of the principal events connected with the Order.

In the year 1172, the Knight Templar Walter du Mesnil was guilty of a foul murder, which created a great sensation in the East. An odious religious sect, supposed to be descended from the Ismaelians of Persia, were settled in the fastnesses of the mountains above Tripoli. They devoted their souls and bodies in blind obedience to a chief who is called by the writers of the crusades "the old man of the mountain," and were employed by him in the most extensive system of murder and assassination known in the history of the world. Both Christian and Moslem writers enumerate with horror the many illustrious victims that fell beneath their daggers. They assumed all shapes and disguises for the furtherance of their deadly designs, and carried, in general, no arms except a small poniard concealed in the folds of their dress, called in the Persian tongue *hassissin*, whence these wretches were called *assassins*, their chief the prince of the assassins; and the word itself, in all its odious import, has passed into most European languages.†

Raimond, son of the count of Tripoli, was slain by these fanatics whilst kneeling at the foot of the altar in the church of the Blessed Virgin at Carchusa or Tortosa; the Templars flew to arms to avenge his death; they penetrated into the fastnesses and strongholds of "the mountain chief," and at last compelled him to purchase peace by the payment of an annual tribute of two thousand crowns into the treasury of the Order. In the ninth year of Amalric's reign, *Sinan Ben Suleiman*, imaun of the assassins, sent a trusty counsellor to Jerusalem, offering, in the name of himself and his people, to embrace the Christian religion, provided the Templars would

---

* Narratio Patriarchæ Hierosolymitani coram summon Pontifice de statu Terræ Sanctæ. Ex M. S. Cod. Bigotiano, apud *Martene thesaur.* nov. anecdot. tom. iii. col. 276, 277.

† Dissertation sur les Assassins, Académic des Inscriptions, tom. xvii. p. 127, 170. *De Guignes.* Hist, des Huns.— *Will. Tyr.* lib. xx. cap. 31.

release them from the tribute money. The proposition was favourably received; the envoy was honourably entertained for some days, and on his departure he was furnished by the king with a guide and an escort to conduct him in safety to the frontier. The Ismaelite had reached the borders of the Latin kingdom, and was almost in sight of the castles of his brethren, when he was cruelly murdered by the Knight Templar Walter du Mesnil, who attacked the escort with a body of armed followers.*

The king of Jerusalem, justly incensed at this perfidious action, assembled the barons of the kingdom at Sidon to determine on the best means of obtaining satisfaction for the injury; and it was determined that two of their number should proceed to Odo de St. Amand to demand the surrender of the criminal. The haughty Master of the Temple bade them inform his majesty the king, that the members of the Order of the Temple were not subject to his jurisdiction, nor to that of his officers; that the Templars acknowledged no earthly superior except the Pope; and that to the holy pontiff alone belonged the cognizance of the offence. He declared, however, that the crime should meet with due punishment; that he had caused the criminal to be arrested and put in irons, and would forthwith send him to Rome, but till judgment was given in his case, he forbade all persons of whatsoever degree to meddle with him.†

ODO DE ST. AMAND A.D. 1177.

Shortly afterwards, however, the Master found it expedient to alter his determination, and insist less strongly upon the privileges of his fraternity. Brother Walter du Mesnil was delivered up to the king, and confined in one of the royal prisons, ultimate fate has not been recorded.

On the death of Noureddin, sultan of Damascus, (A.D. 1175), Saladin raised himself to the sovereignty both of Egypt and of Syria. He levied an immense army, and crossing the desert from Cairo, he again planted the standard of Mahomet upon the sacred territory of Palestine. His forces were composed of twenty-six thousand light infantry, eight thousand horsemen, a host of archers and spearmen mounted on dromedaries, and eighteen thousand common soldiers. The person of Saladin was surrounded by a body-guard of a thousand Mamlook emirs, clothed in yellow cloaks worn over their shirts of mail.

In the great battle fought near Ascalon, (Nov. 1, A.D. 1177), Odo de St. Amand, the Master of the Temple, at the head of eighty of his knights, broke through the guard of Mamlooks, slew their commander, and penetrated to the imperial tent, from whence the sultan escaped with great difficulty, almost naked, upon a fleet dromedary; the infidels, thrown into confusion, were slaughtered or driven into the desert, where they perished from hunger, fatigue, or the inclemency of the weather.* The year

---

* *Jac. De Vitr*. Hist. Orient. Lib. iii. p. 1142. *Will. Tyr*. lib. xx. cap. 32.

† Adjecit etiam et alia a *spiritu superbiæ*, quo ipse plurimum abundabat, dictate, quæ præsenti narrationi no multum necessarium est interserere.— *Will. Tyr*. lib. xx. cap. 32.

following, Saladin collected a vast army at Damascus; and the Templars, in order to protect and cover the road leading from that city to Jerusalem, commenced the erection of a strong fortress on the northern frontier of the Latin kingdom, close to Jacob's ford on the river Jordan, at the spot where now stands *Djiss'r Beni Yakoob*, "the bridge of the sons of Jacob." Saladin advanced at the head of his forces to oppose the progress of the work, and the king of Jerusalem and all the chivalry of the Latin kingdom were gathered together in the plain to protect the Templars and their workmen. The fortress was erected notwithstanding all the exertions of the infidels, and the Templars threw into it a strong garrison. Redoubled efforts were then made by Saladin to destroy the place.

At a given signal from the Mussulman trumpets, "the defenders of Islam" fled before "the avengers of Christ;" the Christian forces became disordered in the pursuit, and the swift cavalry of the desert, wheeling upon both wings, defeated with immense slaughter the entire army of the cross. The Templars and the Hospitallers, with the count of Tripoli, stood firm on the summit of a small hillock, and for a long time presented a bold and undaunted front to the victorious enemy. The count of Tripoli at last cut his way through the infidels, and fled to Tyre; the Master of the Hospital, after seeing most of his brethren slain, swam across the Jordan, and fled, covered with wounds, to the castle of Beaufort; and the Templars, after fighting with their customary zeal and fanaticism around the red-cross banner, which waved to the last over the field of blood, were all killed or taken prisoners, and the Master, Odo de St. Amand, fell alive into the hands of the enemy.† Saladin then laid siege to the newly-erected fortress, which was of some strength, being defended by thick walls, flanked with large towers furnished with military engines. After a gallant resistance on the part of the garrison, it was set on fire, and then stormed. "The Templars," says Abulpharadge, "flung themselves some into the fire, where they were burned, some cast themselves into the Jordan, some jumped down from the walls on to the rocks, and were dashed to pieces: thus were slain the enemy." The fortress was reduced to a heap of ruins, and the enraged sultan, it is said, ordered all the Templars taken in the place to be sawn in two, excepting the most distinguished of the knights, who were reserved for a ransom, and were sent in chains to Aleppo.* ARNOLD DE TORROGE A.D. 1180.

Saladin offered Odo de St. Amand his liberty in exchange for the freedom of his own nephew, who was a prisoner in the hands of the Templars; but the Master of the Temple haughtily replied, that he would never, by

* *Will. Tyr.* lib. xxi. cap. 20, 22, 23. Abulfeda Abulpharadge, Chron. Syr. p. 379.

† Capti sunt ibi de nostris, Otto de Sancto Amando militiæ Templi Magister, homo nequaquam superbus et arrogans, spiritum furoris habens in naribus, nec Deum timens, nec ad hominess habens reverentiam.— *Will. Tyr.* lib. xxi. cp. 29. Abulpharadge, Chron. Syr. p. 380, 381.

his example, encourage any of his knights to be mean enough to surrender, that a Templar ought either to vanquish or die, and that he had nothing to give for his ransom but his girdle and his knife.† The proud spirit of Odo de St. Amand could but ill brook confinement; he languished and died in the dungeons of Damascus, and was succeeded by Brother Arnold de Torroge, who had filled some of the chief situations of the Order in Europe.‡

The affairs of the Latin Christians were at this period in a deplorable situation. Saladin encamped near Tiberias, and extended his ravages into almost every part of Palestine. His light cavalry swept the valley of the Jordan to within a day's march of Jerusalem, and the whole country as far as Panias on the one side, and Beisan, D'Jenneen, and Sebaste, on the other, was destroyed by fire and the sword. The houses of the Templars were pillaged and burnt; various castles belonging to the Order were taken by assault;§ but the immediate destruction of the Latin power was arrested by some partial successes obtained by the Christian warriors, and by the skillful generalship of their leaders. Saladin was compelled to retreat to Damascus, after he had burnt Naplous, and depopulated the whole country around Tiberias. A truce was proposed, (A.D. 1184), and as the attention of the sultan was then distracted by the intrigues of the Turcoman chieftains in the north of Syria, and he was again engaged in hostilities in Mesopotamia, he agreed to a suspension of the war for four years, in consideration of the payment by the Christians of a large sum of money.

ARNOLD DE TORROGE A.D. 1184.

Immediate advantage was taken of this truce to secure the safety of the Latin kingdom. A grand council was called together at Jerusalem, and it was determined that Heraclius, the patriarch of the Holy City, and the Masters of the Temple and Hospital, should forthwith proceed to Europe, to obtain succour from the western princes. The sovereign mostly depended upon for assistance was Henry the Second, king of England,* grandson of Fulk, the late king of Jerusalem, and cousin-german to Baldwin, the then reigning sovereign. Henry had received absolution for the murder of Saint Thomas á Becket, on condition that he should proceed in person at the head of a powerful army to the succour of Palestine, and should, at his own expense, maintain two hundred Templars for the

---

* *Abulpharadge*, Chron. Syr. ut sup. Menologium Cisterciente, p. 194. *Bernardus Thesuurarius* de acq. Terr. Sanc. cap. 139.

† Dicens non esse consuetudinis militum Templi ut aliqua redemptio daretur pro eis prater cingulum et cultellum. Chron. *Trivet* apud *Hall* vol. i. p. 77.

‡ Eodem anno quo captus est in vinculis et squalore carceris, nulli lugendus, dicitur obiisBe.— *Will. Tyr.* lib. xxi. cap. 29. Ib. lib. xxii. cap. 7. Gallia Christiana nova, tom. i. col. 258; ibid p. 172, instrumentorum.

§ *Abulfeda*, ad ann. 1182, 3. *Will. Tyr.* lib. xxii. cap. 16—20.

defence of the holy territory.†

The Patriarch and the two Masters landed in Italy, and after furnishing themselves with the letters of the pope, threatening the English monarch with the judgments of heaven if he did not forthwith perform the penance prescribed him, they set out for England. At Verona, the Master of the Temple fell sick and died,‡ but his companions proceeding on their journey, landed in safety in England at the commencement of the year 1185. They were received by the king at Reading, and throwing themselves at the feet of the English monarch, they with much weeping and sobbing saluted him in behalf of the king, the princes, and the people of the kingdom of Jerusalem. They explained the object of their visit, and presented him with the pope's letters, with the keys of the holy sepulchre, of the tower of David, and of the city of Jerusalem, together with the royal banner of the Latin kingdom.§ Their eloquent and pathetic narrative of the fierce inroads of Saladin, and of the miserable condition of Palestine, drew tears from King Henry and all his court.* The English sovereign gave encouraging assurances to the patriarch and his companions, and promised to bring the whole matter before the parliament, which was to meet the first Sunday in Lent.

The patriarch, in the mean time, proceeded to London, and was received by the Knights Templars at the Temple in that city, the chief house of the Order in Britain, where, in the month of February, he consecrated the beautiful Temple church, dedicated to the blessed Virgin Mary, which had just then been erected.†

---

* Undo propter causas pradictas generali providentia statutum est, ut Jerosoly-mitanus Patriarch a, petendi contra immanissimum hostem Saladinum auxilii gratia, ad christianos principos in Europara mitteretur; sed maxime ad illustrem Anglorum regent, cujus efficacior et promptia opera sperabatur.—*Hemingford,* cap. 33; *Radulph de Diceto,* inter; *Hist. Angl.* X. script, p. 622.

† Concil. Magn. Brit. tom. iv. p. 788,789.

‡ Arnauld of Troy. *Radulph de Diceto,* ut sup. p. 625.

§ Eodem anno (1185), Baldewinus rex Jerusalem, et Templares et Hospitalares, miserunt ad regem Angliae Heraclium, sancto civitatis Jerusalem Patriarcha, et summos Hospitalis et Templi Magistros una cum vexillo regio, et clavibus sepulchri Domini, et tunis David, et civitatis Jerusalem; postulantes ab eo celerem succursum . . . . qui statim ad pedes regis provoluti cum fletu magno et singultu, verba salutationis ex parte regis et principum et universe plebis terra Jerosolymitanae proferebant . . . . tradiderunt ei vexillum regium, etc. etc.—*Hoveden,* ad ann. 1185; *Radulph de Diceto,* p. 626.

** *Matt. Westm.* ad ann. 1185; *Guill. Neubr.* tom. i. lib iii. cap. 12, 13. *Chron. Dunst.*

† † *Speed.* Hist. Britain, p. 506. A.D. 1185.

CHAPTER V.

The Temple at London—The vast possessions of the Templars in England—The territorial divisions of the Order—The different preceptories in this country—The privileges conferred on the Templars by the kings of England—The Masters of the Temple at London—Their power and importance.

Li fiere, li Mestre du Temple
Qu'estoient rempli et ample
D'or et d'argent et de richesse,
Et qui menoient tel noblesse,
Ou sont-il? que sont devenu?
Que tant ont de plait maintenu,
Que nul a elz ne s'ozoit prendre
Tozjors achetoient sans vendre
Nul riche a elz n'estoit de prise;
Tant va pot a eue qu'il brise.
Chron. à la suite du Roman de Favel.

THE Knights Templars first established the chief house of their order in England, without Holborn Bars, on the south side of the street, where Southampton House formerly stood, adjoining to which Southampton Buildings were afterwards erected;* and it is stated, that about a century and a half ago, part of the ancient chapel annexed to this establishment, of a circular form, and built of Caen stone, was discovered on pulling down some old houses near Southampton Buildings in Chancery Lane.†

* *Stowe's* Survey; *Tanner*, Notit. Monast; *Dugd.* Orig. Jund.
† *Herbert*, Antiq. Inns of Court.

This first house of the Temple, established by Hugh de Payens himself, before his departure from England, on his return to Palestine, was adapted to the wants and necessities of the Order in its infant state, when the knights, instead of lingering in the preceptories of Europe, proceeded at once to Palestine, and when all the resources of the society were strictly and faithfully forwarded to Jerusalem, to be expended in defence of the faith; but when the Order had greatly increased in numbers, power, and wealth, and had somewhat departed from its original purity and simplicity, we find that the superior and the knights resident in London began to look abroad for a more extensive and commodious place of habitation. They purchased a large space of ground, extending from the White Friars westward to Essex House without Temple Bar,* and commenced the erection of a convent on a scale of grandeur commensurate with the dignity and importance of the chief house of the great religio-military society of the Temple in Britain. It was called the New Temple, to distinguish it from the original establishment at Holborn, which came thenceforth to be known by the name of the Old Temple.†

This New Temple was adapted for the residence of numerous military monks and novices, serving brothers, retainers, and domestics. It contained the residence of the superior and of the knights, the cells and apartments of the chaplains and serving brethren, the council chamber where the chapters were held, and the refectory or dining-hall, which was connected, by a range of handsome cloisters, with the magnificent church, consecrated by the patriarch. Alongside the river extended a spacious pleasure ground for the recreation of the brethren, who were not permitted to go into the town without the leave of the Master. It was used also for military exercises and the training of the horses.

The year of the consecration of the Temple Church, Geoffrey, the superior of the Order in England, caused an inquisition to be made of the lands of the Templars in this country, and the names of the donors thereof,‡ from which it appears, that the larger territorial divisions of the Order

---

* "Yea, and a part of that too," says Sir William Dugdale, in his *origines juridi- ciales*, as appears from the first grant thereof to Sir William Paget, Knight, Pat. ii. Edward VI. p. 2.

† We read on many old charters and deeds, "Datum apud *vetus* Templum Londoniæ." See an example, *Nichols'* Leicestershire, vol. iii. p. 959; see also the account, in Matt. Par. and Hoveden, of the king's visit to Hugh bishop of Lincoln, who lay sick of a fever at the Old Temple, and died there, the 16th November, A.D. 1200.

‡ Anno ab incarnatione Domini MCLXXXY. facta est ista inquisitio de terrarum donatoribus, et earum possessoribus, ecclesiarum scil. et molendinorum, et terrarum assisarum, et in dominico habitarum, et de redditibus assisis per Angliam, per fratrem Galfridum filium Stephani, quando ipse suscepit balliam de Anglia, qui summo studio pradicta inquirendo curam sollicitam exhibuit, ut majoris notitise posteris expressionem generaret, et pervicacibus omnimodam nocendi rescinderet facultatem. Ex. cod. MS. in Scacc. penes Remor. Regis, fol. i. a.; *Dugd*. Monast. Angl. vol. vi. part ii. p. 820.

were then called bailiwicks, the principal of which were London, Warwic, Couele, Meritune, Gutinge, Westune, Lincolnscire, Lindeseie, Widine, and Eboracisire, (Yorkshire). The number of manors, farms, churches, advowsons, demesne lands, villages, hamlets, windmills, and watermills, rents of assize, rights of common and free warren, and the amount of all kinds of property, possessed by the Templars in England at the period of the taking of this inquisition, are astonishing. Upon the great estates belonging to the Order, prioral houses had been erected, wherein dwelt the procurators or stewards charged with the management of the manors and farms in their neighbourhood, and with the collection of the rents. These prioral houses became regular monastic establishments, inhabited chiefly by sick and aged Templars, who retired to them to spend the remainder of their days, after a long period of honourable service against the infidels in Palestine. They were cells to the principal house at London. There were also under them certain smaller administrations established for the management of the farms, consisting of a Knight Templar, to whom were associated some serving brothers of the Order, and a priest who acted as almoner. The commissions or mandates directed by the Masters of the Temple to the officers at the head of these establishments, were called precepts, from the commencement of them, *Præcipimus tibi* we enjoin or direct you, &c. &c. The knights to whom they were addressed were styled *Præceptores Templi*, or Preceptors of the Temple, and the districts administered by them *Præceptoria*, or preceptories.

It will now be as well to take a general survey of the possessions and organization of the Order both in Europe and Asia, "whose circumstances," saith William archbishop of Tyre, writing from Jerusalem about the period of the consecration at London of the Temple Church, "are in so flourishing a state, that at this day they have in their convent (the Temple on Mount Moriah) more than three hundred knights robed in the white habit, besides serving brothers innumerable. Their possessions indeed beyond sea, as well as in these parts, are said to be so vast, that there cannot now be a province in Christendom which does not contribute to the support of the aforesaid brethren, whose wealth is said to equal that of sovereign princes."*

The eastern provinces of the Order were, 1. Palestine, the ruling province. 2. The principality of Antioch. 3. The principality of Tripoli.

1. PALESTINE.—Some account has already been given of the Temple at Jerusalem, the chief house of the Order, and the residence of the Master. In

---

* Quorum res adeo crevit in immensum, ut hodie, trecentc in conventu habeant equites, albis chlamydibus indutos: exceptis fratribus, quorum pene infinitus est numerus. Possessiones autem, tam ultra quam citra mare, adeo dicuntur immensas habere, ut jam non sit in orbe christiano provincia quæ prædictis fratribus suorum portionem non contulerit, et regiis opulentiis pares hodie dicuntur habere copias.—*Will. Tyr.* lib. xii. cap. 7.

addition to the strong garrison there maintained, the Templars possessed numerous forces, distributed in various fortresses and strongholds, for the preservation and protection of the holy territory.

The following castles and cities of Palestine are enumerated by the historians of the Latin kingdom, as having belonged to the Order of the Temple.

The fortified city of Gaza, the key of the kingdom of Jerusalem on the side next to Egypt, anciently one of the five satrapies of the Lords of the Philistines, and the stronghold of Cambyses when he invaded Egypt.

> "Placed where Judea's utmost bounds extend,
> Towards fair Pelusium, Gaza's towers ascend.
> Fast by the breezy shore the city stands
> A mid unbounded plains of barren sands,
> Which high in air the furious whirlwinds sweep,
> Like mountain billows on the stormy deep,
> That scarce the affrighted traveller, spent with toil,
> Escapes the tempest of the unstable soil."

It was granted to the Templars, in perpetual sovereignty, by Baldwin king of Jerusalem.*

The Castle of Saphet, in the territory of the ancient tribe of Naphtali; the great bulwark of the northern frontier of the Latin kingdom on the side next to Damascus. The Castle of the Pilgrims, in the neighbourhood of Mount Carmel. The Castle of Assur near Jaffa, and the House of the Temple at Jaffa. The fortress of Faba, or La Feue, the ancient Aphek, not far from Tyre, in the territory of the ancient tribe of Asher. The hill-fort Dok, between Bethel and Jericho. The castles of La Cave, Marie, Citern Rouge, Castel Blanc, Trapesach, Sominelleria of the Temple, in the neighbourhood of Acca, now St. John d'Acre. Castrum Planorum, and a place called Gerinum Parvum.† The Templars purchased the castle of Beaufort and the city of Sidon;‡ they also got into their hands a great part of the town of St. Jean d'Acre, where they erected their famous temple, and almost all Palestine was in the end divided between them and the Hospitallers of Saint John.

2. THE PRINCIPALITY OF ANTIOCH.—The principal houses of the Temple in this province were at Antioch itself, at Aleppo, Haram, &c.

*Dominus Baldwinus illustris memorial, Hierosolymorum rex quart us, Gazam munitissimam fratribus militia Templi donavit, *Will. Tyr.* lib. xx. cap. 21. Milites Templi Gazam antiquam Palæetinæ civitatem reædificant, et turribus earn muniunt, *Rob. de Monte,* appen. ad chron. Sig. p. 631.

† *Marin. Sanut,* p.221. *Bernard Thesaur.* p. 768. *Radulph Coggleshale,* p. 249. Hoveden, p. 636. Radulph de Diceto, ut sup. p. 623. Matt. Par. p. 142. Italia sacra, tom. iii. p. 407.

‡ Tunc Julianus Dominus Sydonis vendidit Sydonem et Belfort Templariis, *Marin. Sanut,* cap. vi. p. 221.

3. THE PRINCIPALITY OF TRIPOLI.—The chief establishments herein were at Tripoli, at Tortosa, the ancient Antaradus; Castel-blanc in the same neighbourhood; Laodicea and Beyrout,—all under the immediate super-intendence of the Preceptor of Tripoli. Besides these castles, houses, and fortresses, the Templars possessed farms and large tracts of land, both in Syria and Palestine.

The western nations or provinces, on the other hand, from whence the Order derived its chief power and wealth, were:

1. APULIA AND SICILY, the principal houses whereof were at Palermo, Syracuse, Lentini, Butera, and Trapani. The house of the Temple at this last place has been appropriated to the use of some monks of the Order of St. Augustin. In a church of the city is still to be seen the celebrated statue of the Virgin, which Brother Guerrege and three other Knights Templars brought from the East, with a view of placing it in the Temple Church on the Aventine hill in Rome, but which they were obliged to deposit in the island of Sicily. This celebrated statue is of the most beautiful white marble, and represents the Virgin with the infant Jesus reclining on her left arm; it is of about the natural height, and, from an inscription oil the foot of the figure, it appears to have been executed by a native of the island of Cyprus, A.D. 733.*

The Templars possessed valuable estates in Sicily, around the base of Mount Etna, and large tracts of land between Piazza and Calatagirone, in the suburbs of which last place there was a Temple house, the church whereof, dedicated to the Virgin Mary, still remains. They possessed also many churches in the island, windmills, rights of fishery, of pasturage, of cutting wood in the forests, and many important privileges and immuni-ties. The chief house was at Messina, where the Grand Prior resided.†

2. UPPER AND CENTRAL ITALY.—The houses or preceptories of the Order of the Temple in this province were very numerous, and were all under the immediate superintendence of the Grand Prior or Preceptor of Rome. There were large establishments at Lucca, Milan, and Perugia, at which last place the arms of the Temple are still to be seen on the tower of the holy cross. At Placentia there was a magnificent and extensive convent, called Santa Maria del Tempio, ornamented with a very lofty tower. At Bologna there was also a large Temple house, and on a clock in the city is the following inscription, "*Magister Tosseolus de Miolâ me fecit ... Fr. Petrus de Bon, Procur. Militiœ Templi in curiâ Romanâ*, MCCCIII." In the church of St. Mary in the same place, which formerly belonged to the Knights Templars, is the interesting marble monument of Peter de Rotis, a priest of the Order. He is represented on his tomb, holding

---

* *Atlas Marianus*, p. 156; Siciliæ Antiq., tom. iii. col. 1000.

† Gallia Christiana nova, tom. iii. col. 118; Probat. tom. ix. col. 1067, tom. x. col. 1292, tom. xi. col. 46; *Roccus Pyrrhus*, Sicil. Antiq. tom. iii. col. 1093, 4, 5, 6, 7, &c.

a chalice in his hands with the host elevated above it, and beneath the monumental effigy is the following epitaph:—

> Stirpe Rotis, Petrus, virtutis munere clarus,
> Strenuus ecce pugil Christi, jacet ordine charus;
> Veste ferens, menteque crucem, nunc sidera scandit,
> Exemplum nobis spectandi cælica pandit:
> Annis ter trinis viginti mille trecentis
> Sexta quarte maii fregit lux organa mentis."*

PORTUGAL.—In the province or nation of Portugal, the military power and resources of the Order of the Temple were exercised in almost constant warfare against the Moors, and Europe derived essential advantage from the enthusiastic exertions of the warlike monks in that quarter against the infidels. In every battle, indeed, fought in the south of Europe, after the year 1130, against the enemies of the cross, the Knights Templars are to be found taking an active and distinguished part, and in all the conflicts against the infidels, both in the west and in the east, they were ever in the foremost rank, battling nobly in defence of the Christian faith. With all the princes and sovereigns of the great Spanish peninsula they were extremely popular, and they were endowed with cities, villages, lordships, and splendid domains. Many of the most important fortresses and castles in the land were entrusted to their safe keeping, and some were yielded to them in perpetual sovereignty. They possessed, in Portugal, the castles of Monsento, Idanha, and Tomar; the citadel of Langrovia in the province of Beira, on the banks of the Riopisco; and the fortress of·Miravel in Estremadura, taken from the Moors, a strong place perched on the summit of a lofty eminence.

They had large estates at Castromarin, Almural, and Tavirs in Algarve, and houses, rents, revenues, and possessions, in all parts of the country. The Grand Prior or Preceptor of Portugal resided at the castle of Tomar. It is seated on the river Narboan in Estremadura, and is still to be seen towering in gloomy magnificence on the hill above the town. The castle at present belongs to the Order of Christ, and was lately one of the grandest and richest establishments in Portugal. It possessed a splendid library, and a handsome cloister, the architecture of which was much admired.†

CASTILE AND LEON.—The houses or preceptories of the Temple most known in this province or nation of the Order were those of Cuenca and Guadalfagiara, Tine and Aviles in the diocese of Oviedo, and Pontevreda in Galicia. In Castile alone the Order is said to have possessed

---

* *Petrus Maria Campus* Hist. Placent. part ii. n. 28; *Pauli M. Paciandi* de cultu S. Johannis Bapt. Antiq. p. 297.

† Description et delices d'Espagne, tom. iii. p. 259; Hist Portugal, *La Clede*, tom.i. p. 200, 202, &c.; Hispania illustrata, tom. iii. p. 49.

twenty-four bailiwicks.*

ARAGON.—The sovereigns of Aragon, who had suffered grievously from the incursions of the Moors, were the first of the European princes to recognize the utility of the Order of the Temple. They endowed the fraternity with vast revenues, and ceded to them some of the strongest fortresses in the kingdom. The Knights Templars possessed in Aragon the castles of Dumbel, Cabanos, Azuda, Granena, Chalonere, Remolins, Corbins, Lo Mas de Barbaran, Moncon, and Montgausi, with their territories and dependencies. They were lords of the cities of Borgia and Tortosa; they had a tenth part of the revenues of the kingdom, the taxes of the towns of Huesca and Saragossa, and houses, possessions, privileges, and immunities in all parts.†

The Templars likewise possessed lands and estates in the Balearic Isles, which were under the management of the Prior or Preceptor of the island of Majorca, who was subject to the Grand Preceptor of Aragon.

GERMANY AND HUNGARY.—The houses most known in this territorial division of the Order are those in the electorate of Mayence, at Homburg, Assenheim, Rotgen in the Rhingau, Mongberg in the Marché of Brandenbourg, Nuitz on the Rhine, Tissia Altmunmunster near Ratisbon in Bavaria, Bamberg, Middlebourg, Hall, Brunswick, &c. &c. The Templars possessed the fiefs of Rorich, Pausin and Wildenheuh in *Pomerania*, an establishment at Bach in *Hungary,* several lordships in *Bohemia* and *Moravia*, and lands, tithes, and large revenues, the gifts of pious German crusaders.‡

GREECE.—The Templars were possessed of lands and had establishments in the Morea, and in several parts of the Greek empire. Their chief house was at Constantinople, in the quarter called Ὁμόνια, where they had an oratory dedicated to the holy martyrs Marin and Pentaleon.§

FRANCE.—The principal preceptories and houses of the Temple, in the present kingdom of France, were at Besancon, Dole, Salins, à la Romagne, à la ville Dieu, Arbois in *Franche Comté.***

Bomgarten, Temple Savigné near Corbeil, Dorlesheim near Molsheim, where there still remains a chapel called Templehoff, Ribauvillier, and a Temple house in the plain near Bercheim in Alsace.

---

* Annales Minorum, tom. p. 247; tom. vi. p. 211, 218; tom. viii. p. 26, 27; tom. ix. p. 130, 141.—*Campomanes*.

† *Marem* Hispanicæ, col. 1291, 1292, 1304. Gall christ. nov. tom. i. col. 195. *Mariana*, de. reb. Hisp. lib. ii. cap. 23.

‡ Script, rer. Germ. tom. ii. col. 584. Annales Minorum, tom. vi. p. 6, 95, 177. Suevia and Vertenbergia sacra, p. 74. Annal. Bamb. p. 186. Notitiæ episcopatûs Middelb. p. 11. Scrip, de rebus Marchiæ; Brandeburg,p. 13. *Aventinus annal*. lib. vii. cap. 1. n. 7. Gall. christ. nov. tom. viii. col. 1382; tom. i. col. 1129.

§ Constantinopolis christians, lib. iv. p. 157.

** Hist, de l'Eglise de Besancon, tom. ii. p. 397, 421, 450, 474, 445, 470, 509, &c.

Bures, Voulaine les Templiers, Ville-sous-Gevrey, otherwise St. Philibert, Dijon, Fauverney, where a chapel dedicated to the Virgin still preserves the name of the Temple, Des Feuilles, situate in the parish of Villett, near the chateau de Vernay, St. Martin, Le Chastel, Espesses, Tessones near Bourges, and La Musse, situate between Baujé and Macon in *Burgundy*.*

Montpelier, Sertelage, Nogarade near Pamiers, Falgairas, Narbonne St. Eulalie de Bezieres, Prugnanas, and the parish church of St. Martin d'Ubertas in *Languedoc*.†

Temple Cahor, Temple Marigny, Arras, Le Parc, St. Vaubourg, and Rouen, in *Normandy*. There were two houses of the Temple at Rouen; one of them occupied the site of the present *maison consulaire*, and the other stood in the street now called *La Rue des Hermites*.‡ The preceptories and houses of the Temple in France, indeed, were so numerous, that it would be a wearisome and endless task to repeat the names of them. Hundreds of places in the different provinces are mentioned by French writers as having belonged to the Templars. Between Joinville and St. Dizier may still be seen the remains of Temple Ruet, an old chateau surrounded by a moat; and in the diocese of Meaux are the ruins of the great manorial house of Choisy le Temple. Many interesting tombs are there visible, together with the refectory of the knights, which has been converted into a sheepfold.

The chief house of the Order for France, and also for Holland and the Netherlands, was the Temple at Paris, an extensive and magnificent structure, surrounded by a wall and a ditch. It extended over all that large space of ground, now covered with streets and buildings, which lies between the rue du Temple, the rue St. Croix, and the environs de la Verrerie, as far as the walls and the fosses of the port du Temple. It was ornamented with a great tower, flanked by four smaller towers, erected by the Knight Templar Brother Herbert, almoner to the king of France, and was one of the strongest edifices in the kingdom.§ Many of the modern streets of Paris which now traverse the site of this interesting structure, preserve in the names given to them some memorial of the ancient Temple. For instance, *La rue du Temple, La rue des fossés du Temple, Boulevard du Temple, Faubourg du Temple, rue de Faubourg du Temple, Vieille rue du Temple, &c.&c.*

---

* Hist, de l'Eglise de St. Etienne à Dijon, p. 133, 137, 205. Hist, de Bresse, tom. i. p. 52, 55, 84.

† Hist. gen. de Languedoc, liy. ii. p. 523; liv. xvi, p. 362; liv. xvii. p. 427; liv. xxii. p. 25, 226. Gall, christ. tom. vi. col. 727. *Martene Thesaur.* anecd. tom. i. col. 575.

‡ Gall, christ. nor. tom. i. p. 32; tom. iii. col. 333; tom. ii. col. 46, 47, and 72. *La Martiniere diet, geogr. Mariene*, ampL collect, tom. vi. col. 226. Gloss, nov. tom. iii. col. 223.

§ Histoire de la ville de Paris, tom. i. p. 174. Gall, christ, nov. tom. vii. col. 853.

All the houses of the Temple in Holland and the Netherlands were under the immediate jurisdiction of the Master of the Temple at Paris. The preceptories in these kingdoms were very numerous, and the property dependent upon them was of great value. Those most known are the preceptories of Treves and Dietrich on the Soure, the ruins of which last still remain; Coberne, on the left bank of the Moselle, a few miles from Cob-lentz; Belisch, Temple Spele, Temple Rodt near Vianden, and the Temple at Luxembourg, where in the time of Broverus there existed considerable remains of the refectory, of the church, and of some stone walls covered with paintings; Templehuis near Ghent, the preceptory of Alphen, Braeckel, la maison de Slipes near Ostend, founded by the counts of Flanders; Temple Caestre near Mount Cassel; Villiers le Temple en Condros, between Liege and Huy; Vaillenpont, Walsberge, Haut Avenes near Arras; Temploui near Fleuru in the department of Namur; Vernoi in Hainault; Temple Dieu at Douai; Marles near Valenciennes; St. Symphonier near Mons, &c. &c.*

In these countries, as well as in all parts of Europe wherever they were settled, the Templars possessed vast privileges and immunities, which were conceded to them by popes, kings, and princes.

ENGLAND.—There were in bygone times the following preceptories of Knight Templars in the present kingdom of England:

Aslakeby, Temple Bruere, Egle, Malteby, Mere, Wiiketon, and Witham, in *Lincolnshire.*

North Feriby, Temple Hurst, Temple Newsom, Pafflete, Flaxflete, and Ribstane, in *Yorkshire.*

Temple Cumbe in *Somersetshire.*

Ewell, Strode and Swingfield, near Dover, in *Kent.*

Hadescoe, in *Norfolk.*

Balsall and Warwick, in *Warwickshire.*

Temple Rothley, in *Leicestershire.*

Wilburgham Magna, Daney, and Dokesworth, in *Cambridgeshire.*

Halston, in *Shropshire.*

Temple Dynnesley, in *Hertfordshire.*

Temple Cressing and Sutton, in *Essex.*

Saddlescomb and Chapelay, in *Sussex.*

Schepeley, in *Surrey.*

Temple Cowley, Sandford, Bistelesham, and Chalesey, in *Oxfordshire.*

Temple Hockley, in *Wiltshire.*

Upleden and Garwy, in *Herefordshire.*

South Badeisley, in *Hampshire.*

---

* Annales Trevir. Tom. ii. p. 91, 197, 479. *Prodromus* hist. Trevir. p. 1077 *Bertholet* hist. de Luxembourg, tom. v. p. 145. *Joh. Bapt.* Antiq. Flandriæ Gandavum, p. 24, 207. Antiq. Bredanæ, p. 12, 23. *Austroburgus*, p. 115. *Aub Miræi* Diplomat. tom. ii. p. 1165, &c.

Getinges, in *Worcestershire.*

Giselingham and Dunwich, in *Suffolk.**

There were also several smaller administrations established, as before mentioned, for the management of the farms and lands, and the collection of rent and tithes. Among these were Liddele and Quiely in the diocese of Chichester; Eken in the diocese of Lincoln; Adingdon, Wesdall, Aupledina, Cotona, &c. The different preceptors of the Temple in England had under their management lands and property in every county of the realm.†

In *Leicestershire* the Templars possessed the town and the soke of Rotheley; the manors of Rolle, Babbegrave, Gaddesby, Stonesby, and Melton; Rothely wood, near Leicester; the villages of Beaumont, Baresby, Dalby, North and South Mardefeld, Saxby, Stonesby, and Waldon, with land in above eighty others! They had also the churches of Rotheley, Babbegrave, and Rolle; and the chapels of Gaddesby, Grimston, Wartnaby, Cawdwell, and Wykeham.‡

In *Hertfordshire* they possessed the town and forest of Broxbourne, the manor of Chelsin Templars, (*Chelsin Templariorum*), and the manors of Laugenok, Broxbourne, Letchworth, and Temple Dynnesley; demesne lands at Stanho, Preston, Charlton, Walden, Hiche, Chelles, Levecamp, and Benigho; the church of Broxbourne, two watermills, and a lock on the river Lea: also property at Hichen, Pyrton, Ickilford, Offeley Magna, Offeley Parva, Walden Regis, Furnivale, Ipolitz, Wandsmyll, Watton, Therleton, Weston, Gravele, Wilien, Leccheworth, Baldock, Datheworth, Russenden, Codpeth, Sumershale, Buntynford, &c. &c., and the church of Weston.§

In the county of *Essex* they had the manors of Temple Cressynge, Temple Roydon, Temple Sutton, Odewell, Chingelford, Lideleye, Quarsing, Berwick, and Witham; the church of Roydon, and houses, lands, and farms, both at Roydon, at Rivenhall, and in the parishes of Prittlewall and Great and Little Sutton; an old mansion-house and chapel at Sutton, and an estate called Finchinfelde in the hundred of Hinckford.**

In *Lincolnshire* the Templars possessed the manors of La Bruere, Roston, Kirkeby, Brauncewell, Carleton, Akele, with the soke of Lynderby Aslakeby, and the churches of Bruere, Asheby, Akele, Aslakeby, Donington, Ele, Swinderby, Skarle, &c. There were upwards of thirty churches

---

* *Dugd.* Monast. Angl. vol. vi. part 2, p. 800 to 817. Concilia Magnæ Britanniæ, tom. iii. p. 333 to 382. *Acta Rymeri*, tom. iii. p. 279, 288, 291, 295, &c.

† *Acta Rymeri* tom. iii. p. 279, 288, 291,297, &c.

‡ *Nichols'* hist, of Leicestershire.

§ *Clutterbuck's* hist Hertfordshire. *Chaunoey*, antiq. Hert Acta *Rymeri*, tom. iii. p. 133 134. Dodsworthy M. S. vol xxiv.

** *Morant's* hist. *Essex*, Rymer. tom. iii. p. 290 to 294.

in the county which made annual payments to the Order of the Temple, and about forty windmills. the Order likewise received rents in respect of lands at Bracebrig, Brancetone, Scapwic, Timberlaiid, Weleburne, Eringhton, and a hundred other places; and some of the land in the county was charged with the annual payment of sums of money towards the keeping of the lights eternally burning on the altars of the Temple church.*

William Lord of Asheby gave to the Templars the perpetual advowson of the church of Asheby in Lincolnshire, and they in return agreed to find him a priest to sing for ever twice a week in his chapel of St. Margaret.†

In *Yorkshire* the Templars possessed the manors of temple Werreby, Flaxflete, Etton, South Cave, &c.; the churches of Whitcherche, Kelintune, &c.; numerous windmills and lands and rents at Nehus, Skelture, Pennel, and more than sixty other places besides.‡

In *Warwickshire* they possessed the manors of Barston, Shirburne, Balshale, Wolfhey, Cherlecote, Herbebure, Stodleye, Fechehampstead, Cobington, Tysho and Warwick; lands at Chelverscoton, Herdwicke, Morton, Warwick, Hetherburn, Chesterton, Aven, Derset, Stodley, Napton, and more than thirty other places, the several donors whereof are specified in Dugdale's history of Warwickshire; also the churches of Sireburne, Cardinton, &c., and more than thirteen windmills. In 12 Hen. II., William Earl of Warwick built a new church for them at Warwick.§

In *Kent* they had the manors of Lilleston, Hechewayton, Saunford, Sutton, Dartford, Halgel, Ewell, Cocklescomb, Strode, Swinkfield Mennes, West Greenwich, and the manor of Lydden, which now belongs to the archbishop of Canterbury; the advowsons of the churches of West Greenwich and Kingeswode juxta Waltham; extensive tracts of land in Romney marsh, and farms and assize rents in all parts of the county.**

In *Sussex* they had the manors of Saddlescomb and Shipley; lands and tenements at Compton and other places; and the advowsons of the churches of Shipley, Wodmancote, and Luschwyke.††

In *Surrey* they had the manor form of Temple Elfand or Elfante, and an estate at Merrow in the hundred of Woking. In *Gloucestershire*, the manors of Lower Dowdeswell, Pegsworth, Amford, Nishange, and five

---

* Redditus omnium ecclesiarum et molendinorum et terrarum de bailliâ de Lincolnscire. Inquis. terrar. ut sup. fol. 41 b to 48 b and 49 a. *Peck's* MS. in Museo Britannico, vol. iv. fol. 95 et seq.

† *Peck's* MS. ut sup. fol. 95.

‡ Inquis.ut.sup. 58 b to 65 b.

§ Inquis. terror. ut sup. fol. 12 a to 23 a. Dodsworth MS. vol. xx. p. 65, 67, ex quodam rotulo tangente terras Templariorum. Rot. 42, 46, p. 964. Dugd. Baron, tom. i. p. 70.

** Monast. Angl. ut sup. p. 840. *Hasted*. hist. Kent.

†† Ex cod. MS. in officio armorum, L. xvii. fol. 141 a. Calendarium Inquis. post mortem, p. 13. 18.

others which belonged to them wholly or in part, the church of Down Ammey, and lands in Framton, Temple Guting, and Little Rissington. In *Worcestershire* the manor of Templars Lawern, and lands in Flavel, Temple Broughton, and Hanbury.* In *Northamptonshire*, the manors of Asheby, Thorp, Watervill, &c. &c.; they had the advowson of the church of the manor of Hardwicke in Orlington hundred, and we find that "Robert Saunford, Master of the soldiery of the Temple in England," presented to it in the year 1,238.† In *Nottinghamshire*, the Templars possessed the church of Marnham, lands and rents at Gretton and North Carleton; in *Westmoreland*, the manor of Temple Sowerby; in the Isle of Wight, the manor of Uggeton, and lands in Kerne.‡ But it would be tedious further to continue with a dry detail of ancient names and places; sufficient has been said to give an idea of the enormous wealth of the Order in this country, where it is known to have possessed some hundreds of manors, the advowson or right of presentation to churches innumerable, and thousands of acres of arable land, pasture, and woodland, besides villages, farm-houses, mills, and tithes, rights of common, of fishing, of cutting wood in forests, &c. &c.

There were also several preceptories in Scotland and Ireland, which were dependent on the Temple at London.

The annual income of the Order in Europe has been roughly estimated at six millions sterling! According to Matthew Paris, the Templars possessed *nine thousand* manors or lordships in Christendom, besides a large revenue and immense riches arising from the constant charitable bequests and donations of sums of money from pious persons.§ "They were also endowed," says James of Yitry, bishop of Acre, "with farms, towns, and villages, to an immense extent both in the East and in the West, out of the revenues of which they send yearly a certain sum of money for the defence of the Holy Land to their head Master at the chief house of their order in Jerusalem."** The Templars, in imitation of the other monastic establishments, obtained from pious and charitable people all the advow-

---

* *Manning's* Surrey. *Atkyn's* Gloucestershire; and see the references in Tanner *Nash's* Worcestershire.

† *Bridge's* Northamptonshire, vol. ii. p. 100.

‡ *Thoroton's* Nottinghamshire. *Burn and Nicholson's* Westmoreland. Worsley's Isle of Wight.

§ Habuerunt insuper Templarii in Christianitate *novem millia* maneriorum . . . . . præter emolumenta et varios proventu ex fraternitatibus et prædicationibus provenientes, et per privilegia sua accrescent. *Mat.* Par. p. 615, ed. Lond. 1640.

** Amplis autem possesaionibus tam citra mare quam ultra ditati sunt in immensum, villas, civitates et oppida, ex quibus certam pecuniae summam, pro defensione Terra Sanctse, summo eorum magi ro cujus sedes principalis erat in Jerusalem, mittunt annuatim.—*Jac. de Vitr*. Hist. Hierosol. p. 1084.

sons within their reach, and frequently retained the tithe and the glebe in their own hands, deputing a priest of the Order to perform divine service and administer the sacraments.

The manors of the Templars produced them rent either in money, corn, or cattle, and the usual produce of the soil. By the custom in some of these manors, the tenants were annually to mow three days in harvest, one at the charge of the house; and to plough three days, whereof one at the like charge; to reap one day, at which time they should have a ram from the house, eight-pence, twenty-four loaves, and a cheese of the best in the house, together with a pailful of drink. The tenants were not to sell their horse-colts, if they were foaled upon the land belonging to the Templars, without the consent of the fraternity, nor marry their daughters without their license. There were also various regulations concerning the cocks and hens and young chickens.*

We have previously given an account of the royal donations of King Henry the First, of King Stephen and his queen, to the Order of the Temple. These were far surpassed by the pious benefactions of King Henry the Second. That monarch, for the good of his soul and the welfare of his kingdom, granted the Templars a place situate on the river Fleet, near Barnard's Castle, with the whole current of that river at London, for erecting a mill;† also a messuage near Fleet-street; the church of St. Clement ("quæ dicitur Dacorum extra civitatem Londoniæ") and the churches of Elle, Swinderby and Skarle in Lincolnshire, Kingeswode juxta Waltham in Kent, the manor of Stroder in the hundred of Skamele, the vill of Kele in Staffordshire, the hermitage of Flikeamstede, and all his lands at Lange Cureway, a house in Brosal, and the market of Witham; lands at Berghotte, a mill at the bridge of Pembroke Castle, the vill of Finchingfelde, the manor of Rotheley with its appurtenances, and the advowson of the church and its several chapels, the manor of Blalcolvesley, the park of Haleshall, and three *fat bucks* annually, either from Essex or Windsor Forest. He likewise granted them an annual fair at Temple Bruere, and superadded many rich benefactions

---

* Masculum poll am, si natus sit super terram domus, vendere non possunt sine licentiâ fratrum. Si filiam habent, dare non possunt sine licentiâ fratrum. Inquisitio terrarum, ut supr. fol. 18 a.

† The Templars, by diverting the water, created a great nuisance. In A.D. 1290, the *Prior et fratres de Carmelo* (the white friars) complained to the king in parliament of the putrid exhalations arising from the Fleet river, which were so powerful as to overcome all the frankincense burnt at their altar during divine service, and had occasioned the deaths of many of their brethren. They beg that the stench may be removed, lest they also should perish. The Friars preachers (black friars) and the bishop of Salisbury (whose house stood in Salisbury-court) made a similar complaint; as did also Henry Lacy, Earl of Lincoln, who alleges that the Templars (*ipsi de novo Templo*) had turned off the water of the river to their mills at Castle Baignard.—*Rot. Parl.* vol. i. p. 60, 200.

in Ireland.*

The principal benefactors to the Templars amongst the nobility were William Marshall, earl of Pembroke, and his sons William and Gilbert; Robert, lord de Ros; the earl of Hereford; William, earl of Devon; the king of Scotland; William, archbishop of York; Philip Harcourt, dean of Lincoln; the earl of Cornwall; Philip, bishop of Bayeux; Simon de Senlis, earl of Northampton; Leticia and William, count and countess of Ferrara; Margaret, countess of Warwick; Simon de Montfort, earl of Leicester; Robert de Harecourt, lord of Rosewarden; William de Vernon, earl of Devon, &c. &c.†

The Templars, in addition to their amazing wealth, enjoyed vast privileges and immunities within this realm. In the reign of King John they were freed from all amerciaments in the Exchequer, and obtained the privilege of not being compelled to plead except before the king or his chief justice. King Henry the Third granted them free warren in all their demesne lands; and by his famous charter, dated the 9th of February, in the eleventh year of his reign, he confirmed to them all the donations of his predecessors and of their other benefactors; with soc‡ and sac,§ toll‖ and theam,¶ infangenethef,** and unfangenethef,†† and hamsoca, and grithbrich, and blodwite, and flictwite, and hengewite, and learwite, and flemenefrith, murder, robbery, forestal, ordel, and oreste; and he acquitted them from the royal and sheriff's aids, and from hidage, carucage, danegeld and hornegeld, and from military and wapentake services, scutages, tallages, lastages, stallages, from shires and hundreds, pleas and quarrels, from ward and wardpeny, and averpeni, and hundredespeni, and borethalpeni, and thethingepeni, and from the works of parks, castles, bridges, the building of royal houses and all other works; and also from waste regard and view of foresters, and from toll in all markets and fairs, and at all bridges, and upon all highways throughout the kingdom. And he also gave them the chattels of felons and fugitives, and all waifs within their fee.‡‡

In addition to these particular privileges, the Templars enjoyed, under the authority of the Papal bulls, various immunities and advantages, which gave great umbrage to the clergy. They were freed, as

---

* Ex cod. MS. in officio armorum, L. xvii. fol. 141 a. *Dugd.* Monast. Angl. at sup. p. 838. *Tanner*, Notit. Monast.

† *Dugd.* Baronage. Monast. Angl. p. 800 to 844.

‡ Power to hold courts; § to impose and levy fines and amerciaments upon their tenants; ‖ to buy and sell, or to hold a kind of market; ¶ to judge and punish their villains and vassals; ** to try thieves and malefactors belonging to their manors, and taken within the precincts thereof;

†† to judge foreign thieves taken within the said manors, &c.

‡‡ Cart. 11. Hen. 3. M. 33. *Dugd.* Monast. P. 844.

before mentioned, from the obligation of paying tithes, and might, with the consent of the bishop, receive them. No brother of the Temple could be excommunicated by any bishop or priest, nor could any of the churches of the Order be laid under interdict except by virtue of a special mandate from the holy see. When any brother of the Temple, appointed to make charitable collections for the succour of the Holy Land, should arrive at a city, castle, or village, which had been laid under interdict, the churches, on their welcome coming, were to be thrown open, (once within the year), and divine service was to be performed in honour of the Temple, and in reverence for the holy soldiers thereof. The privilege of sanctuary was thrown around their dwellings; and by various papal bulls it is solemnly enjoined that no person shall lay violent hands either upon the persons or the property of those flying for refuge to the Temple houses.*

Sir Edward Coke, in the second part of the Institute of the Laws of England, observes, that "the Templars did so overspread throughout Christendome, and so exceedingly increased in possessions, revenues, and wealth, and specially in England, as you will wonder to reade in approved histories, and withall obtained so great and large priviledges, liberties, and immunities for themselves, their tenants, and farmers, &c., as no other order had the like."† He further observes, that the Knights Templars were *cruce signati*, and as the cross was the ensign of their profession, and their tenants enjoyed great privileges, they did erect crosses upon their houses, to the end that those inhabiting them might be known to be the tenants of the Order, and thereby be freed from many duties and services which other tenants were subject unto; "and many tenants of other lords, perceiving the state and greatnesse of the knights of the said order, and withall seeing the great priviledges their tenants enjoyed, did set up crosses upon their houses, as their very tenants used to do to the prejudice of their lords."

This abuse led to the passing of the statute of Westminster, the second, *chap*. 33,‡ which recites, that many tenants did set up crosses or cause them to be set up on their lands in prejudice of their lords, that the tenants might defend themselves against the chief lord of the fee by the privileges of Templars and Hospitallers, and enacts that such lands should be forfeited to the chief lords or to the king.

Sir Edward Coke observes, that the Templars were freed from tenths and fifteenths to be paid to the king; that they were discharged of purveyance; that they could not be sued for any ecclesiastical cause before the

* Acta *Rymeri*, tom i. p. 54, 298, 574, 575.
† Page 431.
‡ 13 Edward I.

ordinary, *sed coram conservatoribus suorum privilegiorum;* and that of ancient time they claimed that a felon might take to their houses, having their crosses for his safety, as well as to any church. * And concerning these conservers or keepers of their privileges, he remarks, that the Templars and Hospitallers "held an ecclesiasticall court before a canonist, whom they termed *conservator privilegiorum suorum,* which judge had indeed more authority than was convenient, and did dayly, in respect of the height of these two orders, and at their instance and direction, incroach upon and hold plea of matters determinable by the common law, for *cui plus licet quam par est, plus vult quam licet;* and this was one great mischiefe. Another mischiefe was, that this judge, likewise at their instance, in cases wherein he had jurisdiction, would make general citations as pro salute animœ, and the like, without expressing the matter whereupon the citation was made, which also was against law, and tended to the grievous vexation of the subject."† To remedy these evils, another act of parliament was passed, prohibiting Hospitallers and Templars from bringing any man in plea before the keepers of their privileges, for any matter the knowledge whereof belonged to the king's court, and commanding such keepers of their privileges thenceforth to grant no citations at the instance of Hospitallers and Templars, before it be expressed upon what matter the citation ought to be made.‡

Having given an outline of the great territorial possessions of the Order of the Temple in Europe, it now remains for us to present a sketch of its organisation and government The Master of the Temple, the chief of the entire fraternity, ranked as a sovereign prince, and had precedence of all ambassadors and peers in the general councils of the church. He was elected to his high office by the chapter of the kingdom of Jerusalem, which was composed of all the knights of the East and of the West who could manage to attend. The Master had his general and particular chapters. The first were composed of the Grand Priors of the eastern and western provinces, and of all the knights present in the holy territory. The assembling of these general chapters, however, in the distant land of Palestine, was a useless and almost impracticable undertaking, and it is only on the journeys of the Master to Europe, that we hear of the convocation of the Grand Priors of the West to attend upon their chief. The general chapters called together by the Master in Europe were held at Paris, and the Grand Prior of England always received a summons to attend. The ordinary business and the government of the fraternity in secular matters were conducted by the Master with the assistance of his particular chapter of the Latin kingdom, which was composed of such of the Grand

* 2 Inst. p. 432.
† 2 Inat. p. 465.
‡ Stat. Westr. 2, cap. 43, 13 Ed. I.

Priors and chief dignitaries of the Temple as happened to be present in the East, and such of the knights as were deemed the wisest and most fit to give counsel. In these last chapters visitors-general were appointed to examine into the administration of the western provinces.

The western nations or provinces of the Order were presided over by the provincial Masters,* otherwise Grand Priors or Grand Preceptors, who were originally appointed by the chief Master at Jerusalem, and were in theory mere trustees or bare administrators of the revenues of the fraternity, accountable to the treasurer general at Jerusalem, and removeable at the pleasure of the Chief Master. As the numbers, possessions, and wealth of the Templars, however, increased, various abuses sprang up. The members of the Order, after their admittance to the vows, very frequently, instead of proceeding direct to Palestine to war against the infidels, settled down upon their property in Europe, and consumed at home a large proportion of those revenues which ought to have been faithfully and strictly forwarded to the general treasury at the Holy City. They erected numerous convents or preceptories, with churches and chapels, and raised up in each western province a framework of government similar to that of the ruling province of Palestine.

The chief house of the Temple in England, for example, after its removal from Holborn Bars to the banks of the Thames, was regulated and organised after the model of the house of the Temple at Jerusalem. The superior is always styled "Master of the Temple," and holds his chapters and has his officers corresponding to those of the chief Master in Palestine. The latter, consequently, came to be denominated *Magnus Magister,* or Grand Master,† by our English writers, to distinguish him from the Master at London, and henceforth he will be described by that title to prevent confusion. The titles given indeed to the superiors of the different nations or provinces into which the Order of the Temple was divided, are numerous and somewhat perplexing. In the East, these officers were known only, in the first instance, by the title of Prior, as Prior of England, Prior of France, Prior of Portugal, &c., and afterwards Preceptor of England, preceptor of France, &c.; but in Europe they were called Grand Priors and Grand Preceptors, to distinguish them from the Subpriors and Sub-preceptors, and also Masters of the Temple. The Prior and Preceptor of England, therefore, and the Grand Prior, Grand Preceptor, and Master of the Temple in England, were one and the same person. There were also at the New Temple at London, in imitation of the establishment at the chief house in Palestine, in addition to the Master, the Preceptor of

---

* The title Master of the Temple was so generally applied to the superiors of the western provinces, that we find in the Greek of the lower empire, the words Τέμπλον Μαιστώρ *Ducange* . Gloss

† Also summus magister, magister generalis.

the Temple, the Prior of London, the Treasurer, and the Guardian of the church, who had three chaplains under him, called readers.*

The Master at London had his general and particular, or his ordinary and extraordinary chapters. The first were composed of the grand preceptors of Scotland and Ireland, and all the provincial priors and preceptors of the three kingdoms, who were summoned once a year to deliberate on the state of the Holy Land, to forward succour, to give an account of their stewardship, and to frame new rules and regulations for the management of the temporalities.† The ordinary chapters were held at the different preceptories, which the Master of the Temple visited in succession. In these chapters new members were admitted into the Order; lands were bought, sold, and exchanged; and presentations were made by the Master to vacant benefices. Many of the grants and other deeds of these chapters, with the seal of the Order of the Temple annexed to them, are to be met with in the public and private collections of manuscripts in this country. One of the most interesting and best preserved, is the Harleian charter (83, c. 39), in the British Museum, which is a grant of land made by Brother William de la More, the martyr, the last Master of the Temple in England, to the Lord Milo de Stapleton. It is expressed to be made by him, with the common consent and advice of his chapter, held at the Preceptory of Dynneslee, on the feast of Saint Barnabas the Apostle, and concludes, "In witness whereof, we have to this present indenture placed the seal of our chapter."‡ A facsimile of this seal is given on the page above. On the reverse of it is a man's head, decorated with a long beard, and surmounted by a small cap, and around it are the letters TESTISV-MAGI. The same seal is to be met with on various other indentures made by the Master and Chapter of the Temple.§ The more early seals are surrounded with the words, Sigillum *Militis* Templi, "Seal of the *Knight* of the Temple;" as in the case of the deed of exchange of lands at Normanton in the parish of Botisford, in Leicestershire, entered into between Brother Amadeas de Morestello, Master of the chivalry of the Temple in England, and his chapter, of the one part, and the Lord Henry de Colevile, Knight, of the other part. The seal annexed to this deed has the addition of the word *Militis*, but in other respects it is similar to the one above delineated.**

The Master of the Temple was controlled by the visitors-general of the

---

* Concil. Mag. Brit. tom. ii. p. 335, 339, 340. Monast. Angl. p. 818.

† Concil. Mag. Brit. Tom. ii. p. 355, 356.

‡ Incujus rei testimonium huic præsenti scripto indentato sigillun capituli nostril apposuimus.

§ MS. Apud Belvoir. *Peck's* MS. In Museo Britannico, vol. iv. p. 65.

** *Nicholl's* Hist. Leicestershire, vol. iii. pl. cxxvii. fig. 947, p. 943.; vol. ii. pl. v. fig. 13.

†† Two of these visitors-general have been buried in the Temple Church.

Order,†† who were knights specially deputed by the Grand Master and convent of Jerusalem to visit the different provinces, to reform abuses, make new regulations, and terminate such disputes as were usually reserved for the decision of the Grand Master. These visitors-general sometimes removed knights from their preceptories, and even suspended the masters themselves, and it was their duty to expedite to the East all such knights as were young and vigorous, and capable of fighting. Two regular voyages were undertaken from Europe to Palestine in the course of the year, under the conduct of the Templars and Hospitallers, called the *passagium Martis*, and the *passagium Sancti Johannis*, which took place respectively in the spring and summer, when the newly-admitted knights left the preceptories of the West, taking with them hired foot soldiers, armed pilgrims, and large sums of money, the produce of the European possessions of the fraternity, by which means a continual succour was afforded to the Christian kingdom of Jerusalem. One of the grand priors or grand preceptors generally took the command of these expeditions, and was frequently accompanied by many valiant secular knights, who craved permission to join his standard, and paid large sums of money for a passage to the far East. In the interval between these different voyages, the young knights were diligently employed at the different preceptories in the religious and military exercises necessary to fit them for their high vocation.

On any sudden emergency, or when the ranks of the Order had been greatly thinned by the casualties of war, the Grand Master sent circular letters to the grand preceptors or masters of the western provinces, requiring instant aid and assistance, on the receipt of which collections were made in the churches, and all the knights that could be spared forthwith embarked for the Holy Land.

The Master of the Temple in England sat in parliament as first baron of the realm, (*primus baro Angliæ*), but that is to be understood among priors only. To tbe parliament holden in the twenty-ninth year of King Henry the Third, there were summoned sixty-five abbots, thirty-five priors, and the Master of the Temple.* The oath taken by the grand priors, grand preceptors, or provincial Masters in Europe, on their assumption of the duties of their high administrative office, was drawn up in the following terms:—

"I, *A. B.*, Knight of the Order of the Temple, just now appointed Master of the knights who are in ———— promise to Jesus Christ my Saviour, and to his vicar the sovereign pontiff and his successors, perpetual obedience and fidelity. I swear that I will defend, not only with my lips, but by force of arms and with all my strength, the mysteries of the faith; the seven sacraments, the fourteen articles of the faith, the creed of the

---

* Rot. claus. 49. H. III. m. xi. d. *Acta Rymeri*, tom. iii. p. 802.

Apostles, and that of Saint Athanasius; the books of the Old and the New Testament, with the commentaries of the holy fathers, as received by the church; the unity of God, the plurality of the persons of the holy Trinity; that Mary, the daughter of Joachim and Anna, of the tribe of Judah, and of the race of David, remained always a virgin before her delivery, during and after her delivery. I promise likewise to be submissive and obedient to the Master-general of the Order, in conformity with the statutes prescribed by our father Saint Bernard; that I will at all times in case of need pass the seas to go and fight; that I will always afford succour against the infidel kings and princes; that in the presence of three enemies I will fly not, but cope with them, if they are infidels; that I will not sell the property of the Order, nor consent that it be sold or alienated; that I will always preserve chastity; that I will be faithful to the king of ————; that I will never surrender to the enemy the towns and places belonging to the Order; and that I will never refuse to the religious any succour that I am able to afford them; that I will aid and defend them by words, by arms, and by all sorts of good offices; and in sincerity and of my own free will I swear that I will observe all these things."*

Among the earliest of the Masters, or Grand Priors, or Grand Preceptors of England, whose names figure in history, is Richard de Hastings, who was at the head of the Order in this country on the accession of King Henry the Second to the throne,† (A.D. 1154), and was employed by that monarch in various important negotiations. In the year 1160 he greatly offended the king of France. The Princess Margaret, the daughter of that monarch, had been betrothed to Prince Henry, son of Henry the Second, king of England; and in the treaty of peace entered into between the two sovereigns, it was stipulated that Gizors and two other places, part of the dowry of the princess, should be consigned to the custody of the Templars, to be delivered into King Henry's hands after the celebration of the nuptials. The king of England (A.D. 1160) caused the prince and princess, both of whom were infants, to be married in the presence of Richard de Hastings, the Grand Prior or Master of the Temple in England, and two other Knights Templars, who, immediately after the conclusion of the ceremony, placed the fortresses in King Henry's hands.* The king of France was highly indignant at this proceeding, and some writers accuse the Templars of treachery, but from the copy of the treaty published by

---

* L'histoire des Cisteaux, *Chrisost. Henrique*, p. 479.

† Ricardus de Hastinges, Magister omnium militum et fratrum Templi qui sunt in AngliA, salutem. Notum vobis facimus quod omnis controversia quæ fuit inter nos et monachos de Kirkested . . . . . terminata et finita est assensu et consilio nostro et militum et fratrum, &c., anno ab incarnatione Domini 1155, 11 die kal. Feb. The archbishop of Canterbury, the papal legate, the bishop of Lincoln, and several abbots, are witnesses to this instrument.— *Lansdown* MS. 207 E, fol. 467, p. 162, 163; see also p. 319, where he is mentioned as Master, A.D. 1161.

Lord Littleton† it does not appear that they acted with bad faith.

The above Richard de Hastings was the friend and confidant of Thomas á Becket. During the disputes between that haughty prelate and the king, the archbishop, we are told, withdrew from the council chamber, where all his brethren were assembled, and went to consult with Richard de Hastings, the Prior of the Temple at London, who threw himself on his knees before him, and with many tears besought him to give in his adherence to the famous councils of Clarendon.‡

Richard de Hastings was succeeded by Richard Mallebeench, who confirmed a treaty of peace and concord which had been entered into between his predecessor and the abbot of Kirkested§ and the next Master of the Temple appears to have been Geoffrey son of Stephen, who received the Patriarch Heraclius as his guest at the new Temple on the occasion of the consecration of the Temple church, He styles himself "*Minister* of the soldiery of the Temple in England."**

In consequence of the high estimation in which the Templars were held, and the privilege of sanctuary enjoyed by them, the Temple at London came to be made "a storehouse of treasure." The wealth of the king, the nobles, the bishops, and of the rich burghers of London, was generally deposited therein, under the safeguard and protection of the military friars.†† The money collected in the churches and chapels for the succour of the Holy Land was also paid into the treasury of the Temple, to be forwarded to its destination: and the treasurer was at different times authorised to receive the taxes imposed upon the moveables of the ecclesiastics, also the large sums of money extorted by the rapacious popes from the English clergy, and the annuities granted by the king to the nobles of the kingdom.* The money and jewels of Hubert de Burgh, earl

---

* Et Paulo post rex Angliæ fecut Henricum filium suum desponsare Margaritam filiam regis Franciæ, cum adhuc essent pueruli in cunis vagientes; videntibus et consentientibus Roberto de Pirou et Toster de Sancto Homero et Ricardo de Hastinges, Templariis, qui custodiebant præfata castella, et statim tradiderunt illa castella regi Angilæ, unde rex Franciæ pluimum iratus fugavit illos tres Templarios de regno Franciæ, quos rex Angliæ benigne suscipiens, multis ditavit honoribus.— *Rog. Hoveden*, script. Post Vedam, p. 492. *Guilielmi Neubrigiensis* hist. lib. ii. cap. 4, apud *Hearne*.

† Life of Henry II. tom. iv. p. 203.

‡ Ib. tom. ii. p. 356. Hist. quad. P. 38. *Hoveden*, 453. *Chron. Gervasii*, p. 1386, apud X script.

§ Ricardus Mallebeench, *magister* omnium pauperum militum et fratrum Templi Salomonis in Angliâ, &c. … Confirmavimus pacem et concordiam quam Ricardus de Hastings fecit cum Waltero abbate de Kirkested.— *Lansdown* MS. 207 E., fol. 467.

** Gaufridus, filius Stephant, militiæ Templi in Angliâ Minister, assensu totius capituli nostril dedi, &c., totum illud tenementum in villâ de Scamtrun quod Emma uxor Walteri Cameraii tenet de domo nostrâ, &c. Ib.fol. 201.

†† Post.

of Kent, the chief justiciary, and at one time governor of the king and kingdom of England, were deposited in the Temple, and when that nobleman was disgraced and committed to the Tower, the king attempted to lay hold of the treasure.

Matthew Paris gives the following curious account of the affair:

"It was suggested," says he, "to the king, that Hubert had no small amount of treasure deposited in the New Temple, under the custody of the Templars. The king, accordingly, summoning to his presence the Master of the Temple, briefly demanded of him if it was so. He indeed, not daring to deny the truth to the king, confessed that he had money of the said Hubert, which had been confidentially committed to the keeping of himself and his brethren, but of the quantity and amount thereof he was altogether ignorant. Then the king endeavoured with threats to obtain from the brethren the surrender to him of the aforesaid money, asserting that it had been fraudulently subtracted from his treasury. But they answered to the king, that *money confided to them in trust they would deliver to no man without the permission of him who had intrusted it to he kept in the Temple.* And the king, since the above-mentioned money had been placed under their protection, ventured not to take it by force. He sent, therefore, the treasurer of his court, with his justices of the Exchequer, to Hubert, who had already been placed in fetters in the Tower of London, that they might exact from him an assignment of the entire sum to the king. But when these messengers had explained to Hubert the object of their coming, he immediately answered that he would submit himself and all belonging to him to the good pleasure of his sovereign. He therefore petitioned the brethren of the chivalry of the Temple that they would, in his behalf, present all his keys to his lord the king, that he might do what he pleased with the things deposited in the Temple. This being done, the king ordered all that money, faithfully counted, to be placed in his treasury, and the amount of all the things found to be reduced into writing and exhibited before him. The king's clerks, indeed, and the treasurer acting with them, found deposited in the Temple gold and silver vases of inestimable price, and money and many precious gems, an enumeration whereof would in truth astonish the hearers."†

The kings of England frequently resided in the Temple, and so also did the haughty legates of the Roman pontiffs, who there made contributions in the name of the pope upon the English bishoprics. Matthew Paris gives a lively account of the exactions of the nuncio Martin, who resided for many years at the Temple, and came there armed by the pope with

---

* The money is ordered to be paid "dilecto filio nostro Thesaurario domus militiæ Templi Londonien." Acta *Rymeri*, tom. i. p. 442, 4, 5. *Wilkins Concilia*, tom. ii. p. 230.

† *Matt. Par.* p. 381.

powers such as no legate had ever before possessed. "He made," says he, "whilst residing at London in the New Temple, unheard of extortions of money and valuables. He imperiously intimated to the abbots and priors that they must send him rich presents, desirable palfreys, sumptuous services for the table, and rich clothing; which being done, that same Martin sent back word that the things sent were insufficient, and he commanded the givers thereof to forward him better things, on pain of suspension and excommunication.*

The convocations of the clergy and the great ecclesiastical councils were frequently held at the Temple, and laws were there made by the bishops and abbots for the government of the church and monasteries in England.†

* *Matt. Par.* p. 253, 645.
† *Wilkins*, Concilia Magnæ Britaniæ, tom. ii. p. 19, 26, 93, 239, 253, 272, 292.

CHAPTER VI.

The Patriarch Heraclius quarrels with the king of England—He returns to Palestine without succour—The disappointments and gloomy forebodings of the Templars—They prepare to resist Saladin—Their defeat and slaughter—The valiant deeds of the Marshal of the Temple—The fatal battle of Tiberias—The captivity of the Grand Master and the true Cross—The captive Templars are offered the Koran or death—They choose the latter, and are beheaded—The fall of Jerusalem—The Moslems take possession of the Temple—They purify it with rose-water, say prayers, and hear a sermon—The Templars retire to Antioch—Their letters to the king of England and the Master of the Temple at London—Their exploits at the siege of Acre.

"Gloriosa civitas Dei Jerusalem, ubi dominus passus, ubi sepultus, ubi gloriam resurrectionis ostendit, hosti spurio subjicitur polluenda, nec est dolor sicut dolor iste, cum sepulchrum possideant qui sepulchrum persequuntur, crucem teneant qui crucifixum contemnunt."—*The Lamentation of Geoffrey de Vinisauf over the Fall of Jerusalem.*

"The earth quakes and trembles because the king of heaven hath lost his land, the land on which his feet once stood. The foes of the Lord break into his holy city, even into that glorious tomb where the virgin blossom of Mary was wrapt up in linen and spices, and where the first and greatest flower on earth rose up again."—*St. Bernard*, epist. cccxxii.

ERARD DE ſDERFORT. A.D. 1185. THE Grand Master, Arnold de Torroge, who died on his journey to England, as before mentioned, was succeeded by Brother Gerard de Riderfort.*

On the tenth of the calends of April, a month after the consecration by the patriarch Heraclius of the Temple church, the grand council or parliament of the kingdom, composed of the bishops, earls, and barons, assembled in the house of the Hospitallers at Clerkenwell in London. It was attended by William king of Scotland and David his brother, and many of the counts and barons of that distant land.† The august assembly was

---

* *Bernard Thesaur.* cap. 157, apud *Muratori* script. Rer. Ital. p. 792. *Cotton* MS., Nero E. vi. p. 60, fol. 466.

† *Radulph de Diceto*, ut Bup. p. 626. *Matt. Par.* ad ann. 118.

acquainted, in the king's name, with the object of the solemn embassy just sent to him from Jerusalem, and with the desire of the royal penitent to fulfil his vow and perform his penance; but the barons were at the same time reminded of the old age of their sovereign, of the bad state of his health, and of the necessity of his presence in England. They accordingly represented to King Henry that the solemn oath taken by him on his coronation was an obligation antecedent to the penance imposed on him by the pope; that by that oath he was bound to stay at home and govern his dominions, and that, in their opinion, it was more wholesome for the king's soul to defend his own country against the barbarous French, than to desert it for the purpose of protecting the distant kingdom of Jerusalem. They, however, offered to raise the sum of fifty thousand marks for the levying of troops to be sent into Asia, and recommended that all such prelates and nobles as desired to take the cross should be permitted freely to leave the kingdom on so pious an enterprise.*

Fabian gives the following quaint account of the king's answer to the patriarch, from the Chron. Joan Bromton: "Lasteley, the kynge gaue answere, and sayde that he myghte not leue hys lande wythoute kepynge, nor yet leue yt to the praye and robbery of Frenchemen. But he wolde gyue largely of hys owne to such as wolde take upon theym that vyaffe. Wyth thys answere the patryarke was dyscontente, and sayde, 'We seke a man, and not money; welnere euery crysten regyon sendyth unto us money, but no lande sendyth to us a prince. Therefore we aske a prynce that nedeth money, and not money that nedeth a prynce.' But the kynge layde for hym suche excuses, that the patryarke departed from hym dyscontentyd and comforteless, whereof the kynge beynge aduertysed, entendynge somwhat to recomforte hym wyth pleasaunte wordes, folowed hym unto the see syde. But the more the kynge thought to satysfye liyni wyth hys fay re speche, the more the patryarke was discontented, in so myelin that at the laste he sayde unto hym, 'Hytherto thou haste reygned gloryously, but here after thou shalt be forsaken of him whom thou at thys tyme forsakeste. Thynke on hym what he hath gyuen to thee, and what thou haste yelden to him agayne: howe fyrste thou were false unto the kynge of Fraunce, and after slewe that holy man Thomas of Caunterburye, and lastly thou forsakeste the proteccyon of Crystes faith.' The kynge was amoued wyth these wordes, and sayde unto the patryarke, 'Though all the men of my lande were one bodye, and spake with one mouth, they durste not speke to me such wordys.' 'No wonder,' sayde the patriarke, 'for they loue thyne and not the; that ys to meane, they loue thy goodes temporall, and fere the for losse of promocyon, but they loue not thy soule.' And when he hadde so sayde, he offeryd hys

GERARD]
RIDERFOR
A.D. 1185.

GERARD [
RIDERFOR
A.D. 1185,

* *Hoveden* annal. apud rer. Angl. script, post Bedam, p. 636, 637.

hedde to the kynge, sayenge, 'Do by me ryghte as thou dyddest by that blessed man Thomas of Caunterburye, for I had leur to be slayne of the, then of the Sarasyns, for thou art worse than any Sarasyn.' But the kynge kepte hys pacyence, and sayde, 'I may not wende oute of my lande, for myne own sonnes wyll aryse agayne me whan I were absente.' 'No wonder,' sayde the patryarke, 'for of the deuyll they come, and to the deuyll they shall go,' and so departyd from the kynge in great ire.''*

ERARD DE
IDERFORT.
A.D. 1185.

According to Roger de Hoveden, however, the patriarch, on the 17th of the calends of May, accompanied King Henry into Normandy, where a conference was held between the sovereigns of France and England concerning the proposed succour to the Holy Land. Both monarchs were liberal in promises and fair speeches; but as nothing short of the presence of the king of England, or of one of his sons, in Palestine, would satisfy the patriarch, that haughty ecclesiastic failed in his negotiations, and returned in disgust and disappointment to the Holy Land.† On his arrival at Jerusalem with intelligence of his ill success, the greatest consternation prevailed amongst the Latin christians; and it was generally observed that the true cross, which had been recovered from the Persians by the Emperor Heraclius, was about to be lost under the pontificate, and by the fault of a patriarch of the same name.

ERARD DE
IDERFORT.
A.D. 1185.

A resident in Palestine has given us some curious biographical notices of this worthy consecrator of our Temple church at London. He says that he was a very handsome parson, and, in consequence of his beauty, the mother of the king of Jerusalem fell in love with him, and made him archbishop of Cæsarea, *(biau clerc estoit, et par sa beauté l'ama la mere de roi, et le fist arcevesque de Cesaire).* He then describes how he came to be made patriarch, and how he was suspected to have poisoned the

---

* The above passage is almost literally translated from Abbot Bromton's Chronicle. The Patriarch there says to the king, "Hactenus gloriose regnasti, sed amodo ipse te deseret quem tu deseruisti. Recole quæ dominus tibi contulit, et qualia illi reddidisti; quomodo regi Franciæ infidus fuisti, beatum Thomam occidisti, et nunc protectionem Christianorum abjecisti. Cumque ad hoc rex excandesceret, obtulit patriarcha caput suum et collum ex ten sum, dicens, 'Fac de me quod de *Thomá* fecisti. Adeo libenter volo a te occidi in Anglia, sicut a Saracenis in Syria, quia tu omni Saraceno pejor es.' Cui rex, 'Si omnes homines mei unura corpus essent, unoque ore loquerentur, talia mihi dicere non auderent.' Cui ille, 'Non est mirum, quia tu et non te diligunt, prasdam etiam et non hominem sequitur turba ista.' Recedere non possum, quia filii mei insurgerent in me absentem.' Cui ille, 'Nec mirum, quia de diabolo venerunt, et ad diabolum ibunt.' Et sic demum patriarcha navem ascendens in Galliam reversus est."— *Chron.Joan. Bromton,* abbatis Jornalensis, script. X. p. 1144, ad ann. 1185.

† Sed hæc omnia præfatus Patriarcha parum pendebat, sperabat enim quod esset reducturus secum ad defensionem Ierosolymitanæ terræ præfatum regem Angliae, vel aliquem de filiis suis, vel aliquem virum magna auctoritatis; sed quia hoc esse non potuit, repatriaturus dolens et confusus a curia recessit.—*Hoveden* ut sup. p. 630.

archbishop of Tyre. After his return from Rome he fell in love with the wife of a haberdasher who lived at Naplous, twelve miles from Jerusalem. He went to see her very often, and, not long after the acquaintanceship commenced, the husband died. Then the patriarch brought the lady to Jerusalem, and bought for her a very fine stone house. "Le patriarche la fist venir en Jerusalem, et li acheta bonne maison de pierre. Si la tenoit voiant le siecle ausi com li hons fait sa fame, fors tant que ele n'estoit mie avec lui. Quant ele aloit au mostier, ele estoit ausi atornée de riches dras, com ce fust un emperris, et si serjant devant lui. Quant aucunes gens la veoient qui ne la connoissoient pas, il demandoient qui cele dame estoit. Cil qui la connoissoient, disoient que cestoit la fame du patriarche. Ele avoit nom Pasque de Riveri. Enfans avoit du patriarche, et les barons estoient, que là où il se conseilloient, vint un fol ou patriarche, si li dist; 'Sire Patriarche, dones moi bon don, car je vous aport bones novelles *Pasque de Riveri, vostre fame, a une bele file!*'"* "When Jesus Christ," says the learned author, "saw the iniquity and wickedness which they committed in the very place where he was crucified, he could no longer suffer it."

The Order of the Temple was at this period all-powerful in Palestine, and the Grand Master, Gerard de Riderfort, coerced with the heavy hand of authority the nobles of the kingdom, and even the king himself. Shortly after the return of Heraclius to Palestine, King Baldwin IV. died, and was succeeded by his infant nephew, Baldwin V., who was crowned in the church of the Resurrection, and was afterwards royally entertained by the Templars in the Temple of Solomon, according to ancient custom.† The young king died at Acre after a short reign of only seven months, and the Templars brought the body to Jerusalem, and buried it in the tombs of the Christian kings. The Grand Master of the Temple then raised Sibylla, the mother of the deceased monarch, and her second husband, Guy of Lusignan, to the throne. Gerard de Riderfort surrounded the palace with troops; he closed the gates of Jerusalem, and delivered the regalia to the Patriarch. He then conducted Sibylla and her husband to the church of the Resurrection, where they were both crowned by Heraclius, and were afterwards entertained at dinner in the Temple. Guy de Lusignan was a prince of handsome person, but of such base renown, that his own brother Geoffrey was heard to exclaim, "Since they have made *him* a king, surely they would have made *me* a God!" These proceedings led

GERAR
RIDERF
A.D. 11

---

* *Contin. Hist. Bell. Sacr.* apud *Martene*, tom. v. col. 606. It appears from *Mansi* that this valuable old chronicle, formerly attributed to Hugh Plagon, is the original Freucli work of *Bernard the Treasurer.*

† Quand le roi avoit offert sa corone au Temple Dominus, si avaloit uns degres qui sont dehors le Temple, et entroit en son pales au Temple de Salomon, ou li Templiers manoient. La etoient les tables por mengier, ou le roi s'asseoit, et si baron et tuit cil qui mengier voloient.—Contin. bell. sacr. apud *Martene*, tom. v. col. 586.

to endless discord and dissension; Raymond, Count of Tripoli, withdrew from court; many of the barons refused to do homage, and the state was torn by faction and dissension at a time when all the energies of the population were required to defend the country from the Moslems.*

GERARD DE
RIDERFORT.
A.D. 1186.
Saladin, on the other hand, had been carefully consolidating and strengthening his power, and was vigorously preparing for the reconquest of the Holy City, the long-cherished enterprise of the Mussulraen. The Arabian writers enthusiastically recount his pious exhortations to the true believers, and describe with vast enthusiasm his glorious preparations for the holy war. Bohadin F. Sjeddadi, his friend and secretary, and great biographer, before venturing upon the sublime task of describing his famous and sacred actions, makes a solemn confession of faith, and offers up praises to the one true God.

"Praise be to God," says he, "who hath blessed us with *Islam*, and hath led us to the understanding of the true faith beautifully put together, and hath befriended us; and, through the intercession of our prophet, hath loaded us with every blessing . . . I bear witness that there is no God but that one great God who hath no partner, (a testimony that will deliver our souls from the smoky fire of hell), that Mohammed is his servant and apostle, who hath opened unto us the gates of the right road to salvation . . ."

"These solemn duties being performed, I will begin to write concerning the victorious defender of the faith, the tamer of the followers of the cross, the lifter up of the standard of justice and equity, the saviour of the world and of religion, Saladin Abool-modaffer Joseph, the son of Job, the son of Schadi, Sultan of the Moslems, ay, and of Islam itself; the deliverer of the holy house of God (the Temple) from the hands of the idolaters, the servant of two holy cities, whose tomb may the Lord moisten with the dew of his favour, affording to him the sweetness of the fruits of the faith."†

GERARD DE
RIDERFORT.
A.D. 1187.
On the 10th of May, A.D. 1187, Malek-el-Afdal, "Most excellent prince," one of Saladin's sons, crossed the Jordan at the head of seven thousand Mussulmen. The Grand Master of the Temple immediately despatched messengers to the nearest convents and castles of the Order, commanding all such knights as could be spared to mount and come to him with speed. At midnight, ninety knights of the garrison of La Feue or Faba, forty knights from the garrison of Nazareth, with many others from the convent of Caco, were assembled around their chief, and began their march at the head of the serving brothers and the light cavalry of the Order. They

---

* Contin. Hist. ut sup., col. 593, 4. *Bernard. Thesaur* apud *Muratori* script, rer. Ital., tom. vii. cap. 147, col. 782, cap. 148, col. 173. Assizes de Jerusalem, cap. 287, 288. *Guill Neubr.* cap. 16.

† Vita et res gestæ Saladini by *Bohadin F. Sjeddadi,* apud *Schultens,* ex. MS. Arab. Pref.

joined themselves to the Hospitallers, rashly engaged the seven thousand Moslems, and were cut to pieces in a bloody battle fought near the brook Kishon. The Grand Master of the Temple and two knights broke through the dense ranks of the Moslems, and made their escape. Roger de Molines, the Grand Master of the Hospital, was left dead upon the field, together with all the other brothers of the Hospital and of the Temple.

Jacqueline de Mailly, the Marshal of the Temple, performed prodigies of valour. He was mounted on a white horse, and clothed in the white habit of his order, with the blood-red cross, the symbol of martyrdom, on his breast; he became, through his gallant bearing and demeanour, an object of respect and of admiration even to the Moslems. He fought, say the writers of the crusades, like a wild boar, sending on that day an amazing number of infidels to *hell!* The Mussulmen severed the heads of the slaughtered Templars from their bodies, and attaching them with cords to the points of their lances, they placed them in front of their array, and marched off in the direction of Tiberias.*

The following interesting account is given of the march of another band of holy warriors, who, in obedience to the summons of the Grand Master of the Temple, were hastening to rally around the sacred ensigns of their faith.

GERARD DE RIDERFORT A.D. 1187.

"When they had travelled two miles, they came to the city of Saphet. It was a lovely morning, and they determined to march no further until they had heard mass. They accordingly turned towards the house of the bishop and woke him up, and informed him that the day was breaking. The bishop accordingly ordered an old chaplain to put on his clothes and say mass, after which they hastened forwards. Then they came to the castle of La Feue, (a fortress of the Templars), and there they found, outside the castle, the tents of the convent of Caco pitched, and there was no one to explain what it meant. A varlet was sent into the castle to inquire, but he found no one within but two sick people who were unable to speak. Then they marched towards Nazareth, and after they had proceeded a short distance from the castle of La Feue, they met a brother of the Temple on horseback, who galloped up to them at a furious rate, calling out, Bad news, bad news; and he informed them how that the Master of the Hospital had had his head cut off, and how of all the brothers of the Temple there had escaped but three, the Master of the Temple and two others, and that the knights whom the king had placed in garrison at Nazareth, were all taken and killed."†

In the great battle of Tiberias or of Hittin, fought on the 4th of July, which decided the fate of the Holy City of Jerusalem, the Templars were

---

* Chron. terra Sancta apud *Martene* , tom. v. col. 551. Hist. Hierosol. Gest. Dei, tom. i. pt. ii. p. 1150, 1. *Geoffrey de Vinisauf.*

† Contin. hist. bell. sacr. ut sup., col. 599.

in the van of the Christian army, and led the attack against the infidels. The march of Saladin's host, which amounted to eighty thousand horse and foot, over the hilly country, is compared by an Arabian writer, an eye-witness, to mountains in movement, or to the vast waves of an agitated sea. The same author speaks of the advance of the Templars against them at early dawn in battle array, "horrible in arms, having their whole bodies cased with triple mail." He compares the noise made by their advancing squadrons to the *loud humming of bees!* and describes them as animated with "a flaming desire of vengeance."* Saladin had behind him the lake of Tiberias, his infantry was in the centre, and the swift cavalry of the desert was stationed on either wing, under the command of Faki-ed-deen (teacher of religion). The Templars rushed, we are told, like lions upon the Moslem infidels, and nothing could withstand their heavy and impetuous charge. "Never," says an Arabian doctor of the law, "have I seen a bolder or more powerful army, nor one more to be feared by the believers in the true faith."

Saladin set fire to the dry grass and dwarf shrubs which lay between both armies, and the wind blew the smoke and the flames directly into the faces of the military friars and their horses. The fire, the noise, the gleaming weapons, and all the accompaniments of the horrid scene, have given full scope to the descriptive powers of the oriental writers. They compare it to the last judgment; the dust and the smoke obscured the face of the sun, and the day was turned into night. Sometimes gleams of light darted like the rapid lightning amid the throng of combatants; then you might see the dense columns of armed warriors, now immovable as mountains, and now sweeping swiftly across the landscape like the rainy clouds over the face of heaven. "The sons of paradise and the children of fire," say they, "then decided their terrible quarrel; the arrows rustled through the air like the wings of innumerable sparrows, the sparks flew from the coats of mail and the glancing sabres, and the blood spurting forth from the bosom of the throng deluged the earth like the rains of heaven. . . . The avenging sword of the true believers was drawn forth against the infidels; the faith of the UNITY was opposed to the faith of the TRINITY, and speedy ruin, desolation, and destruction, overtook the miserable sons of baptism!"

The cowardly patriarch Heraclius, whose duty it was to bear the holy cross in front of the Christian array, confided his sacred charge to the bishops of Ptolemais and Lydda†—a circumstance which gave rise to many gloomy forebodings amongst the superstitious soldiers of Christ. In consequence of the treachery, as it is alleged, of the count of Tripoli, who fled from the field with his retainers, both the Templars and

ERARD DE IDERFORT. A.D. 1187.

ERARD DE IDERFORT. A.D. 1187.

---

* *Muhammed F. Muhammed, N. Koreisg. Ispahan,* apud *Schultens,* p. 18.
† *Radulph Coggleshale,* an eye-witness, apud *Martene,* tom. v. col. 553.

Hospitallers were surrounded, and were to a man killed or taken prisoners. The bishop of Ptolemais was slain, the bishop of Lydda was made captive, and the holy cross, together with the king of Jerusalem, and the Grand Master of the Temple, fell into the hands of the Saracens. "Quid plura?" says Radulph, abbot of the monastery of Coggleshale in Essex, who was then on a pilgrimage to the Holy Land, and was wounded in the nose by an arrow. "Capta est crux, et rex, et Magister militiae Templi, et episcopus Liddensis, et frater Regis, et Templarii, et Hospitalarii, et marchio de Montferrat, atque omnes vel mortui vel capti sunt. Plangite super hoc omnes adoratores crucis, et plorate; sublatum est lignum nostra salutis, dignum abindignis indigne heu! heu! asportatum. Væ mihi misero, quod in diebus miserse vitee meae talia cogor videre . . . O dulce lignum, et suave, sanguine filii Dei roratum atque lavatum! O crux alma, in qua sal us nostra pependit! &c.*

"I saw," says the secretary and companion of Saladin, who was present at this terrible fight, and is unable to restrain himself from pitying the disasters of the vanquished—"I saw the mountains and the plains, the hills and the valleys, covered with their dead. I saw their fallen and deserted banners sullied with dust and with blood. I saw their heads broken and battered, their limbs scattered abroad, and the blackened corses piled one upon another like the stones of the builders. I called to mind the words of the Koran, 'The infidel shall say, What am I but *dust?*' . . . I saw thirty or forty tied together by one cord. I saw in one place, guarded by one Mussulman, two hundred of these famous warriors gifted with amazing strength, who had but just now walked forth amongst the mighty; their proud bearing was gone; they stood naked with downcast eyes, wretched and miserable . . . The lying infidels were now in the power of the true believers. Their king and their cross were captured, that cross before which they bow the head and bend the knee; which they bear aloft and worship with their eyes; they say that it is the identical wood to which the God whom they adore was fastened. They had adorned it with fine gold and brilliant stones; they carried it before their armies; they all bowed towards it with respect. It was their first duty to defend it; and he who should desert it would never enjoy peace of mind. The capture of this cross was more grievous to them than the captivity of their king. Nothing can compensate them for the loss of it. It was their God; they prostrated themselves in the dust before it, and sang hymns when it was raised aloft!"†

GERARD D
RIDERFOR'
A.D. 1187.

Among the few Christian warriors who escaped from this terrible encounter, was the Grand Master of the Hospital; he clove his way from

* Chron. Terræ Sanctæ, apud *Martene*, tom. v. col. 558 and 545. A most valuable history.

† *Omad eddin Kateb-Abou-hamed-Mohamed-Benhamed* one of Saladin's secretaries. Extraits Arabes, par *M. Michaud.*

the field of battle, and reached Ascalon in safety, but died of his wounds the day after his arrival. The multitude of captives was enormous, cords could not be found to bind them, the tent-ropes were all used for the purpose, but were insufficient, and the Arabian writers tell us that, on seeing the dead, one would have thought that there could be no prisoners, and on seeing the prisoners, that there could be no dead. As soon as the battle was over, Saladin proceeded to a tent, whither, in obedience to his commands, the king of Jerusalem, the Grand Master of the Temple, and Reginald de Chatillon, had been conducted. This last nobleman had greatly distinguished himself in various daring expeditions against the caravans of pilgrims travelling to Mecca, and had become on that account particularly obnoxious to the pious Saladin. The sultan, on entering the tent, ordered a bowl of sherbet, the sacred pledge amongst the Arabs of hospitality and security, to be presented to the fallen monarch of Jerusalem, and to the Grand Master of the Temple; but when Reginald de Chatillon would have drunk thereof, Saladin prevented him, and reproaching the Christian nobleman with perfidy and impiety, he commanded him instantly to acknowledge the prophet whom he had blasphemed, or be prepared to meet the death he had so often deserved. On Reginald's refusal, Saladin struck him with his scimitar, and he was immediately despatched by the guards.*

Bohadin, Saladin's friend and secretary, an eye-witness of the scene, gives the following account of it: "Then Saladin told the interpreter to say thus to the king, 'It is thou, not I, who givest drink to this man!' Then the sultan sat down at the entrance of the tent, and they brought Prince Reginald before him, and after refreshing the man's memory, Saladin said to him, 'Now then, I myself will act the part of the defender of Mohammed!' He then offered the man the Mohammedan faith, but he refused it; then the king struck him on the shoulder with a drawn scimitar, which was a hint to those that were present to do for him; so they sent his soul to *hell*, and cast out his body before the tent-door!"†

Two days afterwards Saladin proceeded in cold blood to enact the grand concluding tragedy. The warlike monks of the Temple and of the Hospital, the bravest and most zealous defenders of the Christian faith, were, of all the warriors of the cross, the most obnoxious to zealous Mussulmen, and it was determined that death or conversion to Mahometanism should be the portion of every captive of either order, excepting the Grand Master of the Temple, for whom it was expected a heavy ransom would be given. Accordingly, on the Christian Sabbath, at the hour of sunset, the

* Contin. hist. bell. sacr. apud *Martene*, tom. v. col. 608. *Bernard. Thesaur.* apud *Muratori* script, rer. Ital., cap. 46. col. 791.

† *Bohaam*, cap. 35. *Abulfeda. Abulpharag.*

appointed time of prayer, the Moslems were drawn up in battle array under their respective leaders. The Mamlook emirs stood in two ranks clothed in yellow, and, at the sound of the holy trumpet, all the captive knights of the Temple and of the Hospital were led on to the eminence above Tiberias, in full view of the beautiful lake of Gennesareth, whose bold and mountainous shores had been the scene of so many of their Saviour's miracles. There, as the last rays of the sun were fading away from the mountain tops, they were called upon to deny him who had been crucified, to choose God for their Lord, Islam for their faith, Mecca for their temple, the Moslems for their brethren, and Mahomet for their prophet. To a man they refused, and were all decapitated in the presence of Saladin by the devout zealots of his army, and the doctors and expounders of the law. An oriental historian, who was present, says that Saladin sat with a smiling countenance viewing the execution, and that some of the executioners cut off the heads with a degree of dexterity that excited great applause.* "Oh," says Omad'eddin Muhammed, "how beautiful an ornament is the blood of the infidels sprinkled over the followers of the faith and the true religion!"

GERARD D[ ]
RIDERFOR[ ]
A.D. 1187.

If the Mussulmen displayed a becoming zeal in the decapitation and annihilation of the infidel Templars, these last manifested a no less praiseworthy eagerness for martyrdom by the swords of the unbelieving Moslems. The Knight Templar, Brother Nicolas, strove vigorously, we are told, with his companions to be the first to suffer, and with great difficulty accomplished his purpose.† It was believed by the Christians, in accordance with the superstitious ideas of those times, that heaven testified its approbation by a visible sign, and that for three nights, during which the bodies of the Templars remained unburied on the field, celestial rays of light played around the corpses of those holy martyrs.‡

The government of the Order of the Temple, in consequence of the captivity of the Grand Master, devolved upon the Grand Preceptor of the kingdom of Jerusalem, who addressed letters to all the brethren in the West, imploring instant aid and assistance. One of these letters was duly received by Brother Geoffrey, Master of the Temple at London, as follows:

"Brother Terric, Grand Preceptor of the poor house of the Temple, and

---

* *Omad eddin Kateb,* in his book called *Fatah,* celebrates the above exploits of Saladin. Extraits Arabes, *Michaud. Radulph Coggleshale,* Chron. Terr. Sanct. Apud Martene tom. v. col. 553 to 559. *Bohadin,* p. 70. *Jac. de Vitr.* cap. xciv. *Guil. Neubr.* apud Hearne, tom. i. lib. iii. cap. 17, 18. *Chron. Gervasii,* apud X. script, col. 1502. *Abulfeda,* cap. 27. Abulpharag. Chron. Syr. p. 399, 401, 402. *Khondemir. Ben-Schunah.*

† *Geoffrey de Vinisauf* apud *Gale,* script. Antiq. Anglic, p. 15, "O zelus fidei! O fervor animi !" says that admiring historian, cap. xv. p. 251.

‡ *Geoffrey de Vinisauf* ut sup. cap. v. p. 251.

every poor brother, and the whole convent, now, alas! almost annihilated, to all the preceptors and brothers of the Temple to whom these letters may come, salvation through him to whom our fervent aspirations are addressed, through him who causeth the sun and the moon to reign marvellous."

GERARD DE
RIDERFORT.
A.D. 1187.

"The many and great calamities wherewith the anger of God, excited by our manifold sins, hath just now permitted us to be afflicted, we cannot for grief unfold to you, neither by letters nor by our sobbing speech. The infidel chiefs having collected together a vast number of their people, fiercely invaded our Christian territories, and we, assembling our battalions, hastened to Tiberias to arrest their march. The enemy having hemmed us in among barren rocks, fiercely attacked us; the holy cross and the king himself fell into the hands of the infidels, the whole army was cut to pieces, two hundred and thirty of our knights were beheaded, without reckoning the sixty who were killed on the 1st of May. The Lord Reginald of Sidon, the Lord Ballovius, and we ourselves, escaped with vast difficulty from that miserable field. The Pagans, drunk with the blood of our Christians, then marched with their whole army against the city of Acre, and took it by storm. The city of Tyre is at present fiercely besieged, and neither by night nor by day do the infidels discontinue their furious assaults. So great is the multitude of them, that they cover like ants the whole face of the country from Tyre to Jerusalem, and even unto Gaza. The Holy City of Jerusalem, Ascalon and Tyre, and Beyrout, are alone left to us and to the Christian cause, and the garrisons and the chief inhabitants of these places, having perished in the battle of Tiberias, we have no hope of retaining them without succour from heaven and instant assistance from yourselves."*

Saladin, on the other hand, sent triumphant letters to the caliph. "God and his angels," says he, "have mercifully succoured Islam. The infidels have been sent to feed the fires of hell! The cross is fallen into our

GERARD DE
RIDERFORT.
A.D. 1187.

hands, around which they fluttered like the moth round a light; under whose shadow they assembled, in which they boldly trusted as in a wall; the cross, the centre and leader of their pride, their superstition, and their tyranny. . . . "†

After the conquest of between thirty and forty cities and castles, many of which belonged to the Order of the Temple, Saladin laid siege to the holy city. On the 20th of September the Mussulman army encamped on the west of the town, and extended itself from the tower of David to

---

* Epistola Terrici Præceptoris Templi de captione terræ Jerosolymitanæ, *Hoveden* annal. apud rer. Angl. script. post Bedam, p. 636, 637. *Chron.* Gervas. ib. col. 1502. *Radulph de Diceto*, apud X. script. col. 635.

† Saladin's letter to the caliph *Nassir Deldin-Illah Aboul Abbas Ahmed.— Michaud, Extraits Arabes.*

the gate of St. Stephen. The Temple could no longer furnish its brave warriors for the defence of the holy sanctuary of the Christians; two miserable knights, with a few serving brethren, alone remained in its now silent halls and deserted courts.

After a siege of fourteen days, a breach was effected in the walls, and ten banners of the prophet waved in triumph on the ramparts. In the morning a barefoot procession of the queen, the women, and the monks and priests, was made to the holy sepulchre, to implore the Son of God to save his tomb and his inheritance from impious violation. The females, as a mark of humility and distress, cut off their hair and cast it to the winds; and the ladies of Jerusalem made their daughters do penance by standing up to their necks in tubs of cold water placed upon Mount Calvary. But it availed nought; "for our Lord Jesus Christ," says a Syrian Frank, "would not listen to any prayer that they made; for the filth, the luxury, and the adultery which prevailed in the city, did not suffer prayer or supplication to ascend before God."*

On the surrender of the city (October 2, A.D. 1187) the Moslems rushed to the Temple in thousands. "The Imauns and the doctors and expounders of the wicked errors of Mahomet," says Abbot Coggleshale, who was then in Jerusalem suffering from a wound which he had received during the siege, "first ascended to the Temple of the Lord, called by the infidels Beit Allah, (the house of God), in which, as a place of prayer and religion, they place their great hope of salvation. With horrible bellowings they proclaimed the law of Mahomet, and vociferated, with polluted lips, ALLAH *Acbar*—ALLAH *Acbar* (God is victorious). They defiled all the places that are contained within the Temple; i.e., the place of the presentation, where the mother and glorious virgin Mary delivered the Son of God into the hands of the just Simeon; and the place of the confession, looking towards the porch of Solomon, where the Lord judged the woman taken in adultery. They placed guards that no Christian might enter within the seven atria of the Temple; and as a disgrace to the Christians, with vast clamour, with laughter and mockery, they hurled down the golden cross from the pinnacle of the building, and dragged it with ropes throughout the city, amid the exulting shouts of the infidels and the tears and lamentations of the followers of Christ."†

When every Christian had been removed from the precincts of the Temple, Saladin proceeded with vast pomp to say his prayers in the *Beit*

GERARD DE
RIDERFORT.
A.D. 1187.

---

* Les dames de Jerusalem firent prendre cuves et mettere en la place devant le monte Cauviaire, et emplir *d'eue froide*, et firent lors filles entrer jusqu'au col, et couper lor treices et jeter les. — Contin. hist. bell. sacr. apud *Martene* , tom. v. col. 615.

† Chron. Terræ Sanctæ, *Radulphi Coggeshale*, apud Martene , tom. v.col. 572, 573; flentibus christianis, crines et vestes rumpentibus, pectora et capita tundentibus, says the worthy abbot.

Allah, the holy house of God, or "Temple of the Lord," erected by the Caliph Omar.* He was preceded by five camels laden with rose water, which he had procured from Damascus,† and he entered the sacred courts to the sound of martial music, and with his banners streaming in the wind. The *Beit Allah*, "the Temple of the Lord," was then again consecrated to the service of one God and his prophet Mahomet; the walls and pavements were washed and purified with rose water; and a pulpit, the labour of Noureddin, was erected in the sanctuary‡ The following account of these transactions was forwarded to Henry the Second, king of England:

"To the beloved Lord Henry, by the grace of God, the illustrious king of the English, duke of Normandy and Guienne, and count of Anjou, Brother Terric, *formerly* Grand Preceptor of the house of the Temple at Jerusalem, sendeth greeting,— salvation through him who saveth kings.

"Know that Jerusalem, with the citadel of David, hath been surrendered to Saladin. The Syrian Christians, however, have the custody of the Holy Sepulchre up to the fourth day after Michaelmas, and Saladin himself hath permitted ten of the brethren of the Hospital to remain in the house of the hospital for the space of one year, to take care of the sick . . . Jerusalem, alas, hath fallen; Saladin hath caused the cross to be thrown down from the summit of the Temple of the Lord, and for two days to be publicly kicked and dragged in the dirt through the city. He then caused the Temple of the Lord to be washed within and without, upwards and downwards, with rose-water, and the law of Mahomet to be proclaimed throughout the four quarters of the Temple with wonderful clamour. ..."§

Bohadin, Saladin's secretary, mentions as a remarkable and happy circumstance, that the Holy City was surrendered to the sultan of most pious memory, and that God restored to the faithful their sanctuary on the twenty-seventh of the month Regeb, on the night of which very day their most glorious prophet Mahomet performed his wonderful nocturnal journey from the Temple, through the seven heavens, to the throne of God. He also describes the sacred congregation of the Mussulmen gathered together in the Temple and the solemn prayer offered up to God; the shouting and the sounds of applause, and the voices lifted up to heaven, causing the holy buildings to resound with thanks and praises to the most

ERARD DE
RIDERFORT.
A.D. 1187.

ERARD DE
RIDERFORT.
A.D. 1187.

---

* See ante, p. 6.

† Saladin ot mandé a Damas por euë rose assés por le Temple laver ... il avoit quatre chamiex ou cinq tous chargiés.— Contin. Hist. Bell. Sacr. col. 621.

‡ *Bohadin*, cap. xxxvi, and the extracts from *Abulfeda*, apud *Schultens*, cpa. Xxvii. P.42, 43. Ib'n Alatsyr, Michaud, Extraits Arabes.

§ *Hoveden*. annal. apud rer. Angl. Script. post Bedam, p. 645, 646.

** *Bohadin* apud *Schullens*, cap. xxxvi.

bountiful Lord God. He glories in the casting down of the golden cross, and exults in the very splendid triumph of Islam.**

Saladin restored the sacred area of the Temple to its original condition under the first Mussulman conquerors of Jerusalem. The ancient Christian church of the Virgin (otherwise the mosque *Al Acsa*, otherwise the Temple of Solomon) was washed with rose-water, and was once again dedicated to the religious services of the Moslems. On the western side of this venerable edifice the Templars had erected, according to the Arabian writers, an immense building in which they lodged, together with granaries of corn and various offices, which enclosed and concealed a great portion of the edifice. Most of these were pulled down by the sultan to make a clear and open area for the resort of the Mussulmen to prayer. Some new erections placed between the columns in the interior of the structure were taken away, and the floor was covered with the richest carpets. "Lamps innumerable," says Ibn Alatsyr, "were suspended from the ceiling; verses of the Koran were again inscribed on the walls; the call to prayer was again heard; the bells were silenced; the exiled faith returned to its ancient sanctuary; the devout Mussulmen again bent the knee in adoration of the one only God, and the voice of the imaun was again heard from the pulpit, reminding the true believers of the resurrection and the last judgment."*

GERARD DE
RIDERFORT
A.D. 1187.

The Friday after the surrender of the city, the army of Saladin and crowds of true believers, who had flocked to Jerusalem from all parts of the East, assembled in the Temple of the Lord to assist in the religious services of the Mussulman sabbath. Omad, Saladin's secretary, who was present, gives the following interesting account of the ceremony, and of the sermon that was preached. "On Friday morning at daybreak," says he, "every body was asking whom the sultan had appointed to preach. The Temple was full; the congregation was impatient; all eyes were fixed on the pulpit; the ears were on the stretch; our hearts beat fast, and tears trickled down our faces. On all sides were to be heard rapturous exclamations of 'What a glorious sight! What a congregation! Happy are those who have lived to *see the resurrection of Islam.*' At length the sultan ordered the judge (doctor of the law) *Mohieddin Aboulmehali-Mohammed* to fulfil the sacred function of imaun. I immediately lent him the black vestment which I had received as a present from the caliph. He then mounted into the pulpit and spoke. All were hushed. His expressions were graceful and easy; and his discourse eloquent and much admired. He spake of the virtue and the sanctity of Jerusalem, of the purification of the Temple; he alluded to the silence of the bells, and to the flight of

---

* *Ibn-Alatsyr*, hist. Arab, and the *Raoudhatein*, or "the two gardens." *Michaud*, Extraits Arabes. Excerpta ex *Abulfeda* apud *Schuliens*, cap. xxvii. p. 43. *Wilken* Comment. Abulfed. hist. p. 148.

the infidel priests. In his prayer he named the caliph and the sultan, and terminated his discourse with that chapter of the Koran in which God orders justice and good works. He then descended from the pulpit, and prayed in the Mihrah. Immediately afterwards a sermon was preached before the congregation."*

GERARD DE
RIDERFORT.
A.D. 1187.

This sermon was delivered by *Mohammed Ben Zeky*. "Praise be to God," saith the preacher, "who by the power of his might hath raised up Islamism on the ruins of Polytheism; who governs all things according to his will; who overthroweth the devices of the infidels, and causeth the truth to triumph. ... I praise God, who hath succoured his elect; who hath rendered them victorious and crowned them with glory, who hath purified his holy house from the filthiness of idolatry . . . I bear witness that there is no God but that one great God who standeth alone and hath no partner; sole, supreme, eternal; who begetteth not and is not begotten, and hath no equal. I bear witness that Mahomet is his servant, his envoy, and his prophet, who hath dissipated doubts, confounded polytheism, and put down lies, &c. ...

"O men, declare ye the blessings of God, who hath restored to you this holy city, after it has been left in the power of the infidels for a hundred years. ... This holy house of the Lord hath been built, and its foundations have been established, for the glory of God. ... This sacred spot is the dwelling place of the prophets, the *kebla*, (place of prayer), towards which you turn at the commencement of your religious duties, the birthplace of the saints, the scene of the revelation. It is thrice holy, for the angels of God spread their wings over it. This is that blessed land of which God hath spoken in his sacred book. In this house of prayer, Mahomet prayed with the angels who approach God. It is to this spot that all fingers are turned after the two holy places. ... This conquest, O men, hath opened unto you the gates of heaven; the angels rejoice, and the eyes of the prophets glisten with joy. . ."†

GERARD DE
RIDERFORT.
A.D. 1187.

Omad informs us that the marble altar and chapel which had been erected over the sacred rock in the Temple of the Lord, or mosque of Omar, was removed by Saladin, together with the stalls for the priests, the marble statues, and all the abominations which had been placed in the venerated building by the Christians. The Mussulmen discovered with horror that some pieces of the holy stone or rock had been cut off by the Franks, and sent to Europe. Saladin caused it to be immediately surrounded by a grate of iron. He washed it with rose-water and Malek-Afdal covered it with magnificent carpets.‡

---

* Omad eddin Kateb.—*Michaud*, Extraits Arabes.

† *Khotbeh*, or sermon of *Mohammed Ben Zeky*.—*Michaud*, Extraits Arabes.

‡ See the account of this remarkable stone, ante p. 7, 8.

After the conquest of the holy city, and the loss of the Temple at Jerusalem, the Knights Templars established the chief house of their order at Antioch, to which place they retired with Queen Sibylla, the barons of the kingdom, and the patriarch Heraclius.*

The following account of the condition of the few remaining Christian possessions immediately after the conquest of Jerusalem, was conveyed by the before-mentioned Brother Terric, Grand Preceptor of the Temple, and Treasurer General of the Order, to Henry the Second, king of England.

"The brothers of the hospital of Belvoir as yet bravely resist the Saracens; they have captured two convoys, and have valiantly possessed themselves of the munitions of war and provisions which were being conveyed by the Saracens from the fortress of La Feue. As yet, also, Carach, in the neighbourhood of Mount Royal, Mount Royal itself, the Temple of Saphet, the hospital of Carach, Margat, and Castellum Blancum, and the territory of Tripoli, and the territory of Antioch, resist Saladin. ... From the feast of Saint Martin up to that of the circumcision of the Lord, Saladin hath besieged Tyre incessantly, by night and by day, throwing into it immense stones from thirteen military engines. On the vigils of St. Silvester, the Lord Conrad, the Marquis of Montferrat, distributed knights and foot soldiers along the wall of the city, and having armed seventeen galleys and ten small vessels, with the assistance of the house of the Hospital and the brethren of the Temple, he engaged the galleys of Saladin, and vanquishing them he captured eleven, and took prisoners the great admiral of Alexandria and eight other admirals, a multitude of the infidels being slain. The rest of the Mussulman galleys, escaping the hands of the Christians, fled to the army of Saladin, and being run aground by his command, were set on fire and burnt to ashes. Saladin himself, overwhelmed with grief, *having cut off the ears and the tail of his horse, rode that same horse* through his whole army in the sight of all. Farewell!"†

Tyre was valiantly defended against all the efforts of Saladin until the winter had set in, and then the disappointed sultan, despairing of taking the place, burnt his military engines and retired to Damascus. In the mean time, negotiations had been set on foot for the release from captivity of Guy de Lusignan king of Jerusalem, and Gerard de Riderfort, the Grand Master of the Temple. No less than eleven of the most important of the cities and castles remaining to the Christians in Palestine, including Ascalou, Gaza, Jaffa, and Naplous, were yielded up to Saladin by way of ransom for these illustrious personages; and at the commencement of the

GERARD DE RIDERFORT. A.D. 1188.

---

* *Hist. Hierosol.* Gesta Dei per Francos, tom. i, pt. ii. p. 1155.

† *Hoveden* ut sup. p 646. *Schahab'eddin* in the Raoudhatein.—*Michaud.*

‡ *Jac. de Vitr.* cap. xcv. *Vinisauf,* apud XV script, p. 257. *Trivet* ad ann. 1188, apud *Hall*, p. 93.

GERARD DE RIDERFORT. A.D. 1188. year 1188, the Grand Master of the Temple again appeared in arms at the head of the remaining forces of the Order.‡

The torpid sensibility of Christendom had at this time been aroused by the intelligence of the fall of Jerusalem, and of the profanation of the holy places by the conquering infidels. Three hundred knights and a considerable naval force were immediately despatched from Sicily, and all the Templars of the West capable of bearing arms hurried from their preceptories to the sea-ports of the Mediterranean, and embarked for Palestine in the ships of Genoa, Pisa, and Venice. The king of England forwarded a large sum of money to the Order for the defence of the city of Tyre; but as the siege had been raised before its arrival, and as Conrad, the valiant defender of the place, claimed a title to the throne of Jerusalem in opposition to Guy de Lusignan, the Grand Master of the Temple refused to deliver the money into Conrad's hands, in consequence whereof the latter wrote letters filled with bitter complaints to King Henry and the archbishop of Canterbury.*

In the spring of the year 1189, the Grand Master of the Temple marched out of Tyre at the head of the newly-arrived brethren of the Order, and, in conjunction with a large army of crusaders, laid siege to Acre. The "victorious defender of the faith, tamer of the followers of the cross," hastened to its relief, and pitched his tents on the mountains of Carouba.

On the 4th of October, the newly-arrived warriors from Europe, eager to signalize their prowess against the infidels, marched out to attack Saladin's camp. The Grand Master of the Temple, at the head of his knights and the forces of the Order, and a large body of European GERARD DE RIDERFORT. A.D. 1189. chivalry who had ranged themselves under the banner of the Templars, formed a reserve. The Moslem array was broken by the impetuous charge of the soldiers of the cross, who penetrated to the imperial tent, and then abandoned themselves to pillage. The infidels rallied, they were led on by Saladin in person; and the Christian army would have been annihilated but for the Templars. Firm and immovable, they presented, for the space of an hour, an unbroken front to the advancing Moslems, and gave time for the discomfited and panic-stricken crusaders to recover from their terror and confusion; but ere they had been rallied, and had returned to the charge, the Grand Master of the Temple was slain; he fell pierced with arrows at the head of his knights; the seneschal of the Order shared the same fate, and more than half the Templars were numbered with the dead.†

To Gerard de Riderfort succeeded the Knight Templar, Brother

---

* *Radulph de Diceto* ut sup. col. 642, 643. *Matt.* Par. ad ann. 1188.

† *Radulph Coggeshale*, p. 574. Hist. Hierosol. apud Gesta Dei, tom. i. pars 2, p. 1165. *Radulph de Diceto* ut sup, col. 649. *Vinisauf*, cap. xxix. P. 270.

‡ *Ducange* Gloss. tom. vi. p. 1036.

WALTER.‡ Never did the flame of enthusiasm burn with fiercer or more destructive power than at this famous siege of Acre. Nine pitched battles were fought, with various fortune, in the neighbourhood of Mount Carmel, and during the first year of the siege a hundred thousand Christians are computed to have perished. The tents of the dead, however, were replenished by newcomers from Europe; the fleets of Saladin succoured the town, the Christian ships brought continual aid to the besiegers, and the contest seemed interminable.* Saladin's exertions in the cause of the prophet were incessant. The Arab authors compare him to a mother wandering with desperation in search of her lost child, to a lioness who has lost its young. "I saw him," says his secretary Bohadin, "in the fields of Acre afflicted with a most cruel disease, with boils from the middle of his body to his knees, so that he could not sit down, but only recline on his side when he entered into his tent, yet he went about to the stations nearest to the enemy, arranged his troops for battle, and rode about from dawn till eve, now to the right wing, then to the left, and then to the centre, patiently enduring the severity of his pain." ... "O God," says his enthusiastic biographer, "thou knowest that he put forth and lavishly expended all his energies and strength towards the protection and the triumph of thy religion; do thou therefore, O Lord, have mercy upon him."†

WALTER.
A.D. 1190.

At this famous siege died the Patriarch Heraclius.‡

---

* *Geoffrey de Vinisauf,* apud XV script. cap. xxxv. p. 427. *Rad. Coggleshale* apud Martene , tom. v. col. 566, 567. Bohadin, cap. 1. to c.

† *Bohadin,* cap. v. vi.

‡ L'art de verif. tom. i. p 297.

CHAPTER VII.

Richard Cœur de Lion joins the Templars before Acre—The city surrenders, and the Templars establish the chief house of their order within it—Cœur de Lion takes up his abode with them—He sells to them the island of Cyprus— The Templars form the van of his army—Their foraging expeditions and great exploits—Cœur de Lion quits the Holy Land in the disguise of a Knight Templar—The Templars build the Pilgrim's Castle in Palestine—The state of the Order in England—King John resides in the Temple at London— The barons come to him at that place, and demand Magna Charta—The exploits of the Templars in Egypt—The letters of the Grand Master to the Master of the Temple at London—The Templars reconquer Jerusalem.

"Therefore, friends,
As far as to the sepulchre of Christ
(Whose soldier now under whose blessed cross
We are impressed and engag'd to fight),
Forthwith a power of English shall we levy,
Whose arms were moulded in their mother's womb,
To chase these pagans, in those holy fields,
Over whose acres walked those blessed feet,
Which, fourteen hundred years ago, were nail'd,
For our advantage, on the bitter cross."

IN the mean time a third crusade had been preached in Europe. William, archbishop of Tyre, had proceeded to the courts of France and England, and had represented in glowing colours the miserable condition of Palestine, and the horrors and abominations which had been committed by the
infidels in the Holy City of Jerusalem. The English and French monarchs laid aside their private animosities, and agreed to fight under the same banner against the infidels, and towards the close of the month of May, in the second year of the siege of Acre, the royal fleets of Philip Augustus and Richard Cœur de Lion floated in triumph in the bay of Acre. At the period of the arrival of King Richard the Templars had again lost their Grand Master, and Brother Robert de Sablé, or Sabloil, a valiant knight of the Order, who had commanded a division of the English fleet on the

voyage out, was placed at the head of the fraternity.* The proudest of the nobility, and the most valiant of the chivalry of Europe, on their arrival in Palestine, manifested an eager desire to fight under the banner of the Temple. Many secular knights were permitted by the Grand Master to take their station by the side of the military friars, and even to wear the red cross on their breasts whilst fighting in the ranks.

The Templars performed prodigies of valour; "The name of their reputation, and the fame of their sanctity," says James of Vitry, bishop of Acre, "like a chamber of perfume sending forth a sweet odour, was diffused throughout the entire world, and all the congregation of the saints will recount their battles and glorious triumph over the enemies of Christ, knights indeed from all parts of the earth, dukes, and princes, after their example, casting off the shackles of the world, and renouncing the pomps and vanities of this life and all the lusts of the flesh for Christ's sake, hastened to join them, and to participate in their holy profession and religion."† ROBERT DE SABLE. A.D. 1191.

On the morning of the twelfth of July, six weeks after the arrival of the British fleet, the kings of England and France, the Christian chieftains, and the Turkish emirs with their green banners, assembled in the tent of the Grand Master of the Temple, to treat of the surrender of Acre, and on the following day the gates were thrown open to the exulting warriors of the cross. The Templars took possession of three localities within the city by the side of the sea, where they established their famous Temple, which became from thenceforth the chief house of the Order. Richard Coeur de Lion, we are told, took up his abode with the Templars, whilst Philip resided in the citadel.‡ ROBERT DE SABLE. A.D. 1191.

When the fiery monarch of England tore down the banner of the duke of Austria from its staff and threw it into the ditch, it was the Templars who, interposing between the indignant Germans and the haughty Britons, preserved the peace of the Christian army.§

During his voyage from Messina to Acre, King Richard had revenged himself on Isaac Comnenus, the ruler of the island of Cyprus, for the insult offered to the beautiful Berengaria, princess of Navarre, his betrothed bride. The sovereign of England had disembarked his troops, stormed the town of Limisso, and conquered the whole island; and shortly after his arrival at Acre, he sold it to the Templars for three hundred thousand livres d'or.*

---

* Hist, de la maison de Sablé, liv. vi. chap. 5. p. 174, 175. Cotton MS. Nero, E. vi. p. 60. folio 466, where he is called Robert de SambeU. L'art de Verif. p. 347.

† *Jac. de Vitr.* cap. 65.

‡ Le roi de France ot le chastel d'Acre, ot le fist garner et le roi d'Angleterre se herberja en la maison du Temple. — Contin. Hist. bell. Sacr. apud *Martene*, tom. v. col. 634

§ *Chron. Ottonis* a S. Blazio, c. 36. apud Scriptores Italicos, tom. vi. col. 892.

During the famous march of Richard Cœur de Lion from Acre to Ascalon, the Templars generally led the van of the Christian army, and the Hospitallers brought up the rear.† Saladin, at the head of an immense force, exerted all his energies to oppose their progress, and the march to Jaffa formed a perpetual battle of eleven days. On some occasions Cœur de Lion himself, at the head of a chosen body of knights, led the van, and the Templars were formed into a rear-guard.‡ They sustained immense loss, particularly in horses, which last calamity, we are told, rendered them nearly desperate.§

ROBERT DE SABLE. A.D. 1191.

The Moslem as well as the Christian writers speak with admiration of the feats of heroism performed. "On the sixth day," says Bohadin, "the sultan rose at dawn as usual, and heard from his brother that the enemy were in motion. They had slept that night in suitable places about Caesarea, and were now dressing and taking their food. A second messenger announced that they had begun their march; our brazen drum was sounded, all were alert, the sultan came out, and I accompanied him: he surrounded them with chosen troops, and gave the signal for attack.".... "Their foot soldiers were covered with thick-strung pieces of cloth, fastened together with rings so as to resemble coats of mail. I saw with my own eyes several who had not one nor two but *ten darts sticking in their backs!* and yet marched on with a calm and cheerful step, without any trepidation!" **

Every exertion was made to sustain the courage and enthusiasm of the Christian warriors. When the army halted for the night, and the soldiers were about to take their rest, a loud voice was heard from the midst of the camp, exclaiming, "ASSIST THE HOLY SEPULCHRE," which words were repeated by the leaders of the host, and were echoed and re-echoed along their extended lines.†† The Templars and the Hospitallers, who were well acquainted with the country, employed themselves by night in marauding and foraging expeditions. They frequently started off at midnight, swept the country with their turcopoles or light cavalry, and returned to the camp

ROBERT DE SABLE. A.D. 1191.

---

* *Contin. Hist. bell. sacr.* Martene, tom. v. col. 633. *Trivet*, ad. ann. 1191. *Chron. de S. Denis*, lib. ii. cap. 7. *Vinisauf*, p. 328.

† Primariam aciem deducebant Templarii et ultimam Hospitalarii, quorum utrique strenue agents magnarum virtutum prætendebant imaginem.— *Vinisauf*, cap. xii. P. 350.

‡ Ibi rex præordinaverat quod die sequenti primam aciem ipse deduceret, et quod Templarii extremæ agminis agerent custodiam.— *Vinisauf* cap. xiv. p. 351.

§ Deducendæ extremæ legioni præfuerant Templarii, qui tot equos eâ die Turcis irruentibus, a tergo amiserunt, quod fere desperati sunt.—Ib.

** *Bohadin*, cap. cxvi. p. 189.

†† Singulis noctibus antequam dormituri cubarent, quidam ad hoc deputatus voce magnâ clamaret fortiter in medio exercitu dicens, ADJUVA SKPULCHRUM SANCTUM; ad hanc vocem clamabant universi eadem verba repetentes, et manus suas cum lacrymis uberrimis tendentes in caelum, Dei misericordiam poetulantes et adjutorium.—*Vinisauf* cap. xii. p. 351.

at morning's dawn with rich prizes of oxen, sheep, and provisions.*

In the great plain near Ramleh, when the Templars led the van of the Christian army, Saladin made a last grand effort to arrest their progress, which was followed by one of the greatest battles of the age. Geoffrey de Vinisauf, the companion of King Richard on this expedition, gives a lively and enthusiastic description of the appearance of the Moslem array in the great plain around Jaffa and Ramleh. On all sides, far as the eye could reach, from the sea-shore to the mountains, nought was to be seen but a forest of spears, above which waved banners and standards innumerable. The wild Bedouins,† the children of the desert, mounted on their fleet Arab mares, coursed with the rapidity of the lightning over the vast plain, and darkened the air with clouds of missiles. Furious and unrelenting, of a horrible aspect, with skins blacker than soot, they strove by rapid movement and continuous assaults to penetrate the well-ordered array of the Christian warriors. They advanced to the attack with horrible screams and bellowings, which, with the deafening noise of the trumpets, horns, cymbals, and brazen kettledrums, produced a clamour that resounded through the plain, and would have drowned even the thunder of heaven.

ROBERT DE
SABLE.
A.D. 1191.

The engagement commenced with the left wing of the Hospitallers, and the victory of the Christians was mainly owing to the personal prowess of King Richard. Amid the disorder of his troops, Saladin remained on the plain without lowering his standard or suspending the sound of his brazen kettle-drums, he rallied his forces, retired upon Ramleh, and prepared to defend the road leading to Jerusalem. The Templars and Hospitallers, when the battle was over, went in search of Jacques d'Asvesnes, one of the most valiant of King Richard's knights, whose dead body, placed on their spears, they brought into the camp amid the tears and lamentations of their brethren.‡

The Templars, on one of their foraging expeditions, were surrounded by a superior force of four thousand Moslem cavalry; the Earl of Leicester, with a chosen body of English, was sent by Cœur de Lion to their assistance, but the whole party was overpowered and in danger of being cut to pieces, when Richard himself hurried to the scene of action with his famous battle-axe, and rescued the Templars from their perilous situation.§ By the valour and exertions of the lion-hearted king, the city of Gaza, the ancient fortress of

---

* Ibid. cap. xxxii. p. 369.

† *Bedewini* horridi, fuligine obscuriores, pedites improbissimi, arcus gestantes cum pharetris, et ancilia rotunda, gene quidem acerrima et expedita.—*Vinisauf*, cap. xviii. p. 355.

‡ *Vinisauf* cap. xxii. p. 360. *Bohadin*, cap. cxx.

§ Expedite descenderunt (Templarii) ex equis suis, et dorsa singuli dorsis sociorum habentes haerentia, facie versâ in hostes, sese viriliter defendere cœperunt. Ibi videri fuit pugnam acerrimam, ictus validissimos, tinniunt galea a percutientium collisione gladiorum, igneæ exsiliunt scintillæ, crepitant arma tumultuantium, perstrepunt voces; Turci se viriliter ingerunt, Templarii strenuissime defendunt.—Ib. cap. xxx. p. 366, 367.

the Order, which had been taken by Saladin soon after the battle of Tiberias, was recovered to the Christian arms, the fortifications were repaired, and the place was restored to the Knights Templars, who again garrisoned it with their soldiers.

As the army advanced, Saladin fell back towards Jerusalem, and the vanguard of the Templars was pushed on to the small town of Ramleh.

At midnight of the festival of the Holy Innocents, a party of them sallied out of the camp in company with some Hospitallers on a foraging expedition; they scoured the mountains in the direction of Jerusalem, and at morning's dawn returned to Ramleh with more than two hundred oxen.*

When the Christian army went into winter quarters, the Templars established themselves at Gaza, and King Richard and his army were stationed in the neighbouring town of Ascalon, the walls and houses of which were rebuilt by the English monarch during the winter. Whilst the Christian forces were reposing in winter quarters, an arrangement was made between the Templars, King Richard, and Guy de Lusignan, "the king without a kingdom," for the cession to the latter of the island of Cyprus, previously sold by Richard to the Order of the Temple, by virtue of which arrangement, Guy de Lusignan took possession of the island and ruled the country by the magnificent title of emperor.†

When the winter rains had subsided, the Christian forces were again put in motion, but both the Templars and Hospitallers strongly advised Cœur de Lion not to march upon Jerusalem, and the latter appears to have had no strong inclination to undertake the siege of the holy city, having manifestly no chance of success. The English monarch declared that he would be guided by the advice of the Templars and Hospitallers, who were acquainted with the country, and were desirous of recovering their ancient inheritances. The army, however, advanced within a day's jour-

ROBERT DE ney of the holy city, and then a council was called together, consisting of
SABLE.   five Knights Templars, five Hospitallers, five eastern Christians, and five
A.D. 1192.   western Crusaders, and the expedition was abandoned.‡

The Templars took part in the attack upon the great Egyptian convoy, wherein four thousand and seventy camels, five hundred horses, provisions, tents, arms, and clothing, and a great quantity of gold and silver, were captured, and then fell back upon Acre; they were followed by Saladin, who immediately commenced offensive operations, and laid siege to Jaffa. The Templars marched by land to the relief of the place, and Cœur de Lion hurried by sea. Many valiant exploits were performed, the town was relieved, and the campaign was concluded by the ratification of a treaty

---

* *Vtnisauf* cap. xxxii. p. 369.

† Ib. cap. xxxvii. p. 392. *Contin. Hist. Bell. Sacr.* apud *Martene* , r. col. 638.

‡ *Vinisauf*, lib. v. cap. l,p. 403. Ibid. lib. vi. cap. 2, p. 404.

whereby the Christians were to enjoy the privilege of visiting Jerusalem as pilgrims. Tyre, Acre, and Jaffa, with all the sea-coast between them, were yielded to the Latins, but it was stipulated that the fortifications of Ascalon should be demolished.*

After the conclusion of this treaty, King Richard being anxious to take the shortest and speediest route to his dominions by traversing the continent of Europe, and to travel in disguise to avoid the malice of his enemies, made an arrangement with his friend Robert de Sable, the Grand Master of the Temple, whereby the latter undertook to place a galley of the Order at the disposal of the king, and it was determined that whilst the royal fleet pursued its course with Queen Berengaria through the Straits of Gibraltar to Britain, Cœur de Lion himself, disguised in the habit of a Knight Templar, should secretly embark and make for one of the ports of the Adriatic. The plan was carried into effect on the night of the 26th of October, and King Richard set sail, accompanied by some attendants, and four trusty Templars.† The habit he had assumed, however, protected him not, as is well known, from the cowardly vengeance of the base duke of Austria.

The lion-hearted monarch was one of the many benefactors to the Order of the Temple. He granted to the fraternity his manor of Calow, with various powers and privileges.‡

Shortly after his departure from Palestine, the Grand Master, Robert de Sablé, was succeeded by Brother Gilbert Horal or Erail, who had previously filled the high office of Grand Preceptor of France.§ The Templars, to retain and strengthen their dominion in Palestine, commenced the erection of various strong fortresses, the stupendous ruins of many of which remain to this day. The most famous of these was the Pilgrim's Castle,** which commanded the coast-road from Acre to Jerusalem. It derived its name from a solitary tower erected by the early Templars to protect the passage of the pilgrims through a dangerous pass in the mountains bordering the sea-coast, and was commenced shortly after the removal of the chief house of the Order from Jerusalem to Acre. A small promontory which juts out into the sea a few miles below Mount Carmel, was converted into

GILBERT
HORAL.
A.D. 1195.

* Ib. cap. iv. v. p. 406, 407, &c. &c.; cap. xi. p. 410; cap. xiv. p. 412. King Richard was the first to enter the town. Tunc rex per cocleam quandaxn, quam forte prospexerat in domibus Templariorum solus primus intravit villam.—*Vinisauf*, p. 413, 414.

† *Contin. Hist Bell. Sacr,* apud *Martene* , tom. v. col. 641.

‡ Concessimus omne jus, omne dominium quod ad nos pertinet et pertineat, omnem potestatem, omnes libertates et liberas consuetudines quas regia potestas conferre potest. *Cart. Ric.* 1. ann. 5, regni sui.

§ *Hispania Illustrata,* tom. iii. p. 59. *Hist, gen. de Languedoc,* tom. iii. p. 409. Cotton, MS. Nero E. VI. 23. i.

** Castrum nostrum quod Peregrinorum dicitur, see the letter of the Grand Master *Matt. Par.* p. 312, and *Jac. de Vitr.* lib. iii. apud Gest. Dei, p. 1131.

GILBERT
HORAL.
A.D. 1195.
a fortified camp. Two gigantic towers, a hundred feet in height and seventy-four feet in width, were erected, together with enormous bastions connected together by strong walls furnished with all kinds of military engines. The vast inclosure contained a palace for the use of the Grand Master and knights, a magnificent church, houses and offices for the serving brethren and hired soldiers, together with pasturages, vineyards, gardens, orchards, and fishponds. On one side of the walls was the salt sea, and on the other, within the camp, delicious springs of fresh water. The garrison amounted to four thousand men in time of war.* Considerable remains of this famous fortress are still visible on the coast, a few miles to the south of Acre. It is still called by the Levantines, *Castel Pellegrino.* Pococke describes it as "very magnificent, and so finely built, that it may be reckoned one of the things that are best worth seeing in these parts. . . . It is encompassed," says he, "with two walls fifteen feet thick, the inner wall on the east side cannot be less than forty feet high, and within it there appear to have been some very grand apartments. The offices of the fortress seem to have been at the west end, where I saw an oven fifteen feet in diameter. In the castle there are remains of a fine lofty church of ten sides, built in a light gothic taste: three chapels are built to the three eastern sides, each of which consists of five sides, excepting the opening to the church; in these it is probable the three chief altars stood."† Irby and Mangles referring at a subsequent period to the ruins of the church, describe it as a double hexagon, and state that the half then standing had six sides. Below the cornice are human heads and heads of animals in alto relievo, and the walls are adorned with a double line of arches in the gothic style, the architecture light and elegant. To narrate all the exploits of the Templars, and all the incidents and events connected with the Order, would be to write the history of the Latin kingdom of Palestine, which was preserved and maintained for the period of ninety-nine years after the departure of Richard Cœur de Lion, solely by the exertions of the Templars and the Hospitallers. No action of importance was ever fought with the infidels, in which the Templars did not take an active and distinguished part, nor was the atabal of the Mussulmen ever sounded in defiance on the frontier, without the trumpets of the Templars receiving and answering the challenge.

GILBERT
HORAL.
A.D. 1195.

PHILIP
DUPLESS-
IES.
A.D. 1201.
The Grand Master, Gilbert Horal, was succeeded by Philip Dulplessies or De Plesseis.‡ We must now refer to a few events connected with the Order of the Temple in England.

---

* "Opus egregium," says *James of Vitry*," ubi tot et tantas effuderunt divitias, quod mirum est undo eas accipiunt."—*Hist. Orient.* lib. iii. apud Gest. Dei, tom. i. pars 9, p. 1131, *Martene* , tom. iii. col. 288. Hist. capt. Damietæ, apud Hist. Angl. script. XV. p. 437, 438, where it is called Castrum Filii Dei.

† *Pococke*, Travels in the East, book i. chap. 15.

‡ *Dufresne, Gloss. Archives d'Arles.* Cotton, MS. Nero E. VI.

Brother Geoffrey, who was Master of the Temple at London at the period of the consecration of the Temple Church by the Patriarch of Jerusalem, died shortly after the capture of the Holy City by Saladin, and was succeeded by Brother Amaric de St. Maur, who is an attesting witness to the deed executed by King John, A.D. 1203, granting a dowry to his young queen, the beautiful Isabella of Angouleme.* Philip Augustus, king of France, placed a vast sum of gold and silver in the Temple at Paris, and the treasure of John, king of England, was deposited in the Temple at London.† King John, indeed, frequently resided, for weeks together, at the Temple in London, and many of his writs and precepts to his lieutenants, sheriffs, and bailiffs, are dated therefrom.‡ The orders for the concentration of the English fleet at Portsmouth, to resist the formidable French invasion instigated by the pope, are dated from the Temple, and the convention between the king and the count of Holland, whereby the latter agreed to assist King John with a body of knights and men-at-arms, in case of the landing of the French, was published at the same place.§

In all the conferences and negotiations between the mean-spirited king and the imperious and overbearing Roman pontiff, the Knights Templars took an active and distinguished part. Two brethren of the Order were sent by Pandulph, the papal legate, to King John, to arrange that famous conference between them which ended in the complete submission of the latter to all the demands of the holy see. By the advice and persuasion of the Templars, King John repaired to the preceptory of Temple Ewell, near Dover, where he was met by the legate Pandulph, who crossed over from France to confer with him, and the mean-hearted king was there frightened into that celebrated resignation of the kingdoms of England and Ireland, "to God, to the holy apostles Peter and Paul, to the holy Roman church his mother, and to his lord, Pope Innocent the Third, and his catholic successors, for the remission of all his sins and the sins of all his people, as well the living as the dead."** The following year the commands of King John for the extirpation of the heretics in Gascony, addressed to the seneschal of that province, were issued from the Temple at London,†† and about the same period the Templars were made the depositaries of various private and confidential matters pending between

---

* Acta et Fœdera, *Rymeri*, tom. i. p. 134, ad. ann. 1203, ed. 1704.

† *Rigord* in Gest. Philippi. Acta *Rymeri*, tom. i. p. 165, 173.

‡ Itinerarium regis Johannis, compiled from the grants and precepts of that monarch, *by Thomas Duff Hardy*, published by the Record Commissioners.

§ Acta *Rymeri*, tom. i. p. 170, ad. ann. 1213.

** *Matt. Par.* ad. ann. 1213, p. 234, 236, 237. *Matt. Westr.* p. 271, 2. *Bib. Cotton.* Nero C. 2. Acta *Rymeri tom.* i. p. 172, 173. King John resided at Temple Ewell from the 7th to the 28th of May.

†† Teste meipso apud Novum Templum London . . . . Acta *Rymeri,* tom. i. p . 105. ad. ann. 1214, ed. 1704.

PHILIP
DUPLESSIES.
A.D. 1215.

King John and his illustrious sister-in-law, "the royal, eloquent, and beauteous" Berengaria of Navarre, the youthful widowed queen of Richard Cœur *de Lion** The Templars in England managed the money transactions of that fair princess. She directed her dower to be paid in the house of the New Temple at London, together with the arrears due to her from the king, amounting to several thousand pounds.†

John was resident at the Temple when he was compelled by the barons of England to sign MAGNA CHARTA. Matthew Paris tells us that the barons came to him, whilst he was residing in the New Temple at London, "in a very resolute manner, clothed in their military dresses, and demanded the liberties and laws of King Edward, with others for themselves, the kingdom, and the church of England.‡

King John was a considerable benefactor to the Order. He granted to the fraternity the Isle of Lundy, at the mouth of the river Severn; all his land at Radenach and at Harewood, in the county of Hereford; and he conferred on the Templars numerous privileges.§

WILLIAM DE
CHARTRES.
A.D. 1217.

The Grand Master Philip Duplessies was succeeded by Brother WILLIAM DE CHARTRES, as appears from the following letter to the Pope:

"To the very reverend father in Christ, the Lord Honorius, by the providence of God chief pontiff of the Holy Roman Church, William de Chartres, humble Master of the poor chivalry of the Temple, proffereth all due obedience and reverence, with the kiss of the foot.

WILLIAM DE
CHARTRES.
A.D. 1217.

"By these our letters we hasten to inform your paternity of the state of that Holy Land which the Lord hath consecrated with his own blood. Know that, at the period of the departure of these letters, an immense number of pilgrims, both knights and foot soldiers, marked with the emblem of the life-giving cross, arrived at Acre from Germany and other parts of Europe. Saphadin, the great sultan of Egypt, hath remained closely within the confines of his own dominions, not daring in any way to molest us. The arrival of the king of Hungary, and of the dukes of Austria and Moravia, together with the intelligence just received of the near approach of the fleet of the Friths, has not a little alarmed him. Never do we recollect the power of the Pagans so low as at the present time; and may the omnipotent God, O holy father, make it grow weaker and weaker day by day. But we must inform you that in these parts corn and barley, and all the necessaries of life, have become extraordinarily dear. This year the harvest has utterly

---

* "Formam autem rei prolocutae inter nos et ipsoa, scriptam et sigillo nostro sigillatam. ... in custodiam Templariorum commisimus."—*Literæ Regis sorori suæ Reginæ Berengariæ*, ib. p. 194.

† Berengaria Dei gratiâ, quondam humilis Angliæ Regina. Omnibus, &c. salutem. ... Hanc pecuniam solvet in domo Novi Templi London. Ib. p. 208, 209, ad. ann. 1215.

‡ *Matt. Par.* p. 253, ad. ann. 1215.

§ *Monast. Angl.* vol. vi. part ii.

disappointed the expectations of our husbandmen, and has almost totally failed. The natives, indeed, now depend for support altogether upon the corn imported from the West, but as yet very little foreign grain has been received; and to increase our uneasiness, nearly all our knights are dismounted, and we cannot procure horses to supply the places of those that have perished. It is therefore of the utmost importance, O holy father, to advertise all who design to assume the cross of the above scarcity, that they may furnish themselves with plentiful supplies of grain and horses.

"Before the arrival of the king of Hungary and the duke of Austria, we had come to the determination of marching against the city of Naplous, and of bringing the Saracen chief Coradin to an engagement if he would have awaited our attack, but we have all now determined to undertake an expedition into Egypt to destroy the city of Damietta, and we shall then march upon Jerusalem. ..."* WILLIAM DE CHARTRES. A.D. 1218.

It was in the month of May, A.D. 1218, that the galleys of the Templars set sail from Acre on the above-mentioned memorable expedition into Egypt. They cast anchor in the mouth of the Nile, and, in conjunction with a powerful army of crusaders, laid siege to Damietta. A pestilence broke out shortly after their arrival, and hurried the Grand Master, William de Chartres, to his grave.† He was succeeded by the veteran warrior, Brother Peter de Montaigu, Grand Preceptor of Spain .‡

James of Vitry, bishop of Acre, who accompanied the Templars on this expedition, gives an enthusiastic account of their famous exploits, and of the tremendous battles fought upon the Nile, in one of which a large vessel of the Templars was sunk, and every soul on board perished. He describes the great assault on their camp towards the middle of the year 1219, when the trenches were forced, and all the infantry put to flight. "The insulting shouts of the conquering Saracens," says he, "were heard on all sides, and a panic was rapidly spreading through the disordered ranks of the whole army of the cross, when the Grand Master and brethren of the Temple made a desperate charge, and bravely routed the first ranks of the infidels. The spirit of Gideon animated the Templars, and the rest of the army, stimulated by their example, bravely advanced to their support. ... Thus did the Lord on that day, through the valour of the Templars, save those who trusted in Him."§ Immediately after the surrender of Damietta, the Grand Master of the Temple returned to Acre to repel the forces of the sultan of Damascus, who had invaded the Holy Land, as PETER DE MONTAIGU. A.D. 1218.

PETER DE MONTAIGU. A.D. 1222.

* Ital. et Raven. Historiarum *Hieronymi Rubei*, lib. vi. p. 380, 381, ad ann. 1217. ed, Ven. 1603.

† *Jac. de Vitr.* lib. iii. ad. ann. 1218. Gesta Dei, tom i. 1, para2, p. 1133, 4, 5.

‡ *Gall. Christ nov.* tom. ii. col. 714, torn vii. col. 229.

§ *Jac. de Vitr.* Hist. Orient, ut sup. p. 1138. Bernard Thesaur. apud Muratori, cap. 190 to 200.

appears from the following letter to the bishop of Ely.

"Brother Peter de Montaigu, Master of the Knights of the Temple, to the reverend brother in Christ, N., by the grace of God bishop of Ely, health. We proceed by these letters to inform your paternity how we have managed the affairs of our Lord Jesus Christ since the capture of Damietta and of the castle of Taphneos." The Grand Master describes various military operations, the great number of galleys fitted out by the Saracens to intercept the supplies and succour from Europe, and the arming of the galleys, galliots, and other vessels of the Order of the Temple to oppose them, and clear the seas of the infidel flag. He states that the sultan of Damascus had invaded Palestine, had ravaged the country around Acre and Tyre, and had ventured to pitch his tents before the castle of the Pilgrims, and had taken possession of Cæsarea. "If we are disappointed," says he, "of the succour we expect in the ensuing summer, all our newly-acquired conquests, as well as the places that we have held for ages past, will be left in a very doubtful condition. We ourselves, and others in these parts, are so impoverished by the heavy expenses we have incurred in prosecuting the affairs of Jesus Christ, that we shall be unable to contribute the necessary funds, unless we speedily receive succour and subsidies from the faithful. Given at Acre, xii. kal. October, A.D. 1222."*

The troops of the sultan of Damascus were repulsed and driven beyond the frontier, and the Grand Master then returned to Damietta, to superintend the preparations for a march upon Cairo. The results of that disastrous campaign are detailed in the following letter to Brother Alan Marcel, Preceptor of England, and Master of the Temple at London. "Brother Peter de Montaigu, humble Master of the soldiers of Christ, to our vicegerent and beloved brother in Christ, Alan Marcel, Preceptor of England.

PETER DE
MONTAIGU.
A.D. 1222.

"Hitherto we have had favourable information to communicate unto you touching our exertions in the cause of Jesus Christ; now, alas! such have been the reverses and disasters which our sins have brought upon us in the land of Egypt, that we have nothing but ill news to announce. After the capture of Damietta, our army remained for some time in a state of inaction, which brought upon us frequent complaints and reproaches from the eastern and the western Christians. At length, after the feast of the holy apostles, the legate of the holy pontiff, and all our soldiers of the cross, put themselves in march by land and by the Nile, and arrived in good order at the spot where the sultan was encamped, at the head of an immense number of the enemies of the cross. The river Taphneos, an arm of the great Nile, flowed between the camp of the sultan and our forces, and being unable to ford this river, we pitched our tents on its banks, and prepared bridges to enable us to force the passage. In the mean time, the

* Epist. Magni Magistri Templi apud Matt. Par. p. 312, 313.

annual inundation rapidly increased, and the sultan, passing his galleys and armed boats through an ancient canal, floated them into the Nile below our positions, and cut off our communications with Damietta." ... "Nothing now was to be done but to retrace our steps. The sultans of Aleppo and Damascus, the two brothers of the sultan, and many chieftains and kings of the pagans, with an immense multitude of infidels who had come to their assistance, attempted to cut off our retreat. At night we commenced our march, but the infidels cut through the embankments of the Nile, the water rushed along several unknown passages and ancient canals, and encompassed us on all sides. We lost all our provisions, many of our men were swept into the stream, and the further progress of our Christian warriors was forthwith arrested. The waters continued to increase upon us, and in this terrible inundation we lost all our horses and saddles, our carriages, baggage, furniture, and moveables, and everything that we had. We ourselves could neither advance nor retreat, and knew not whither to turn. We could not attack the Egyptians on account of the great lake which extended itself between them and us; we were without food, and being caught and pent up like fish in a net, there was nothing left for us but to treat with the sultan. PETER DE MONTAIGU. A.D. 1222.

"We agreed to surrender Damietta, with all the prisoners which we had in Tyre and at Acre, on Condition that the sultan restored to us the wood of the true cross and the prisoners that he detained at Cairo and Damascus. We, with some others, were deputed by the whole army to announce to the people of Damietta the terms that had been imposed upon us. These were very displeasing to the bishop of Acre,* to the chancellor, and some others, who wished to defend the town, a measure which we should indeed have greatly approved of, had there been any reasonable chance of success; for we would rather have been thrust into perpetual imprisonment than have surrendered, to the shame of Christendom, this conquest to the infidels. But after having made a strict investigation into the means of defence, and finding neither men nor money wherewith to protect the place, we were obliged to submit to the conditions of the sultan, who, after having exacted from us an oath and hostages, accorded to us a truce of eight years. During the negotiations the sultan faithfully kept his word, and for the space of fifteen days furnished our soldiers with the bread and corn necessary for their subsistence. "Do you, therefore, pitying our misfortunes, hasten to relieve them to the utmost of your ability. Farewell."† PETER DE MONTAIGU. A.D. 1223.

Brother Alan Marcell, to whom the above letter is addressed, succeeded Amaric de St. Maur, and was at the head of the Order in England for the space of sixteen years. He was employed by King Henry the Third in

* Our historian, James de Vitry; he subsequently became one of the hostages. Contin. Hist. apud. *Martene*, tom. v. col. 698

† Matt. Par. ad. ann. 1222, p. 314. See also another letter, p. 313.

various important negotiations; and was Master of the Temple at London, when Reginald, king of the island of Man, by the advice and persuasion of the legate Pandulph, made a solemn surrender at that place of his island to the pope and his Catholic successors, and consented to hold the same from thenceforth as the feudatory of the church of Rome.*

At the commencement of the reign of Henry the Third, the Templars in England appear to have been on bad terms with the king. The latter made heavy complaints against them to the pope, and the holy pontiff issued (A.D. 1223) the bull "DE INSOLENTIA TEMPLARIORUM REPRIMENDA," in which he states that his very dear son in Christ, Henry, the illustrious king of the English, had complained to him of the usurpations of the Templars on the royal domains; that they had placed their crosses upon houses that did not belong to them, and prevented the customary dues and services from being rendered to the crown; that they undutifully set at nought the customs of the king's manors, and involved the bailiffs and royal officers in lawsuits before certain judges of their own appointment. The pope directs two abbots to inquire into these matters, preparatory to further proceedings against the guilty parties;† but the Templars soon became reconciled to their sovereign, and on the 28th of April of‡the year following, the Master, Brother Alan Marcell, was employed by King Henry to negotiate a truce between himself and the king of France. The king of England appears at that time to have been resident at the Temple, the letters of credence being made out at that place, in the presence of the archbishop of Canterbury, several bishops, and Hubert, the chief justiciary.§ The year after, the same Alan Marcell was sent into Germany, to negotiate a treaty of marriage between King Henry and the daughter of the duke of Austria.**

PETER DE MONTAIGU. A.D. 1224.

At this period, Brother Hugh de Stocton and Richard Ranger, knights of the convent of the New Temple at London, were the guardians of the royal treasure in the Tower, and the former was made the depositary, of the money paid annually by the king to the count of Flanders. He was also entrusted by Henry the Third with large sums of money, out of which he was commanded to pay ten thousand marks to the emperor of Constantinople.††

Among the many illustrious benefactors to the Order of the Temple

---

* Actum London in domo Militiæ Templi, II. kal. Octob. *Acta Rymeri,* tom. i. p. 234, ad ann. 1219.

† *Acta Rymeri,* tom. i. ad ann 1223, p. 258.

‡ Mittimua ad vos dilect. nobis in Christo, fratrem Alanum Marcell Magistrum militiæ Templi in Angliâ, &c. . . . . Teste meipso apud Novum Templum London coram Domino Cantuar—archiepiscopo, Huberto de Burgo justitiario et J. Bath—Sarum episcopis. *Acta Rymeri,* tom. i. p. 270, ad ann. 1224.

§ Ib. p. 275.

** Ib. p. 311, 373, 380.

at this period was Philip the Second, king of France, who bequeathed the sum of one hundred thousand pounds to the Grand Master of the Temple.*

The Grand Master, Peter de Montaigu, was succeeded by Brother Hermann de Perigord.† Shortly after his accession to power, William de Montserrat, Preceptor of Antioch, being "desirous of extending the Christian territories, to the honour and glory of Jesas Christ," besieged a fortress of the infidels in the neighbourhood of Antioch. He refused to retreat before a superior force, and was surrounded and overwhelmed; a hundred knights of the Temple and three hundred cross-bowmen were slain, together with many secular warriors, and a large number of foot soldiers. The *Balcanifer,* or standard-bearer, on this occasion, was an English Knight Templar, named Reginald d'Argenton, who performed prodigies of valour. He was disabled and covered with wounds, yet he unflinchingly bore the Beauseant, or war-banner, aloft with his bleeding arms into the thickest of the fight, until he at last fell dead upon a heap of his slaughtered comrades. The Preceptor of Antioch, before he was slain, *"sent sixteen infidels to hell."*‡

HERMANN D
PERIGORD.
A.D. 1236.

HERMANN D
PERIGORD.
A.D. 1237.

As soon as the Templars in England heard of this disaster, they sent, in conjunction with the Hospitallers, instant succour to their brethren. "The Templars and the Hospitallers," says Matthew Paris, "eagerly prepared to avenge the blood of their brethren so gallantly poured forth in the cause of Christ. The Hospitallers appointed Brother Theodore, their prior, a most valiant soldier, to lead a band of knights and of stipendiary troops, with an immense treasure, to the succour of the Holy Land. Having made their arrangements, they all started from the house of the Hospitallers at Clerkenwell in London, and passed through the city with spears held aloft, shields displayed, and banners advanced. They marched in splendid pomp to the bridge, and sought a blessing from all who crowded to see them pass. The brothers indeed uncovered, bowed their heads from side to side, and recommended themselves to the prayers of all."§

HERMANN DI
PERIGORD.
A.D. 1239.

Whilst the Knights Templars were thus valiantly sustaining the cause of the cross against the infidels in the East, one of the holy brethren of

---

* Sanut, lib. iii. c x. p. 210.

† *Cotton, MS.* Nero E. VI. p. 60. fol. 466. Nero E. VI. 23. i.

‡ Cecidit autem in illo infausto certnmine illustris miles Templarius Anglicus natione, Reginaldus de Argentomio, eâ die Balcanifer; ... indefessus vero vexillum sustinebat, donec tibiæ cum cruribus et manibus frangerentur. Solus quoque eorum Preceptor priusquam trucidaretur, sexdecim hostium ad inferos destinavit.—*Matt.* Par. p. 443, ad ann. 1237.

§ A *Clerkenwelle* domo sua, quæ est Londoniis, per medium civitatis, clypeis circiter triginta detectis, hastis ele vat is, et prævio vexillo, versus pontem, ut ab omnibus viden-tibus, benedictionem obtinerent, perrexerunt eleganter. Fratres vero inclinatis capitibus, hinc et inde caputiis depositis, se omnium precibus commendaverunt.—*Matt.* Par. p. 443, 444.

the Order, the king's special counsellor, named Geoffrey, was signalising his zeal against infidels at home in England, (A.D. 1239), by a fierce destruction and extermination of the Jews. According to Matthew Paris, he seized and incarcerated the unhappy Israelites, and extorted from them immense sums of money.* Shortly afterwards, Brother Geoffrey fell into disgrace and was banished from court, and Brother Roger, another Templar, the king's almoner, shared the same fate, and was forbidden to approach the royal presence.† Some of the brethren of the Order were always about the court, and when the English monarch crossed the seas, he generally wrote letters to the Master of the Temple at London, informing him of the state of the royal health.‡

It was at this period, (A.D. 1240), that the oblong portion of the Temple church was completed and consecrated in the presence of King Henry the Third.§

HERMANN DE
PERIGORD.
A.D. 1236. The Grand Mastership of Brother Hermann de Perigord is celebrated for the treaty entered into with the infidels, whereby the Holy City was again surrendered to the Christians. The patriarch returned thither with all his clergy, the churches were reconsecrated, and the Templars and Hospitallers emptied their treasuries in rebuilding the walls.

The following account of these gratifying events was transmitted by the Grand Master of the Temple to Robert de Sanford, Preceptor of England, and Master of the Temple at London.

"Brother Hermann de Perigord, humble *minister* of the knights of the poor Temple, to his beloved brother in Christ, Robert de Sanford, Preceptor in England, salvation in the Lord.

"Since it is our duty, whenever an opportunity offers, to make known to the brotherhood, by letters or by messengers, the state and prospects of the Holy Land, we hasten to inform you, that after our great successes against the sultan of Egypt, and Nassr his supporter and abettor, the great persecutor of the Christians, they were reluctantly compelled to negotiate a truce, promising us to restore to the followers of Jesus Christ all the territory on this side Jordan. We despatched certain of our brethren, noble and discreet personages, to Cairo, to have an interview with the Sultan upon these matters. . . . . ."

The Grand Master proceeds to relate the progress of the negotiations, and the surrender of the Holy City and the greater part of Palestine to the

---

* Et eodem anno (1239) … passi sunt Judæi exterminium magnum et destructionem, eosdem arctante et incarcerante, et pecuniam ab eisdem extorquente Galfrido Templario, Regis speciali consiliario.—*Matt.* Par. p. 489, ad ann. 1239.

† In ipsâ irâ aufugavit fratrem Rogerum Templarium ab officio eleemosynariæ, et a curiâ jussit elongari.—Ib.

‡ *Rymer*, tom. i. p. 404.

§ Post.

soldiers of Christ. ... "whence, to the joy of angels and of men," says he, "Jerusalem is now inhabited by Christians alone, all the Saracens being driven out. The holy places have been reconsecrated and purified by the prelates of the churches, and in those spots where the name of the Lord has not been invoked for fifty-six years, now, blessed be God, the divine mysteries are daily celebrated. To all the sacred places there is again free access to the faithful in Christ, nor is it to be doubted but that in this happy and prosperous condition we might long remain, if our Eastern Christians would from henceforth live in greater concord and unanimity. But, alas! opposition and contradiction arising from envy and hatred have impeded our efforts in the promotion of these and other advantages for the land. With the exception of the prelates of the churches, and a few of the barons, who afford us all the assistance in their power, the entire burthen of its defence rests upon our house alone.

"For the safeguard and preservation of the holy territory, we propose to erect a fortified castle near Jerusalem, which will enable us the more easily to retain possession of the country, and to protect it against all enemies. But indeed we can in nowise defend for any great length of time the places that we hold, against the sultan of Egypt, who is a most powerful and talented man, unless Christ and his faithful followers extend to us an efficacious support."*

* *Matt. Par.* p. 615.

CHAPTER VIII.

The conquest of Jerusalem by the Carizmians —The slaughter of the Templars, and the death of the Grand Master—The exploits of the Templars in Egypt— King Louis of France visits the Templars in Palestine—He assists them in putting the country into a defensible state—Henry II., king of England, visits the Temple at Paris—The magnificent hospitality of the Templars in England and France—Benocdar, sultan of Egypt, invades Palestine—He defeats the Templars, takes their strong fortresses, and decapitates six hundred of their brethren—The Grand Master comes to England for succour—The renewal of the war—The fall of Acre, and the final extinction of the Templars in Palestine.

"The Knights of the Temple ever maintained their fearless and fanatic character; if they neglected to *live* they were prepared to die in the service of Christ."—*Gibbon.*

HERMANN DE PERIGORD. A.D. 1242.

Shortly after the recovery of the holy city, Djemal'eddeen, the Mussulman, paid a visit to Jerusalem. "I saw," says he, "the monks and the priests masters of the Temple of the Lord. I saw the vials of wine prepared for the sacrifice. I entered into the Mosque al Acsa, (the Temple of Solomon), and I saw a bell suspended from the dome. The rites and ceremonies of the Mussulmen were abolished; the call to prayer was no longer heard. The infidels publicly exercised their idolatrous practices in the sanctuaries of the Mussulmen."[*]

HERMANN DE PERIGORD. A.D. 1243.

By the advice of Benedict, bishop of Marseilles, who came to the Holy City on a pilgrimage, the Templars rebuilt their ancient and formidable castle of Saphet. Eight hundred and fifty work-men, and four hundred slaves were employed in the task. The walls were sixty *French* feet in width, one hundred and seventy in height, and the circuit of them was two thousand two hundred and fifty feet. They were flanked by seven large round towers, sixty feet in diameter, and seventy-two feet higher than the walls. The fosse surrounding the fortress was thirty-six feet wide, and was pierced in the solid rock to a depth of forty-three feet The garrison, in

[*] *Michaud* Extraits Arabes, p. 549.

time of peace, amounted to one thousand seven hundred men, and to two thousand two hundred in time of war.* The ruins of this famous castle crowning the summit of a lofty mountain, torn and shattered by earthquakes, still present a stupendous appearance. In Pococke's time "two particularly fine large round towers" were entire, and Van Egmont and Heyman describe the remains of two moats lined with freestone, several fragments of walls, bulwarks, and turrets, together with corridors, winding staircases, and internal apartments. Ere this fortress was completed, the Templars again lost the holy city, and were well-nigh exterminated in a bloody battle fought with the Carizmians. These were a fierce, pastoral tribe of Tartars, who, descending from the north of Asia, and quitting their abodes in the neighbourhood of the Caspian, rushed headlong upon the nations of the south. They overthrew with frightful rapidity, and the most terrific slaughter, all who had ventured to oppose their progress; and, at the instigation of Saleh Ayoub, sultan of Egypt, with whom they had formed an alliance, they turned their arms against the Holy Land. In a great battle fought near Gaza, which lasted two days, the Grand Masters of the Temple and the Hospital were both slain, together with three hundred and twelve Knights Templars, and three hundred and twenty-four serving brethren, besides hired soldiers in the pay of the Order.† The following account of these disasters was forwarded to Europe by the Vice-Master of the Temple, and the bishops and abbots of Palestine.

HERMANN DE PERIGORD. A.D. 1244.

"To the reverend Fathers in Christ, and to all our friends, archbishops, bishops, abbots, and other prelates of the church in the kingdoms of France and England, to whom these letters shall come;— Robert, by the grace of God, patriarch of the holy church of Jerusalem; Henry, archbishop of Nazareth; J. elect of Cæsarea; R. bishop of Acre; *William de Rochefort, Vice-Master of the house of the soldiery of the* TEMPLE, and of the convent of the *same house*; H. prior of the sepulchre of the Lord; B. of the Mount of Olives, &c. &c. Health and prosperity."

"The cruel barbarian, issuing forth from the confines of the East, hath turned his footsteps towards the kingdom of Jerusalem, that holy land, which, though it hath at different periods been grievously harassed by the Saracen tribes, hath yet in these latter days enjoyed ease and tranquillity, and been at peace with the neighbouring nations. But, alas! the sins of our Christian people have just now raised up for its destruction an unknown people, and an avenging sword from afar . . ." They proceed to describe the destructive progress of the Carizmians from Tartary, the devastation of Persia, the fierce extermination by those savage hordes of all races and nations, without distinction of religion, and their sudden entry into the Holy Land by the side of Saphet and Tiberias, "when," say they, "*by*

---

* *Sleph. Baluz* Miscell., lib. vi. p. 357.
† *Marin Sanut,* p. 217.

the common advice, and at the unanimous desire of the Masters of the religious houses of the chivalry of the Temple and the Hospital, we called in the assistance of the sultans of Damascus and Carac, who were bound to us by treaty, and who bore especial hatred to the Carizmians; they promised and solemnly swore to give us their entire aid, but the succour came slow and tardy; the Christian forces were few in number, and were obliged to abandon the defence of Jerusalem . . .''

After detailing the barbarous and horrible slaughter of five thousand three hundred Christians, of both sexes—men, women, children, monks, priests, and nuns—they thus continue their simple and affecting narrative:

"At length, the before-mentioned perfidious savages having penetrated within the gates of the Holy City of Israel, the small remnant of the faithful left therein, consisting of children, women, and old men, took refuge in the church of the sepulchre of our Lord. The Carizrnians rushed to that holy sanctuary; they butchered them all before the very sepulchre itself, and cutting off the heads of the priests who were kneeling with uplifted hands before the altars, they said one to another, 'Let us here shed the blood of the Christians *on the very place where they offer up wine to their God, who they say was hanged here.*' Moreover, in sorrow be it spoken, and with sighs we inform you, that laying their sacrilegious hands on the very sepulchre itself, they sadly disturbed it, utterly battering to pieces the marble shrine which was built around that holy sanctuary. They have defiled, with every abomination of which they were capable, Mount Calvary, where Christ was crucified, and the whole church of the resurrection. They have taken away, indeed, the sculptured columns which were placed as a decoration before the sepulchre of the Lord, and as a mark of victory, and as a taunt to the Christians, they have sent them to the sepulchre of the wicked Mahomet. They have violated the tombs of the happy kings of Jerusalem in the same church, and they have scattered, to the hurt of Christendom, the ashes of those holy men to the winds, irreverently profaning the revered Mount Sion. The Temple of the Lord, the church of the Valley of Jehoshapliat, where the Virgin lies buried, the church of Bethlehem, and the place of the nativity of our Lord, they have polluted with enormities too horrible to be related, far exceeding the iniquity of all the Saracens, who, though they frequently occupied the land of the Christians, yet always reverenced and preserved the holy places . . .''

They then describe the subsequent military operations, the march of the Templars and Hospitallers, on the 4th of October, A.D. 1244, from Acre to Cæsarea; the junction of their forces with those of the Moslem sultans; the retreat of the Carizmians to Gaza, where they received succour from the sultan of Egypt; and the preparation of the Hospitallers and Templars for the attack before that place.

"Those holy warriors," say they, "boldly rushed in upon the enemy, but the Saracens who had joined us, having lost many of their men, fled, and the warriors of the cross were left alone to withstand the united attack of the Egyptians and Carizmians. Like stout champions of the Lord, and true defenders of catholicity, whom the same faith and the same cross and passion make true brothers, they bravely resisted; but as they were few in number in comparison with the enemy, they at last succumbed, so that of the convents of the house of the chivalry of the Temple, and of the house of the Hospital of Saint John at Jerusalem, only thirty-three Templars and twenty-six Hospitallers escaped; the archbishop of Tyre, the bishop of Saint George, the abbot of Saint Mary of Jehoshaphat, and the Master of the Temple, with many other clerks and holy men, being slain in that sanguinary fight. We ourselves, having by our sins provoked this dire calamity, fled half dead to Ascalon; from thence we proceeded by sea to Acre, and found that city and the adjoining province filled with sorrow and mourning, misery and death. There was not a house or a family that had not lost an inmate or a relation. . . .

"The Carizmians have now pitched their tents in the plain of Acre, about two miles from the city. The whole country, as far as Nazareth and Saphet, is overrun by them, so that the churches of Jerusalem and the Christian kingdom have now no territory, except a few fortifications, which are defended with great difficulty and labour by the Templars and Hospitallers. ...

"To you, dearest Fathers, upon whom the burthen of the defence of the cause of Christ justly resteth, we have caused these sad tidings to be communicated, earnestly beseeching you to address your prayers to the throne of grace, imploring mercy from the Most High; that he who consecrated the Holy Land with his own blood in redemption of all mankind, may compassionately turn towards it and defend it, and send it succour. Do ye yourselves, dearest Fathers, as far as ye are able, take sage counsel and speedily assist us, that ye may receive a heavenly reward. But know, assuredly, that unless, through the interposition of the Most High, or by the aid of the faithful, the Holy Land is succoured in the next spring passage from Europe, its doom is sealed, and utter ruin is inevitable.

"Since it would be tedious to explain by letter all our necessities, we have sent to you the venerable father bishop of Beirout, and the holy man Arnulph, of the Order of Friars Preachers, who will faithfully and truly unfold the particulars to your venerable fraternity. We humbly entreat you liberally to receive and patiently to hear the aforesaid messengers, who have exposed themselves to great dangers for the church of God, by navigating the seas in the depth of winter. Given at Acre, this fifth day of November, in the year of our Lord one thousand twelve hundred and forty-four."*

The above letter was read before a general council of the church, which had been assembled at Lyons by Pope Innocent IV., and it was re-

HERMANN L
PERIGORD.
A.D. 1244.

HERMANN
DE
PERIGORD.
A.D. 1244.

solved that a new crusade should be preached. It was provided that those who assumed the cross should assemble at particular places to receive the Pope's blessing; that there should be a truce for four years between all Christian princes; that during all that time there should be no tournaments, feasts, nor public rejoicings; that all the faithful in Christ should be exhorted to contribute, out of their fortunes and estates, to the defence of the Holy Land; and that ecclesiastics should pay towards it the tenth, and cardinals the twentieth, of all their revenues, for the term of three years successively. The ancient enthusiasm, however, in favour of distant expeditions to the East had died away; the addresses and exhortations of the clergy now fell on unwilling ears, and the Templars and Hospitallers received only some small assistance in men and money.

The temporary alliance between the Templars and the Mussulman sultans of Syria, for the purpose of insuring their common safety, did not escape animadversion. The emperor Frederick the Second, the nominal king of Jerusalem, in a letter to Richard earl of Cornwall, the brother of Henry the Third, king of England, accuses the Templars of making war upon the sultan of Egypt, in defiance of a treaty entered into with that monarch, of compelling him to call in the Carizmians to his assistance; and he compares the union of the Templars with the infidel sultans, for purposes of defence, to an attempt to extinguish a fire by pouring upon it a quantity of oil. "The proud religion of the Temple," says he, in continuation, "nurtured amid the luxuries of the barons of the land, waxeth wanton. It hath been made manifest to us, by certain religious persons lately arrived from parts beyond sea, that the aforesaid sultans and their trains were received with pompous alacrity within the gates of the houses of HERMANN the Temple, and that the Templars suffered them to perform within them DE their superstitious rites and ceremonies, with invocation of Mahomet, PERIGORD. and to indulge in secular delights."† The Templars, notwithstanding their A.D. 1245. disasters, successfully defended all their strong fortresses in Palestine against the efforts of the Carizmians, and gradually recovered their footing in the Holy Land. The galleys of the Order kept the command of the sea, and succour speedily arrived to them from their western brethren. A general chapter of knights was assembled in the Pilgrim's Castle, and the veteran warrior, brother was chosen Grand Master of the Order.* Circular mandates were, at the same time, sent to the western preceptories, summoning all the brethren to Palestine, and directing the immediate transmission of all the money in the different treasuries to the headquarters of the Order at Acre. These calls appear to have been promptly attended to, and the Pope praises both the Templars and Hospitallers for

---

* *Matt. Par.* p. 631 to 633, ad ann. 1244. "Huic scripto originali, quod erat hujus exemplum, appensa fuerunt duodecim sigilla.

† *Matt. Par.* p. 618—620.

the zeal and energy displayed by them in sending out the newly-admitted knights and novices with armed bands and a large amount of treasure to the succour of the holy territory.† The aged knights, and those whose duties rendered them unable to leave the western preceptories, implored the blessings of heaven upon the exertions of their brethren; they observed extraordinary fasts and mortification, and directed continual prayers to be offered up throughout the Order.‡ Whilst the proposed crusade was slowly progressing, the holy pontiff wrote to the sultan of Egypt, the ally of the Carizmians, proposing a peace or a truce, and received the following grand and magnificent reply to his communication:

"To the Pope, the noble, the great, the spiritual, the affectionate, the holy, the thirteenth of the apostles, the leader of the sons of baptism, the high priest of the Christians, (may God strengthen him, and establish him, and give him happiness!) from the most powerful sultan ruling over the necks of nations; wielding the two great weapons, the sword and the pen; possessing two pre-eminent excellencies—that is to say, learning and judgment; king of two seas; ruler of the South and North; king of the region of Egypt and Syria, Mesopotamia, Media, Idumea, and Ophir; King Saloph Beelpheth, Jacob, son of Sultan Camel, Hemevafar Mehameth, son of Sultan Hadel, Robethre, son of Jacob, whose kingdom may the Lord God make happy.

"IN THE NAME OF GOD THE MOST MERCIFUL AND COMPASSIONATE.

"The letters of the Pope, the noble, the great, &c. &c. . . . have been presented to us. May God favour him who earnestly seeketh after righteousness and doeth good, and wisheth peace and walketh in the ways of the Lord. May God assist him who worshippeth him in truth. We have considered the aforesaid letters, and have understood the matters treated of therein, which have pleased and delighted us; and the messenger sent by the holy Pope came to us, and we caused him to be brought before us with honour, and love, and reverence; and we brought him to see us face to face, and inclining our ears towards him, we listened to his speech, and we have put faith in the words he hath spoken unto us concerning Christ, upon whom be salvation and praise. But we know more concerning that same Christ than ye know, and we magnify him more than ye magnify him. And as to what you say concerning your desire for peace, tranquillity, and quiet, and that you wish to put down war, so also do we; we desire and wish nothing to the contrary. But let the Pope know, that

WILLI
DE
SONN/
A.D. 1

WILLI
DE
SONN
A.D. 1

---

* Cotton MS. Nero E. VI. p. 60, fol. 466, vir discretus et circumspectus; in negotiis quoque bellicis peritus.

† Hospitalarii et Templarii militea neophitos et manum armatam cum thesauro non modico illuc ad consolationem et auxilium ibi commorantium festinanter transmiserunt. Epist. Pap. Innocent IV.

‡ *Matt. Par.* p. 697, 698.

between ourselves and the Emperor (Frederick) there hath been mutual love, and alliance, and perfect concord, from the time of the sultan, my father, (whom may God preserve and place in the glory of his brightness;) and between you and the Emperor there is, as ye know, Btrife and warfare; whence it is not fit that we should enter into any treaty with the Christians until we have previously had his advice and assent. We have therefore written to our envoy at the imperial court upon the propositions made to us by the Pope's messenger, &c. ...

"This letter was written on the seventh of the month *Maharan*. Praise be to the one only God, and may his blessing rest upon our master Mahomet."*

The year following, (A.D. 1247), the Carizmians were annihilated; they were cut up in detail by the Templars and Hospitallers, and were at last slain to a man. Their very name perished from the face of the earth, but the traces of their existence were long preserved in the ruin and desolation they had spread around them.† The Holy Land, although happily freed from the destructive presence of these barbarians, had yet everything to fear from the powerful sultan of Egypt, with whom hostilities still continued; and Brother William de Sonnac, the Grand Master of the Temple, for the purpose of stimulating the languid energies of the English nation, and reviving their holy zeal and enthusiasm in the cause of the Cross, despatched a distinguished Knight Templar to England, charged with the duty of presenting to King Henry the Third a magnificent crystal vase, containing a portion of the blood of our Lord Jesus Christ, which had been poured forth upon the sacred soil of Palestine for the remission of the sins of all the faithful.

WILLIAM DE SONNAC. A.D. 1249. A solemn attestation of the genuineness of this precious relic, signed by the patriarch of Jerusalem, and the bishops, the abbots, and the barons of the Holy Land, was forwarded to London for the satisfaction of the king and his subjects, and was deposited, together with the vase and its inestimable contents, in the cathedral church of Saint Paul.‡

In the month of June, A.D. 1249, the galleys of the Templars left Acre with a strong body of forces on board, and joined the expedition undertaken by the French king, Louis IX., against Egypt. The following account of the capture of Damietta was forwarded to the Master of the Temple at London.

"Brother William de Sonnac, by the grace of God Master of the poor chivalry of the Temple, to his beloved brother in Christ, Robert de Sanford, Preceptor of England, salvation in the Lord.

---

* Literæ Soldani Babyloniæ ad Papam missæ, a quodam Cardinali ex Arabico translatæ.— *Matt. Par.* p. 711.

† Ibid. p. 733.

‡ *Matt. Par.* p. 735.

"We hasten to unfold to you by these presents agreeable and happy intelligence." (He details the landing of the French, the defeat of the infidels with the loss of one Christian soldier, and the subsequent capture of the city.) "Damietta, therefore, has been taken, not by our deserts, nor by the might of our armed bands, but through the divine power and assistance. Moreover, be it known to you that King Louis, with God's favour, proposes to march upon Alexandria or Cairo for the purpose of delivering our brethren there detained in captivity, and of reducing, with God's help, the whole land to the Christian worship. Farewell."*

The Lord de Joinville, the friend of King Louis, and one of the bravest of the French captains, gives a lively and most interesting account of the campaign, and of the famous exploits of the Templars. During the march towards Cairo, they led the van of the Christian army, and on one occasion, when the king of France had given strict orders that no attack should be made upon the infidels, and that an engagement should be avoided, a body of Turkish cavalry advanced against them. "One of these Turks," says Joinville, "gave a Knight Templar in the first rank so heavy a blow with his battle-axe, that it felled him under the feet of the Lord Reginald de Vichier's horse, who was Marshall of the Temple; the Marshall, seeing his man fall, cried out to his brethren, 'At them in the name of God, for I cannot longer stand this.' He instantly stuck spurs into his horse, followed by all his brethren, and as their horses were fresh, not a Saracen escaped." On another occasion, the Templars marched forth at the head of the Christian army, to make trial of a ford across the Tanitic branch of the Nile. "Before we set out," says Joinville, "the king had ordered that the Templars should form the van, and the Count d'Artois, his brother, should command the second division after the Templars; but the moment the Compte d'Artois had passed the ford, he and all his people fell on the Saracens, and putting them to flight, galloped after them. The Templars sent to call the Compte d'Artois back, and to tell him that it was his duty to march behind and not before them; but it happened that the Count d'Artois could not make any answer by reason of my Lord Foucquault du Melle, who held the bridle of his horse, and my Lord Foucquault, who was a right good knight, being deaf, heard nothing the Templars were saying to the Count d'Artois, but kept bawling out, 'Forward ! forward !' (*"Or a eulz! or a eulz!"*) When the Templars perceived this, they thought they should be dishonoured if they allowed the Count d'Artois thus to take the lead; so they spurred their horses more and more, and faster and faster, and chased the Turks, who fled before them, through the town of Massoura, as far as the plains towards Babylon; but on their return, the Turks shot at them plenty of arrows, and attacked them in the narrow

WILLIAM DE SONNAC. A.D. 1249.

---

* Ib. in additamentis, p. 168, 169.

streets of the town. The Count d'Artois and the Earl of Leicester were there slain, and as many as three hundred other knights. The Templars lost, as their chief informed me, full fourteen score men-at-arms, and all his horsemen."*

WILLIAM DE SONNAC. A.D. 1250.

The Grand Master of the Temple also lost an eye, and cut his way through the infidels to the main body of the Christian army, accompanied only by two Knights Templars.† There he again mixed in the affray, took the command of a vanguard, and is to be found fighting by the side of the Lord de Joinville at sunset. In his account of the great battle fought on the first Friday in Lent, Joinville thus commemorates the gallant bearing of the Templars:

"The next battalion was under the command of Brother William de Sonnac, Master of the Temple, who had with him the small remnant of the brethren of the Order who survived the battle of Shrove Tuesday. The Master of the Temple made of the engines which we had taken from the Saracens a sort of rampart in his front, but when the Saracens marched up to the assault, they threw Greek fire upon it, and as the Templars had piled up many planks of fir wood amongst these engines, they caught fire immediately; and the Saracens, perceiving that the brethren of the Temple were few in number, dashed through the burning timbers, and vigorously attacked them. In the preceding battle of Shrove Tuesday, Brother William, the Master of the Temple, lost one of his eyes, and in this battle the said lord lost his other eye, and was slain. God have mercy on his soul! And know that immediately behind the place where the battalion of the Templars stood, there was a good acre of ground, so covered with darts, arrows, and missiles, that you could not see the earth beneath them, such showers of these had been discharged against the Templars by the Saracens!"‡

REGINALD DE VICHIER. A.D. 1252.

The Grand Master, William de Sonnac, was succeeded by the Marshall of the Temple, Brother Reginald de Vichier.* King Louis, after his release from captivity, proceeded to Palestine, where he remained two years. He repaired the fortifications of Jaffa and Cæsarea, and assisted the Templars in putting the country into a defensible state. The Lord de Joinville remained with him the whole time, and relates some curious events that took place during his stay. It appears that the scheik of the assassins still

---

* Quant les Templiers virent-ce, il se penserent que il seroient honniz se il lessoient le Compte d'Artois aler devant eulz; si ferirent des esperons qui plus plus, et qui miex miex, et chasserent les Tures. Hist. de San Louis par Jehan Sire de Joinville, p. 47.

† Nec evasit de tatâ il'â gloriosâ militia nisi duo Templarii.— Matt. Par. ad ann. 1250. Chron. Nangis, p. 790.

‡ Et à celle bataille frere Guillaume le Mestre du Temple perdi l'un des yex, et l'autre avoit il perdu le jour de quaresm pernant, et en fu mort ledit seigneur, que Dieux absoille.— *Joinville*, p. 58.

continued to pay tribute to the Templars; and during the king's residence at Acre, the chief sent ambassadors to him to obtain a remission of the tribute. He gave them an audience, and declared that he would consider of their proposal. "When they came again before the king," says Joinville, "it was about vespers, and they found the Master of the Temple on one side of him, and the Master of the Hospital on the other. The ambassadors refused to repeat what they had said in the morning, but the Masters of the Temple and the Hospital commanded them so to do. Then the Masters of the Temple and Hospital told them that their lord had very foolishly and impudently sent such a message to the king of France, and had they not been invested with the character of ambassadors, they would have thrown them into the filthy sea of Acre, and have drowned them in despite of their master. 'And we command you,' continued the masters, 'to return to your lord, and to come back within fifteen days with such letters from your prince, that the king shall be contented with him and with you.'"

The ambassadors accordingly did as they were bid, and brought back from their scheik a shirt, the symbol of friendship, and a great variety of rich presents, "crystal elephants, pieces of amber, with borders of pure gold," &c. &c.† "You must know that when the ambassadors opened the case containing all these fine things, the whole apartment was instantly embalmed with the odour of their sweet perfumes."

The Lord de Joinville accompanied the Templars in several marches and expeditions against the infidel tribes on the frontiers of Palestine, and was present at the storming of the famous castle of Panias, situate near the source of the Jordan.

At the period of the return of the king of France to Europe, (A.D. 1254), Henry the Third, king of England, was in Gascony with Brother Robert de Sanford, Master of the Temple at London, who had been previously sent by the English monarch into that province to appease the troubles which had there broken out.‡ King Henry proceeded to the French capital, and was magnificently entertained by the Knights Templars at the Temple in Paris, which Matthew Paris tells us was of such immense extent that it could contain within its precincts a numerous army. The day after his arrival, King Henry ordered an innumerable quantity of poor people to be regaled at the Temple with meat, fish, bread, and wine; and at a later hour the King of France and all his nobles came to dine with the English monarch. "Never," says Matthew Paris, "was there at any period in bygone times so noble and so celebrated an entertainment. They

REGINALD DE VICHIER. A.D. 1254.

---

* Et sachez que il avoit bien un journel de terre dariere les Templiers, qui estoit si chargé de pyles que les Sarrazins leur avoient lanciées, que il n'I paroit point de terre pour la grant foison de pyles.—Ib.

† Joinville, p. 95, 96.

‡ Acta *Rymeri*, tom. i. p. 474, ad ann. 1252.

Reginald de Vichier. A.D. 1252.

feasted in the great hall of the Temple, where hang the shields on every side, as many as they can place along the four walls, according to the custom of the Order beyond sea. . .."[*] The Knights Templars in this country likewise exercised a magnificent hospitality, and constantly entertained kings, princes, nobles, prelates, and foreign ambassadors, at the Temple. Immediately after the return of King Henry to England, some illustrious ambassadors from Castile came on a visit to the Temple at London; and as the king "greatly delighted to honour them," he commanded three pipes of wine to be placed in the cellars of the Temple for their use,[†] and ten fat bucks to be brought them at the same place from the royal forest in Essex.[‡] He, moreover, commanded the mayor and sheriffs of London, and the commonalty of the same city, to take with them a respectable assemblage of the citizens, and to go forth and meet the said ambassadors without the city, and courteously receive them, and honour them, and conduct them to the Temple.[§]

Thomas Berard. A.D. 1256.

The Grand Master, Reginald de Vichier, was succeeded by Brother Thomas Berard,[**] who wrote several letters to the king of England, displaying the miserable condition of the Holy Land, and earnestly imploring succour and assistance.[††] The English monarch, however, was too poor to assist him, being obliged to borrow money upon his crown jewels, which he sent to the Temple at Paris. The queen of France, in a letter

Thomas Berard. A.D. 1261.

"to her very dear brother Henry, the illustrious king of England," gives a long list of golden wands, golden combs, diamond buckles, chaplets, and circlets, golden crowns, imperial beavers, rich girdles, golden peacocks, and rings innumerable, adorned with sapphires, rubies, emeralds, topazes, and carbuncles, which she says she had inspected in the presence of the treasurer of the Temple at Paris, and that the same were safely deposited in the coffers of the Templars.[*]

The military power of the Orders of the Temple and the Hospital in Palestine was at last completely broken by Bibars, or Benocdar, the fourth Mamlook sultan of Egypt, who, from the humble station of a Tartar slave, had raised himself to the sovereignty of that country, and through his valour and military talents had acquired the title of "the Conqueror."

---

[*] *Matt. Par.* ad ann. 1254, p. 899, 900.

[†] . . . Mandatum est Johanni de Eynfort, camerario regis London, quod sine dilatione capiat quatuor dolia boni vini, et ea liberet Johanni de Suwerk,ponenda in cellaria Novi Templi London, ad opus nuntiorum ipsorum.—Acta *Rymeri*, tom i. p. 5.57, ad ann. 1255.

[‡] Et mandatum est Ricardo de Muntfichet, custodi forestæ Regis Essex, quod eadem forestâ sine dilatione capiat X. damos, et eos usque ad Novum Templum London cariari faciat, liberandos prædicto Johanni, ad opus prædictorum nuntiorum.—Ib.

[§] Acta Rymeri, p. 557, 558.

[**] MCCLVI. morut frère Renaut de Vichieres Maistre du Temple. Apres lui fu fait Maistre frère Thomas Berard.—Contin. hist, apud Martene, tom. v. col. 736.

[††] Acta Rymeri, tom. i. p. 698, 699, 700.

He invaded Palestine (A.D. 1262) at the head of thirty thousand cavalry, and defeated the Templars and Hospitallers with immense slaughter.[†] After several years of continuous warfare, during which the most horrible excesses were committed by both parties, all the strongholds of the Christians, with the solitary exception of the Pilgrim's Castle and the city of Acre, fell into the hands of the infidels.

On the last day of April, (A.D. 1265), Benocdar stormed Arsuf, one of the strongest of the castles of the Hospitallers; he slew ninety of the garrison, and led away a thousand into captivity. The year following he stormed Castel Blanco, a fortress of the Knights Templars, and immediately after laid siege to their famous and important castle of Saphet. After an obstinate defence, the Preceptor, finding himself destitute of provisions, agreed to capitulate, on condition that the surviving brethren and their retainers, amounting to six hundred men, should be conducted in safety to the nearest fortress of the Christians. The terms were acceded to, but as soon as Benocdar had obtained possession of the castle, he imposed upon the whole garrison the severe alternative of the Koran or death. They chose the latter, and, according to the Christian writers, were all slain.[‡] The Arabian historian Schafi Ib'n Ali Abbas, however, in his life of Bibars, or Benocdar, states that one of the garrison named *Effreez Lyoub*, embraced the Mahommetan faith, and was circumcised, and that another was sent to Acre to announce the fall of the place to his brethren. This writer attempts to excuse the slaughter of the remainder, on the ground that they had themselves first broken the terms of the capitulation, by attempting to carry away arms and treasure.[§] "By the death of so many knights of both orders," says Pope Clement IV., in one of his epistles, "the noble college of the Hospitallers, and the illustrious chivalry of the Temple, are almost destroyed, and I know not how we shall be able, after this, to find gentlemen and persons of quality sufficient to supply the places of such as have perished.[*] The year after the fall of Saphet, (A.D. 1267), Benocdar captured the cities of Homs, Belfort, Bagras, and Sidon, which belonged to the Order of the Temple; the maritime towns of Laodicea, Gabala, Tripoli, Beirout, and Jaffa, successively fell into his hands, and the fall of the princely city of Antioch was signalized by the slaughter of seventeen and the captivity of one hundred thousand of her inhabitants.[†] The utter ruin of the Latin kingdom, however, was

THOM/
BERAF
A.D. 12

THOM
BERAF
A.D. 1[

---

* Acta Rymeri, tom. i. p. 730, 878, 879, ad ann. 1261.

† Furent mors et pris, et perdirent les Templiers tot lor hernois, et le commandeor du Temple frère Matthieu le Sauvage.— Contin. hist. bell. sacr. ut sup. col. 737. Marin Sanut, cap. 6.

‡ *Marin Sanut Torsell,* lib. iii. pars 12, cap. 6, 7, 8. Contin. hist. bell. sacr. apud *Martene,* tom. v. col. 742. See also Abulfed. Hist. Arab. Apud Wilkens, p. 223. De Guignes, Hist. des Huns, tom. iv. p. 141.

§ *Michaud,* Extraites Arabes, p. 668.

averted by the timely assistance brought by Edward Prince of Wales, son of Henry the Second, king of England, who appeared at Acre with a fleet and an army. The infidels were once more defeated and driven back into Egypt, and a truce for ten years between the sultan and the Christians was agreed upon.‡ Prince Edward then prepared for his departure, but, before encountering the perils of the sea on his return home, he made his will; it is dated at Acre, June 18th, A.D. 1272, and Brother Thomas Berard, Grand Master of the Temple, appears as an attesting witness.§ Whilst the prince was pursuing his voyage to England, his father, the king of England, died, and the council of the realm, composed of the archbishops of Canterbury and York, and the bishops and barons of the kingdom, assembled in the Temple at London, and swore allegiance to the prince. They there caused him to be proclaimed king of England, and, with the consent of the queen-mother, they appointed Walter Giffard, archbishop of York, and the earls of Cornwall and Gloucester, guardians of the realm. Letters were written from the Temple to acquaint the young sovereign with the death of his father, and many of the acts of the new government emanated from the same place.**

King Henry the Third was a great benefactor to the Templars. He granted them the manors of Lilleston, Hechewayton, Saunford, Sutton, Dartfeld, and Halgel, in Kent; several lands, and churches and annual fairs at Baldok, Walnesford, Wetherby, and other places, and various weekly markets.††

WILLIAM DE BEAUJEU. A.D. 1273.

The Grand Master, Thomas Berard, was succeeded by Brother William de Beaujeu,* who came to England for the purpose of obtaining succour, and called together a general chapter of the Order at London. Whilst resident at the Temple in that city, he received payment of a large sum of money which Edward, the young king, had borrowed of the Templars during his residence in Palestine.† The Grand Master of the Hospital also came to Europe, and every exertion was made to stimulate the languid energies of the western Christians, and revive their holy zeal in the cause

---

* De Vertot, liv. iii. Preuve. xiii. See also epist. Ccccii. Apud Martene thesaur. anec. Tom. ii. col. 422.

† Facta est civitas tam famosa quaasi solitude deserti.—Martin Sanut, lib. iii. pars. 12, cap. 9. De Guignes, Hist. des Huns, tom. iv. p. 143. Contin. Hist. apud Martene, tom. v. col. 743. Abulpharag. Chron. Syr. p. 546. Michaud, Extraits Arabes, p. 681.

‡ Marin Sanut ut sup. cap. II, 12. Contin. Hist, apud Martene, col. 745,746.

§ En testimoniaunce de la queu chose, a ceo testament avons fet mettre nostre sel, et avoms pries les honurables Ben frere Hue, Mestre de l'Hospital, et frere Thomas Berard, Mestre du Temple, ke a cest escrit meisent ausi lur seus, etc. Acta Rymeri, tom. i. p. 885, 886, ad ann. 1272.

** Trivet ad ann. 1272. Walsingham, p. 43. Acta Rymeri, tom. i. p. 889, ad ann. 1272, tom. ii. p. 2.

†† Monast. Angl., vol. vi. part 2, p. 800—844.

of the Cross. A general council of the church was opened at Lyons by the Pope in person; the two Grand Masters were present, and took precedence of all the ambassadors and peers at that famous assembly. It was determined that a new crusade should be preached, that all ecclesiastical dignities and benefices should be taxed to support an armament, and that the sovereigns of Europe should be compelled by ecclesiastical censures to suspend their private quarrels, and afford succour to the desolate city of Jerusalem. The Pope, who had been himself resident in Palestine, took a strong personal interest in the promotion of the crusade, and induced many nobles, princes, and knights to assume the Cross; but the holy pontiff died in the midst of his exertions, and with him expired all hope of effectual assistance from Europe. A vast change had come over the spirit of the age; the fiery enthusiasm of the holy war had expended itself, and the Grand Masters of the Temple and Hospital returned without succour, in sorrow and disappointment, to the East.

WILLIAM D BEAUJEU. A.D. 1275.

William de Beaujeu arrived at the Temple of Acre on Saint Michael's Day, A.D. 1275, and immediately assumed the government of Palestine.‡ As there was now no hope of recovering the lost city of Jerusalem, he bent all his energies to the preservation of the few remaining possessions of the Christians in the Holy Land. At the expiration of the ten years' truce he entered into a further treaty with the infidels, called "the peace of Tortosa." It is expressed to be made between sultan Malek-Mansour and his son Malek-Saleh Ali, "honour of the world and of religion," of the one part, and Afryz Dybadjouk (William de Beaujeu) Grand Master of the Order of the Templars, of the other part. The truce is further prolonged for ten years and ten months from the date of the execution of the treaty, (A.D. 1282); and the contracting parties strictly bind themselves to make no irruptions into each other's territories during the period. To prevent mistakes, the towns, villages, and territory belonging to the Christians in Palestine are specified and defined, together with the contiguous possessions of the Moslems.* This treaty, however, was speedily broken, the war was renewed with various success, and another treaty was concluded, which was again violated by an unpardonable outrage. Some European adventurers, who had arrived at Acre, plundered and hung nineteen Egyptian merchants, and the sultan of Egypt immediately

---

* MCCLXXIII. a viii. Jors d'Avri morut frere Thomas Berart, Maistre du Temple le jor de la notre dame de Mars, et fu fait Maistre a xiii. jors de May, frere Guillaume de Bieaujcu qui estoit outré *Commendeor* du Temple en Pouille, et alerent por lui querire frere Guillaume de Poucon, qui avait tenu lieu de Maistre, et frere Bertrand de Fox; et frere Gonfiere fu fait *Commandeor* gran tenant lieu de Maistre.—Contin. Hist. apud Martene, tom. v. col. 746, 747. This is the earliest instance I have met with of the application of the term COMMANDER to the high officers of the Temple.

† Acta *Rymeri*, tom. ii. p. 34, ad ann. 1274.

‡ Contin. hist. bell. sacr. apud *Martene*, tom. v. col. 748.

WILLIAM
DE
BEAUJEU.
A.D. 1291. resumed hostilities, with the avowed determination of crushing for ever the Christian power in the East. The fortress of Margat was besieged and taken; the city of Tripoli shared the same fate; and in the third year from the re-commencement of the war, the Christian dominions in Palestine were reduced within the narrow confines of the strong city of Acre and the Pilgrim's Castle. In the spring of the year 1291, the sultan Khalil marched against Acre at the head of sixty thousand horse and a hundred and forty thousand foot.

"An innumerable people of all nations and every tongue," says a chronicle of the times, "thirsting for Christian blood, were assembled together from the deserts of the East and the South; the earth trembled beneath their footsteps, and the air was rent with the sound of their trumpets and cymbals. The sun's rays, reflected from their shields, gleamed on the distant mountains, and the points of their spears shone like the innumerable stars of heaven. When on the march, their lances presented the appearance of a vast forest rising from the earth, and covering all the landscape." ... "They wandered round about the walls, spying out their weaknesses and defects; some barked like dogs, some roared like lions, some lowed and bellowed like oxen, some struck drums with twisted sticks after their fashion, some threw darts, some cast stones, some shot arrows and bolts from cross-bows."† On the 5th of April, the place was regularly invested. No rational hope of saving it could be entertained; the sea was open; the harbour was filled with Christian vessels, and with the galleys of the Temple and the Hospital; yet the two great monastic and military orders scorned to retire to the neighbouring and friendly island of Cyprus; they refused to desert, even in its last extremity, that cause which they had sworn to maintain with the last drop of their blood. For
WILLIAM
DE
BEAUJEU.
A.D. 1291. a hundred and seventy years their swords had been constantly employed in defending the Holy Land from the profane tread of the unbelieving Moslem; the sacred territory of Palestine had been everywhere moistened with the blood of the best and bravest of their knights, and, faithful to their vows and their chivalrous engagements, they now prepared to bury themselves in the ruins of the last stronghold of the Christian faith.

William de Beaujeu, the Grand Master of the Temple, a veteran warrior of a hundred fights, took the command of the garrison, which amounted to about twelve thousand men, exclusive of the forces of the Temple and the Hospital, and a body of five hundred foot and two hundred horse, under the command of the king of Cyprus. These forces were distributed along the walls in four divisions, the first of which was commanded by Hugh de Grandison, an English knight. The old and the feeble, women and children, were sent away by sea to the Christian island of Cyprus,

---

* Life of Malek Muusour Kelaoun. *Michaud*, Extruits Arabes, p. 685, 686, 687.

† De excidio urbis Aconis apud *Martene* vet. script, tom. v. col. 767.

and none remained in the devoted city but those who were prepared to fight in its defence, or to suffer martyrdom at the hands of the infidels. The siege lasted six weeks, during the whole of which period the sallies and the attacks were incessant. Neither by night nor by day did the shouts of the assailants and the noise of the military engines cease; the walls were battered from without, and the foundations were sapped by miners, who were incessantly labouring to advance their works. More than six hundred catapults, balistæ, and other instruments of destruction, were directed against the fortifications; and the battering machines were of such immense size and weight, that a hundred wagons were required to transport the separate timbers of one of them.* Moveable towers were erected by the Moslems, so as to overtop the walls; their workmen and advanced parties were protected by hurdles covered with raw hides, and all the military contrivances which the art and the skill of the age could produce, were used to facilitate the assault. For a long time their utmost efforts were foiled by the valour of the besieged, who made constant sallies upon their works, burnt their towers and machines, and destroyed their miners. Day by day, however, the numbers of the garrison were thinned by the sword, whilst in the enemy's camp the places of the dead were constantly supplied by fresh warriors from the deserts of Arabia, animated with the same wild fanaticism in the cause of *their* religion as that which so eminently distinguished the military monks of the Temple. On the fourth of May, after thirty-three days of constant fighting, the great tower, considered the key of the fortifications, and called by the Moslems *the cursed tower*, was thrown down by the military engines. To increase the terror and distraction of the besieged, sultan Khalil mounted three hundred drummers, with their drums, upon as many dromedaries, and commanded them to make as much noise as possible whenever a general assault was ordered. From the 4th to the 14th of May, the attacks were incessant. On the 15th, the double wall was forced, and the king of Cyprus, panic-stricken, fled in the night to his ships, and made sail for the island of Cyprus, with all his followers, and with near three thousand of the best men of the garrison. On the morrow the Saracens attacked the post he had deserted; they filled up the ditch with the bodies of dead men and horses, piles of wood, stones, and earth, and their trumpets then sounded to the assault. Ranged under the yellow banner of Mahomet, the Mamlooks forced the breach, and penetrated sword in hand to the very centre of the city; but their victorious career and insulting shouts were there stopped by the mail-clad Knights of the Temple and the Hospital, who charged on horseback through the narrow streets, drove them back

WILLIAM ⅱ
BEAUJEU.
A.D. 1291.

WILLIAM ⅰ
BEAUJEU.
A.D. 1291.

---

* The famous Abul-feda, prince of Hamah, surnamed Amod-ed-deen, (Pillar of Religion), the great historian and astronomer, superintended the transportation of the military engines from Hasn-el-Akrah to St. Jean d'Aere.

with immense carnage, and precipitated them head-long from the walls.

At sunrise the following morning the air resounded with the deafening noise of drums and trumpets, and the breach was carried and recovered several times, the military friars at last closing up the passage with their bodies, and presenting a wall of steel to the advance of the enemy. Loud appeals to God and to Mahomet, to heaven and the saints, were to be heard on all sides; and after an obstinate engagement from sunrise to sunset, darkness put an end to the slaughter. On the third day, (the 18th), the infidels made the final assault on the side next the gate of St. Anthony. The Grand Masters of the Temple and the Hospital fought side by side at the head of their knights, and for a time successfully resisted all the efforts of the enemy. They engaged hand to hand with the Mamlooks, and pressed like the meanest of the soldiers into the thick of the battle. But as each knight fell beneath the keen scimitars of the Moslems, there were none in reserve to supply his place, whilst the vast hordes of the infidels pressed on with untiring energy and perseverance. The Marshall of the Hospital fell covered with wounds, and William de Beaujeu, as a last resort, requested the Grand Master of that order to sally out of an adjoining gateway at the head of five hundred horse, and attack the enemy's rear. Immediately after the Grand Master of the Temple had given these orders, he was himself struck down by the darts and the arrows of the enemy; the panic-stricken garrison fled to the port, and the infidels rushed on with tremendous shouts of *Allah acbar! Allah acbar!* ("God is victorious!") Three hundred Templars, the sole survivors of their illustrious order in Acre, were now left alone to withstand the shock of the victorious Mamlooks. In a close and compact column they fought their way, accompanied by several hundred Christian fugitives, to the Temple, and shutting their gates, they again bade defiance to the advancing foe.

GAUDINI.
A.D. 1291.
The surviving knights now assembled together in solemn chapter, and appointed the Knight Templar Brother Gaudini Grand Master.* The Temple at Acre was a place of great strength, and surrounded by walls and towers of immense extent. It was divided into three quarters, the first and principal of which contained the palace of the Grand Master, the church, and the habitation of the knights; the second, called the Bourg of the Temple, contained the cells of the serving brethren; and the third, called the Cattle Market, was devoted to the officers charged with the duty of procuring the necessary supplies for the Order and its forces.

The following morning very favourable terms were offered to the Templars by the victorious sultan, and they agreed to evacuate the Temple on condition that a galley should be placed at their disposal, and that they should be allowed to retire in safety with the Christian fugitives under

---

* Ex ipsis fratrem monachum Gaudini elegerunt ministrum generalem. De excidio urbis Acconia apud *Martene*, tom. v. col 782.

their protection, and to carry away as much of their effects as each person could load himself with. The Mussulman conqueror pledged himself to the fulfilment of these conditions, and sent a standard to the Templars, which was mounted on one of the towers of the Temple. A guard of three hundred Moslem soldiers, charged to see the articles of capitulation properly carried into effect, was afterwards admitted within the walls of the convent. Some Christian women of Acre, who had refused to quit their fathers, brothers, and husbands, the brave defenders of the place, were amongst the fugitives, and the Moslem soldiers, attracted by their beauty, broke through all restraint, and violated the terms of the surrender. The enraged Templars closed and barricaded the gates of the Temple; they set upon the treacherous infidels, and put every one of them, "from the greatest to the smallest," to death.* Immediately after this massacre the Moslem trumpets sounded to the assault, but the Templars successfully defended themselves until the next day (the 20th). The Marshall of the Order and several of the brethren were then deputed by Gaudini with a flag of truce to the sultan, to explain the cause of the massacre of his guard. The enraged monarch, however, had no sooner got them into his power than he ordered every one of them to be decapitated, and pressed the siege with renewed vigour. In the night, Gaudini, with a chosen band of his companions, collected together the treasure of the Order and the ornaments of the church, and sallying out of a secret postern of the Temple which communicated with the harbour, they got on board a small vessel, and escaped in safety to the island of Cyprus.† The residue of the Templars retired into the large tower of the Temple, called "The Tower of the Master," which they defended with desperate energy. The bravest of the Mamlooks were driven back in repeated assaults, and the little fortress was everywhere surrounded with heaps of the slain. The sultan, at last, despairing of taking the place by assault, ordered it to be undermined. As the workmen advanced, they propped the foundations with beams of wood, and when the excavation was completed, these wooden supports were consumed by fire; the huge tower then fell with a tremendous crash, and buried the brave Templars in its ruins. The sultan set fire to the town in four places, and the last stronghold of the Christian power in Palestine

GAUDI
A.D. 12

GAUDI
A.D. 129

---

* Videntes pulchros Francorum filios acfilias, manus his injecerunt.— *Abulfarag*, Chron. Syr. p. 595. Maledicti Saraceni mulieres et pueros ad loca domus secretiora ex eisdem abusuri distrahere conabantur, turpibus ecclesiam obscœnitatibus cum nihil possent aliud maculantes. Quod videntes christiani, clauses portis, in perfidos viriliter irruerunt, et omnes a minimo usque ad maximum occiderunt, muros, turres, atque portas Templi munientes ad defensam.— De excid. Acconis ut sup. col. 782. *Martin Sanut* ut sup. cap. xxii. P. 231.

† Per totam noctem illam, dum fideles vigilarent contra perfidorum astutiam, domum contra eos defensuri, fratrum adjustorio de thesauris quod potuit cun sacrosanctis reliquiis ecclesiæ Templi, ad mare salubriter deportavit. Inde quidem cum fratribus paucis auspicato remigio, in Cyprum cum cautelâ transfretavit.— De excid. Acconis, col. 782.

was speedily reduced to a smoking solitude.* A few years back the ruins of the Christian city of Acre were well worthy of the attention of the curious. You might still trace the remains of several churches; and the quarter occupied by the Knights Templars continued to present many interesting memorials of that proud and powerful order.

* De excidio urbis Acconis apud *Martene*, tom. v. col. 757. *De Guignes*, Hist, ties Huna, tom. iv. p. 162. *Michaud*, Extraits Arabes, p. 762, 808. Abulfarag. Chron. Syr. p. 595. Wilkens, Comment. Abulfed. Hist. p. 231—234. *Marin. Sanut Torsell,* lib. iii. pars 12, cap. 21.

CHAPTER IX.

The downfall of the Templars—The cause thereof—The Grand Master comes to Europe at the request of the Pope—He is imprisoned, with all the Templars in France, by command of King Philip—They are put to the torture, and confessions of the guilt of heresy and idolatry are extracted from them—Edward II. king of England stands up in defence of the Templars, but afterwards persecutes them at the instance of the Pope—The imprisonment of the Master of the Temple and all his brethren in England—Their examination upon eighty-seven horrible and ridiculous articles of accusation before foreign inquisitors appointed by the Pope—A council of the church assembles at London to pass sentence upon them—The curious evidence adduced as to the mode of admission into the Order, and of the customs and observances of the fraternity.

En cel an qu'ai dist or endroit,
Et ne sait a tort ou a droit,
Furent li Templiers, sans doutance,
Tous pris par le royaume de France.
Au mois d'Octobre, au point du jor,
Et un vendredi fu le jor.

Chron. MS.

It now only remains for us to describe the miserable fate of the surviving brethren of the Order of the Temple, and to tell of the ingratitude they encountered from their fellow Christians in the West. Shortly after the fall of Acre, a general chapter of the fraternity was called together, and James de Molay, the Preceptor of England, was chosen Grand Master.* He attempted once more (A.D. 1302) to plant the banners of the Temple upon the sacred soil of Palestine, but was defeated by the sultan of Egypt with the loss of a hundred and twenty of his brethren.* This

JAMES DE MOLAY. A.D. 1297.

JAMES DE MOLAY. A.D. 1302.

* *Raynald*, tom. xiv. ad ann. 1298. Cotton MS. Nero E. vi. p. 60. fol. 466.

disastrous expedition was speedily followed by the downfall of the fraternity. Many circumstances contributed to this memorable event.

With the loss of all the Christian territory in Palestine had expired in Christendom every serious hope and expectation of recovering and retaining the Holy City. The services of the Templars were consequently no longer required, and men began to regard with an eye of envy and of covetousness their vast wealth and immense possessions. The privileges conceded to the fraternity by the popes made the church their enemy. The great body of the clergy regarded with jealousy and indignation their exemption from the ordinary ecclesiastical jurisdiction. The bull *omne datum optimum* was considered a great inroad upon the rights of the church, and broke the union which had originally subsisted between the Templars and the ecclesiastics. Their exemption from tithe was a source of considerable loss to the parsons, and the privilege they possessed of celebrating divine service during interdict brought abundance of offerings and alms to the priests and chaplains of the Order, which the clergy looked upon as so many robberies committed upon themselves. Disputes arose between the fraternity and the bishops and priests, and the hostility of the latter to the Order was manifested in repeated acts of injustice, which drew forth many severe bulls and indignant animadversions from the Roman pontiffs. Pope Alexander, in a bull fulminated against the clergy, tells them that if they would carefully reflect upon the contests which his beloved sons, the brethren of the chivalry of the Temple, continually maintained in Palestine for the defence of Christianity, and their kindness to the poor, they would not only cease from annoying and injuring them, but would strictly restrain others from so doing. He expresses himself to be grieved and astonished to hear that many ecclesiastics had vexed them with grievous injuries, had treated his apostolic letters with contempt, and had refused to read them in their churches; that they had subtracted the customary alms and oblations from the fraternity, and had admitted aggressors against the property of the brethren to their familiar friendship, insufferably endeavouring to press down and discourage those whom they ought assiduously to uphold. From other bulls it appears that the clergy interfered with the right enjoyed by the fraternity of collecting alms; that they refused to bury the brethren of the Order when deceased without being paid for it, and arrogantly claimed a right to be entertained with sumptuous hospitality in the houses of the Temple. For these delinquencies, the bishops, archdeacons, priests, and the whole body of the clergy, are threatened with severe measures by the

JAMES DE
MOLAY.
A.D. 1302.

---

* *Marin Sanut Torsell.* lib. iii. pars. 13, cap. x. p. 242. *De Guignes*, Hist des Huns, tom. iv. p. 184.

† Acta *Rymeri* tom. i. p. 575, 576—579, 582, tom. ii. p. 250. *Martene*, vet. script, tom. vii. col. 156.

Roman pontiff.†

The Templars, moreover, towards the close of their career, became unpopular with the European sovereigns and their nobles. The revenues of the former were somewhat diminished through the immunities conceded to the Templars by their predecessors, and the paternal estates of the latter had been diminished by the grant of many thousand manors, lordships, and fair estates to the Order by their pious and enthusiastic ancestors. Considerable dislike also began to be manifested to the annual transmission of large sums of money, the revenues of the Order, from the European states to be expended in a distant warfare in which Christendom now took comparatively no interest. Shortly after the fall of Acre, and the total loss of Palestine, Edward the First, king of England, seized and sequestered to his own use the monies which had been accumulated by the Templars, to forward to their brethren in Cyprus, alleging that the property of the Order of the Temple had been granted to it by the kings of England, his predecessors, and their subjects, for the defence of the Holy Land, and that since the loss thereof, no better use could be made of the money than by appropriating it to the maintenance of the poor. At the earnest request of the pope however, the king afterwards permitted their revenues to be transmitted to them in the island of Cyprus in the usual manner.* King Edward had previously manifested a strong desire to lay hands on the property of the Templars. On his return from his victorious campaign in Wales, finding himself unable to disburse the arrears of pay due to his soldiers, he went with Sir Robert Waleran and some armed followers to the Temple, and calling for the treasurer, he pretended that he wanted to see his mother's jewels, which were there kept. Having been admitted into the house, he deliberately broke open the coffers of the Templars, and carried away ten thousand pounds with him to Windsor Castle.† His son, Edward the Second, on his accession to the throne, committed a similar act of injustice. He went with his favourite, Piers Gavaston, to the Temple, and took away with him fifty thousand pounds of silver, with a quantity of gold, jewels, and precious stones, belonging to the bishop of Chester.‡ The impunity with which these acts of violence were committed, manifests that the Templars then no longer enjoyed the power and respect which they possessed in ancient times.

As the enthusiasm, too, in favour of the holy war diminished, large numbers of the Templars remained at home in their western preceptories,

---

* Acta *Rymeri*, tom. ii. p. 683. ad ann. 1295.

† Chron. *Dunmow*. Annals of St. *Augutin. Rapin.*

‡ Ipse yero Rex et Petras thesaurum ipsius episcopi, apud Novum Templum Londoniis reconditum, ceperunt, ad sum mam quinquaginta millia librarum argenti, præter aurum multum, jocalia et lapides preciosos. … Erant enim ambo præsentes, cum cistæ frangerentur, et adhuc non erat sepultum corpus patris sui.—*Hemingford*, p. 244.

and took an active part in the politics of Europe. They interfered in the quarrels of Christian princes, and even drew their swords against their fellow-Christians. Thus we find the members of the Order taking part in the war between the houses of Anjou and Aragon, and aiding the king of England in his warfare against the king of Scotland. In the battle of Falkirk, fought on the 22nd of July, A.D. 1298, seven years after the fall of Acre, perished both the Master of the Temple at London, and his vice-gerent the Preceptor of Scotland.* All these circumstances, together with the loss of the Holy Land, and the extinction of the enthusiasm of the crusades, diminished the popularity of the Templars in Europe.

At the period of the fall of Acre, Philip the Fair, son of St. Louis, occupied the throne of France. He was a needy and avaricious monarch,† and had at different periods resorted to the most violent expedients to replenish his exhausted exchequer. On the death of Pope Benedict XI., (A.D. 1304), he succeeded, through the intrigues of the French Cardinal Dupre, in raising the archbishop of Bourdeaux, a creature of his own, to the pontifical chair. The new pope removed the Holy See from Rome to France; he summoned all the cardinals to Lyons, and was there conse-crated, (A.D. 1305), by the name of Clement V., in the presence of King Philip and his nobles. Of the ten new cardinals then created nine were Frenchmen, and in all his acts the new pope manifested himself the obe-JAMES DE dient slave of the French monarch. The character of this pontiff has been MOLAY. painted by the a woe ecclesiastical historians in the darkest colours: they A.D. 1306. represent him as wedded to pleasure, eaten up with ambition, and greedy for money; they accuse him of indulging in a criminal intrigue with the beautiful countess of Perigord, and of trafficking in holy things.‡

On the 6th of June, A.D. 1306, a few months after his coronation, this new French pontiff addressed letters from Bourdeaux to the Grand Mas-ters of the Temple and Hospital, expressing his earnest desire to consult them with regard to the measures necessary to be taken for the recovery of the Holy Land. He tells them that they are the persons best qualified to give advice upon the subject, and to conduct and manage the enterprize, both from their great military experience and the interest they had in the success of the expedition. "We order you," says he, "to come hither with-out delay, with as much secrecy as possible, and with a *very little retinue*, since you will find on this side the sea a sufficient number of your knights

---

* Chron. *Triveti*, ad ann. 1298. *Hemingford*, vol. i. p. 159.

† *Dante* styles him *il mal di Francia,* Del. Purgat. cant. 20, 91.

‡ Questo Papa fue huomo molto cupido di moneta, e fue lusurioso, si dice ache tenea per amica la contessa di Paragordo, bellissima donna ! ! *Villani*, lib. ix. Cap. 58. Fuit nimis cupiditatibus deditus. . . Sanct. Ant. Flor. De Concil. Vien. Tit. 21. sec. 3. Circa thesaurus colligendos insudavit, says *Knighton* apud X script. col. 2494. *Fleuri,* 1. 92. p. 239. *Chron. de Namgis,* ad ann. 1305.

§ *Rainald.* Tom. xv. ad ann. 1306, n. 12. *Fleuri*, Hist. Eccles. Tom. xix. p. 111.

to attend upon you."§ The Grand Master of the Hospital declined obeying this summons; but the Grand Master of the Temple forthwith accepted it, and unhesitatingly placed himself in the power of the pope and the king of France. He landed in France, attended by sixty of his knights, at the commencement of the year 1307, and deposited the treasure of the Order which he had brought with him from Cyprus, in the Temple at Paris. He was received with distinction by the king, and then took his departure for Poictiers to have an interview with the pope. He was there detained with various conferences and negotiations relative to a pretended expedition for the recovery of the Holy Land. JAMES DE MOLAY. A.D. 1307.

Among other things, the pope proposed an union between the Templars and Hospitallers, and the Grand Master handed in his objections to the proposition. He says, that after the fall of Acre, the people of Italy and of other Christian nations clamoured loudly against Pope Nicholas, for having afforded no succour to the besieged, and that he, by way of screening himself, had laid all the blame of the loss of the place on pretended dissensions between the Templars and Hospitallers, and projected an union between them. The Grand Master declares that there had been no dissensions between the Orders prejudicial to the Christian cause; that there was nothing more than a spirit of rivalry and emulation, the destruction of which would be highly injurious to the Christians, and advantageous to the Saracens; for if the Hospitallers at any time performed a brilliant feat of arms against the infidels, the Templars would never rest quiet until they had done the same or better, and *e converso*. So also if the Templars made a great shipment of brethren, horses, and other beasts across sea to Palestine, the Hospitallers would always do the like or more. He at the same time positively declares, that a member of one order had never been known to raise his hand against a member of the other.* The Grand Master complains that the reverence and respect of the Christian nations for both orders had undeservedly diminished, that everything was changed, and that most persons were then more ready to take from them than to give to them, and that many powerful men, both clergy and laity, brought continual mischiefs upon the fraternities.

In the mean time, the secret agents of the French king industriously circulated various dark rumours and odious reports concerning the Templars, and it was said that they would never have lost the Holy Land if they had been good Christians. These rumours and accusations were soon put into a tangible shape. JAMES DE MOLAY. A.D. 1307.

According to some writers, Squin de Florian, a citizen of Bezieres, who had been condemned to death or perpetual imprisonment in one of the royal castles for his iniquities, was brought before Philip, and received a free pardon, and was well rewarded in return, for an accusation on

* *Bal. Pap. Aven*, tom. ii. p. 176.

oath, charging the Templars with heresy, and with the commission of the most horrible crimes. According to others, Nosso de Florentin, an apostate Templar, who had been condemned by the Grand Preceptor and chapter of France to perpetual imprisonment for impiety and crime, made in his dungeon a voluntary confession of the sins and abominations charged against the Order.* Be this as it may, upon the strength of an information sworn to by a condemned criminal, King Philip, on the 14th of September, despatched secret orders to all the baillis of the different provinces in France, couched in the following extravagant and absurd terms:

"Philip, by the grace of God king of the French, to his beloved and faithful knights. ... &c. &c.

"A deplorable and most lamentable, matter, full of bitterness and grief, a monstrous business, a thing that one cannot think on without affright, cannot hear without horror, transgressions unheard of, enormities and atrocities contrary to every sentiment of humanity, &c. &c., have reached our ears." After a long and most extraordinary tirade of this kind, Philip accuses the Templars of insulting Jesus Christ, and making him suffer more in those days than he had suffered formerly upon the cross; of renouncing the Christian religion; of mocking the sacred image of the Saviour; of sacrificing to idols; and of abandoning themselves to impure practices and unnatural crimes. He characterises them as ravishing wolves in sheep's clothing; a perfidious, ungrateful, idolatrous society, whose words and deeds were enough to pollute the earth and infect the air; to dry up the sources of the celestial dews, and to put the whole church of Christ into confusion.

JAMES DE
MOLAY.
A.D. 1307.

"We being charged," says he, "with the maintenance of the faith; after having conferred with the pope, the prelates, and the barons of the kingdom, at the instance of the inquisitor, from the informations already laid, from violent suspicions, from probable conjectures, from legitimate presumptions, conceived against the enemies of heaven and earth; and because the matter is important, and it is expedient to prove the just like gold in the furnace by a rigorous examination, have decreed that the members of the Order who are our subjects shall be arrested and detained to be judged by the church, and that all their real and personal property shall be seized into our hands, and be faithfully preserved," &c. To these orders are attached instructions requiring the baillis and seneschals accurately to inform themselves, with great secrecy, and without exciting suspicion, of the number of the houses of the Temple within their respective jurisdictions; they are then to provide an armed force sufficient to overcome all resistance, and on the 13th of October are to surprise the Templars in their preceptories, and make them prisoners. The inquisition

---

* *Bal. Pap. Aven.* tom. i. p. 99. Sexta Vita, Clem. V. apud *Balux*, tom. i. col. 100.

is then directed to assemble to examine the guilty, and to employ *torture* if it be necessary. "Before proceeding with the inquiry," says Philip, "you are to inform them (the Templars) that the pope and ourselves have been convinced, by irreproachable testimony, of the errors and abominations which accompany their vows and profession; you are to promise them pardon and favour if they *confess* the truth, but if not, you are to acquaint them that they will be condemned to death."*

JAMES DE MOLAY.
A.D. 1307.

As soon as Philip had issued these orders, he wrote to the principal sovereigns of Europe, urging them to follow his example,† and sent a confidential agent, named Bernard Peletin, with a letter to the young king, Edward the Second, who had just then ascended the throne of England, representing in frightful colours the pretended sins of the Templars. On the 22nd of September, King Edward replied to this letter, observing that he had considered of the matters mentioned therein, and had listened to the statements of that discreet man, Master Bernard Peletin; that he had caused the latter to unfold the charges before himself, and many prelates, earls, and barons of his kingdom, and others of his council; but that they appeared so astonishing as to be beyond belief; that such abominable and execrable deeds had never before been heard of by the king and the aforesaid prelates, earls, and barons, and it was therefore hardly to be expected that an easy credence could be given to them. The English monarch, however, informs King Philip that by the advice of his council he had ordered the seneschal of Agen, from whose lips the rumours were said to have proceeded, to be summoned to his presence, that through him he might be further informed concerning the premises; and he states that at the fitting time, after due inquiry, he will take such steps as will redound to the praise of God, and the honour and preservation of the catholic faith.‡

On the night of the 13th of October, all the Templars in the French dominions were simultaneously arrested. Monks were appointed to preach against them in the public places of Paris, and in the gardens of the Palais Royale; and advantage was taken of the folly, the superstition, and the credulity of the age, to propagate the most horrible and extravagant charges against the Order. They were accused of worshipping an idol covered with an old skin, embalmed, having the appearance of a piece of polished oil-cloth. "In this idol," we are assured, "there were two carbuncles for eyes, bright as the brightness of heaven, and it is certain that all the hope of the Templars was placed in it; it was their sovereign god, and they trusted in it with all their heart." They are accused of burning the bodies of the deceased brethren, and making the ashes into a powder,

JAMES DE MOLAY.
A.D. 1307.

* Hist. de la Condemnation des Templiers.—*Dupuy*, tom. ii. p. 309.

† Mariana Hispan. Illustr. Tom. iii. p. 152. *Le Gendre* Hist. de France, tom. ii. p. 499.

‡ Acta *Rymerti*, tom. iii. p. 18. ad ann. 1307.

which they administered to the younger brethren in their food and drink, to make them hold fast their faith and idolatry; of cooking and roasting infants, and anointing their idols with the fat; of celebrating hidden rites and mysteries, to which young and tender virgins were introduced, and of a variety of abominations too absurd and horrible to be named.* Guillaume Paradin, in his history of Savoy, seriously repeats these monstrous accusations, and declares that the Templars had "un lieu creux ou cave en terre, fort obscur, en laquelle ils avoient un image en forme d'un homme, sur lequel ils avoient appliqué la peau d'un corps humain, et mis deux clairs et lui sans escarboucles au lieu des deux yeux. A cette horrible statue etoient contraints de sacrifier ceux qui vouloient etre de leur damnable religion, lesquels avant toutes ceremonies ils contragnoient de renier Jesus Christ, et fouler la croix avec les pieds, et apres ce maudit sacre auquel assistoient femmes et filles (seduites pour etre de ce secte) ils estegnoient les lampes et lumieres qu'ils avoient en cett cave. ... Et s'il advenoit que d'un Templier et d'un pucelle nasquit, un fils, ils se rangoit tous en un rond, et se jettoient cet enfant de main en main, et ne cessoient de le letter lusquacequil fu mort entre leurs mains: etant mort ils se rotissoient (chose execrable) etde la graisse ils en ognoient leur grand statue!"† The character of the charges preferred against the Templars proves that their enemies had no serious crimes to allege against the Order. Their very virtues indeed were turned against them, for we are told that "*to conceal the iniquity of their lives* they made much almsgiving, constantly frequented church, comported themselves with edification, frequently partook of the holy sacrament, and manifested always much modesty and gentleness of deportment in the house, as well as in public."‡

During twelve days of severe imprisonment, the Templars remained constant in the denial of the horrible crimes imputed to the fraternity. The king's promises of pardon extracted from them no confession of guilt, and they were therefore handed over to the tender mercies of the brethren of St. Dominic, who were the most refined and expert torturers of the day.

On the 19th of October, the grand inquisitor proceeded with his myrmidons to the Temple at Paris, and a hundred and forty Templars were one after another put to the torture. Days and weeks were consumed in the examination, and thirty-six Templars perished in the hands of their tormentors, maintaining with unshaken constancy to the very last the entire innocence of their order. Many of them lost the use of their feet from the application of the torture of fire, which was inflicted in the following manner: their legs were fastened in an iron frame, and the soles of their

JAMES DE MOLAY. A.D. 1307.

* Les forfaits pourquoi les Templiers furent ars et condamnez, pris et contre eux approuvez *Chron. S. Denis.* Sexta vita, Clem. V. *Dupuy,* p. 24. edition de 1713.

† Liv. ii. chap. 106, chez *Dupuy.*

‡ Sexta vita, Clem. V. col. 102.

feet were greased over with fat or butter; they were then placed before the fire, and a screen was drawn backwards and forwards, so as to moderate and regulate the heat. Such was the agony produced by this roasting operation, that the victims often went raving mad. Brother Bernarde de Vado, on subsequently revoking a confession of guilt, wrung from him by this description of torment, says to the commissary of police, before whom he was brought to be examined, "They held me so long before a fierce fire that the flesh was burnt off my heels, two pieces of bone came away, which I present to you."* Another Templar, on publicly revoking his confession, declared that four of his teeth were drawn out, and that he confessed himself guilty to save the remainder.† Others of the fraternity deposed to the infliction on them of the most revolting and indecent torments‡ and, in addition to all this, it appears that forged letters from the Grand Master were shown to the prisoners, exhorting them to confess themselves guilty. Many of the Templars were accordingly compelled to acknowledge whatever was required of them, and to plead guilty to the commission of crimes which in the previous interrogatories they had positively denied. §

These violent proceedings excited the astonishment and amazement of Europe.

On the 20th of November, the king of England summoned the seneschal of Agen to his presence, and examined him concerning the truth of the horrible charges preferred against the Templars; and on the 4th of December the English monarch wrote letters to the kings of Portugal, Castile, Aragon, and Sicily, to the following effect:

"To the magnificent prince the Lord Dionysius, by the grace of God the illustrious king of Portugal, his very dear friend Edward, by the same grace king of England, &c. Health and prosperity.

"It is fit and proper, inasmuch as it conduceth to the honour of God and the exaltation of the faith, that we should prosecute with benevolence those who come recommended to us by strenuous labours and incessant exertions in defence of the Catholic faith, and for the destruction of the enemies of the cross of Christ. Verily, a certain clerk, (Bernard Peletin), drawing nigh unto our presence, applied himself, with all his might, to the destruction of the Order of the brethren of the Temple of Jerusalem. He dared to publish before us and our council certain horrible and detestable enormities repugnant to the Catholic faith, to the prejudice of the aforesaid brothers, endeavouring to persuade us, through his own all-

JAMES DE MOLAY. A.D. 1307.

JAMES DE MOLAY. A.D. 1307.

---

* Ostendei duo ossa quod dicebat ilia esse qua ceciderunt de talis suis. *Processus contra Templarios. Raynouard* Monumens Historiques, p. 73, ed. 1813.

† In quibus tormentis dicebat se quatuor dentes perdidisse. Ib p. 35.

‡ Fuit quaestionibus ponderibus appensis in genitalibus, et in aliis membris usque ad exanimationem. Ib.

§ Tres des Chart. TEMPLIERS, cart 3, n. 20.

egations, as well as through certain leters which he had caused to be addressed to us for that purpose, that by reason of the premises, and without a due examination of the matter, we ought to imprison all the brethren of the aforesaid order abiding in our dominions. But, considering that the Order, which hath been renowned for its religion and its honour, and in times long since passed away was instituted, as we have learned, by the Catholic Fathers, exhibits, and hath from the period of its first foundation exhibited, a becoming devotion to God and his holy church, and also, up to this time, hath afforded succour and protection to the Catholic faith in parts beyond sea, it appeared to us that a ready belief in an accusation of this kind, hitherto altogether unheard of against the fraternity, was scarcely to be expected. We affectionately ask, and require of your royal majesty, that ye, with due diligence, consider of the premises, and turn a deaf ear to the slanders of ill-natured men, who are animated, as we believe, not with the zeal of rectitude, but with a spirit of *cupidity* and envy, permitting no injury unadvisedly to be done to the persons or property of the brethren of the aforesaid order, dwelling within your kingdom, until JAMES DE they have been legally convicted of the crimes laid to their charge, or it MOLAY. shall happen to be otherwise ordered concerning them in these parts."*
A.D. 1307.

A few days after the transmission of this letter, King Edward wrote to the pope, expressing his disbelief of the horrible and detestable rumours spread abroad concerning the Templars. He represents them to his holiness as universally respected by all men in his dominions for the purity of their faith and morals. He expresses great sympathy for the affliction and distress suffered by the master and brethren, by reason of the scandal circulated concerning them; and he strongly urges the holy pontiff to clear, by some fair course of inquiry, the character of the Order from the unjust and infamous aspersions cast against it† On the 22nd of November, however, a fortnight previously, the Pope had issued the following bull to King Edward.

"Clement, bishop, servant of the servants of God, to his very dear son in Christ, Edward, the illustrious king of England, health and apostolical blessing.

"Presiding, though unworthy, on the throne of pastoral pre-eminence, by the disposition of him who disposeth all things, we fervently seek after this one thing above all others; we with ardent wishes aspire to this, that shaking off the sleep of negligence, whilst watching over the Lord's flock, by removing that which is hurtful, and taking care of such things as are profitable, we may be able, by the divine assistance, to bring souls

---

* Dat. Apud Redyng, 4 die Decembris. Consimiles litteræ diriguntur Ferando regi Castillæ et Ligionis, consanguineo Regis, domino Karolo, regi Siciliæ, et Jacobo regi Aragoniæ, amico Regis. Acta *Rymeri*, tom. iii. ad ann. 1307, p. 35, 36.

† Acta *Rymeri*, tom. iii. p. 37, ad ann. 1307.

to God."

"In truth, a long time ago, about the period of our first promotion to the summit of the apostolical dignity, there came to our ears a light rumour, to the effect that the Templars, though fighting ostensibly under the guise of religion, have hitherto been secretly living in perfidious apostasy, and in detestable heretical depravity. But, considering that their order, in times long since passed away, shone forth with the grace of much nobility and honour, and that they were for a length of time held in vast reverence by the faithful, and that we had then heard of no suspicion concerning the premises, or of evil report against them; and also, that from the beginning of their religion, they have publicly borne the cross of Christ, exposing their bodies and goods against the enemies of the faith, for the acquisition, retention, and defence of the Holy Land, consecrated by the precious blood of our Lord and Saviour Jesus Christ, we were unwilling to yield a ready belief to the accusation. . . ."

JAMES DE MOLAY. A.D. 1307.

The holy pontiff then states, that afterwards, however, the same dreadful intelligence was conveyed to the king of France, who, animated by a lively zeal in the cause of religion, took immediate steps to ascertain its truth. He describes the various confessions of the guilt of idolatry and heresy made by the Templars in France, and requires the king forthwith to cause all the Templars in his dominions to be taken into custody on the same day. He directs him to hold them, in the name of the pope, at the disposition of the Holy See, and to commit all their real and personal property to the hands of certain trustworthy persons, to be faithfully preserved until the holy pontiff shall give further directions concerning it.* King Edward received this bull immediately after he had despatched his letter to the pope, exhorting his holiness not to give ear to the accusation against the Order. The young king was now either convinced of the guilt of the Templars, on the high authority of the sovereign pontiff, or hoped to turn the proceedings against them to a profitable account, as he yielded a ready and prompt compliance with the pontifical commands. An order in council was made for the arrest of the Templars, and the seizure of their property. Inventories were directed to be taken of their goods and chattels, and provision was made for the sowing and tilling of their lands during the period of their imprisonment.† This order in council was carried into effect in the following manner:

JAMES DE MOLAY. A.D. 1307.

On the 20th of December, the king's writs were directed to each of the sheriffs throughout England, commanding them to make sure of certain trustworthy men of their bailiwicks, to the number of ten or twelve in each county, such as the king could best confide in, and have them at a certain place in the county, on pain of forfeiture of everything that could

---

* Dat. Pictavis 10, kal. Dec. Acta *Rymeri*, tom. iii. ad ann. 1307, p. 30—32.

† Acta *Rymeri*, tom. iii. p. 34, 35, ad ann. 1307.

be forfeited to the king; and commanding the sheriffs, on pain of the like forfeiture, to be in person at the same place, on the Sunday before the feast of Epiphany, to do certain things touching the king's peace, which the sheriff would find contained in the king's writ about to be directed to him. And afterwards the king sent sworn clergymen with his writs, containing the said order in council to the sheriffs, who, before they opened them, were to take an oath that they would not disclose the contents of such writs until they proceeded to execute them.* The same orders, to be acted upon in a similar manner in Ireland, were sent to the justiciary of that country, and to the treasurer of the Exchequer at Dublin; also, to John de Richemund, guardian of Scotland; and to Walter de Pederton, justiciary of West Wales; Hugh de Aldithelegh, justiciary of North Wales; and to Robert de Holland, justiciary of Chester, who were strictly commanded to carry the Orders into execution before the king's proceedings against the Templars in England were noised abroad. All the king's faithful subjects were commanded to aid and assist the officers in the fulfilment of their duty.†

JAMES DE
MOLAY.
A.D. 1308.

On the 26th of December the king wrote to the Pope, informing his holiness that he would carry his commands into execution in the best and speediest way that he could; and on the 8th of January, A.D. 1308, the Templars were suddenly arrested in all parts of England, and their property was seized into the king's hands.‡ Brother William de la More was at this period Master of the Temple, or Preceptor of England. He succeeded the Master Brian le Jay, who was slain, as before mentioned, in the battle of Falkirk, and was taken prisoner, together with all his brethren of the Temple at London, and committed to close custody in Canterbury Castle. He was afterwards liberated on bail at the instance of the bishop of Durham.§

On the 12th of August, the Pope addressed the bull *faciens misericordiam* to the English bishops as follows: "Clement, bishop, servant of the servants of God, to the venerable brethren the archbishop of Canterbury and his suffragans, health and apostolical benediction. The Son of God, the Lord Jesus Christ, *using mercy* with his servant, would have us taken up into the eminent mirror of the apostleship, to this end, that being, though unworthy, his vicar upon Earth, we may, as far as human frailty will permit in all our actions and proceedings, follow his footsteps." He describes the rumours which had been spread abroad in France against the Templars, and his unwillingness to believe them, "because it was not likely, nor did seem credible, that such religious men, who particularly

* Ibid. p. 34, 35.
† Ibid. p. 45.
‡ *Knyghton*, apud X. script, col. 2494, 2531.
§ Acta *Rymeri* tom. iii. p. 83.

often shed their blood for the name of Christ, and were thought very frequently to expose their persons to danger of death for his sake; and who
often showed many and great signs of devotion, as well in the divine offices as in fasting and other observances, should be so unmindful of their
salvation as to perpetrate such things; we were un- willing to give ear to   JAMES DE
the insinuations and impeachments against them, being taught so to do   MOLAY.
by the example of the same Lord of ours, and the writings of canonical   A.D. 1308.
doctrine. But afterwards, our most dear son in Christ, Philip, the illustrious king of the French, to whom the same crimes had been made known,
not from motives of avarice, (since he does not design to apply or to
appropriate to himself any portion of the estates of the Templars, nay, has
washed his hands of them!) but inflamed with zeal for the orthodox faith,
following the renowned footsteps of his ancestors, getting what information he properly could upon the premises, gave us much instruction in the
matter by his messengers and letters." The holy pontiff then gives a long
account of the various confessions made in France, and of the absolution
granted to such of the Templars as were truly contrite and penitent; he
expresses his conviction of the guilt of the Order, and makes provision
for the trial of the fraternity in England.* King Edward, in the mean time,
had begun to make free with their property, and the Pope, on the 4th of
October, wrote to him to the following effect:

"Your conduct begins again to afford us no slight cause of affliction,
inasmuch as it hath been brought to our knowledge from the report of
several barons, that in contempt of the Holy See, and without fear of
offending the divine Majesty, you have, of your own sole authority, distributed to different persons the property which belonged formerly to
the Order of the Temple in your dominions, which you had got into your
hands at our command, and which ought to have remained at our disposition. ... We have therefore ordained that certain fit and proper persons
shall be sent into your kingdom, and to all parts of the world where the
Templars are known to have had property, to take possession of the same
conjointly with certain prelates specially deputed to that end, and to make   JAMES DE
an inquisition concerning the execrable excesses which the members of   MOLAY.
the Order are said to have committed."†   A.D. 1308.

To this letter of the supreme pontiff, King Edward sent the following
short and pithy reply:

"As to the goods of the Templars, we have done nothing with them
up to the present time, nor do we intend to do with them aught but
what we have a right to do, and what we know will be acceptable to the
Most High."‡

---

* Acta *Rymeri*, tom. iii. p. 101, 2, 3.
† Acta Rymeri, tom. iii. p. 110, 111. Vitœ paparum Avenion, tom. ii. p. 107
‡ Ibid., tom. iii. p. 121, 122.

On the 13th of September, A.D. 1309, the king granted letters of safe conduct "to those discreet men, the abbot of Lagny, in the diocese of Paris, and Master Sicard de Vaur, canon of Narbonne," the inquisitors appointed by the Pope to examine the Grand Preceptor and brethren of the Temple in England;* and the same day he wrote to the archbishop of Canterbury, and the bishops of London and Lincoln, enjoining them to be personally present with the papal inquisitors, at their respective sees, as often as such inquisitors, or any one of them, should proceed with their inquiries against the Templars.†

On the 14th of September writs were sent, in pursuance of an order in council, to the sheriffs of Kent and seventeen other counties, commanding them to bring all their prisoners of the Order of the Temple to London, and deliver them to the constable of the Tower; also to the sheriffs of Northumberland and eight other counties, enjoining them to convey their prisoners to York Castle; and to the sheriffs of Warwick and seven other counties, requiring them, in like manner, to conduct their prisoners to the Castle of Lincoln. ‡ Writs were also sent to John de Cumberland, constable of the Tower, and to the constables of the castles of York and Lincoln, commanding them to receive the Templars, to keep them in safe custody, and hold them at the disposition of the inquisitors.§ The total number of Templars in custody was two hundred and twenty-nine. Many, however, were still at large, having successfully evaded capture by obliterating all marks of their previous profession, and some had escaped in disguise to the wild and mountainous parts of Wales, Scotland, and Ireland. Among the prisoners confined in the Tower were brother William de la More, Knight, Grand Preceptor of England, otherwise Master of the Temple; Brother Himbert Blanke, Knight, Grand Preceptor of Auvergne, one of the veteran warriors who had fought to the last in defence of Palestine, had escaped the slaughter at Acre, and had accompanied the Grand Master from Cyprus to France, from whence he crossed over to England, and was rewarded for his meritorious and memorable services, in defence of the Christian faith, with a dungeon in the Tower.** Brother *Radulph de Barton*, priest of the Order of the Temple, custos or guardian of the Temple church, and prior of London; Brother *Michael de Baskeville*, Knight, Preceptor of London; Brother *John de Stoke*, Knight, Treasurer of the Temple at London; together with many other knights and serving brethren of the same house. There were also in custody in the Tower the knights preceptors of the preceptories of Ewell in Kent, of Daney

JAMES DE MOLAY.
A.D. 1309.

---

* Ibid. p. 168.
† Ibid. p. 168, 169.
‡ Ibid. p. 174.
§ Acta *Rymeri*, tom. iii. p. 173, 175.
** *Rainald*, tom. xv. ad ann. 1306.

and Dokesworth in Cambridgeshire, of Getinges in Gloucestershire, of Cumbe in Somersetshire, of Schepeley in Surrey, of Samford and Bistelesham in Oxfordshire, of Garwy in Herefordshire, of Cressing in Essex, of Pafflet, Hippleden, and other preceptories, together with several priests and chaplains of the Order.* A general scramble appears to have taken place for possession of the goods and chattels of the imprisoned Templars; and the king, to check the robberies that were committed, appointed Alan de Goldyngham and John de Medefeld to inquire into the value of the property that had been carried off, and to inform him of the names of the parties who had obtained possession of it. The sheriffs of the different counties were also directed to summon juries, through whom the truth might be better obtained.†

On the 22nd of September, the archbishop of Canterbury transmitted letters apostolic to all his suffragans, enclosing copies of the bull *faciens misericordiam*, and also the articles of accusation to be exhibited against the Templars, which they are directed to copy and deliver again, under their seals, to the bearer, taking especial care not to reveal the contents thereof.‡ At the same time the archbishop, acting in obedience to the papal commands, before a single witness had been examined in England, caused to be published in all churches and chapels a papal bull, wherein the Pope declares himself perfectly convinced of the guilt of the Order, and solemnly denounces the penalty of excommunication against all persons, of whatever rank, station, or condition in life, whether clergy or laity, who should knowingly afford, either publicly or privately, assistance, counsel, or kindness to the Templars, or should dare to shelter them, or give them countenance or protection, and also laying under interdict all cities, castles, lands, and places, which should harbour any of the members of the proscribed order.§ At the commencement of the month of October, the inquisitors arrived in England, and immediately published the bull appointing the commission, enjoining the citation of the criminals, and of witnesses, and denouncing the heaviest ecclesiastical censures against the disobedient, and against every person who should dare to impede the inquisitors in the exercise of their functions. Citations were made in St. Paul's Cathedral, and in all the churches of the ecclesiastical province of Canterbury, at the end of high mass, requiring the Templars to appear before the inquisitors at a certain time and place, and the articles of accusation were transmitted to the constable of the Tower, in Latin, French, and English, to be read to all the Templars imprisoned in that fortress. On Monday, the 20th of October, after the Templars had

---

* Concil. Mag. Brit. tom. ii. p. 346, 347.

† Acta *Rymeri*, tom. iii. p. 178, 179.

‡ Concil. Mag. Brit. tom. ii. p. 304—311.

§ *Processus contra Templarios, Dugd.* Monast. Angl. vol. vi. part 2, p. 844—846 ed. 1830.

been languishing in the English prisons for more than a year and eight months, the tribunal constituted by the Pope to take the inquisition in the province of Canterbury assembled in the episcopal hall of London. It was composed of the bishop of London, Dieudonné, abbot of the monastery of Lagny, in the diocese of Paris, and Sicard de Vaur, canon of Narbonne, the Pope's chaplain, and hearer of causes in the pontifical palace. They were assisted by several foreign notaries. After the reading of the papal bulls, and some preliminary proceedings, the monstrous and ridiculous articles of accusation, a monument of human folly, superstition, and credulity, were solemnly exhibited as follows:

"*Item.* At the place, day, and hour aforesaid, in the presence of the aforesaid lords, and before us the above-mentioned notaries, the articles inclosed in the apostolic bull were exhibited and opened before us, the contents whereof are as underwritten.

"These are the articles upon which inquisition shall be made against the brethren of the military order of the Temple, &c.

"1. That at their first reception into the Order, or at some time afterwards, or as soon as an opportunity occurred, they were induced or admonished by those who had received them within the bosom of the fraternity, to deny Christ or Jesus, or the crucifixion, or at one time God, and at another time the blessed virgin, and sometimes all the saints.

"2. That the brothers jointly did this.

"3. That the greater part of them did it.

"4. That they did it sometimes after their reception.

"5. That the receivers told and instructed those that were received, that Christ was not the true God, or sometimes Jesus, or sometimes the person crucified.

"6. That they told those they received that he was a false prophet.

"7. That they said he had not suffered for the redemption of mankind, nor been crucified but for his own sins.

"8. That neither the receiver nor the person received had any hope of obtaining salvation through him, and this they said to those they received, or something equivalent, or like it.

"9. That they made those they received into the Order spit upon the cross, or upon the sign or figure of the cross, or the image of Christ, though they that were received did sometimes spit aside.

"10. That they caused the cross itself to be trampled under foot.

"11. That the brethren themselves did sometimes trample on the same cross.

"12. Item quod mingebant interdum, et alios mingere faciebant, super ipsam crucem, et hoc fecerunt aliquotiens in die veneris sanctâ!!

"13. Item quod nonnulli eorum ipsâ die, vel alia septimanæ sanctæ pro conculcatione et minctione prædictis consueverunt convenire!

"14. That they worshipped a cat which was placed in the midst

JAMES DE
MOLAY.
A.D. 1309.

of the congregation.

"15. That they did these things in contempt of Christ and the orthodox faith. JAMES DE MOLAY. A.D. 1309.

"16. That they did not believe the sacrament of the altar.

"17. That some of them did not.

"18. That the greater part did not.

"19. That they believed not the other sacraments of the church.

"20. That the priests of the Order did not utter the words by which the body of Christ is consecrated in the canon of the mass.

"21. That some of them did not.

"22. That the greater part did not.

"23. That those who received them enjoined the same.

"24. That they believed, and so it was told them, that the Grand Master of the Order could absolve them from their sins.

"25. That the visitor could do so.

"26. That the preceptors, of whom many were laymen, could do it.

"27. That they in fact did do so.

"28. That some of them did.

"29. That the Grand Master confessed these things of himself, even before he was taken, in the presence of great persons.

"30. That in receiving brothers into the Order, or when about to receive them, or some time after having received them, the receivers and the persons received kissed one another on the mouth, the navel. ... !!

"36. That the receptions of the brethren were made clandestinely.

"37. That none were present but the brothers of the said order.

"38. That for this reason there has for a long time been a vehement suspicion against them. JAMES DE MOLAY. A.D. 1309.

The succeeding articles proceed to charge the Templars with crimes and abominations too horrible and disgusting to be named.

"46. That the brothers themselves had idols in every province, viz. heads; some of which had three faces, and some one, and some a man's skull.

"47. That they adored that idol, or those idols, especially in their great chapters and assemblies.

"48. That they worshipped it.

"49. As their God.

"50. As their Saviour.

"51. That some of them did so.

"52. That the greater part did.

"53. That they said that that head could save them.

"54. That it could produce riches.

"55. That it had given to the Order all its wealth.

"56. That it caused the earth to bring forth seed.

"57. That it made the trees to flourish.

"58. That they bound or touched the head of the said idols with cords, wherewith they bound themselves about their shirts, or next their skins.

"59. That at their reception the aforesaid little cords, or others of the same length, were delivered to each of the brothers.

"60. That they did this in worship of their idol.

"61. That it was enjoined them to gird themselves with the said little cords, as before mentioned, and continually to wear them.

"62. That the brethren of the Order were generally received in that manner.

JAMES DE
MOLAY.
A.D. 1309.

"63. That they did these things out of devotion.

"64. That they did them everywhere.

"65. That the greater part did.

"66. That those who refused the things above mentioned at their reception, or to observe them afterwards, were killed or cast into prison."*

The remaining articles, twenty-one in number, are directed principally to the mode of confession practised amongst the fraternity, and to matters of heretical depravity. Such an accusation as this, justly remarks Voltaire, *destroys itself.*

Brother William de la More, and thirty more of his brethren, being interrogated before the inquisitors, positively denied the guilt of the order, and affirmed that the Templars who had made the confessions alluded to in France *had lied.* They were ordered to be brought up separately to be examined.

On the 23rd of October, brother William Raven, being interrogated as to the mode of his reception into the Order, states that he was admitted by brother William de la More, the Master of the Temple at Temple Coumbe, in the diocese of Bath; that he petitioned the brethren of the Temple that they would be pleased to receive him into the Order to serve God and the blessed Virgin Mary, and to end his life in their service; that he was asked if he had a firm wish so to do; and replied that he had; that two brothers then expounded to him the strictness and severity of the Order,

JAMES DE
MOLAY.
A.D. 1309.

and told him that he would not be allowed to act after his own will, but must follow the will of the preceptor; that if he wished to do one thing, he would be ordered to do another; and that if he wished to be at one place, he would be sent to another; that having promised so to act, he swore upon the holy gospels of God to obey the Master, to hold no property,

---

* The original draft of these articles of accusation, with the corrections and alterations, is preserved in the Tresor des Chartres *Raynouard*, Monumens Historiques, p. 50, 51. The proceedings against the Templars in England are preserved in MS. in the British Museum, Harl. No. 252, 62, f. p. 113; No. 247, 68, f. p. 144. Bib. Cotton Julius, b. xii. p. 70; and in the Bodleian Library and Ashmolean Museum. The principal part of them has been published by *Wilkins* in the Concilia Magna Britanniæ, tom. ii. p. 329—401, and by *Dugdale*, in the Monast. Angl. vol. vi. part 2. p. 844—848.

to preserve chastity, never to consent that any man should be unjustly despoiled of his heritage, and never to lay violent hands on any man, except in self-defence, or upon the Saracens. He states that the oath was administered to him in the chapel of the preceptory of Temple Coumbe, in the presence only of the brethren of the Order; that the rule was read over to him by one of the brothers, and that a learned serving brother, named John de Walpole, instructed him, for the space of one month, upon the matters contained in it. The prisoner was then taken back to the Tower, and was directed to be strictly separated from his brethren, and not to be suffered to speak to any one of them.

The two next days (Oct. 24 and 25) were taken up with a similar examination of Brothers Hugh de Tadecastre and Thomas le Chamberleyn, who gave precisely the same account of their reception as the previous witness. Brother Hugh de Tadecastre added, that he swore to succour the Holy Land with all his might, and defend it against the enemies of the Christian faith; and that after he had taken the customary oaths and the three vows of chastity, poverty, and obedience, the mantle of the order and the cross with the coif on the head were delivered to him in the church, in the presence of the Master, the knights, and the brothers, all seculars being excluded. Brother Thomas le Chamberleyn added, that there was the same mode of reception in England as beyond sea, and the same mode of taking the vows; that all seculars are excluded, and that when he himself entered the Temple church to be professed, the door by which he entered was closed after him; that there was another door looking into the cemetery, but that no stranger could enter that way. On being asked why none but the brethren of the Order were permitted to be present at the reception and profession of brothers, he said he knew of no reason, but that it was so written in their book of rules.

JAMES DE MOLAY. A.D. 1309.

Between the 25th of October and the 17th of November, thirty-three knights, chaplains, and serving brothers, were examined, all of whom positively denied every article imputing crime or infidelity to their order. When Brother Himbert Blanke was asked why they had made the reception and profession of brethren secret, he replied, *Through their own unaccountable folly.* They avowed that they wore little cords round their shirts, but for no bad end; they declared that they never touched idols with them, but that they were worn by way of penance, or according to a knight of forty-three years' standing, by the instruction of the holy father St. Bernard. Brother Richard de Goldyngham says that he knows nothing further about them than that they were called *girdles of chastity.* They state that the receivers and the party received kissed one another on the face, but everything else regarding the kissing was false, abominable, and had never been done.

Brother Radulph de Barton, priest of the Order of the Temple, and custos or guardian of the Temple church at London, stated, with regard to

Article 24, that the Grand Master in chapter could absolve the brothers from offences committed against the rules and observances of the Order, but not from private sin, as he was not a priest; that it was perfectly true that those who were received into the Order swore not to reveal the secrets of the chapter, and that when any one was punished in the chapter, those who were present at it durst not reveal it to such as were absent; but if any brother revealed the mode of his reception, he would be deprived of his chamber, or else stripped of his habit. He declares that the brethren were not prohibited from confessing to priests not belonging to the Order of the Temple; and that he had never heard of the crimes and iniquities mentioned in the articles of inquiry previous to his arrest, except as regarded the charges made against the Order by Bernard Peletin, when he came to England from King Philip of France. He states that he had been guardian of the Temple church for ten years, and for the last two years had enjoyed the dignity of preceptor at the same place. He was asked about the death of Brother Walter le Bachelor, knight, formerly Preceptor of Ireland, who died at the Temple at London, but he declares that he knows nothing about it, except that the said Walter was fettered and placed in prison, and there died; that he certainly had heard that great severity had been practised towards him, but that he had not meddled with the affair on account of the danger of so doing; he admitted also that the aforesaid Walter was not buried in the cemetery of the Temple, as he was considered excommunicated on account of his disobedience of his superior, and of the rule of the Order.

JAMES DE MOLAY. A.D. 1309.

Many of the brethren thus examined had been from twenty to thirty, forty, forty-two, and forty-three years in the Order, and some were old veteran warriors who had fought for many a long year in the East, and richly merited a better fate. Brother Himbert Blanke, knight, Preceptor of Auvergne, had been in the Order thirty-eight years. He was received at the city of Tyre in Palestine, had been engaged in constant warfare against the infidels, and had fought to the last in defence of Acre. He makes in substance the same statements as the other witnesses; declares that no religious order believes the sacrament of the altar better than the Templars; that they truly believed all that the church taught, and had always done so, and that if the Grand Master had confessed the contrary, *he had lied*. Brother Robert le Scott, knight, a brother of twenty-six years' standing, had been received at the Pilgrim's Castle, the famous fortress of the Knights Templars in Palestine, by the Grand Master, Brother William de Beaujeu, the hero who died so gloriously at the iiead of his knights at the last siege and storming of Acre. He states that from levity of disposition he quitted the Order after it had been driven out of Palestine, and absented himself for two years, during which period he came to Rome, and confessed to the Pope's penitentiary, who imposed on him a heavy penance, and enjoined him to return to his brethren in the East, and that he

JAMES DE MOLAY. A.D. 1309.

went back and resumed his habit at Nicosia in the island of Cyprus, and was re-admitted to the Order by command of the Grand Master, James de Molay, who was then at the head of the convent. He adds, also, that Brother Himbert Blanke (the previous witness) was present at his first reception at the Pilgrim's Castle. He fully corroborates all the foregoing testimony.

Brother Richard de Peitevyn, a member of forty-two years' standing, deposes that, in addition to the previous oaths, he swore that he would never bear arms against Christians except in his own defence, or in defence of the rights of the Order; he declares that the enormities mentioned in the articles were never heard of before Bernard Peletin brought letters to his lord, the king of England, against the Templars.

On the 22nd day of the inquiry, the following entry was made on the record of the proceedings:

"Memorandum. Brothers Philip de Mewes, Thomas de Burton, and Thomas de Staundon, were advised and earnestly exhorted to abandon their religious profession, who severally replied that *they would rather die* than do so."*

On the 19th and 20th of November, seven lay witnesses, un-connected with the Order, were examined before the inquisitors in the chapel of the monastery of the Holy Trinity, but could prove nothing against the Templars that was criminal or tainted with heresy.

JAMES DE MOLAY. A.D. 1309.

Master William le Dorturer, notary public, declared that the Templars rose at midnight, and held their chapters before dawn, and he *thought* that the mystery and secrecy of the receptions were owing to a bad rather than a good motive, but declared that he had never observed that they had acquired, or had attempted to acquire, anything unjustly. Master Gilbert de Bruere, clerk, said that he had never suspected them of anything worse than an *excessive correction* of the brethren. William Lambert, formerly a "messenger of the Temple," (nuntius Templi), knew nothing bad of the Templars, and thought them perfectly innocent of all the matters alluded to. And Richard de Barton, priest, and Radulph de Rayndon, an old man, both declared that they knew nothing of the Order, or of the members of it, but what was good and honourable.

On the 25th of November, a provincial council of the church, summoned by the archbishop of Canterbury, in obedience to a papal bull, assembled in the cathedral church of St. Paul. It was composed of the bishops, abbots, priors, heads of colleges, and all the principal clergy, who were called together to treat of the reformation of the English church, of the recovery and preservation of the Holy Land, and to pronounce sentence of absolution or of condemnation against singular persons of

---

* Actum in Capella infirmariæ prioratus Sanctæ Trinitatis præsentibus etc. Concilia Magnæ Britanniæ, tom. iii. p. 344. Ibid. p. 334—343.

the Order of the chivalry of the Temple in the province of Canterbury, according to the tenor of the apostolical mandate. The council was opened by the archbishop of Canterbury, who rode to St. Paul's on horseback. The bishop of Norwich celebrated the mass of the Holy Ghost at the great altar, and the archbishop preached a sermon in Latin upon the 20th chapter of the Acts of the Apostles; after which a papal bull was read, in which the holy pontiff dwells most pathetically upon the awful sins of the Templars, and their great and tremendous fall from their previous high estate. Hitherto, says he, they have been renowned throughout the world as the special champions of the faith, and the chief defenders of the Holy Land, whose affairs have been mainly regulated by those brothers. The church, following them and their order with the plenitude of its especial favour and regard, armed them with the emblem of the cross against the enemies of Christ, exalted them with much honour, enriched them with wealth, and fortified them with various liberties and privileges. The holy pontiff displays the sad report of their sins and iniquities which reached his ears, filled him with bitterness and grief, disturbed his repose, smote him with horror, injured his health, and caused his body to waste away! He gives a long account of the crimes imputed to the Order, of the confessions and depositions that had been made in France, and then bursts out into a paroxysm of grief, declares that the melancholy affair deeply moved all the faithful, that all Christianity was shedding bitter tears, was overwhelmed with grief, and clothed with mourning. He concludes by decreeing the assembly of a general council of the church at Vienne to pronounce the abolition of the Order, and to determine on the disposal of its property, to which council the English clergy are required to send representatives.*

After the reading of the bulls and the closing of the preliminary proceedings, the council occupied themselves for six days with ecclesiastical matters; and on the seventh day, being Tuesday, Dec. 2nd, all the bishops and members assembled in the chamber of the archbishop of Canterbury in Lambeth palace, in company with the papal inquisitors, who displayed before them the depositions and replies of the forty-three Templars, and of the seven witnesses previously examined. It was decreed that a copy of these depositions and replies should be furnished to each of the bishops, and that the council should stand adjourned until the next day, to give time for deliberation upon the premises.

On the following day, accordingly, (Wednesday, December the 3rd), the council met, and decided that the inquisitors and three bishops should seek an audience of the king, and beseech him to permit them to proceed against the Templars in the way that should seem to them the best

JAMES DE MOLAY. A.D. 1309.

JAMES DE MOLAY. A.D. 1309.

---

* *Concil. Mag.* Brit, tom. ii. p. 305—308.

and most expedient for the purpose of eliciting the truth. On Sunday, the 7th, the bishops petitioned his majesty in writing, and on the following Tuesday they went before him with the inquisitors, and besought him that they might proceed against the Templars according to the ecclesiastical constitutions, and that he would instruct his sheriffs and officers to that effect. The king gave a written answer complying with their request, which was read before the council,* and, on the 16th of December, orders were sent to the gaolers, commanding them to permit the prelates and inquisitors to do with the bodies of the Templars that which should seem expedient to them according to ecclesiastical law. Many Templars were at this period wandering about the country disguised as secular persons, successfully evading pursuit, and the sheriffs were strictly commanded to use every exertion to capture them.† On Wednesday, the ecclesiastical council again met, and adjourned for the purpose of enabling the inquisitors to examine the prisoners confined in the castles of Lincoln and of York.

In Scotland, in the mean time, similar proceedings had been instituted against the Order.‡ On the 17th of November, Brother Walter de Clifton being examined in the parish church of the Holy Cross at Edinburgh, before the bishop of St. Andrews and John de Solerio, the pope's chaplain, states that the brethren of the Order of the Temple in the kingdom of Scotland received their orders, rules, and observances from the Master of the Temple in England, and that the Master in England received the rules and observances of the Order from the Grand Master and the chief convent in the East; that the Grand Master or his deputy was in the habit of visiting the Order in England and elsewhere; of summoning chapters, and making regulations for the conduct of the brethren and the administration of their property. Being asked as to the mode of his reception, he states that when William de la More, the Master, held his chapter at the preceptory of Temple Bruere in the county of Lincoln, he sought of the assembled brethren the habit and the fellowship of the Order; that they told him that he little knew what it was he asked, in seeking to be. admitted to their fellowship; that it would be a very hard matter for him, who was then his own master, to become the servant of another, and to have no will of his own; but notwithstanding their representations of the rigour of their rules and observances, he still continued earnestly to seek their habit and fellowship. He states that they then led him to the chamber of the Master, where they held their chapter, and that there, on his bended knees, and with his hands clasped, he again prayed for the habit and the fellowship of the Temple; that the Master and the brethren then required him to

JAMES DE MOLAY. A.D. 1309.

* Concil. Mag. Brit., tom. ii. p. 312—314.
† Acta Rymeri, tom. iii. p. 194, 195.
‡ Ibid., p. 182.

answer questions to the following effect: Whether he had a dispute with any man, or owed any debts? whether he was betrothed to any woman? and whether he had any secret infirmity of body? or knew of anything to prevent him from remaining within the bosom of the fraternity? And having answered all those questions satisfactorily, the Master then asked of the surrounding brethren, "Do ye give your consent to the reception of brother Walter?" who unanimously answered that they did; and the Master and the brethren then standing up, received the said Walter in this manner. On his bended knees, and with his hands joined, he solemnly promised that he would be the perpetual servant of the Master, and of the Order, and of the brethren, for the purpose of defending the Holy Land. Having done this, the Master took out of the hands of a brother chaplain of the Order the book of the holy gospels, upon which was depicted a cross, and laying his hands upon the book and upon the cross, he swore to God and the blessed Virgin Mary to be for ever thereafter chaste, obedient, and to live without property. And then the Master gave to him the white mantle, and placed the coif on his head, and admitted him to the kiss on the mouth, after which he made him sit down on the ground, and admonished him to the following effect: that from thenceforth he was to sleep in his shirt, drawers, and stockings, girded with a small cord over his shirt; that he was never to tarry in a house where there was a woman in the family way; never to be present at a marriage, nor at the purification of women; and likewise instructed and informed him upon several other particulars. Being asked where he had passed his time since his reception, he replied that he had dwelt three years at the preceptory of Blancradok in Scotland; three years at Temple Newsom in England; one year at the Temple at London, and three years at Aslakeby. Being asked concerning: the other brothers in Scotland, he stated that John de Hueflete was Preceptor of Blancradok, the chief house of the Order in that country, and that he and the other brethren, having heard of the arrest of the Templars, threw off their habits and fled, and that he had not since heard aught concerning them.

Brother William de Middleton, being examined, gave the same account of his reception, and added that he remembered that brother William de la More, the Master in England, went, in obedience to a summons, to the Grand Master beyond sea, as the superior of the whole order, and that in his absence Brother Hugh de Peraut, the visitor, removed several preceptors from their preceptories in England, and put others in their places. He further states, that he swore he would never receive any service at the hands of a woman, not even water to wash his hands with.

After the examination of the above two Templars, forty-one witnesses, chiefly abbots, priori, monks, priests, and serving men, and retainers of the Order in Scotland, were examined upon various interrogatories, but nothing of a criminatory nature was elicited. The monks observed that the receptions of other orders were public, and were celebrated as great religious solemnities, and the friends, parents, and neighbours of the party about to take the vows were invited to attend; that the Templars, on the other hand, shrouded their proceedings in mystery and secrecy, and therefore they *suspected* the worst. The priests thought them guilty, because they were always *against the church!* Others condemned them because (as they say) the Templars closed their doors against the poor and the humble, and extended hospitality only to the rich and the powerful. The abbot of the monastery of the Holy Cross at Edinburgh declared that they appropriated to themselves the property of their neighbours, right or wrong. The abbot of Dumferlyn knew nothing of his own knowledge against them, but had *heard* much, and *suspected* more. The serving men and the tillers of the lands of the Order stated that the chapters were held sometimes by night and sometimes by day, with extraordinary secrecy; and some of the witnesses had heard old men say that the Templars would *never have lost the Holy Landy if they had been good Christians!* *

On the 9th of January, A.D. 1310, the examination of witnesses was resumed at London, in the parish church of St. Dunstan's West, near the Temple. The rector of the church of St. Mary de la Strode declared that he had strong suspicions of the guilt of the Templars; he had, however, often been at the Temple church, and had observed that the priests performed divine service there just the same as elsewhere. William de Cumbrook, of St. Clement's church, near the Temple, the vicar of St. Martin's-in-the-Fields, and many other priests and clergymen of different churches in London, all declared that they had nothing to allege against the Order.† *[margin: JAMES DE MOLAY. A.D. 1310.]*

On the 27th of January, Brother John de Stoke, a serving brother of the Order of the Temple, of seventeen years' standing, being examined by the inquisitors in the chapel of the Blessed Mary of Berkyngecherclie at London, states, amongst other things, that secular persons were allowed to be present at the burial of Templars; that the brethren of the Order all received the sacraments of the church at their last hour, and were attended to the grave by a chaplain of the Temple. Being interrogated concerning the death and burial of the Knight Templar Brother Walter le Bachelor, he deposes that the said knight was buried like any other Chris-

---

*Et ad evidentius præmissorum testimonium reverendus in Christo pater dominus Willielmus, providentiâ divinâ S. Andreæ episcopus, et magister Johannes de Solerio prædicti sigilla sua præsenti inquisitioni appenderunt, et eisdem sigillis post subscriptionem meam eandem inquisitionem clauserunt. In quorum etiam firmius testimonium ego Willielmus de Spottiswod auctoritate imperiali notarius qui prædictæ inquisitioni interfui die, anno, et loco prædictis, testibus præsentibus supra dictis, signum meum solitum eidem apposui requisitas, et propriâ manu scripsi rogatus.—*Acta contra Templarios. Concil. Mag. Brit.,* tom. ii. p. 380, 383.

† Act. in ecclesiâ parochiali S. Dunstani prope Novum Templum.—Ib., p. 349.

tian, except that he was not buried in the buryingground, but in the court, of the house of the Temple at London; that he confessed to Brother Richard de Grafton, a priest of the Order, then in the island of Cyprus, and partook, as he believed, of the sacrament. He states that he himself and Brother Radulph de Barton carried him to his grave at the dawn of day, and that JAMES DE the deceased knight was in prison, as he believes, for the space of eight MOLAY. weeks; that he was not buried in the habit of his order, and was interred A.D. 1310. without the cemetery of the brethren, because he was considered to be excommunicated, in pursuance, as he believed, of a rule or statute among the Templars, to the effect that every one who privily made away with the property of the Order, and did not acknowledge his fault, was deemed excommunicated. Being asked in what respect he considered that his order required reformation, he replied, "By the establishment of a probation of one year, and by making the receptions public."

Two other Templars were examined on the same 27th day of January, from whose depositions it appears that there were at that time many brethren of the Order, natives of England, in the island of Cyprus.

On the 29th of January, the inquisitors exhibited twenty-four fresh articles against the prisoners, drawn up in an artful manner. They were asked if they knew anything of the crimes mentioned in the papal bulls, and *confessed* by the Grand Master, the heads of the Order, and many knights in France; and whether they knew of anything sinful or dishonourable against the Master of the Temple in England, or the preceptors, or any of the brethren. They were then required to say whether the same rules, customs, and observances did not prevail throughout the entire order; whether the Grand Preceptors, and especially the Grand Preceptor of England, did not receive all the observances and regulations from the Grand Master; and whether the Grand Preceptors and all the brethren of the Order in England did not observe them in the same mode as the Grand Master, and visitors, and the brethren in Cyprus and in Italy, and in the other kingdoms, provinces, and preceptories of the Order; whether the observances and regulations were not commonly delivered by the visitors JAMES DE to the Grand Preceptor of England; and whether the brothers received in MOLAY. England or elsewhere had not of their own free will confessed what these A.D. 1310. observances were. They were, moreover, required to state whether a bell was rung, or other signal given, to notify the time of the assembling of the chapter; whether all the brethren, without exception, were summoned and in the habit of attending; whether the Grand Master could relax penances imposed by the regular clergy; whether they believed that the Grand Preceptor or visitor could absolve a layman who had been excommunicated for laying hands on a brother or lay servant of the Order; and whether they believed that any brother of the Order could absolve from the sin of perjury a lay servant, when he came to receive the discipline in the Temple-hall, and the serving brother scourged him in the name of the

Father, and of the Son, and of the Holy Ghost, &c. &c.

Between the 29th of January and the 6th of February, thirty-four Templars, many of whom appeared for the first time before the inquisitors, were examined upon these articles in the churches of St. Botolph without Aldgate, St. Alphage near Cripplegate, and St. Martin de Ludgate, London. They deny everything of a criminatory nature, and declare that the abominations mentioned in the confessions and depositions made in France were not observances of the Order; that the Grand Master, Preceptors, visitors, and brethren in France had never observed such things, and if they said they had, *they lied*. They declare that the Grand Preceptor and brethren in England were all good men, worthy of faith, and would not deviate from the truth by reason of hatred of any man, for favour, reward, or any other cause; that there had been no suspicion in England against them, and no evil reports current against the Order before the publication of the papal bull, and they did not think that any *good man* would believe the contents of the articles to be true. From the statements of the prisoners, it appears that the bell of the Temple was rung to notify the assembling of the chapter, that the discipline was administered in the hall, in the presence of the assembled brethren, by the Master, who punished the delinquent on the bare back with a scourge made of leathern thongs, after which he himself absolved the offender from the guilt of a transgression against the rule of the Order; but if he had been guilty of immoral conduct, he was sent to the priest for absolution. It appears also, that Brother James de Molay, before his elevation to the office of Grand Master, was visitor of the Order in England, and had held chapters or assemblies of the brethren, at which he had enforced certain rules and regulations; that all the Orders came from the Grand Master and chief convent in the East to the Grand Preceptor of England, who caused them to be published at the different preceptories.*

On the 1st of March, the king sent orders to the constable of the Tower, and to the sheriffs of Lincoln and of York, to obey the directions of the inquisitors, or of one bishop and of one inquisitor, with regard to the confinement of the Templars in separate cells, and he assigns William de Diene to assist the inquisitors in their arrangements. Similar orders were shortly afterwards sent to all the gaolers of the Templars in the English dominions.†

On the 3rd of March five fresh interrogatories were exhibited by the inquisitors, upon which thirty-one Templars were examined at the palace of the bishop of London, the chapel of St. Alphage, and the chapter-house of the Holy Trinity. They were chiefly concerning the reception and profession of the brethren, the number that each examinant had

JAMES DE MOLAY. A.D. 1310.

---

* *Acta contra Templarios. Concil. Mag. Brit.*, tom. ii. p. 350, 351, 352.

† Acta *Rymeri*, tom, iii. ad ann. 1310. p. 202, 203.

seen received, their names, and as to whether the burials of the Order were conducted in a clandestine manner. From the replies it appears that JAMES DE MOLAY. A.D. 1310. many Templars had died during their imprisonment in the Tower. The twenty-sixth prisoner examined was the Master of the Temple, Brother William de la More, who gives an account of the number of persons he had admitted into the Order during the period of his mastership, specifying their names. It is stated that many of the parishioners of the parish adjoining the New Temple had been present at the interment of the brethren of the fraternity, and that the burials were not conducted in a clandestine manner.

In Ireland, in the mean time, similar proceedings against the Order had been carried on. Between the 11th of February and the 23rd of May, thirty Templars were examined in Saint Patrick's Church, Dublin, by Master John de Mareshall, the pope's commissary, but no evidence of their guilt was obtained. Forty-one witnesses were then heard, nearly all of whom were monks. They spoke merely from hearsay and suspicion, and the gravest charges brought by them against the fraternity appear to be, that the Templars had been observed to be inattentive to the reading of the holy Gospels at church, and to have cast their eyes on the ground at the period of the elevation of the host.*

On the 30th of March the papal inquisitors opened their commission at Lincoln, and between that day and the 10th of April twenty Templars were examined in the chapter-house of the cathedral, amongst whom were some of the veteran warriors of Palestine, men who had moistened with their blood the distant plains of the far East in defence of that faith which they were now so infamously accused of having repudiated. Brother William de Winchester, a member of twenty-six years' standing, had been received into the Order at the castle *de la Roca Guille* in the prov- JAMES DE MOLAY. A.D. 1310. ince of Armenia, bordering on Palestine, by the valiant Grand Master William de Beaujeu. He states that the same mode of reception exist- ed there as in England, and everywhere throughout the Order. Brother Robert de Hamilton declares that the girdles were worn from an honour- able motive, that they were called the girdles of Nazareth, because they had been pressed against the column of the Virgin at that place, and were worn in remembrance of the blessed Mary; but he says that the brethren were not compelled to wear them, but might make use of any girdle that they liked. With regard to the confessions made in France, they all say that if their brethren in that country confessed such things, *they lied !*†

At York the examination commenced on the 28th of April, and lasted until the 4th of May, during which period twenty-three Templars, prison- ers in York Castle, were examined in the chapter-house of the cathedral,

---

* Acta *Rymeri* tom. iii. p. 179, 180. *Concil. Mag, Brit.,* tom. ii. p. 373 to 380.

† Terrore tormentorum confessi sunt et *mentiti.—Concil. Mag. Brit.,* tom. ii. p. 365, 366, 367.

and followed the example of their brethren in maintaining their innocence. Brother Thomas de Stanford, a member of thirty years' standing,
had been received in the East by the Grand Master William de Beaujeu,
and Brother Radulph de Rostona, a priest of the Order, of twenty-three
years' standing, had been received at the preceptory of Lentini in Sicily
by Brother William de Canello, the Grand Preceptor of Sicily. Brother
Stephen de Radenhall refused to reveal the mode of reception, because
it formed part of the secrets of the chapter, and if he discovered them
he would lose his chamber, be stripped of his mantle, or be committed
to prison.*

On the 20th of May, in obedience to the mandate of the archbishop of
York, an ecclesiastical council of the bishops and clergy assembled in the
cathedral. The mass of the Holy Ghost was solemnly celebrated, after
which the archbishop preached a sermon, and then caused to be read to
the assembled clergy the papal bulls fulminated against the Order of the
Temple.† He exhibited to them the articles upon which the Templars had
been directed to be examined; but as the inquiry was still pending, the
council was adjourned until the 23rd of June of the following year, when
they were to meet to pass sentence of condemnation, or of absolution,
against all the members of the Order in the province of York, in conformity with ecclesiastical law.‡

On the 1st of June the examination was resumed before the
papal inquisitors at Lincoln. Sixteen Templars were examined upon
points connected with the secret proceedings in the general and particular
chapters of the Order, the imposition of penances therein, and the nature
of the absolution granted by the Master. From the replies it appears that
the penitents were scourged three times with leathern thongs, in the name
of the Father, and of the Son, and of the Holy Ghost, after which they
were absolved either by the Master or by a priest of the Order, according
to the particular circumstances of each case. It appears, also, that none
but preceptors were present at the general chapters of the Order, which
were called together principally for the purpose of obtaining money to
send to the Grand Master and the chief convent in Palestine.§

---

* Despositiones Templariorum in Provinciâ Eboracensi.—*Concil. Mag. Brit.*, tom. ii.
p. 371—373.

† Eodem anno (1310) XIX. Die Maii apud Eborum in ecclesia cathedrali, ex amndato
speciali Domini Papæ, enuit dominus Archiepiscopus concilium provinciale. Prædicavitque
et erat suum thema; *omnes isti conregati venerunt tibi, factoque sermone, recitavit et legi
fecit sequentem bullam horribilem contra Templarios, &c. &c. Hemingford apud Hearne,*
vol. i. p. 249.

‡ Processus observatus in concilio provinciali Eboracensi in ecclesia beati Petri Ebor.
contra Templarios celebrato A.D. 1310, ex. Reg. Will. Grenefeld Archiepiscopi Eborum, fol.
179, p. 1.—*Concil. Mag. Brit.,* tom. ii. p. 393.

§ *Concil. Mag. Brit.,* tom. ii. p. 367.

JAMES DE
MOLAY.
A.D. 1310.

After closing the examinations at Lincoln, the abbot of Lagny and the canon of Narbonne returned to London, and immediately resumed the inquiry in that city. On the 8th and 9th days of June, Brother William de la More, the Master of the Temple, and thirty-eight of his knights, chaplains, and sergeants, were examined by the inquisitors in the presence of the bishops of London and Chichester, and the before-mentioned public notaries, in the priory of the Holy Trinity. They were interrogated for the most part concerning the penances imposed, and the absolution pronounced in the chapters. The Master of the Temple was required to state what were the precise words uttered by him, as the president of the chapter, when a penitent brother, having bared his back and acknowledged his fault, came into his presence and received the discipline of the leathern thongs. He states that he was in the habit of saying, "Brother, pray to God that he may forgive you and to the bystanders he said, "And do ye, brothers, beseech the Lord to forgive him his sins, and say a *paternoster;*" and that he said nothing further, except to warn the offender against sinning again. He declares that he did not pronounce absolution in the name of the Father, and of the Son, and of the Holy Ghost! and relates, that in a general chapter, and as often as he held a particular chapter, he was accustomed to say, after prayers had been offered up, that all those who did not acknowledge their sins, or who appropriated to their own use the alms of the house, could not be partakers in the spiritual blessings of the Order; but that which through shame-facedness, or through fear of the justice of the Order, they dared not confess, he, out of the power conceded to him by God and the pope, forgave him as far as he was able. Brother William de Sautre, however, declares that the president of the chapter, after he had finished the flagellation of a penitent brother, said, "I forgive you, in the name of the Father, and of the Son, and of the Holy Ghost," and then sent him to a priest of the Order for absolution; and the other witnesses vary in their account of the exact words uttered, either because they were determined, in obedience to their oaths, not to reveal what actually did take place, or else (which is very probable) because the same form of proceeding was not always rigidly adhered to.

JAMES DE
MOLAY.
A.D. 1310.

When the examination was closed, the inquisitors drew up a memorandum, showing that, from the apostolical letters, and the depositions and attestations of the witnesses, it was to be collected that certain practices had crept into the Order of the Temple, which were not consistent with the orthodox faith.*

---

* *Acta contra Templarios. Concil. Mag. Brit.,* tom. ii. p. 358.

CHAPTER X.

The Templars in France revoke their rack-extorted confessions—They are tried as relapsed heretics, and burnt at the stake—The progress of the inquiry in England—The curious evidence adduced as to the mode of holding the chapters of the Order—As to the penance enjoined therein, and the absolution pronounced by the Master—The Templars draw up a written defence, which they present to the ecclesiastical council—They are placed in separate dungeons, and put to the torture—Two serving brethren and a chaplain of the Order then make confessions—Many other Templars acknowledge themselves guilty of heresy in respect of their belief in the religious authority of their Master—They make their recantations, and are reconciled to the church before the south door of Saint Paul's cathedral—The order of the Temple is abolished by the Pope—The last of the Masters of the Temple in England dies in the Tower—The disposal of the property of the Order—Observations on the downfall of the Templars.

Veggio '1 nuovo Pilato sì crudele,
Che cio nol sazia, ma, senza decreto
Porta nel Tempio le cupide vele.
Dante. Del Purgatorio. Canto xx. 91.

In France, on the other hand, the proceedings against the Order had assumed a most sanguinary character. Many Templars, both in the capital and the provinces, had made confessions of guilt whilst suffering upon the rack, but they had no sooner been released from the hands of their tormentors, and had recovered their health, than they disavowed their confessions, maintained the innocence of their order, and appealed to all their gallant actions, in ancient and modern times, in refutation of the calumnies of their enemies. The enraged Philip caused these Templars to be brought before an ecclesiastical tribunal convoked at Paris, and sentence of death was passed upon them by the archbishop of Sens, in the following terms:

"You have avowed," said he, "that the brethren who are received into the Order of the Temple are compelled to renounce Christ and spit upon the cross, and that you yourselves have participated in that crime: you have thus acknowledged that you have fallen into the sin of heresy. By your confession and repentance you had merited absolution, and had once more become reconciled to the church. As you have revoked your confession, the church no longer regards you as reconciled, but as having fallen back to your first errors. You are, therefore, relapsed heretics (!) and as such, we condemn you to the fire."*

The following morning, (Tuesday, May 12), in pursuance of this absurd and atrocious sentence, fifty-four Templars were handed over to the secular arm, and were led out to execution by the king's officers. They were conducted into the open country, in the environs of the Porte St. Antoine des Champs at Paris, and were burnt to death in a most cruel manner before a slow fire. All historians speak with admiration of the heroism and intrepidity with which they met their fate.†

Many hundred other Templars were dragged from the dungeons of Paris before the archbishop of Sens and his council. Those whom neither the agony of the torture nor the fear of death could overcome, but who remained stedfast amid all their trials in the maintenance of the innocence of their Order, were condemned to perpetual imprisonment as *unreconciled heretics;* whilst those who, having made the required confessions of guilt, continued to persevere in them, received absolution, were declared reconciled to the church, and were set at liberty. Notwithstanding the terror inspired by these executions, many of the Templars still persisted in the revocation of their confessions, which they stigmatized as the result of insufferable torture, and boldly maintained the innocence of their order.

On the 18th of August, four other Templars were condemned as relapsed heretics by the council of Sens, and were likewise burned by the Porte St. Antoine; and it is stated that a hundred and thirteen Templars were from first to last burnt at the stake in Paris. Many others were burned in Lorraine; in Normandy; at Carcassone, and nine, or, according to some writers, twenty-nine, were burnt by the archbishop of Rheims at Senlis! King Philip's officers, indeed, not content with their inhuman cruelty towards the living, invaded the sanctity of the tomb; they dragged a dead Templar, who had been Treasurer of the Temple at Paris, from his grave, and burnt the mouldering corpse as a heretic.‡ In the midst of all these sanguinary atrocities, the examinations continued before the ecclesiastical tribunals. Many aged and illustrious warriors,

---

* *Joan. can. Sanct. Vict. Contin. De Nangis* ad ann. 1310. Ex secundâ vitâ *Clem.* V. p. 37.

† Chron. *Cornel. Zanfliet,* apud *Martene,* tom. v. col. 159. *Bocat.* de cas. vir. illustr. Lib. 9. chap. xxi. *Raynouard,* Monumens historiques. *Dupuy,* Condemnation de Templiers.

‡ Vit. prim, et tert. Clem. V. col. 57, 17. Bern. *Guac.* apud *Muratori,* tom. iii. p. 676. Contin. Chron. de *Nangis* ad ann 1310. *Raynouard,* p. 120.

who merited a better fate, appeared before their judges pale and trembling. At first they revoked their confessions, declared their innocence, and were remanded to prison; and then, panic-stricken, they demanded to be led back before the papal commissioners, when they abandoned their retractations, persisted in their previous avowals of guilt, humbly expressed their sorrow and repentance, and were then pardoned, absolved, and reconciled to the church! The torture still continued to be applied, and out of thirty-three Templars confined in the chateau d'Alaix, four died in prison, and the remaining twenty confessed, amongst other things, the following absurdities:—that in the provincial chapter of the Order held at Montpelier, the Templars set up a head and worshipped it; that the devil often appeared there in the shape of a cat, and conversed with the assembled brethren, and promised them a good harvest, with the possession of riches, and all kinds of temporal property. Some asserted that the head worshipped by the fraternity possessed a long beard; others that it was a woman's head; and one of the prisoners declared that as often as this wonderful head was adored, a great number of devils made their appearance in the shape of beautiful women . . . !!* James de Molay. A.D. 1310.

We must now unfold the dark page in the history of the Order in England. All the Templars in custody in this country had been examined separately and apart, and had, notwithstanding, deposed in substance to the same effect, and given the same account of their reception into the Order, and of the oaths that they took. Any reasonable and impartial mind would consequently have been satisfied of the truth of their statements; but it was not the object of the inquisitors to obtain evidence of the *innocence*, but proof of the *guilt*, of the Order. At first, king Edward the Second, to his honour, forbade the infliction of torture upon the illustrious members of the Temple in his dominions—men who had fought and bled for Christendom, and of whose piety and morals he had a short time before given such ample testimony to the principal sovereigns of Europe. But the virtuous resolution of the weak king was speedily overcome by the all-powerful influence of the Roman pontiff, who wrote to him in the month of June, upbraiding him for preventing the inquisitors from submitting the Templars to the discipline of the rack.† Influenced by the admonitions of the pope, and the solicitations of the clergy, King Edward, on the 26th of August, sent orders to John de Crumbewell, constable of James de Molay. A.D. 1310.

---

* *Raynouard*, p. 155.

† Inhibuisti ne contra ipsas personas et ordinem per quœstiones ad inquirendum super eisdem criminibus procedatur, quam vis iidem Templarii diffiteri dicuntur super eisdem articulis veritatem . . . . . Attende, quæsumus, fili carissime, et prudenti deliberatione considera, si hoc tuo honori et saluti conveniat, et statui congruat regni tui. Arch. Secret. Vatican. Registr. Literar. curiæ anno 5 domini Clementis Papæ 5. — *Raynourad*, p. 152.

‡ Acta *Rymeri*, tom. iii. ad ann. 1310, p. 224.

the Tower, to deliver up all the Templars in his custody, at the request of the inquisitors, to the sheriffs of London, in order that the inquisitors might be able to proceed more conveniently and effectually with their inquisition.‡ And on the same day he directed the sheriffs to receive the prisoners from the constable of the Tower, and cause them to be placed in the custody of gaolers appointed by the inquisitors, to be confined in prisons or such other convenient places in the city of London as the inquisitors and bishops should think expedient, and generally to permit them to do with the bodies of the Templars whatever should seem fitting, in accordance with ecclesiastical law. He directs, also, that from thenceforth the Templars should receive their sustenance at the hands of such newly-appointed gaolers.*

On the Tuesday after the feast of St. Matthew, (Sept. 21st), the ecclesiastical council again assembled at London, and caused the inquisitions and depositions taken against the Templars to be read, which being done, great disputes arose touching various alterations observable in them. It was at length ordered that the Templars should be again confined in separate cells in the prisons of London; that fresh interrogatories should be prepared, to see if by such means the *truth* could be extracted, and if by straitenings and confinement they would confess nothing *further*, then the torture was to be applied; but it was provided that the examination by torture should be conducted without the perpetual mutilation or disabling of any limb, and without a violent effusion of blood! and the inquisitors and the bishops of London and Chichester were to notify the result to the archbishop of Canterbury, that he might again convene the assembly for the purpose of passing sentence, either of absolution or of condemnation. These resolutions having been adopted, the council was prorogued, on the following Saturday, *de die in diem,* until the feast of the Exaltation of the Holy Cross, A.D. 1311.†

On the 6th of October, a fortnight after the above resolution had been formed by the council, the king sent fresh instructions to the constable of the Tower, and the sheriffs of London, directing them to deliver up the Templars, one at a time, or altogether, and receive them back in the same way, at the will of the inquisitors.‡ The gaolers of these unhappy gentlemen seem to have been more merciful and considerate than their judges, and to have manifested the greatest reluctance to act upon the Orders sent from the king. On the 23rd of

JAMES DE
MOLAY.
A.D. 1310.

---

* Ib., p. 224, 225. claus. 4. E. 2. M. 22.

† Et si per hujusmodi arctationes et separations nihil aliud, quam prius, vellent confiteri, quod extunc *quæstionarentur;* ita quod *quæstiones* illæ fierent ABSQUE MUTILATIONE ET DEBILITATIONE PERPETUA ALICUJUS MEMBRI, ET SINE VIOLENTA SANGUINIS EFFUSIONE. —*Concil. Mag. Brit.,* tom. ii. p. 314.

‡ Acta *Rymeri,* tom. iii. p. 227, 228.

October, further and more preremptory commands were forwarded to the constable of the Tower, distinctly informing him that the king, on account of his respect for the holy apostolic see, had lately conceded to the prelates and inquisitors deputed to take inquisition against the Order of the Temple, and the Grand Preceptor of that order in England, the power of ordering and disposing of the Templars and their bodies, of examining them by torture or otherwise, and of doing to them whatever they should deem expedient, according to the ecclesiastical law; and he again strictly enjoins the constable to deliver up all the Templars in his custody, either together or separately, or in any way that the inquisitors or one bishop and one inquisitor may direct, and to receive them back when required so to do.* Corresponding orders were again sent to the sheriffs, commanding them, at the requisition of the inquisitors, to get the Templars out of the hands of the constable of the Tower, to guard them in convenient prisons, and to permit certain persons deputed by the inquisitors to see that the imprisonment was properly carried into effect, to do with the bodies of the Templars whatever they should think fit according to ecclesiastical law. When the inquisitors, or the persons appointed by them, had done with the Templars what they pleased, they were to deliver them back to the constable of the Tower, or his lieutenant, there to be kept in custody as before.† Orders were likewise sent to the constable of the castle of Lincoln, and to the mayor and bailiffs of the city of Lincoln, to the same effect. The king also directed Roger de Wyngefeld, clerk, guardian of the lands of the Templars, and William Plummer, sub-guardian of the manor of Cressing, to furnish to the king's officers the sums required for the keep, and for the expenses of the detention of the brethren of the Order.‡

On the 22nd of November the king condescended to acquaint the mayor, aldermen, and commonalty of his faithful city of London, that out of reverence to the pope he had authorised the inquisitors, sent over by his holiness, to question the Templars by torture; he puts them in possession of the Orders he had sent to the constable of the Tower, and to the sheriffs; and he commands them, in case it should be notified to them by the inquisitors that the prisons provided by the sheriffs were insufficient for their purposes, to procure without fail fit and

---

* Cum nuper, OB REVERIENTIAM SEDIS APOSTOLICÆ, concessimus prælatis et inquisitoribus ad inquirendum contra ordinem Templariorum, et contra Magnum Præceptorem ejusdem ordinis in regno nostra Angliæ, quod iidem prælati et inquisitores, de ipsis Templariis et eorum corporibus in quÆstionibus, et aliis ad hoc convenientibus ordinent et faciant, quoties voluerint, id quod eis secundum legem ecclesiasticam, videbitur faciendum, &c. — Teste rege apud Linliscu in Scotiâ, 23 die Octobris. Ibid. tom. iii. p. 228, 229.

† Acta Rymeri, tom. iii. p. 229.

‡ Ibid. p. 230.

§ Acta Rymeri, tom. iii. p. 231.

convenient houses in the city, or near thereto, for carrying into effect the contemplated measures; and he graciously informs them that he will reimburse them all the expenses that may be incurred by them or their officers in fulfilling his commands.§ Shortly afterwards the king again wrote to the mayor, aldermen, and commonalty of London, acquainting them that the sheriffs had made a return to his writ, to the effect that the four gates (prisons) of the city were not under their charge, and that they could not therefore obtain them for the purposes required; and he commands the mayor, aldermen, and commonalty, to place those four gates at the disposal of the sheriffs.*

On the 12th of December, all the Templars in custody at Lincoln were, by command of the king, brought up to London, and placed in solitary confinement in different prisons and private houses provided by the mayor and sheriffs. Shortly afterwards orders were given for all the Templars in custody in London to be loaded with chains and fetters; the myrmidons of the inquisitors were to be allowed to make periodical visits to see that the imprisonment was properly carried into effect, and were to be allowed to torture the bodies of the Templars in any way that they might think fit.†

JAMES DE MOLAY. A.D. 1311. On the 30th of March, A.D. 1311, after some months' trial of the above severe measures, the examination was resumed before the inquisitors, and the bishops of London and Chichester, at the several churches of St. Martin's, Ludgate, and St. Botolph's, Bishopsgate. The Templars had now been in prison in England for the space of three years and some months. During the whole of the previous winter they had been confined in chains in the dungeons of the city of London, compelled to receive their scanty supply of food from the officers of the inquisition, and to suffer from cold, from hunger, and from torture. They had been made to endure all the horrors of solitary confinement, and had none to solace or to cheer them during the long hours of their melancholy captivity. They had been already condemned collectively by the pope, as members of an heretical and idolatrous society, and as long as they continued to persist in the truth of their first confessions, and in the avowal of their innocence, they were treated as obstinate, unreconciled heretics, living in a state of excommunication, and doomed, when dead, to everlasting punishment in hell. They had heard of the miserable fate of their brethren in France, and they knew that those who had confessed crimes of which they had never been guilty, had been immediately declared reconciled to the church, had been absolved and set at liberty, and they knew that freedom, pardon, and peace could be immediately purchased by a confession of guilt; notwithstanding all which, every Templar, at this last examina-

* Ibid. p. 231, 232.
† Ibid. tom. iii. p. 232—235.

tion, persisted in the maintenance of his innocence, and in the denial of all knowledge of, or participation in, the crimes and heresies imputed to the Order. They declare that everything that was done in their chapters, in respect of absolution, the reception of brethren, and other matters, was honourable and honest, and might well and lawfully be done; that it was in no wise heretical or vicious; and that whatever was done was from the appointment, approbation, and regulation of all the brethren.* JAMES DE MOLAY. From their statements, it appears that the Master of the Temple in England was in the habit of summoning a general chapter of the Order once A.D. 1311. a year, at which the preceptors of Ireland and of Scotland were present. These were always called together to take into consideration the affairs of the Holy Land, and to determine on sending succour to their brethren in the East. At the close of their examination the Templars were again sent back to their dungeons, and loaded with chains; and the inquisitors, disappointed of the desired confessions, addressed themselves to the enemies of the Order for the necessary proofs of guilt.

During the month of April, seventy-two witnesses were examined in the chapter-house of the Holy Trinity. They were nearly all monks, Carmelites, Augustinians, Dominicans, and Minorites; their evidence is all hearsay, and the nature of it will be seen from the following choice specimens.

Henry Thanet, an Irishman, had *heard* that Brother Hugh de Nipurias, a Templar, deserted from the castle of Tortosa in Palestine, and went over to the Saracens, abjuring the Christian faith; and that a certain preceptor of the Pilgrim's Castle was in the habit of making all the brethren he received into the Order deny Christ; but the witness was unable to give either the name of the preceptor or of the persons so received. He had also heard that a certain Templar had in his custody a brazen *head* with two faces, which would answer all questions put to it!

Master John de Nassington declared that Milo de Stapelton and Adam de Everington, knights, told him that they had once been invited to a great feast at the preceptory of Templehurst, and were there informed that the Templars celebrated a solemn festival once a year, at which they worshipped a *calf!*

John de Eure, knight, sheriff of the county of York, deposed that he JAMES DE had once invited Brother William de la Fenne, Preceptor of Wesdall, to MOLAY. dine with him, and that after dinner the preceptor drew a book out of his A.D. 1311. bosom, and delivered it to the knight's lady to read, who found a piece of paper fastened into the book, on which were written abominable, heretical doctrines, to the effect that Christ was not the Son of God, nor born of a virgin, but conceived of the seed of Joseph, the husband of Mary, after the manner of other men, and that Christ was not a true but a false

* Acta contra Templartos, Concil. Mag. Brit. tom. ii. p. 368—371.

prophet, and was not crucified for the redemption of mankind, but for his own sins, and many other things contrary to the Christian faith. On the production of this important evidence, Brother William de la Fenne was called in and interrogated; he admitted that he had dined with the sheriff of York, and had lent his lady a book to read, but he swore that he was ignorant of the piece of paper fastened into the book, and of its contents. It appears that the sheriff of York had kept this dangerous secret to himself for the space of six years!

William de laForde, a priest, rector of the church of Crofton in the diocese of York, had *heard* William de Reynbur, priest of the Order of St. Augustine, who was then dead, say, that the Templar, Brother Patrick of Rippon, son of William of Gloucester, had confessed to him, that at his entrance into the Order, he was led, clothed only in his shirt and trousers, through a long passage to a secret chamber, and was there made to deny his God and his Saviour; that he was then shown a representation of the crucifixion, and was told that since he had previously honoured that emblem he must now dishonour it and spit upon it, and that he did so. "Item dictum fuitei quod, depositis brachis, dorsum verteret ad crucifixum," and this he did bitterly weeping. After this they brought an image, as it were, of a calf, placed upon an altar, and they told him he must kiss that image, and worship it, and he did so, and after all this they covered up his eyes and led him about, kissing and being kissed by all the brethren, but he could not recollect in what part. The worthy priest was asked when he had first *heard* all these things, and he replied after the arrest of the brethren by the king's orders!

JAMES DE MOLAY. A.D. 1311.

Robert of Oteringham, senior of the Order of Minorites, stated that on one occasion he was partaking of the hospitality of the Templars at the preceptory of Ribstane in Yorkshire, and that when grace had been said after supper, the chaplain of the Order reprimanded the brethren of the Temple, saying to them, "The devil will burn you," or some such words; and hearing a bustle amongst them, he got up to see what was the matter, and, as far as he recollects, he saw one of the brothers of the Temple, "brachis depositis, tenentem faciem versus occidentem et posteriora versus altare!" Being asked who it was that did this, he says he does not exactly remember. He then goes on to state, that about twenty years before that time! he was again the guest of the Templars, at the preceptory of Wetberby (query Feriby) in Yorkshire, and when evening came he heard that the preceptor was not coming to supper, as he was arranging some relics that he had brought with him from the Holy Land, and afterwards at midnight he heard a confused noise in the chapel, and getting up he looked through the keyhole, and saw a great light therein, either from a fire or from candles, and on the morrow he asked one of the brethren of the Temple the name of the saint in whose honour they had celebrated so grand a festival during the night, and that brother, aghast and turning pale, thinking he had seen what had been done amongst them, said to him, "Go thy way, and if you love me, or have any regard for your own life, never speak of this matter." This same "Senior of the Minorites" declares also that he had seen, in the chapel of the preceptory of Ribstane, a cross, with the image of our Saviour nailed upon it, thrown carelessly upon the altar, and he observed to a certain brother of the Temple, that the cross was in a most indecent and improper position, and he was about to lift it up and stand it erect, when that same brother called out to him, "Lay down the cross and depart in peace!" JAMES DE MOLAY. A.D. 1311.

Brother John de Wederal, another Minorite, sent to the inquisitors a written paper, wherein he stated that he had lately heard in the country, that a Templar, named Robert de Baysat, was once seen running about a meadow uttering, "Alas! alas! that ever I was born, seeing that I have denied God and sold myself to the devil!" Brother N. de Chinon, another Minorite, had heard that a certain Templar had a son who peeped through a chink in the wall of the chapter-room, and saw a person who was about to be professed, slain because he would not deny Christ, and afterwards the boy was asked by his father to become a Templar, but refused, and he immediately shared the same fate. Twenty witnesses, who were examined in each other's presence, merely repeated the above absurdities, or related similar ones.*

At this stage of the proceedings, the papal inquisitor, Sicard de Yaur, exhibited two rack-extorted confessions of Templars which had been obtained in France. The first was from Robert de St. Just, who had been received into the Order by brother Himbert, Grand Preceptor of England, but had been arrested in France, and there tortured by the myrmidons of Philip. In this confession, Robert de St. Just states that, on his admission to the vows of the Temple, he denied Christ, and spat *beside* the cross. The second confession had been extorted from Geoffrey de Gonville, Knight of the Order of the Temple, Preceptor of Aquitaine and Poitou, and had been given on the 15th of November, A.D. 1307, before the grand inquisitor of France. In this confession, (which had been afterwards revoked, but of which revocation no notice was taken by the inquisitors), Sir Qeoffrey de Gonville states that he was received into the Order in England in the house of the Temple at London, by Brother Robert de Torvibe, knight, the Master of all England, about twenty-eight years before that time; that the master showed him on a missal the image of Jesus Christ on the cross, and commanded him to deny him who was crucified; that, terribly alarmed, he exclaimed, "Alas! my lord, why should JAMES DE MOLAY. A.D. 1311.

---

* Suspicio (quæ loco testis 21, in MS. allegatur), probare videtur, quod omnes examinati in aliquo dejeraverunt (pejeraverunt), ut ex inspectione processuum apparet.—MS. Bodl. Oxon. f. 5. 2. *Concil* tom. ii. p. 359.

I do this? I will on no account do it." But the master said to him, "Do it boldly; I swear to thee that the act shall never harm either thy soul or thy conscience and then proceeded to inform him that the custom had been introduced into the Order by a certain bad Grand Master, who was imprisoned by a certain sultan, and could escape from prison only on condition that he would establish that form of reception in his order, and compel all who were received to deny Christ Jesus! but the deponent remained inflexible; he refused to deny his Saviour, and asked where were his uncle and the other good people who had brought him there, and was told that they were all gone; and at last a compromise took place between him and the Master, who made him take his oath that he would tell all his brethren that he had gone through the customary form, and never reveal that it had been dispensed with! He states also that the ceremony was instituted in memory of St. Peter, who three times denied Christ!*

JAMES DE MOLAY. A.D. 1311. Ferinsius le Mareschal, a secular knight, being examined, declared that his grandfather entered into the Order of the Temple, active, healthy, and blithesome as the birds and the dogs, but on the third day from his taking the vows he was dead, and, as he now suspects, was killed because he refused to participate in the iniquities practised by the brethren. An Augustine monk declared that he had heard a Templar say that a man after death had no more soul than a dog. Roger, rector of the church of Godmersham, swore that about fifteen years before he had an intention of entering into the Order of the Temple himself, and consulted Stephen Queynterel, one of the brothers, on the subject, who advised him not to do so, and stated that they had three articles amongst themselves in their order, known only to God, the devil, and the brethren of the Temple, and the said Stephen would not reveal to the deponent what those articles were.

The vicar of the church of Saint Clement at Sandwich had *heard* that a boy had secreted himself in the large hall where the Templars held their chapter, and heard the Master preach to the brethren, and explain to them in what mode they might enrich themselves; and after the chapter was concluded, one of the brothers, in going out of the hall, dropped his girdle, which the boy found and carried to the brother who had so dropped it, when the latter drew his sword and instantly slew him! But to crown all, Brother John de Gertia, a Minorite, had *heard* from a certain woman called Cacocaca! who had it from Exvalettus, Preceptor of London, that one of the servants of the Templars entered the hall where the chapter was

---

* This knight had been tortured in the Temple at Paris, by the brothers of St Dominic, in the presence of the grand inquisitor, and he made his confession when suffering on the rack; he afterwards revoked it, and was then tortured into a withdrawal of his revocation, notwithstanding which the inquisitor made the unhappy wretch, in common with others, put his signature to the following interrogatory, "Interrogatus utrum *vi vel metu carceris* aut *tormentorum*, immiscuit in suâ depositione aliquam falsitatem, dicit *quod non!*"

held, and secreted himself, and after the door had been shut and locked by the last Templar who entered, and the key had been brought by him to the superior, the assembled Templars jumped up and went into another room, and opened a closet, and drew therefrom a certain black figure with shining eyes, and a cross, and they placed the cross before the Master, and the "culum idoli vel figuræ" they placed upon the cross, and carried it to the Master, who kissed the said image, (in ano), and all the others did the same after him; and when they had finished kissing, they all spat three times upon the cross, except one, who refused, saying, "I was a bad man in the world, and placed myself in this order for the salvation of my soul; what could I do worse? I will not do it;" and then the brethren said to him, "Take heed, and do as you see the Order do but he answered that he would not do so, and then they placed him in a well which stood in the midst of their house, and covered the well up, and left him to perish. Being asked as to the time when the woman heard this, the deponent stated that she told it to him about fourteen years back at London, where she kept a shop for her husband, Robert Cotacotal. This witness also knew a certain Walter Salvagyo of the family of Earl Warrenne, grandfather of the then earl, who, having entered into the Order of the Temple, was about two years afterwards entirely lost sight of by his family, and neither the earl nor any of his friends could ever learn what had become of him.

John Walby de Bust, another Minorite, had *heard* John de Dingeston say that *he had heard* that there was in a secret place of the house of the Templars at London a gilded head, and that when one of the Masters was on his deathbed, he summoned to his presence several preceptors, and told them that if they wished for power, and dominion, and honour, they must worship that head.

Brother Richard de Koefeld, a monk, had *heard* from John de Borna, who had it from the Knight Templar Walter le Bacheler, that every man who entered into the Order of the Temple had to sell himself to the devil; he had also *heard* from the priest Walter, rector of the church of Hodlee, who had it from a certain who was a priest of the said Walter le Bacheler, that there was one article in the profession of the Templars which might not be revealed to any living man.

Gasper de Nafferton, chaplain of the parish of Ryde, deposed that three years back he was in the employ of the Templars for about six months, during which period William de Pokelington was received into the Order; that he well recollected that the said William made his appearance at the Temple on Sunday evening, with the equipage and habit of a member of the Order, accompanied by Brother William de la More, the Master of the Temple, Brother William de Grafton, Preceptor of Ribbestane and Fontebriggs; and other brethren: that the same night, during the first watch, they assembled in the church, and caused the deponent to be awakened to say mass; that, after the celebration of the mass, they made the deponent with his clerk go out into the hall beyond the cloister, and then sent for the person who was to be received; and on his entry into the church one of the brethren immediately closed all the doors opening into the cloister, so that no one within the chambers could get out, and thus they remained till daylight; but what was done in the church the deponent knew not; the next day, however, he saw the said William clothed in the habit of a Templar, looking very sorrowful. The deponent also declared that he had threatened to peep through a secret door to see what was going on, but was warned that it was inevitable death so to do. He states that the next morning he went into the church, and found the books and crosses all removed from the places in which he had previously left them; that he afterwards saw the knight Templar Brother William deliver to the newly-received brother a large roll of paper, containing the rule of the Order, which the said newly-received brother was directed to transcribe in private; that after the departure of the said Brother William, the deponent approached the said newly-received brother, who was then diligently writing, and asked to be allowed to inspect the roll, but was told that none but members of the Order could be allowed to read it; that he was then about to depart, when Brother William made his appearance, and, astonished and confounded at the sight of the deponent, snatched up the roll and walked away with it, declaring, with a great oath, that he would never again allow it to go out of his hands.

Brother John de Donyngton, of the Order of the Minorites, the seventy-sixth witness examined, being sworn, deposed that some years back an old veteran of the Temple (whose name he could not recollect) told him that the Order possessed four chief idols in England, one at London in the sacristy of the Temple; another at the preceptory of Bistelesham; a third at Bruere in Lincolnshire; and the fourth in some place beyond the Humber (the name of which he had forgotten;) that Brother William de la More, the Master of the Temple, introduced the melancholy idolatry of the Templars into England, and brought with him into the country a great roll, whereon were inscribed in large characters the wicked practices and observances of the Order. The said old veteran also told the deponent that many of the Templars carried idols about with them in boxes, &c. &c.

The deponent further states that he recollected well that a private gentleman, Master William de Shokerwyk, a short time back, had prepared to take the vows of the Order, and carried his treasures and all the property he had to the Temple at London; and that as he was about to deposit it in the treasury, one of the brethren of the Temple heaved a profound sigh, and Master William de Shokerwyk having asked what ailed him, he immediately replied, "It will be the worse for you, brother, if you enter our order. "That the said Master William asked why, and the Templar replied, "You see us externally, but not internally; take heed what you do; but I shall say no more;" and the deponent further declares, that on another occasion the said Master William entered into the Temple Hall, and found there an old Templar, who was playing at the game called Daly; and the old Templar observing that there was no one in the hall besides himself and the said Master William, said to the latter, "If you enter into our order, it will be the worse for you."

The witness then goes into a rambling account of various transactions in the East, tending to show that the Templars were in alliance with the Saracens, and had acted with treachery towards the Christian cause!*

After the delivery of all this hearsay, these vague suspicions and monstrous improbabilities, the notaries proceeded to arrange the valuable testimony adduced, and on the 22nd of April all the Templars in custody in the Tower and in the prisons of the city were assembled before the inquisitors and the bishops of London and Chichester, in the church of the Holy Trinity, to hear the depositions and attestations of the witnesses publicly read. The Templars required copies of these depositions, which were granted them, and they were allowed eight days from that period to bring forward any defences or privileges they wished to make use of. Subsequently, before the expiration of the eight days, the officer of the bishop of London was sent to the Tower with scriveners and witnesses, to know if they would then set up any matters of defence, to whom the Templars replied that they were unlettered men, ignorant of law, and that all means of defence were denied them, since they were not permitted to employ those who could afford them fit counsel and advice. They observed, however, that they were desirous of publicly proclaiming the faith, and the religion of themselves and of the Order to which they belonged, of showing the privileges conceded to them by the chief pontiffs, and their own dépotions taken before the inquisitors, all which they said they wished to make use of in their defence. *JAMES DE MOLAY. A.D. 1311.*

On the eighth day, being Thursday the 29th of April, they appeared before the papal inquisitors and the bishops of London and Chichester, in the church of All Saints of Berkyngecherche, and presented to them the following declaration, which they had drawn up amongst themselves, as the only defence they had to offer against the injustice, the tyranny, and the persecution of their powerful oppressors; adding, that if they had in any way done wrong, they were ready to submit themselves to the Orders of the church.

This declaration is written in the Norman French of that day, and is as follows:

"Conue chese seit a nostre honurable pere, le ercevesque de Canterbiere, primat de toute Engletere, e a touz prelaz de seinte Eglise, e a touz Cristiens, qe touz les freres du Temple que sumes ici assemblez et chescune singulere persone par sen sumes cristien nostre seignur Jesu

---

* *Acta contra Templarios.— Cocil. Mag. Brit.* tom. ii. p. 358—364.

Crist, e creoms en Dieu Pere omnipotent, qui fist ciel e terre, e en Jesu soen fiz, qui fust conceu du Seint Esperit, nez de la Virgine Marie, soeffrit peine e passioung morut sur la croiz pour touz peccheours, descendist e enferns, e le tierz jour releva de mort en vie, e mounta en ciel, siet au destre soen Pere, e vendra au jour de juise, ,juger les vifs e les morz, qui fu saunz commencement, e serra saunz fyn; e creoms comme seynte eglise crets, e nous enseigne. E que nostre religion est foundee sus obe-dience, chastete, vivre sans propre, aider a conquere la seint terre de Jerusalem, a force e a poer, qui Dieu nous ad preste. E nyorms e firme-ment en countredioms touz e chescune singulere persone, par sei toutes maneres de heresies e malvaistes, que sount encountre la foi de Seinte Eglise. E prioms pour Dieu e pour charite a vous, que estes en lieu nostre

seinte pere l' apostoile, que nous puissoms aver lez drettures de seinte eglise, comme ceus que sount les filz de sainte eglise, que bien avoms garde, e tenu la foi, e la lei de seinte eglise, e nostre religion, la quele est bone, honeste e juste, solom ordenaunces, e les privileges de la court de Rome avons grauntez, confermez, e canonizez par commun concile, priviliges ensemblement ou lestablisement, e la regie sount en la dite court enregistrez. E mettoms en dur e en mal eu touz Cristiens saune noz anoisourz, par la ou nous avoms este conversaunt, comment nous avoms nostre vie demene. E se nous avoms rien mesprys de aucun parole en nos examinations par ignorance de seu, si comme nous sumes genz laics prest sumes, a ester a lesgard de seint eglise, comme cely que mourust pour nouz en la beneite de croiz. E nous creoms fermement touz les sacre-menz de seinte eglise. E nous vous prioms pour Dieu e pour salvacioun de vous almes, que vous nous jugez si comme vous volez respoundre pour vous et pour nous devaunt Dieu: e que nostre examinement puet estre leu e oii devaunt nous e devaunt le people, solom le respouns e le langage que fust dit devaunt vous, e escrit en papier*

"Be it known to our honourable father, the archbishop of Canterbury, primate of all England, and to all the prelates of holy church, and to all Christians, that all we brethren of the Temple here assembled, and every of one of us are Christians, and believe in our Saviour Jesus Christ, in God the Father omnipotent, &c. &c. ..."

"And we believe all that the holy church believes and teaches us. We declare that our religion is founded on vows of obedience, chastity, and poverty, and of aiding in the conquest of the Holy Land of Jerusalem, with all the power and might that God affordeth us. And we firmly deny and contradict, one and all of us, all manner of heresy and evil doings,

contrary to the faith of holy church. And for the love of God, and for charity, we beseech you, who represent our holy father the pope, that we

---

* *Concil. Mag. Brit.* tom. ii. p. 364.

may be treated like true children of the church, for we have well guarded and preserved the faith and the law of the church, and of our own religion, the which is good, honest, and just, according to the ordinances and the privileges of the court of Rome, granted, confirmed, and canonized by common council; the which privileges, together with the rule of our order, are enregistered in the said court. And we would bring forward all Christians, (save our enemies and slanderers), with whom we are conversant, and among whom we have resided, to say how and in what manner we have spent our lives. And if, in our examinations, we have said or done anything wrong through ignorance of a word, since we are unlettered men, we are ready to suffer for holy church like him who died for us on the blessed cross. And we believe all the sacraments of the church. And we beseech you, for the love of God, and as you hope to be saved, that you judge us as you will have to answer for yourselves and for us before God; and we pray that our examination may be read and heard before ourselves and all the people, *in the very language and words in which it was given before you, and written down on paper."*

The above declaration was presented by Brother William de la More, the Master of the Temple; the Knights Templars Philip de Mewes, Preceptor of Garwy; William de Burton, Preceptor of Cumbe; Radulph de Maison, Preceptor of Ewell; Michael de Baskevile, Preceptor of London; Thomas de Wothrope, Preceptor of Bistelesham; William de Warwick, Priest; and Thomas de Burton, Chaplain of the Order; together with twenty serving brothers. The same day the inquisitors and the two bishops proceeded to the different prisons of the city to demand if the prisoners confined therein wished to bring forward anything in defence of the Order, who severally answered that they would adopt and abide by the declaration made by their brethren in the Tower. JAMES DE MOLAY. A.D. 1311.

It appears that in the prison of Aldgate there were confined Brother William de Sautre, Knight, Preceptor of Samford; Brother William de la Ford, Preceptor of Daney; Brother John de Coningeston, Preceptor of Getinges; Roger de Norreis, Preceptor of Cressing; Radulph de Barton, priest, Prior of the New Temple; and several serving brethren of the Order. In the prison of Crepelgate were detained William de Egendon, Knight, Preceptor of Schepeley; John de Moun, Knight, Preceptor of Dokesworth; and four serving brethren. In the prison of Ludgate were five serving brethren; and in Newgate was confined Brother Himbert Blanke, Knight, Grand Preceptor of Auvergne.

The above declaration of faith and innocence was far from agreeable to the papal inquisitors, who required a confession of guilt, and the torture was once more directed to be applied. The king sent fresh orders to the mayor and the sheriffs of the city of London, commanding them to place the Templars in separate dungeons; to load them with chains and fetters; to permit the myrmidons of the inquisitors to pay periodical visits to see that the wishes and intentions of the inquisitors, with regard to the severity of the confinement, were properly carried into effect; and, lastly, to inflict torture upon the bodies of the Templars, and generally to do whatever should be thought fitting and expedient in the premises, according to ecclesiastical law.* In conformity with these orders, we learn from the record of the proceedings, that the Templars were placed in solitary confinement in loathsome dungeons; that they were placed on a short allowance of bread and water, and periodically visited by the agents of the inquisition; that they were moved from prison to prison, and from dungeon to dungeon; were now treated with rigour, and anon with indulgence; and were then visited by learned prelates, and acute doctors in theology, who, by exhortation, persuasion, and by menace, attempted in every possible mode to wring from them the required avowals. We learn that all the engines of terror wielded by the church were put in force, and that torture was unsparingly applied "*usque ad judicium sanguinis!*" The places in which these atrocious scenes were enacted were the Tower, the prisons of Aldgate, Ludgate, Newgate, Bishopsgate, and Crepelgate, the house formerly belonging to John de Banguel, and the tenements once the property of the brethren of penitence.† It appears that some French monks were sent over to administer the torture to the unhappy captives, and that they were questioned and examined in the presence of notaries whilst suffering under the torments of the rack. The relentless perseverance and the incessant exertions of the foreign inquisitors were at last rewarded by a splendid triumph over the powers of endurance of two poor serving brethren, and one chaplain of the Order of the Temple, who were at last induced to make the longdesired avowals.

On the 23rd of June, Brother Stephen de Stapelbrugge, described as an apostate and fugitive of the Order of the Temple, captured by the king's officers in the city of Salisbury, deposed in the house of the head gaoler of Newgate, in the presence of the bishops of London and Chichester, the chancellor of the archbishop of Canterbury, Hugh de Walkeneby, doctor of theology, and other clerical witnesses, that there were two modes of profession in the Order of the Temple, the one good and lawful, and the other contrary to the Christian faith; that he himself was received into the Order by Brother Brian le Jay, Grand Preceptor of England at Dynneslee, and was led into the chapel, the door of which was closed as soon as he had entered; that a cross was placed before the Master, and that

JAMES DE MOLAY. A.D. 1311.

JAMES DE MOLAY. A.D. 1311.

---

* Vobis, præfati vicecomites, mandamus quod illos, quos dicti prælati et inquisitors, seu aliquis eorum, cum uno saltem inquisitore, deputaverint ad supervidendum quod dicta custodia bene fiat, id supervidere; et corpora dictroum Templariorum in QUÆSTIONIBUS et aliis ad hoc convenientibus, ponere; et alia, quæ in hac parte secundum legem ecclesiasticam fueint facienda, facere permittatis. Claus. 4, E. 2. m. 8. Acta *Rymeri*, tom. iii. p. 290.

† *M. S. BodL F.* 5, 2. *Concil.* p. 364, 365. Acta *Rymeri*, tom. iii. p. 228, 231,232.

a brother of the Temple, with a drawn sword, stood on either side of him; that the Master said to him, "Do you see this image of the crucifixion?" to which he replied, "I see it, my lord," that the Master then said to him, "You must deny that Christ Jesus was God and man, and that Mary was his mother; and you must spit upon this cross which the deponent, through immediate fear of death, did with his mouth, but not with his heart, and he spat beside the cross, and not on it; and then falling down upon his knees, with eyes uplifted, with his hands clasped, with bitter tears and sighs, and devout ejaculations, he besought the mercy and the favour of holy church, declaring that he cared not for the death of the body, or for any amount of penance, but only for the salvation of his soul.

On Saturday, the 25th of June, Brother Thomas Tocci de Thoroldeby serving brother of the Order of the Temple, described as an apostate who had escaped from Lincoln after his examination at that place by the papal inquisitors, but had afterwards surrendered himself to the king's officers, was brought before the bishops of London and Chichester, the arch-deacon of Salisbury, and others of the clergy in St. Martin's Church in Vinetria; and being again examined, he repeated the statement made in his first deposition, but added some particulars with regard to penances imposed and absolutions pronounced in the chapter, showing the differ-ence between sins and defaults, the priest having to deal with the one, and the Master with the other. He declared that the little cords were worn from honourable motives, and relates a story of his being engaged in a battle against the Saracens, in which he lost his cord, and was punished by the Grand Master for a default in coming home without it. He gives the same account of the secrecy of the chapters as all the other breth-ren, states that the members of the Order were forbidden to confess to the friars mendicants, and were enjoined to confess to their own chap-lains; that they did nothing contrary to the Christian faith, and as to their endeavouring to promote the advancement of the Order by any means, right or wrong, that exactly the contrary was the case, as there was a statute in the Order to the effect, that if any one should be found to have acquired anything unjustly, he should be deprived of his habit, and be ex-pelled the Order. Being asked what induced him to become an apostate, and to fly from his order, he replied that it was through fear of death, because the abbot of Lagny, (the papal inquisitor), when he examined him at Lincoln, asked him if he would not confess anything further, and he answered that he knew of nothing further to confess, unless he were to say things that were not true; and that *the abbot, laying his hand upon his breast, swore by the word of God that he would make him confess before he had done with him!* and that being terribly frightened he afterwards bribed the gaoler of the castle of Lincoln, giving him forty florins to let him make his escape.

The abbot of Lagny, indeed, was as good as his word, for on the 29th

JAMES
MOLAY
A.D. 13

of June, four days after this imprudent avowal, Brother Thomas Tocci de Thoroldeby was brought back to Saint Martin's Church, and there, in the presence of the same parties, he made a third confession, in which he declares that, coerced by two Templars with drawn swords in their hands, he denied Christ with his mouth, but not with his heart; and spat *beside* the cross, but not on it; that he was required to spit upon the image of the Virgin Mary, but contrived, instead of doing so, to give her a kiss on the foot. He declares that he had heard Brian le Jay, the Master of the Temple at London, say a hundred times over, that Jesus Christ was not the true God, but a man, and that the smallest hair out of the beard of one Saracen was of more worth than the whole body of any Christian. He declares that he was once standing in the presence of Brother Brian, when some poor people besought charity of him for the love of God and our lady the blessed Virgin Mary; and he answered, "*Que dame, alez vous pendre a vostre dame*"—"What lady? go and be hanged to your lady," and violently casting a halfpenny into the mud, he made the poor people hunt for it, although it was in the depth of a severe winter. He also relates that at the chapters the priest stood like a beast, and had nothing to do but to repeat the psalm, "God be merciful unto us, and bless us," which was read at the closing of the chapter. (The Templars, by the way, must have been strange idolaters to have closed their chapters, in which they are accused of worshipping a cat, a man's head, and a black idol, with the reading of the beautiful psalm, "God be merciful unto us, and bless us, and show us the light of thy countenance, that *thy way may be known upon earth,* thy saving health among all nations," &c. Psalm lxvii.) This witness further states, that the priest had no power to impose a heavier penance than a day's fast on bread and water, and could not even do that without the permission of the brethren. He is made also to relate that the Templars always favoured the Saracens in the holy wars in Palestine, and oppressed the Christians! and he declares, speaking of himself, that for three years before he had never seen the body of Christ without thinking of the devil, nor could he remove that evil thought from his heart by prayer, or in any other way that he knew of; but that very morning he had heard mass with great devotion, and since then had thought only of Christ, and thinks there is no one in the Order of the Temple whose soul will be saved, unless a reformation takes place.*

Previous to this period, the ecclesiastical council had again assembled, and these last depositions of Brothers Stephen de Stapelbrugge and Thomas Tocci de Thoroldeby having been produced before them, the following solemn farce was immediately publicly enacted. It is thus described in the record of the proceedings:

JAMES DE MOLAY. A.D. 1311.

JAMES DE MOLAY. A.D. 1311.

* *Concil. Mag. Brit.,* tom. ii. p. 383—387.

"To the praise and glory of the name of the most high Father, and of the Son, and of the Holy Ghost, to the confusion of heretics, and the strengthening of all faithful Christian begins the public record of the reconciliation of the penitent heretics, returning to the orthodox faith published in the council, celebrated at London in the year 1311.

"In the name of God, Amen. In the year of the incarnation of our Lord 1311, on the twenty-seventh day of the month of June, in the hall of the palace of the bishop of London, before the venerable fathers the Lord Robert by the grace of God archbishop of Canterbury, primate of all England, and his suffragans in provincial council assembled, appeared Brother Stephen de Stapelbrugge, of the Order of the chivalry of the Temple; and the denying of Christ and the blessed Virgin Mary his mother, the spitting upon the cross, and the heresies and errors acknowledged and confessed by him in his deposition being displayed, the same Stephen asserted in full council, before the people of the City of London, introduced for the occasion, that all those things so deposed by him were true, and that to that confession he would wholly adhere; humbly confessing his error on his bended knees, with his hands clasped, with much lamentation and many tears, he again and again besought the mercy and pity of holy mother church, offering to abjure all heresies and errors, and praying them to impose on him a fitting penance, and then the book of the holy gospels being placed in his hands, he abjured the aforesaid heresies in this form: JAMES DE MOLAY. A.D. 1311.

"I, brother Stephen de Stapelbrugge, of the Order of the chivalry of the Temple, do solemnly confess," &c. &c. (he repeats his confession, makes his abjuration, and then proceeds); "and if at any time hereafter I shall happen to relapse into the same errors, or deviate from any of the articles of the faith, I will account myself *ipso facto* excommunicated; I will stand condemned as a manifest perjured heretic, and the punishment inflicted on perjured relapsed heretics shall be forthwith imposed upon me without further trial or judgment!!"

He was then sworn upon the holy gospels to stand to the sentence of the church in the matter, after which Brother Thomas Tocci de Thoroldeby was brought forward to go through the same monstrous ceremony, which being concluded, these two poor serving brothers of the Order of the Temple, who were so ignorant that they could not write, were made to place their mark (*loco subscriptionis*) on the record of the abjuration.

"And then our lord the archbishop of Canterbury, for the purpose of absolving and reconciling to the unity of the church the aforesaid Thomas and Stephen, conceded his authority and that of the whole council to the bishop of London, in the presence of me the notary, specially summoned for the occasion, in these words: 'We grant to you the authority of God, of the blessed Mary, of the blessed Thomas the Martyr our patron, and of all the saints of God (*sanctorum atque sanctarum* Dei) to us conceded, and also the authority of the pres-

ent council to us transferred, to the end that thou mayest reconcile to
the unity of the church these miserables, separated from her by their
repudiation of the faith, and now brought back again to her bosom,
reserving to ourselves and the council the right of imposing a fit
penance for their transgressions!'" And as there were two penitents,
the bishop of Chichester was joined to the bishop of London for the
purpose of pronouncing the absolution, which two bishops, putting
on their mitres and pontificals, and being assisted by twelve priests
in sacerdotal vestments, placed themselves in seats at the western
entrance of the cathedral church of Saint Patil, and the penitents, with
bended knees, humbly prostrating themselves in prayer upon the steps
before the door of the church, the members of the council and the people of the city standing around; and the psalm, *"Have mercy upon me,
O God, after thy great goodness,"* having been chaunted from the beginning to the end, and the subjoined prayers and sermon having, been gone
through, they absolved the said penitents, and received them back to the
unity of the church in the following form:

"In the name of God, Amen. Since by your confession we find that
you, Brother Stephen de Stapelbrugge, have denied Christ Jesus and the
blessed Virgin Mary, and have spat beside the cross, and now taking better advice wishest to return to the unity of the holy church with a true
heart and sincere faith, as you assert, and all heretical depravity having for that purpose been previously abjured by you according to the
form of the church, we, by the authority of the council, absolve you from
the bonds of excommunication wherewith you were held fast, and we
reconcile you to the unity of the church, if you shall have returned to
her in sincerity of heart, and shall have obeyed her injunctions imposed
upon you."

Brother Thomas Tocci de Thoroldeby was then absolved and reconciled to the church in the same manner, after which various psalms (Gloria
Patri, Kyrie Eleyson, Christe Eleyson, &c. &c.) were sung, and prayers
were offered up, and then the ceremony was concluded.*

On the 1st of July, an avowal of guilt was wrung by the inquisitors
from Brother John de Stoke, chaplain of the Order, who, being brought
before the bishops of London and Chichester in St. Martin's church,
deposed that he was received in the mode mentioned by him on his first
examination; but a year and fifteen days after that reception, being at the
preceptory of Garwy in the diocese of Hereford, he was called into the
chamber of Brother James de Molay, the Grand Master of the Order, who,
in the presence of two other Templars of foreign extraction, informed
him that he wished to make proof of his obedience, and commanded him
to take a seat at the foot of the bed, and the deponent did so. The Grand

* *Concil. Mag. Brit.,* tom. ii, p. 388, 389.

Master then sent into the church for the crucifix, and two serving brothers, with naked swords in their hands, stationed themselves on either side of the doorway. As soon as the crucifix made its appearance, the Grand Master, pointing to the figure of our Saviour nailed thereon, asked the deponent whose image it was, and he answered, "The image of Jesus Christ, who suffered on the cross for the redemption of mankind;" but the Grand Master exclaimed, "Thou sayest wrong, and are much mistakened, for he was the son of a certain woman, and was crucified because he called himself the Son of God, and I myself have been in the place where he was born and crucified, and thou must now deny him whom this image represents." The deponent exclaimed, "Far be it from me to deny my Saviour but the Grand Master told him he must do it, or he would be put into a sack and be carried to a place which he would find by no means agreeable, and there were swords in the room, and brothers ready to use them, &c. &c.; and the deponent asked if such was the custom of the Order, and if all the brethren did the same; and being answered in the affirmative, he, through fear of immediate death, denied Christ with his tongue, but not with his heart. Being asked in whom he was told to put his faith after he had denied Christ Jesus, he replies, "In that great Omnipotent God who created the heaven and the earth."*

JAMES DE MOLAY. A.D. 1311.

Such, in substance, was the whole of the criminatory evidence that could be wrung by torture, by a long imprisonment, and by hardships of every kind, from the Templars in England. It amounts simply to an assertion that they compelled all whom they received into their order to renounce the Christian religion, a thing perfectly incredible. Is it to be supposed that the many good Christians of high birth, and honour, and exalted piety, who entered into the Order of the Temple, taking the cross for their standard and their guide, would thus suddenly have cast their faith and their religion to the winds? Would they not 'rather have denounced the impiety and iniquity to the officers of the Inquisition, and to the pope, the superior of the Order?

"Ainsi que la vertu, le crime a ses degrés
Et jamais on n'a vu la timide innocence
Passer subitement à l'extreme licence.
Un seul jour ne fait point d'un mortel vertueux
Un perfide apostat, un traitre audacieux."

Phedre, Acte iv. Scene 2.

On Saturday, the 3rd of July, the archbishop of Canterbury, and the

* Acta fuerunt hæc die et loco prædictis, præsentibus patribus antedictis, et venerandæ discretionis viris magistris Michaele de Bercham, cancellario domini archiepiscipi Cantuar. . . . et me Ranulpho de Waltham, London, episcoporum notaries publicis.—*Acta contra Templarios. Concil. Mag. Brit.*, tom. ii. p. 387, 388.

bishops, the clergy, and the people of the city of London, were again assembled around the western door of Saint Paul's cathedral, and Brother John de Stoke, chaplain of the Order of the Temple, made his public recantation of the heresies confessed by him, and was then absolved and reconciled to the church in the same manner as Brothers Thomas de Stapelbrugge and Tocci de Thoroldeby, after which a last effort was made to bend the remaining Templars to the wishes of the papal inquisitors.

JAMES DE MOLAY. A.D. 1311.

On Monday, July 5th, at the request of the ecclesiastical council, the bishop of Chichester had an interview with Sir William de la More, the Master of the Temple, taking with him certain learned lawyers, theologians, and scriveners. He exhorted and earnestly pressed him to abjure the heresies of which he stood convicted, by his own confessions and those of his brethren, respecting the absolutions pronounced by him in the chapters, and submit himself to the disposition of the church; but the Master declared that he had never been guilty of the heresies mentioned, and that he would not abjure crimes which he had never committed; so he was sent back to his dungeon.

The next day, (Tuesday, July the 6th), the bishops of London, Winchester, and Chichester, had an interview in Southwark with the Knight Templar, Philip de Mewes, Preceptor of Garwy, and some serving brethren of the New Temple at London, and told them that they were manifestly guilty of heresy, as appeared from the pope's bulls, and the depositions taken against the Order both in England and France, and also from their own confessions regarding the absolutions pronounced in their chapters, explaining to them that they had grievously erred in believing that the Master of the Temple, who was a mere layman, had power to absolve them from their sins by pronouncing an absolution in the mode previously described, and they warned them that if they persisted in that error they would be condemned as heretics, and that as they could not clear themselves therefrom, it behoved them to abjure all the heresies of which they were accused. The Templars replied that they were ready to abjure the error they had fallen into respecting the absolution, and *all heresies of every hind*, before the archbishop of Canterbury and the prelates of the council, whenever they should be required so to do, and they humbly and reverently submitted themselves to the Orders of the church, beseeching pardon and grace.

JAMES DE MOLAY. A.D. 1311.

A sort of compromise was then made with most of the Templars in custody in London. They were required publicly to repeat a form of confession and abjuration drawn up by the bishops of London and Chichester, and were then solemnly absolved and reconciled to the church in the following terms:

"In the name of God, Amen. Since you have confessed in due form before the ecclesiastical council of the province of Canter, bury that you have gravely erred concerning the sacrament of repentance, in believing that the absolution pronounced by the Master in chapter had as much efficacy as is implied in the words pronounced by bim, that is to say, 'The sins which you have omitted to confess through shamefacedness, or through fear of the justice of the Order, we, by virtue of the power delegated to us by God and our lord the pope, forgive you, as far as we are able and since you have confessed that you cannot entirely purge yourselves from the heresies set forth under the apostolic bull, and taking sage counsel with a good heart and unfeigned faith, have submitted yourselves to the judgment and the mercy of the church, having previously abjured the aforesaid heresies, and all heresies of every description, we, by the authority of the council, absolve you from the chain of excommunication wherewith you have been bound, and reconcile you once more to the unity of the church, &c. &c."

On the 9th of July, Brother Michael de Baskevile, Knight, Preceptor of London, and seventeen other Templars, were absolved and reconciled in full council, in the Episcopal Hall of the see of London, in the presence of a vast concourse of the citizens. On the 10th of the same month, the Preceptors of Dokes-worth, Getinges, and Samford, the guardian of the Temple church at London, Brother Radulph de Evesham, chaplain, with other priests, knights, and serving brethren of the Order, were absolved by the bishops of London, Exeter, Winchester, and Chichester, in the presence of the archbishop of Canterbury and the whole ecclesiastical council. *JAMES DE MOLAY. A.D. 1311.*

The next day many more members of the fraternity were publicly reconciled to the church on the steps before the south door of Saint Pauls cathedral, and were afterwards present at the celebration of high mass in the interior of the sacred edifice, when they advanced in a body towards the high altar bathed in tears, and falling down on their knees, they devoutly kissed the sacred emblems of Christianity.

The day after, (July 12), nineteen other Templars were publicly absolved and reconciled to the church at the same place, in the presence of the earls of Leicester, Pembroke, and Warwick, and afterwards assisted in like manner at the celebration of high mass. The priests of the Order made their confessions and abjurations in Latin; the knights pronounced them in Norman French, and the serving brethren for the most part repeated them in English.* The vast concourse of people collected together could have comprehended but very little of what was uttered, whilst the appearance of the penitent brethren, and the public spectacle of their recantation, answered the views of the papal inquisitors, and doubtless impressed the commonalty with a conviction of the guilt of the Order. Many of the Templars were too sick (suffering doubtless from the effect of torture) to be brought down to St. Paul's, and were therefore absolved

* *Concil. Mag. Brit.,* tom. ii. p. 390, 391.

and reconciled to the church by the bishops of London, Winchester, and Chichester, at Saint Mary's chapel near the Tower.

Among the prisoners absolved at the above chapel were many old veteran warriors in the last stage of decrepitude and decay. "They were so old and so infirm," says the public notary who recorded the proceedings, "that they were unable to stand their confessions were consequently made before two masters in theology; they were then led before the west door of the chapel, and were publicly reconciled to the church by the bishop of Chichester; after which they were brought into the sacred building, and were placed on their knees before the high altar, which they devoutly kissed, whilst the tears trickled down their furrowed cheeks. All these penitent Templars were now released from prison, and directed to do penance in different monasteries. Precisely the same form of proceeding was followed at York: the reconciliations and absolution being there carried into effect before the south door of the cathedral.*

Thus terminated the proceedings against the Order of the Temple in England.

Similar measures had, in the mean time, been prosecuted against the Templars in all parts of Christendom, but no better evidence of their guilt than that above mentioned was ever discovered. The councils of Tarragona and Aragon, after applying the torture, pronounced the Order free from heresy. In Portugal and in Germany the Templars were declared innocent, and in no place situate beyond the sphere of the influence of the king of France and his creature the pope was a single Templar condemned to death.†

On the 16th of October a general council of the Church, which had been convened by the pope to pronounce the abolition of the Order, assembled at Vienne near Lyons in France. It was opened by the holy

pontiff in person, who caused the different confessions and avowals of the Templars to be read over before the assembled nobles and prelates, and then moved the suppression of an order wherein had been discovered such crying iniquities and sinful abominations; but the entire council, with the exception of an Italian prelate, nephew of the pope, and the three French bishops of Rheims, Sens, and Rouen, all creatures of Philip, who had severally condemned large bodies of Templars to be burnt at the stake in their respective dioceses, were unanimously of opin-

---

* *Concil. Mag. Brit.*, tom. ii. p. 394—401.

† *Concilia Hispaniæ*, tom. v. p. 233. *Zurita*, lib. v. c. 73. 101. *Mariana*, lib. xv. cap. 10. *Mutius, chron.* lib. xxii. p. 211. *Raynouard*, p. 199—204.

‡ Ut det Templariis audientiuam sive defensionem. In hac sentential concordant omnes prælati Italiæ præter unum, Hispaniæ, Theutoniæ, Daniæ, Angliæ, Scotiæ, Hiberni æ, etc. etc., ex second. Vit. Clem. V. p. 43.—*Rainald* ad ann. 1311, n. 55. *Walsingham*, p. 99. *Antiq. Britann.*, p. 210.

ion, that before the suppression of so celebrated and illustrious an order, which had rendered such great and signal services to the Christian faith, the members belonging to it ought to be heard in their own defence.‡ Such a proceeding, however, did not suit the views of the pope and king Philip, and the assembly was abruptly dismissed by the holy pontiff, who declared that since they were unwilling to adopt the necessary measures, he himself, out of the plenitude of the papal authority, would supply every defect. Accordingly, at the commencement of the following year, the pope summoned a private consistory; and several cardinals and French bishops having been gained over, the holy pontiff abolished the Order by an apostolical ordinance, perpetually prohibiting every one from thenceforth entering into it, or accepting or wearing the habit thereof, or representing themselves to be Templars, on pain of excommunication.*

On the 3rd of April, the second session of the council was opened by the pope at Vienne. King Philip and his three sons were present, accompanied by a large body of troops, and the papal decree abolishing the Order was published before the assembly.† The members of the council appear to have been called together merely to hear the decree read. History does not inform of any discussion with reference to it, nor of any suffrages having been taken.

JAMES DE MOLAY. A.D. 1312.

A few months after the close of these proceedings, Brother William de la More, the Master of the Temple in England, died of a broken heart in his solitary dungeon in the Tower, persisting with his last breath in the maintenance of the innocence of his order. King Edward, in pity for his misfortunes, directed the constable of the Tower to hand over his goods and chattels, valued at the sum of 4*l.* 19*s.* 11*d.*, to his executors, to be employed in the liquidation of his debts, and he commanded Geoffrey de la Lee, guardian of the lands of the Templars, to pay the arrears of his prison pay (2*s.* per diem) to the executor, Roger Hunsingon.‡

Among the Cotton MS. is a list of the Masters of the Temple, otherwise the Grand Priors or Grand Preceptors of England, compiled under the direction of the prior of the Hospital of Saint John at Clerkenwell, to the intent that the brethren of that fraternity might remember the ancient Masters of the Temple in their prayers.§ A few names have been omitted which are supplied in the following list:

Magister R. de Pointon.1

Rocelinus de Fossa.²

JAMES DE MOLAY. A.D. 1312.

---

* *Muratorii* collect. Tom. iii. p. 448; tom. x. col. 377. *Mariana.* Tom. iii. p. 157. *Raynouard*, p. 191, 192.

† *Raynouard* ut supra. Tertia vita Clem. V.

‡ Pro executoribus testamenti Wilielmi de la More, quondam Magistri militiæ Templi in Anglia, claus 6. E. 2. m. 15. Acta *Rymeri*, tom. iii. p. 380.

§ Registr. Hosp. S. Joh. Jerus. *Cotton* MS. Nero E. vi. p. 60. fol. 466.

Richard de Hastings,[3] A.D. 1160.
Richard Mallebeench.[4]
Geoffrey, son of Stephen,[5] A.D. 1180.
Thomas Berard, A.D. 1200.
Amaric de St. Maur[6], A.D. 1203.
Alan Marcel,[7] A.D. 1224.
Amberaldus, A.D. 1229.
Robert Mountforde,[8] A.D. 1234.
Robert Sanford,[9] A.D. 1241.
Amadeus de Morestello, A.D. 1254.
Himbert Peraut,[10] A.D. 1270.
Robert Turvile,[11] A.D. 1290.
Guido de Foresta,[12] A.D. 1292.
James de Molay, A.D. 1293.
Brian le Jay,[13] A.D. 1295.
WILLIAM DE LA MORE THE MARTYR.

JAMES DE MOLAY. A.D. 1313.

The only other Templar in England whose fate merits particular attention is Brother Himbert Blanke, the Grand Preceptor of Auvergne. He appears to have been a knight of high honour and of stern unbending pride. From first to last he had boldly protested against the violent proceedings of the inquisitors, and had fearlessly maintained, amid all trials, his own innocence and that of his order. This illustrious Templar had fought under four successive Grand Masters in defence of the Christian faith in Palestine, and after the fall of Acre, had led in person several daring expeditions against the infidels. For these meritorious services he was rewarded in the following manner:—After having been tortured and half-starved in the English prisons for the space of five years, he was condemned, as he would make no confession of guilt, to be shut up in a loathsome dungeon, to be loaded with double chains, and to be occasionally visited by the agents of the inquisition, to

[1] *Lansdown*, MS. 207. E. vol. v. fol. 317.

[2] Ib., fol. 284.

[3] Ib., fol. 162, 163, 317.

[4] Ib., fol. 467.

[5] Ib., fol. 201.

[6] Acta Rymeri, tom. i. p. 134, ad ann. 1203. He was one of those who advised king John to sign Magna Charta.—*Matt.* Par., p. 253—255.

[7] Ib., p. 258, 270. *Matt.* Par., p. 314.

[8] Acta *Rymeri*, tom. i. p. 342, 344, 345. He was employed to negotiate a marriage between King Henry the Third and the fair Eleanor of Provence.

[9] *Matt. Par.*, p. 615, et in additamentis, p. 480.

[10] Concil. Mag. Brit., tom. ii. p. 340.

[11] Ib., p. 339, 341, 344.

[12] Ib., p. 335, 343. *Prynne*, collect 3, 143.

[13] Acta *Rymeri*, tom. i. part iii. p. 104.

see if he would confess *nothing further!** In this miserable situation he remained until death at last put an end to his sufferings.

James de Molay, the Grand Master of the Temple, Guy, the Grand Preceptor, a nobleman of illustrious birth, brother to the prince of Dauphiny, Hugh de Peralt, the Visitor-general of the Order, and the Grand Preceptor of Aquitaine, had now languished in the prisons of France for the space of five years and a half. The Grand Master had been compelled to make a confession which he afterwards disowned and stigmatized as a forgery, swearing that if the cardinals who had subscribed it had been of a different cloth, he would have proclaimed them liars, and would have challenged them to mortal combat.† The other knights had also made confessions which they had subsequently revoked. The secrets of the dark prisons of these illustrious Templars have never been brought to light, but on the 18th of March, A.D. 1313, a public scaffold was erected before the cathedral church of Notre Dame, at Paris, and the citizens were summoned to hear the Order of the Temple convicted by the mouths of its chief officers, of the sins and iniquities charged against it. The four knights, loaded with chains and surrounded by guards, were then brought upon the scaffold by the provost, and the bishop of Alba read their confessions aloud in the presence of the assembled populace. The papal legate then, turning towards the Grand Master and his companions, called upon them to renew, in the hearing of the people, the avowals which they had previously made of the guilt of their order. Hugh de Peralt, the Visitor-General, and the Preceptor of the Temple of Aquitaine, signified their assent to whatever was demanded of them, but the Grand Master raising his arms bound with chains towards heaven, and advancing to the edge of the scaffold, declared in a loud voice, that to say that which was untrue was a crime, both in the sight of God and man. "I do," said he, "confess my guilt, which consists in having, to my shame and dishonour, suffered myself, through the pakn of torture and the fear of death, to give utterance to falsehoods, imputing scandalous sins and iniquities to an illustrious order," which hath nobly served the cause of Christianity. I disdain to seek a wretched and disgraceful existence by engrafting another lie upon the original falsehood." He was here interrupted by the provost and his officers, and Guy, the Grand Preceptor, having commenced with strong asseverations of his innocence, they were both hurried back to prison.

King Philip was no sooner informed of the result of this strange proceeding, than, upon the first impulse of his indignation, without consulting either pope, or bishop, or ecclesiastical council, he commanded

<small>JAMES DE
MOLAY.
A.D. 1313.</small>

---

* In vilissimo carcere, ferro duplici constrictus, jussus est recludi, et ibidem, donec aliud ordinatum extiterit, reservari; et interim visitari, ad videndum si vellet *alterius aliqua confiteri!* —Concil. Mag. Brit., tom. ii. p. 393.

† *Processus contra Templarios. Dupuy,* p. 128, 139. *Raynourard,* p. 60.

JAMES DE
MOLAY.
A.D. 1313.
the instant execution of both these gallant noblemen. The same day at dusk they were led out of their dungeons, and were burned to death in a slow and lingering manner upon small fires of charcoal which were kindled on the little island in the Seine, between the king's garden and the convent of St. Augustine, close to the spot where now stands the equestrian statue of Henri IV.*

Thus perished the last Grand Master of the Temple.

The fate of the persecutors of the Order is not unworthy of notice.

A year and one month after the above horrible execution, the pope was attacked by a dysentery, and speedily hurried to his grave. The dead body was transported to Carpentras, where the court of Rome then resided; it was placed at night in a church which caught fire, and the mortal remains of the holy pontiff were almost entirely consumed. His relations quarrelled over the immense treasures he left behind him, and a vast sum of money, which had been deposited for safety in a church at Lucca, was stolen by a daring band of German and Italian freebooters.

Before the close of the same year, King Philip died of a lingering disease which baffled all the art of his medical attendants, and the condemned criminal, upon the strength of whose information the Templars were originally arrested, was hanged for fresh crimes. "History attests," says Monsieur Raynouard, "that all those who were foremost in the persecution of the Templars, came to an untimely and miserable death." The last days of Philip were embittered by misfortune; his nobles and clergy leagued against him to resist his exactions; the wives of his three sons were accused of adultery, and two of them were publicly convicted of that crime. The misfortunes of Edward the Second, king of England, and his horrible death in Berkeley Castle, are too well known to be further alluded to.

To save appearances, the pope had published a bull transferring the property, late belonging to the Templars, to the Order of the Hospital of Saint John,† which had just then acquired additional renown and popularity in Europe by the conquest from the infidels of the island of Rhodes. This, bull, however, remained for a considerable period nearly a dead letter, and the Hospitallers never obtained a twentieth part of the ancient possessions of the Templars.

The kings of Castile, Aragon, and Portugal, created new military orders in their own dominions, to which the estates of the late order of the Temple were transferred, and, annexing the Grand Masterships thereof to their own persons, by the title of Perpetual Administrators, they succeeded

---

* *Villani*, lib. vii. cap. 92. Contin. Chron. de *Nangis*, ad ann. 1313. *Pap. Mass.* in Philip. pulchr. lib. iii. p. 393. *Mariana* de reb. Hisp. lib. xv. cap. 10. *Dupuy*, ed. 1700, p. 71. Chron. *Corn. Zanfliet* apud *Martene*, tom. v. col. 160. *Raynouard*, p. 209, 210.

† Acta Rymeri, tom. iii. p. 323,4, 5, ad ann. 1312.

in drawing to themselves an immense revenue.* The kings of Bohemia, Naples, and Sicily, retained possession of many of the houses and strong-holds of the Templars in their dominions, and various religious orders of monks succeeded in installing themselves in the convents of the frater-nity. The heirs of the donors of the property, moreover, claimed a title to it by escheat, and in most cases where the Hospitallers obtained the lands and estates granted them by the pope, they had to pay large fines to adverse claimants to be put into peaceable possession.†

"The chief cause of the ruin of the Templars," justly remarks Fuller, "was their extraordinary wealth. As Naboth's vineyard was the chief-est ground of his blasphemy, and as in England Sir John Cornwall Lord Fanhope said merrily, not he, but his stately house at Ampthill in Bed-fordshire was guilty of high treason, so certainly their wealth was the principal cause of their overthrow. ... We may believe that King Philip would never have taken away their lives if he might have taken their lands without putting them to death, but the mischief was, he could not get the honey unless he burnt the bees."‡

King Philip, the pope, and the European sovereigns, appear to have disposed of all the personalty of the Templars, the ornaments, jew-els, and treasure of their churches and chapels, and during the period of five years, over which the proceedings against the Order exten-ded, they remained in the actual receipt of the vast rents and revenues of the fraternity. After the promulgation of the bull, assigning the prop-erty of the Templars to the Hospitallers, King Philip put forward a claim upon the land to the extent of two hundred thousand pounds for the expenses of the prosecution, and Louis Hutin, his son, required a further sum of sixty thousand pounds from the Hospitallers, before he would consent to surrender the estates into their hands."§ "J'ignore," says Voltaire, "ce qui revint au pape, mais je vois evidemment que les frais des cardinaux, des inquisiteurs délégués pour faire ce procès épouvant-able monterent à des *sommés immenses*."** The holy pontiff, according to his own account, received only a small portion of the personalty of the Order,†† but others make him a large participator in the good things of the fraternity.‡‡

---

* *Zurita*, lib. v. c. 101. Institut. milit. Christi apud *Henriquez*, p. 534.

† Annales Minorum. Gall. Christ nov. *Aventinus*, Annal. *De Vertot*, liv. 3.

‡ *Fuller's* Hist. Holy War, book v. ch. iii.

§ *Dupuy*, p. 179, 184.

** Essai sur les mœurs, &c., tom. ii. p. 242.

†† Nihil ad nos unquam pervenit nisi modica bona mobilia. Epist. ad Philip, 2 non. May, 1309. *Raynouard*, p. 198. De Vertot, liv. iii.

‡‡ *Raynouard* 197, 198, 199.

On the imprisonment of the Templars in England, the Temple at London, and all the preceptories dependent upon it, with the manors, farms, houses, lands, and revenues of the fraternity, were placed under the survey of the Court of Exchequer, and extents* were directed to be taken of the same, after which they were confided to the care of certain trustworthy persons, styled "Guardians of the lands of the Templars," who were to account for the rents and profits to the king's exchequer. The bishop of Lichfield and Coventry had the custody of all the lands and tenements in the county of Hants. John de W burgham had those in the counties of Norfolk and Suffolk, and there were thirty-two other guardians entrusted with the care of the property in the remaining counties of England.† These guardians were directed to pay various pensions to the old servants and retainers of the Templars dwelling in the different preceptories,‡ also the expenses of the prosecution against the Order, and they were at different times required to provide for the exigencies of the public service, and to victual the king's castles and strongholds. On the 12th of January, A.D. 1312, William de Slengesby, guardian of the manor of Ribbestayn in the county of York, was commanded to forward to the constable of the castle of Knaresburgh a hundred quarters of corn, ten quarters of oats, twenty fat oxen, eighty sheep, and two strong carts, towards the victualling of the said fortress, and the king tells him that the same shall be duly deducted when he renders his account to the exchequer of the rents and profits of the said manor.§ The king, indeed, began to dispose of the property as if it was wholly vested in the crown, and made munificent donations to his favourites and friends. In the month of February of the same year, he gave the manors of Etton and Cave to David Earl of Athol, directing the guardians of the lands and tenements of the Templars in the county of York to hand over to the said earl all the corn in those manors, the oxen, calves, ploughs, and all the goods and chattels of the Templars existing therein, together with the ornaments and utensils of the chapel of the Temple.**

On the 16th of May, however, the pope addressed bulls to the king, and to all the earls and barons of the kingdom, setting forth the proceedings of the council of Vienne and the publication of the papal decree, vesting the property late belonging to the Templars in the brethren of the Hospital of

* The extents of the lands of the Templars are amongst the unarranged records in the Queen's Remembrancer's office, and various sheriffs' accounts are in the third chest in the Pipe Office.

† Acta *Rymeri*, tom. iii. p. 130, 134, 139, 279, 288, 290, 1, 2, 297, 321. *Dodsworth*. MS. vol. xxxv. p. 65, 67.

‡ Acta *Rymeri*, tom. iii. p. 292, 3, 4, 5.

§ Ib tom. iii. p. 299.

** Acta Rymeri, tom. iii. p. 303.

St. John, and he commands them forthwith to place the members of that order in possession thereof. Bulls were also addressed to the archbishops of Canterbury and York and their suffragans, commanding them to enforce by ecclesiastical censures the execution of the papal commands,* King Edward and his nobles very properly resisted this decree, and on the 21st of August the king wrote to the Prior of the Hospital of St. John at Clerkenwell, telling him that the pretensions of the pope to dispose of property within the realm of England, without the consent of parliament, were derogatory to the dignity of the crown and the royal authority; and he commands him, under severe pains and penalties, to refrain from attempting to obtain any portion of the possessions of the Templars.† The king, indeed, continued to distribute the lands and rents amongst his friends and favourites. At the commencement of the year 1313, he granted the Temple at London, with the church and all the buildings therein, to Aymer de Valence earl of Pembroke;‡ and on the 5th of May of the same year he caused several merchants, from whom he had borrowed money, to be placed in possession of many of the manors of the Templars.§

Yielding, however, at last to the exhortations and menaces of the pope, the king, on the 21st of Nov. A.D. 1313, granted the property to the Hospitallers,** and sent orders to all the guardians of the lands of the Templars, and to various powerful barons who were in possession of the estates, commanding them to deliver them up to certain parties deputed by the Grand Master and chapter of the Hospital of Saint John to receive them.†† At this period, however, many of the heirs of the donors, whose title had been recognized by the law, were in possession of the lands, and the judges held that the king had no power of his own sole authority to transfer them to the Order of the Hospital.‡‡ The thunders of the Vatican were consequently vigorously made use of, and all the detainers of the property were doomed by the Roman pontiff to everlasting damnation.§§ Pope John, in one of his bulls, dated A.D. 1322, bitterly complains of the disregard by all the king's subjects of the papal commands. He laments that they had hardened their hearts and despised the sentence of excommunication fulminated against them, and declares that his heart was riven with grief to find that even the ecclesiastics, who ought to have been as a wall of defence to the Hospitallers, had them-

---

* Ib , tom. iii. p. 326, 327.

† Ib., tom. iii. p. 337.

‡ Cart. 6. E. 2. No. 4. 41.

§ Acta *Rymeri*, tom. iii. p. 409, 410.

** Acta *Rymeri*, tom. iii. p. 451.

†† Ib., p. 451, 454, 455, 457, 459—463. *Dugd. Monast.* Angl., vol. vi. part 2. p. 809.

‡‡ Rolls of Parliament, vol. ii. p. 41.

§§ *Dugd. Monast.* Angl., vol. vi. part 2, p. 849, 850. *Concil. Mag. Brit.*, tom. ii. 9. 499.

*** Acta *Rymeri*, tom. iii. p. 956—959, ad ann. 1322.

selves been heinously guilty in the premises.***

At last (A.D. 1324) the pope, the bishops, and the Hospitallers, by their united exertions, succeeded in obtaining an act of parliament, vesting all the property late belonging to the Templars in the brethren of the Hospital of Saint John, in order that the intentions of the donors might be carried into effect by the appropriation of it to the defence of the Holy Land and the succour of the Christian cause in the East.* This statute gave rise to the greatest discontent. The heirs of the donors petitioned parliament for its repeal, alleging that it had been made against law and against reason, and contrary to the opinion of the judges;† and many of the great barons who held the property by a title recognised by the common law, successfully resisted the claims of the Order of the Hospital, maintaining that the parliament had no right to interfere with the tenure of private property, and to dispose of their possessions without their consent.

This struggle between the heirs of the donors on the one hand, and the Hospitallers on the other, continued for a lengthened period; and in the reign of Edward the Third it was found necessary to pass another act of parliament, confirming the previous statute in their favour, and writs were sent to the sheriffs (A.D. 1334) commanding them to enforce the execution of the acts of the legislature, and to take possession, in the king's name, of all the property unjustly detained from the brethren of the Hospital.‡

Whilst the vast possessions, late belonging to the Templars, thus continued to be the subject of contention, the surviving brethren of that dissolved order continued to be treated with the utmost inhumanity and neglect. The ecclesiastical council had assigned to each of them a pension of fourpence a day for subsistence, but this small pittance was not paid, and they were consequently in great danger of dying of hunger. The king, pitying their miserable situation, wrote to the prior of the hospital of St. John at Clerkenwell, earnestly requesting him to take their hard lot into his serious consideration, and not suffer them to come to beggary in the streets.§ The archbishop of Canterbury also exerted himself in their behalf, and sent letters to the possessors of the property, reproving them for the non-payment of the allotted stipends. "This inhumanity," says he, "awakens our compassion, and penetrates us with the most lively grief. We pray and conjure you in kindness to furnish them, for the love of God and for

---

* *Statutes at Large,* vol. ix. Appendix, p. 23.
† *Rolls of Parliament,* vol. ii. p. 41. No. 52.
‡ *Monast. Angl.,* p. 810.
§ Acta *Rymeri,* tom. iii. p. 472.
** Concil. Mag. Brit., tom. ii.
†† Walsingham, p. 99.

charity, with the means of subsistence."** The archbishop of York caused many of them to be supported in the different monasteries of his diocese.††

Many of the quondam Templars, however, after the dissolution of their order, assumed a secular habit; they blended themselves with the laity, mixed in the pleasures of the world, and even presumed to contract matrimony, proceedings which drew down upon them the severe indignation of the Roman pontiff. In a bull addressed to the archbishop of Canterbury, the pope stigmatises these marriages as unlawful concubinages; he observes that the late Templars remained bound, notwithstanding the dissolution of their order, by their vows of perpetual chastity, and he orders them to be separated from the women whom they had married, and to be placed in different monasteries, where they are to dedicate themselves to the service of God, and the strict performance of their religious vows.*

The Templars adopted the oriental fashion of long beards, and during the proscription of the fraternity, when the fugitives who had thrown off their habits were hunted out like wild beasts, it appears to have been dangerous for laymen to possess beards of more than a few weeks' growth.

Papers and certificates were granted to men with long beards, to prevent them from being molested by the officers of justice as suspected Templars, as appears from the following curious certicate given by king Edward the Second to his valet, who had made a vow not to shave himself until he had performed a pilgrimage to a certain place beyond sea.

"Rex, etc. Cum dilectus valettus noster Petrus Auger, exhibitor presentium, nuper voverit quod barbam suam radi non faciat, quousque peregrinationem fecerit in certo loco in partibus transmarinis; et idem Petrus sibi timeat, quod aliqui ipsum, ratione barbae suae prolixæ fuisse Templarium imponere sibi velint, et ei inferre impedimenta seu gravamina ex hac causa; Nos ventati volentes testimonium pertulere, vobis tenore praesentium intimamus, quod preedictus Petrus est valettus camera nostra, *nec unquam fait Templarius, sed barbam suam sic prolixam esse permittit, ex causa superius annotata,* etc. Teste Rege, &c."†

---

* Monast. Angl., vol. vi. port ii. p. 848.
† Pat. 4, E. 2, p. 2; m. 20. *Dugdale,* Hiat. Warwickshire, vol. i. p. 962, ed. 1730.

CHAPTER XI.

THE TEMPLE CHURCH.

The restoration of the Temple Church—The beauty and magnificence of the venerable building—The various styles of architecture displayed in it—The discoveries made during the recent restoration—The sacrarium—The marble piscina—The sacramental niches—The penitential cell—The ancient Chapel of St. Anne—Historical matters connected with the Temple Church—The holy relics anciently preserved therein—The interesting monumental remains.

"If a day should come when pew lumber, preposterous organ cases, and pagan altar screens, are declared to be unfashionable, no religious building, stript of such nuisances, would come more fair to the sight, or give more general satisfaction to the antiquary, than the chaste and beautiful Temple Church."—*Gentleman's Magazine* for May, 1808, p. 1087.

"AFTER three centuries of demolition, the solemn structures raised by our Catholic ancestors are being gradually restored to somewhat of their original appearance, and buildings, which, but a few years since, were considered as unsightly and barbarous erections of ignorant times, are now become the theme of general eulogy and models for imitation."*

It has happily been reserved for the present generation, after a lapse of two centuries, to see the venerable Temple Church, the chief ecclesiastical edifice of the Knights Templars in Britain, and the most beautiful and perfect relic of the Order now in existence, restored to the simple majesty it possessed near seven hundred years ago; to see it once again presenting the appearance which it wore when the patriarch of Jerusalem exercised his sacred functions within its walls, and when the mailed knights of the most holy order of the Temple of Solomon, the sworn champions of the Christian faith, unfolded the red-cross banner amid "the long-drawn aisles" and offered their swords upon the altar to be blessed by the ministers of religion.

* Dublin Review for May, 1841, p. 301.

From the period of the reign of Charles the First down to our own times, the Temple Church has remained sadly disfigured by incongruous innovations and modern *embellishments*, which entirely changed the ancient character and appearance of the building, and clouded and obscured its elegance and beauty.

Shortly after the Reformation, the Protestant lawyers, from an over-anxious desire to efface all the emblems of the popish faith, covered the gorgeously-painted ceiling of this venerable structure with an uniform coating of simple whitewash; they buried the antique tesselated pavement under hundreds of cart-loads of earth and rubbish, on the surface of which, two feet above the level of the ancient floor, they placed another pavement, formed of old grave-stones. They, moreover, disfigured all the magnificent marble columns with a thick coating of plaster and paint, and destroyed the beauty of the elaborately-wrought mouldings of the arches, and the exquisitely-carved marble ornaments with thick incrustations of whitewash, clothing the whole edifice in one uniform garb of plain white, in accordance with the puritanical ideas of those times.

Subsequently, in the reign of Charles the Second, the fine open area of the body of the church was filled with long rows of stiff and formal pews, which concealed the bases of the columns, while the plain but handsome stone walls of the sacred edifice were encumbered, to a height of eight feet from the ground, with oak wainscoting, which was carried entirely round the church, so as to shut out from view the elegant marble piscina on the south side of the building, the interesting arched niches over the high altar, and the *sacrarium* on the eastern side of the edifice. The elegant gothic arches connecting the Round with the oblong portion of the building were filled up with an oak screen and glass windows and doors, and with an organ-gallery adorned with Corinthian columns and pilastres and Grecian ornaments, which divided the building into two parts, altogether altered its original character and appearance, and sadly marred its architectural beauty. The eastern end of the church was, at the same time, disfigured with an enormous altarpiece in the *classic* style, decorated with Corinthian columns and Grecian cornices and entablatures, and with enrichments of cherubims and wreaths of fruit, leaves, and flowers, exquisitely carved and beautiful in themselves, but heavy and cumbrous, and quite at variance with the gothic character of the edifice. A huge pulpit and sounding-board, elaborately carved, were also erected in the middle of the nave, forming a great obstruction to the view of the interior of the building, and the walls and all the columns were thickly clustered and disfigured with mural monuments.

All these unsightly and incongruous additions to the ancient fabric have, thanks to the good taste and the public spirit of the Masters of the Benches of the societies of the Inner and Middle Temple, been recently removed; the ceiling of the church has been repainted; the marble columns and the tesselated pavement have been restored, and the venerable structure has now been brought back to its ancient condition.

The historical associations and recollections connected with the Temple Church throw a powerful charai around the venerable building. During the holy fervour of the crusades, the kings of England and the haughty legates of the pope were wont to mix with the armed bands of the Templars in this their chief ecclesiastical edifice in Britain. In the twelfth and thirteenth centuries some of the most remarkable characters of the age were buried in the Round, and their mail-clad marble monumental effigies, reposing side by side on the cold pavement, still attract the wonder and admiration of the inquiring stranger.

The solemn ceremonies attendant in days of yore upon the admission of a novice to the holy vows of the Temple, conducted with closed doors during the first watch of the night; the severe religious exercises performed by the stern military friars; the vigils that were kept up at night in the church, and the reputed terrors of the penitential cell, all contributed in times past to throw an air of mystery and romance around the sacred building, and to create in the minds of the vulgar a feeling of awe and of superstitious terror, giving rise to those strange and horrible tales of impiety and crime, of magic and sorcery, which led to the unjust and infamous execution at the stake of the Grand Master and many hundred Knights of the Temple, and to the suppression and annihilation of their proud and powerful order.

The first and most interesting portion of the Temple Church, denominated by the old writers "The Round," was consecrated in the year 1186 by Heraclius, the Patriarch of Jerusalem, on his arrival in England from Palestine, as before mentioned, to obtain succour from King Henry the Second against the formidable power of the famous Saladin.* The old inscription which formerly stood over the small door of the Round leading into the cloisters, and which was broken and destroyed by the workmen whilst repairing the church, in the year 1695, was to the following effect:

"On the 10th of February, in the year from the incarnation of our Lord 1185, this church was consecrated in honour of the blessed Mary by our lord Heraclius, by the grace of God patriarch of the church of the Resurrection, who hath granted an indulgence of fifty days to those yearly seeking it."†

---

* See ante, p. 80. On the 10th of March, before his departure from this country, Heraclius consecrated the church of the Hospitallers at Clerkenwell, and the altars of St. John and St. Mary. Ex registr. S. John Jerus, in Bib. *Cotton*, fol. 1.

† A fac-simile of this inscription was faithfully delineated by Mr. Geo. Holmes, the antiquary, and was published by Strype, A.D. 1670. The earliest copy I have been able to fine of it is in a manuscript history of the Temple, in the Inner Temple library, supposed to have been written at the commencement of the reign of Charles the First by John Wilde, Esq., a bencher of the society, and Lent reader in the year 1630.

The oblong portion of the church, which extendeth eastwards from the Round, was consecrated on Ascension-day, A.D. 1240, as appears from the following passage in the history of Matthew Paris, the monk of St. Alban's, who was probably himself present at the ceremony.

"About the same time (A.D. 1240) was consecrated the noble church of the New Temple at London, an edifice worthy to be seen, in the presence of the king and much of the nobility of the kingdom, who, on the same day, that is to say, the day of the Ascension, after the solemnities of the consecration had been completed, royally feasted at a most magnificent banquet, prepared at the expense of the Hospitallers."*

It was after the promulgation, A.D. 1162 and 1172, of the famous bull *omne datum optimum*, exempting the Templars from the ordinary ecclesiastical jurisdiction, and enabling them to admit priests and chaplains into their order, and appoint them to their churches without installation and induction, and free from the interference of the bishops, that the members of this proud and powerful fraternity began to erect at great cost, in various parts of Christendom, churches of vast splendour and magnificence, like the one we now see at London. It is probable that the earlier portion of this edifice was commenced immediately after the publication of the above bull, so as to be ready (as churches took a long time in building in those days) for consecration by the Patriarch on his arrival in England with the Grand Master of the Temple.

As there is a difference in respect of the time of the erection, so also is there a variation in the style of the architecture of the round and oblong portions of the church; the one presenting to us a most beautiful and interesting specimen of that mixed style of ecclesiastical architecture termed the semi-Norman, and by some writers the intermediate, when the rounded arch and the short and massive column became mingled with, and were gradually giving way to, the early Gothic; and the other affording to us a pure and most elegant example of the latter style of architecture, with its pointed arches and light slender columns. These two portions of the Temple Church, indeed, when compared together, present features of peculiar interest to the architect and the antiquary. The oblong portion of the venerable fabric affords, perhaps, the first specimen of the complete conquest of the pointed style over the massive circular or Norman architecture which preceded its erection, whilst the Round displays the different changes which the latter style underwent previous to its final subversion.

---

* Tempore quoque Templi *Londinensis*, præsente Rege et multis regni Magnatibus; quieodem die, scilicet die Ascensionis, completes dedicationis solemniis, convivium in mensâ nimis laute celebrarunt, sumptibus Hospitaliorum.—*Matt. Par.* ad ann. 1240, p. 526, ed. 1640.

The Temple Church is entered by a beautiful semicircular arched doorway, an exquisite specimen of the Norman style of architecture, still unfortunately surrounded and smothered by the smoke-dried buildings of studious lawyers. It is deeply recessed and ornamented on either side with columns bearing foliated capitals, from whence spring a series of arched mouldings, richly carved and decorated. Between these columns project angular piers enriched with lozenges, roses, foliage, and ornaments of varied pattern and curious device. The upper part of these piers between the capitals of the columns is hollowed out, and carved half-length human figures, representing a king and queen, monks and saints, have been inserted. Some of these figures hold scrolls of paper in their hands, and others rest in the attitude of prayer. Over them, between the ribs of the arch, are four rows of enriched foliage springing from the mouths of human heads.

Having passed this elegant and elaborately-wrought doorway, we enter that portion of the church called by the old writers

The Round,

which consists of an inner circular area formed by a round tower resting on six clustered columns, and of a circular external aisle or cloister, connected with the round tower by a sloping roof on the outside, and internally by a groined vaulted ceiling. The beauty and elegance of the building from this point, with its circular colonnades, storied windows, and long perspective of architectural magnificence, cannot be described—it must be seen.

From the centre of the Round, the eye is carried upward to the vaulted ceiling of the inner circular tower with its groined ribs and carved bosses. This tower rests on six clustered marble columns, from whence spring six pointed arches enriched with numerous mouldings. The clustered columns are composed of four marble shafts, surmounted by foliated capitals, which are each of a different pattern, but correspond in the general outline, and display great character and beauty. These shafts are connected together by bands at their centres; and the bases and capitals run into each other, so as to form the whole into one column. Immediately above the arches resting on these columns, is a small band or cornice, which extends around the interior of the tower, and supports a most elegant arcade of interlaced arches. This arcade is formed of numerous small Purbeck marble columns, enriched with ornamented bases and capitals, from whence spring a series of arches which intersect one another and produce a most pleasing and striking combination of the round and pointed arch. Above this elegant arcade is another cornice surmounted by six circular-headed windows pierced at equal intervals through the thick walls of the tower. These windows are ornamented at the angles with small columns, and in the time of the Knights Templars they were filled with stained glass. Between each window is a long slender circular shaft of Purbeck marble, which springs from the clustered columns, and terminates in a bold foliated capital, whereon rest the groined ribs of the ceiling of the tower.

From the tower, with its marble columns, interlaced arches, and elegant decorations, the attention will speedily be drawn to the innumerable small columns, pointed arches, and grotesque human countenances which extend around the lower portion of the exter-nal aisle or cloister encircling the Round. The more these human countenances are scrutinised, the more astonishing and extraordinary do they appear. They seem for the most part distorted and agonised with pain, and have been supposed, not without reason, to represent the writh-ings and grimaces of the damned. Unclean beasts may be observed gnaw-ing the ears and tearing with their claws the bald heads of some of them, whose firmly-compressed teeth and quivering lips plainly denote intense bodily anguish. These sculptured visages display an astonishing vari-ety of character, and will be regarded with increased interest when it is remembered, that an arcade and cornice decorated in this singular man-ner have been observed among the ruins of the Temple churches at Acre, and in the Pilgrim's Castle. This circular aisle or cloister is lighted by a series of semi-circular-headed windows, which are ornamented at the angles with small columns.

Over the western doorway leading into the Round, is a beautiful Norman wheel-window, which was uncovered and brought to light by the workmen during the recent reparation of this interesting building. It is considered a masterpiece of masonry.

The entrance from the Round to the oblong portion of the Temple Church is formed by three lofty pointed arches, which open upon the nave and the two aisles. The mouldings of these arches display great beauty and elegance, and the central arch, which forms the grand entrance to the nave, is supported upon magnificent Purbeck marble columns.

Having passed through one of these elegant and richly-embellished archways, we enter a large, lofty, and light structure, consisting of a nave and two aisles of equal height, formed by eight clustered marble columns, which support a groined vaulted ceiling richly and elaborately painted. This chaste and graceful edifice presents to us one of the most pure and beautiful examples in existence of the early pointed style, which immediately succeeded the mixed order of architecture visible in the Round. The numerous elegantly-shaped windows which extend around this portion of the building, the exquisite proportions of the slim marble columns, the beauty and richness of the architectural decorations, and the extreme lightness and airiness of the whole structure, give us the idea of a fairy palace.

The marble columns supporting the pointed arches of the roof, four in number on each side, do not consist of independent shafts banded together, as in the Hound, but form solid pillars which possess vast elegance and beauty. Attached to the walls of the church, in a line with these pillars, are a series of small clustered columns, composed of three slender shafts, the central one being of Purbeck marble, and the others of Caen stone; they are bound together by a band at their centres and their bases, which are of Purbeck marble, rest on a stone seat or plinth, which extends the whole length of the body of the church. These clustered columns, which are placed parallel to the large central pillars, are surmounted by foliated capitals, from whence spring the groined ribs which traverse the vaulted ceiling of the roof. The side walls are thus divided into five compartments on either side, which are each filled up with a triple lancet-headed window, of a graceful form, and richly orna-mented. It is composed of three long narrow openings surmounted by pointed arches, the central arch rising above the lateral ones. The mould-ings of the arches rest upon four slender marble columns which run up in front of the stone mullions of the windows, and impart to them great elegance and beauty. The great number of these windows, and the small intervening spaces of blank wall between them, give a vast lightness and airiness to the whole structure.

Immediately beneath them is a small cornice or stringing course of Purbeck marble, which runs entirely round the body of the church, and supports the small marble columns which adorn the windows.

The roof is composed of a series of pointed arches supported by groined ribs, which, diverging from the capitals of the columns, cross one another at the centre of the arch, and are ornamented at the point of intersection with richly-carved bosses. This roof is composed principally of chalk, and previous to the late restoration, had a plain and somewhat naked appearance, being covered with an uniform coat of humble whitewash. On the recent removal of this whitewash, extensive remains of an ancient painted ceiling were brought to light, and it was consequently determined to repaint the entire roof of the body of the church according to a design furnished by Mr. Willement.

At the eastern end of the church are three elegant windows opening upon the three aisles; they are similar in form to the side windows, but the central one is considerably larger than any of the others, and has in the spandrels formed by the line of groining two small quatrefoil pan-els. The label mouldings on either side of this central window termi-nate in two crowned heads, which are supposed to represent King Henry the Third and his queen. These windows are to be filled with stained glass as in the olden time, and will, when finished, present a most gor-geous and magnificent appearance. Immediately beneath them, above the high altar, are three niches, in which were deposited in days of yore the sacred vessels used during the celebration of the mass. The central recess, surmounted by a rounded arch, contained the golden chalice and patin covered with the veil and bursa; and the niches on either side received the silver cruets, the ampullæ, the subdeacon's veil, and all the paraphernalia used during the sacrament. In the stonework around them may be observed the marks of the locks and fastenings of doors.

These niches were uncovered and brought to light on the removal of the large heavy oak screen and altar-piece, which disfigured the eastern end of the church.

On the southern side of the building, near the high altar, is an elegant marble *piscina* or *lavacrum*, which was in like manner discovered on pulling down the modern oak wainscoting. This interesting remnant of antiquity has been beautifully restored, and well merits attention. It was constructed for the use of the priest who officiated at the adjoining altar, and was intended to receive the water in which the chalice had been rinsed, and in which the priest washed his hands before the consecration of the bread and wine. It consists of two perforated hollows or small basins, inclosed in an elegant marble niche, adorned with two graceful arches, which rest on small marble columns. The holes at the bottom of the basins communicate with two conduits or channels for draining off the water, which anciently made its exit through the thick walls of the church. In the olden time, before the consecration of the host, the priest walked to the piscina, accompanied by the clerk, who poured water over his hands, that they might be purified from all stain before he ventured to touch the body of our Lord. One of these channels was intended to receive the water in which the priest washed his hands, and the other that in which he had rinsed the chalice. The piscina, consequently, served the purposes of a sink.*

Adjoining the piscina, towards the eastern end of the church, is a small elegant niche, in which the ewer, basin, and towels were placed; and immediately opposite, in the north wall of the edifice, is another niche, which appears to have been a *sacrarium* or tabernacle for holding the eucharist preserved for the use of the sick brethren.†

In the centre of the northern aisle of the church, a large recess has been erected for the reception of the organ, as no convenient place could be found for it in the old structure. Below this recess, by the side of the archway communicating with the Round, is a small Norman doorway, opening upon a dark circular staircase which leads to the summit of the round tower, and also to

* A large piscina, similar to the one in the Temple Church, may be seen in Cowling church, Kent. Archoelogia, vol. zi. pl. xiv. p. 320.

† Ib p. 347 to 359.

THE PENITENTIAL CELL.

This dreary place of solitary confinement is formed within the thick wall of the church, and is only four feet six inches long, and two feet six inches wide, so that it would be impossible for a grown person to lie down with any degree of comfort within it. Two small apertures, or loop-holes, four feet high and nine inches wide, have been pierced through the walls to admit light and air. One of these apertures looks eastward into the body of the church towards the spot where stood the high altar, in order that the prisoner might see and hear the performance of divine service, and the other looks southward into the Round, facing the west entrance of the church. The hinges and catch of a door, firmly attached to the doorway of this dreary prison, still remain, and at the bottom of the staircase is a stone recess or cupboard, where bread and water were placed for the prisoner.

In this miserable cell were confined the refractory and disobedient brethren of the Temple, and those who were enjoined severe penance with solitary confinement. Its dark secrets have long since been buried in the silence of the tomb, but one sad tale of misery and horror, probably connected with it, has been brought to light.

Several of the brethren of the Temple at London, who were examined before the papal inquisitors, tell us of the miserable death of Brother Walter le Bacheler, Knight, Grand Preceptor of Ireland, who, for disobedience to his superior the Master of the Temple, was fettered and cast into prison, and there expired from the rigour and severity of his confinement. His dead body was taken out of the solitary cell in the Temple at morning's dawn, and was buried by Brother John de Stoke and Brother Radulph de Barton, in the midst of the court, between the church and the hall.*

The discipline of the Temple was strict and austere to an extreme. An eye-witness tells us that disobedient brethren were confined in chains and dungeons for a longer or a shorter period, or perpetually, according as it might seem expedient, in order that their souls might be saved at the last from the eternal prison of hell.† In addition to imprisonment, the Templars were scourged on their bare backs, by the hand of the Master himself, in the Temple Hall, and were frequently whipped on Sundays in the church, in the presence of the whole congregation.

Brother Adam de Valaincourt, a knight of a noble family, quitted the Order of the Temple, but afterwards returned, smitten with remorse for his disobedience, and sought to be admitted to the society of his quondam brethren. He was compelled by the Master to eat for a year on the ground

* Acta contra Templarios. Concil. Mag. Brit. tom. ii. p. 336, 350, 351.
† Jac. de Vitr. De Religione fratrum militiæ Templi, cap. 65.
‡ Processus contra Templarios, apud Dupuy, p. 65 ; ed. 1700.

with the dogs; to fast four days in the week on bread and water, and every Sunday to present himself naked in the church before the high altar, and receive the discipline at the hands of the officiating priest, in the presence of the whole congregation.‡

On the opposite side of the church, corresponding with the doorway and staircase leading to the penitential cell, there was formerly another doorway and staircase communicating with a very curious ancient structure, called the chapel of St. Anne, which stood on the south side of the Bound, but was removed during the repairs in 1827. It was two stories in height. The lower story communicated with the Round through a doorway formed under one of the arches of the arcade, and the upper story communicated with the body of the church by the before-mentioned doorway and staircase, which have been recently stopped up. The roofs of these apartments were vaulted, and traversed by cross-ribs of stone, ornamented with bosses at the point of intersection.* This chapel anciently opened upon the cloisters, and formed a private medium of communication between the convent of the Temple and the church. It was here that the papal legate and the English bishops frequently had conferences respecting the affairs of the English clergy, and in this chapel Almaric de Montforte, the pope's chaplain, who had been imprisoned by King Edward the First, was set at liberty at the instance of the Roman pontiff, in the presence of the archbishop of Canterbury, and the Bishops of London, Lincoln, Bath, Worcester, Norwich, Oxford, and several other prelates, and of many distinguished laymen; the said Almeric having previously taken an oath that he would forthwith leave the kingdom, never more to return without express permission.† In times past, this chapel of St. Anne, situate on the south of "the round about walles," was widely celebrated for its productive powers. It was resorted to by barren women, and was of great repute for making them "joyful mothers of children!"‡

There were formerly numerous priests attached to the Temple church, the chief of whom was styled *custos* or guardian of the sacred edifice. King Henry the Third, for the salvation of his own soul, and the souls of his ancestors and heirs, gave to the Templars eight pounds per annum, to be paid out of the ex-chequer, for the maintenance of three chaplains in the Temple to say mass daily for ever; one was to pray in the church for

---

* See the plan of this chapel and of the Temple Church, in the vetusta monumenta of the Society of Antiquaries.

† Acta fuerunt he in capellâ juxta ecclesiam, apud Novum Templum London, ex parte Australi ipsius ecclesiae sitâ, coram reverendis patribus domino archiepiscopo et episcopis, &c. &. Acta Rymeri, tom. ii. p. 193, ad ann. 1282.

‡ Anecdotes and Traditions published by the Camden Society. No. clxxxi. p. 110.

§ *De tribus Capellanis inveniendis, apud Novum Templum, Londoniarum, pro animâ Regis Henrici Tertii. Ex regist Hosp. S. Johannis Jerus. in Angliâ. Bib. Cotton, f. 25. a. f*

the king himself, another for all Christian people, and the third for the faithful departed.§ Idonea de Veteri Ponte also gave thirteen bovates of her land, at Ostrefeld, for the support of a chaplain in the house of the Temple at London, to pray for her own soul and that of her deceased husband, Robert de Veteri Ponte.*

The *custos* or guardian of the Temple church was appointed by the Master and Chapter of the Temple, and entered upon his spiritual duties, as did all the priests and chaplains of the Order, without any admission, institution, or induction. He was exempt from the ordinary ecclesiastical authority, and was to pay perfect obedience in all matters, and upon all occasions, to the Master of the Temple, as his lord and bishop. The priests of the Order took precisely the same vows as the rest of the brethren, and enjoyed no privileges above their fellows. They remained, indeed, in complete subjection to the knights, for they were not allowed to take part in the consultations of the chapter, unless they had been enjoined so to do, nor could they occupy themselves with the cure of souls unless required. The Templars were not permitted to confess to priests who were strangers to the Order, without leave so to do.

"Et les freres chapeleins du Temple dovinent oyr la confession desfreres, ne nul ne se deit confesser a autre chapelein saunz counge, car il ount greigneur poer du Pape, de els assoudre que un evesque."

The particular chapters of the Master of the Temple, in which transgressions were acknowledged, penances were enjoined, and quarrels were made up, were frequently held on a Sunday morning in the above chapel of St. Anne, on the south side of the Temple church, when the following curious form of absolution was pronounced by the Master of the Temple in the Norman French of that day.

"La manere de tenir chapitre e d'assoudre."

"Apres chapitre dira le mestre, ou cely qe tendra le chapitre. 'Beaus seigneurs freres, le pardon de nostre chapitre est tiels, qe cil qui ostast les almones de la meson a tout e maie resoun, ou tenist aucune chose en noun de propre, ne prendreit u tens ou pardoun de nostre chapitre. Mes toutes les choses qe vous lessez a dire pour hounte de la char, ou pour poour de la justice de la mesoun qe lein ne la prenge requer Dieu, e de par la poeste, que nostre sire otria a sein pere, la quele nostre pere le pape lieu tenaunt a terre a otrye a la maison, e a noz sovereyns, e nous de par Dieu, e de par nostre mestre, e de tout nostre chapitre tiel pardoun come ieo vous puis fere, ieo la vous faz, de bon quer, e de bone volonte. E prioms nostre sire, qe issi veraiement come il pardona a la glorieuse Magdaléyne, quant ele plura ses pechez. E al larron en la croiz mis pardona il ses pechez, e a vous face les vos a pardone a moy les miens. Et pry vous

* *Ibid., 30. b.*
† Acta contra Tempiarios. Concil. Mag. Brit., tom. ii. p. 383.

que se ieo ouges meffis oudis a mil de vous que vous depleise que vous le me pardonez.'"†

At the close of the chapter, the Master or the President of the chapter shall say, "Good and noble brethren, the pardon of our chapter is such, that he who unjustly maketh away with the alms of the house, or holdeth anything as his own property, hath no part in the pardon of our chapter, or in the good works of our house. But those things which through shame-facedness, or through fear of the justice of the Order, you have neglected to confess before God, I, by the power which our Lord obtained from his Father, and which our father the pope, his vicar, has-granted to the house, and to our superiors, and to us, by the authority of God and our Master, and all our chapter, grant unto you, with hearty good will, such pardon as I am able to give. And we beseech our Lord, that as he forgave the glorious Mary Magdalene when she bewailed her sins, and pardoned the robber on the cross, that he will in like manner mercifully pardon both you and me. And if I have wronged any of you, I beseech you to grant me forgiveness."

The Temple Church in times past contained many holy and valuable relics, which had been sent over by the Templars from Palestine. Numerous indulgences were granted by the bishops of London to all devout Christians who went with a lively faith to adore these relics. The bishop of Ely also granted indulgences to all the faithful of his diocese, and to all pious Christians who attended divine worship in the Temple Church, to the honour and praise of God, and his glorious mother the Virgin Mary, the resplendent Queen of Heaven, and also to all such as should contribute, out of their goods and possessions, to the maintenance and support of the lights which were kept eternally upon the altars.*

The circular form of the oldest portion of the Temple Church imparts an additional interest to the venerable fabric, as there are only three other ancient churches in England of this shape. It has been stated that all the churches of the Templars were built in the circular form, after the model of the church of the holy sepulchre at Jerusalem; but this was not the case. The numerous remains of these churches, to be met with in various parts of Christendom, prove them to have been built of all shapes, forms, and sizes.

We must now say a word concerning the ancient monuments in the Temple Church.

In a recess in the south wall, close to the elegant marble piscina, reposes the recumbent figure of a bishop clad in pontifical robes, having a mitre on his head and a crosier in his hand. It rests upon an altar-tomb, and has been beautifully carved out of a single block of Purbeck marble.

* E registro mun. eviden. Prior. Hosp. Sanc. Joh. fol. 23, b.; fo. 24, a.

On the 7th of September, 1810, this tomb was opened, and beneath the figure was found a stone coffin, about three feet in height and ten feet in length, having a circular cavity to receive the head of the corpse. Within the coffin was found a human skeleton in a state of perfect preservation. It was wrapped in sheet-lead, part of which had perished. On the left side of the skeleton were the remains of a crosier, and among the bones and around the skull were found fragments of sackcloth and of garments wrought with gold tissue. It was evident that the tomb had been previously violated, as the sheet-lead had been divided longitudinally with some coarse cutting instrument, and the bones within it had been displaced from their proper position. The most remarkable discovery made on the opening of this tomb was that of the skeleton of an infant a very few months old, which was found lying at the feet of the bishop.

Nichols, the antiquary, tells us that Brown Willis ascribed the above monument to Silvester de Everdon, bishop of Carlisle, who was killed in the year 1255 by a fall from a mettlesome horse, and was buried in the Temple Church.*

All the monumental remains of the ancient Knights Templars, formerly existing in the Temple Church, have unfortunately long since been utterly destroyed. Burton, the antiquary, who was admitted a member of the Inner Temple in the reign of Queen Elizabeth, on the 20th of May, 1593, tells us that in the body of the church there was "a large blue marble inlaid with brasse," with this circumscription—"Hic requiescit Constantius de Houerio, quondam visitator generalis ordinis militiæ Templi in Angliâ, Franciâ, et Italiâ."† "Here lies Constance de Hover, formerly visitor-general of the Order of the Temple, in England, France, and Italy." Not a vestige of this interesting monument now remains. During the recent excavation in the churchyard for the foundations of the new organ gallery, two very large stone coffins were found at a great depth below the present surface, which doubtless enclosed the mortal remains of distinguished Templars. The churchyard appears to abound in ancient stone coffins.

In the Round of the Temple Church, the oldest part of the present fabric, are the famous monuments of secular warriors, with their legs crossed, in token that they had assumed the cross, and taken the vow to march to the defence of the Christian faith in Palestine. These cross-legged effigies have consequently been termed "the monuments of the crusaders," and are so singular and interesting, that a separate chapter must be devoted to the consideration of them.

* Nicholls' Hist. Leicestershire, vol. iii. p. 960, note. Malcolm, Londinium Redivivum, vol. ii. p. 294.

† Burton's Leicestershire, p. 235, 236.

CHAPTER XII.

THE TEMPLE CHURCH.

THE MONUMENTS OF THE CRUSADERS—The tomb and effigy of Sir Geoffrey de Magnaville, earl of Essex, and constable of the Tower—His life and death, and famous exploits—Of William Marshall, earl of Pembroke, Protector of England—Of the Lord de Ross—Of William and Gilbert Marshall, earls of Pembroke—Of William Plantagenet, fifth son of Henry the Third—The anxious desire manifested by King Henry the Third, Queen Eleanor, and various persons of rank, to be buried in the Temple Church.

"The knights are dust,
And their good swords are rust,
Their souls are with the saints, we trust."

THE mail-clad monumental effigies reposing side by side on the pavement of "the Round" of the Temple Church, have been supposed to be monuments of Knights Templars, but this is not the case. The Templars were always buried in the habit of their order, and are represented in it on their tombs. This habit was a long white mantle, as before mentioned, with a red cross over the left breast; it had a short cape and a hood behind, and fell down to the feet unconfined by any girdle. In a long mantle of this description, with the cross of the Order carved upon it, is represented the Knight Templar Brother Jean de Dreux, in the church of St. Yvod de

Braine in France, with this inscription, in letters of gold, carved upon the monument—F. Jean li Templier fuis au comte Jean de Dreux.*

Although not monuments of Knight Templars, yet these interesting cross-legged effigies have strong claims to our attention upon other grounds. They appear to have been placed in the Temple Church, to the memory of a class of men termed "Associates of the Temple," who, though not actually admitted to the holy vows and habit of the Order, were yet received into a species of spiritual connexion with the Templars, curiously illustrative of the superstition and credulity of the times.

Many piously-inclined persons of rank and fortune, bred up amid the pleasures and the luxuries of the world, were anxiously desirous of participating in the spiritual advantages and blessings believed to be enjoyed by the holy warriors of the Temple, in respect of the good works done by the fraternity, but could not bring themselves to submit to the severe discipline and gloomy life of the regularly-professed brethren. For the purpose of turning the tendencies anil peculiar feelings of such persons to a good account, the Master and Chapter of the Temple assumed the power of admitting them into a spiritual association and connexion with the Order, so that, without renouncing their pleasures and giving up their secular mode of life, they might share in the merit of the good works performed by the brethren. The mode in which this was frequently done is displayed to us by the following public authentic document, extracted by Ducange from the Royal Registry of Provence.

"Be it known to all persons present and to come, that in the year of the incarnation 1209, in the month of December, I, William D. G., count of Forcalquier, and son of the deceased Gerald, being inspired with the love of God, of my own free will, and with hearty desire, dedicate my body and soul to the Lord, to the most blessed Virgin Mary, and to the house of the chivalry of the Temple, in manner following. If at any time I determine on taking the vows of a religious order, I will choose the religion of the Temple, and none other; but I will not embrace it except in sincerity, of my own free will, and without constraint. Should I happen to end my days amid the pleasures of the world, I will be buried in the cemetery of the house of the Temple. I promise, through love of God, for the repose of my soul, and the souls of my parents, and of all the dead faithful in Christ, to give to the aforesaid house of the Temple and to the brethren, at my decease, my own horse, with two other saddle-horses, all my equipage and armour complete, as well iron as wood, fit for a knight, and a hundred marks of silver. Moreover, in acknowledgment of this donation, I promise to give to the aforesaid house of the Temple and to the brethren, as long as I lead a secular life, a hundred pennies a year at the

---

* Monumens de la monarchie Françoise, par *Monifaucon*, tom. ii. p. 184, plate p. 185. Hist, de la Maison de Dreux, p. 86, 276.

feast of the nativity of our Lord; and all the property of the aforesaid house, wheresoever situate, I take under my safeguard and protection, and will defend it in accordance with right and justice against all men.

"This donation I have made in the presence of Brother Peter de Montaigu, Preceptor of Spain; Brother Peter Cadelli, Preceptor of Provence; and many other brothers of the Order."

"And we, Brother Peter de Montaigu, Master, with the advice and consent of the other brothers, receive you, the aforesaid Lord William, count of Fourcalquier, as a benefactor and brother (*in donatum et confratrem*) of our house, and grant you a bountiful participation in all the good works that are done in the house of the Temple, both here and beyond sea. Of this our grant are witnesses, of the brethren of the Temple, Brother William Cadelli, Preceptor of Provence; Brother Bermond, Preceptor of Rue; the reverend Brother Chosoardi, Preceptor of Barles; Brother Jordan de Mison, Preceptor of Embrun; Brother G. de la Tour, Preceptor of the hpuse of Limaise. Of laymen are witnesses, the lady countess, the mother of the aforesaid count; Gerald, his brother, &c. &c."*

William of Asheby in Lincolnshire was admitted into this species of spiritual confraternity with the Templars, as appears from the following grant to the Order:

"William of Asheby, to all the barons and vavasors of Lincolnshire, and to all his friends and neighbours, both French and English, Salvation. Be it known to all present and to come, that since the knights of the Temple have received me into confraternity with them, and have taken me under their care and protection, I the said William have, with the consent of my Brothers Ingram, Gerard, and Jordan, given and granted to God and the blessed Mary, and to the aforesaid knights of the Temple, all the residue of my waste and heath land, over and above what I have confirmed to them by my previous grant ... &c &c."†

By these curious arrangements with secular persons, the Templars succeeded in attaching men of rank and influence to their interests, and in obtaining bountiful alms and donations, both of land and money. It is probable that the cross-legged monuments in the Temple Church were erected to the memory of secular warriors who had been admitted amongst the class of associated brethren of the Temple, and had bequeathed their bodies to be buried in the Temple cemetery.

During the recent repairs it became necessary to make an extensive excavation in the Round, and beneath these monumental effigies were found two enormous stone coffins, together with five-leaden coffins curiously and beautifully ornamented with a device

---

* *Ducange*. Gloss. tom. iii. p. 16, 17 ; ed. 1678, verb. *Oblati*
† *Peck*. MS. vol. iv. p. 67.

resembling the one observable on the old tesselated pavement of the church; and an arched vault, which had been formed in the inner circular foundation, supporting the clustered columns and the round tower. The leaden coffins had been inclosed in small vaults, the walls of which had perished. The skeletons within them were entire and undisturbed; they were enveloped in coarse sackcloth, which crumbled to dust on being touched. One of these skeletons measured six feet four inches in length, and another six feet two inches! The large stone coffins were of immense thickness and weight; they had long previously been broken open and turned into charnel-houses. In the one nearest the south window were found three skulls, and a variety of bones, amongst which were those of some young person. Upon the lid, which was composed of Purbeck marble, was a large and elegantly-shaped cross, beautifully sculptured, and in an excellent state of preservation. The vault constructed in the solid foundations of the pillars of the round tower, on the north side of the church, contained the remains of a skeleton wrapped in sackcloth; the skull and the upper part of it were in a good state of preservation, but the lower extremities had crumbled to dust.

Neither the number nor the position of the coffins below corresponded with the figures above, and it is quite clear that these last have been removed from their original position.

In Camden's Britannia, the first edition of which was published in the 38th of Eliz., A.D. 1586, we are informed that many noblemen lie buried in the Temple Church, whose effigies are to be seen crosslegged, among whom were William the father, and William and Gilbert his sons, earls of Pembroke and marshals of England.* Stow, in his Survey of London, the first edition of which was published A.D. 1598, speaks of them as follows:

"In the round walk (which is the west part without the quire) there remain monuments of noblemen there buried, to the number of eleven. *Eight* of them are images of armed knights; five *lying* cross-legged, as men vowed to the Holy Land against the infidels and unbelieving Jews, the other three straight-legged The rest are coped stones, all of gray marble."† A manuscript history of the Temple in the Inner Temple library, written at the commencement of the reign of Charles the First, tells us that "the crossed-legged images or portraitures remain in carved stone in *the middle of the round walke, environed with barres of iron.*"‡ And Dug-

---

* Plurimique nobiles apud eos humati fuerunt, quorum imagines visuntur in hoc Templo, tibiis in crucem transversis (sic enim sepulti fuerunt quotquot illo sæculo nomina bello sacro dedissent, vel qui ut tunc temporis sunt locuti crucem suscepissent.)

E quibus fuerunt Guilielmus Pater, Guilielmus et Gilberti ejus filii, onines marescalli Angliæ, comitesque Pembrochiæ .—Camden's Britannia, p. 375.

† Stow's Survey.

‡ MS. Inner Temple Library, No. 17. fol. 402.

dale, in his Origines Juridiciales, published 1666, thus describes them: "Within a spacious *grate of iron* in *the midst of the round walk* under the steeple, do lye *eight* statues in military habits, each of them having large and deep shields on their left armes, of which five are cross-legged. There are also three other gravestones lying about five inches above the level of the ground, on one of which is a large escocheon, with a lion rampant graven thereon."* Such is the ancient account of these monuments; now, however, six instead of five cross-legged statues are to be seen, making nine armed knights, whilst only *one* coped gravestone remains. The effigies are no longer inclosed "within a spacious grate of iron," but are divided into two groups environed by iron railings, and are placed on either side of the entrance to the oblong portion of the church.

Whatever change was made in their original position appears to have been effected at the time that the church was so shamefully disfigured by the Protestant lawyers, either in the year 1682, when it was "thoroughly repaired," or in 1695, when "the ornamental screen was set up in itinas-much, as we are informed by a newspaper, called the Flying Post, of the date of the 2nd of January, 1696, that Roger Gillingham, Esq., treasurer of the Middle Temple, who died on the 29th of December, 1695, aet. seventy, had the credit of facing the Temple Church with New Portland stone, and of *"marshalling the Knights Templars in uniform order."*† Stow tells us that "the first of the crossed legged was William Marshall, the elder, earl of Pembroke," but the effigy of that nobleman now stands the second; the additional figure appears to have been placed the first, and seems to have been brought from the western doorway and laid by the side of the others.

During the recent restoration of the church, it was necessary to excavate the earth in every part of the Round, and just beneath the pavement of the external circular aisle or portico environing the tower, was found a broken sarcophagus of Purbeck marble, containing a skull and some bones apparently of very great antiquity; the upper surface of the sarcophagus was on a level with the ancient pavement; it had no mark or inscription upon it, and seemed originally to have been decorated with a monumental effigy.

From two ancient manuscript accounts of the foundation of Walden Abbey, written by the monks of that great religious house, we learn that Geoffrey de Magnaville, earl of Essex, the founder of it, being slain by an arrow, in the year 1144, was taken by the Knights Templars to the Old Temple, that he was afterwards removed to the cemetery of the New Temple, and that his body was buried in the portico before the western door of the church.* The sarcophagus lately found in that position is of

---

* Origines Juridiciales, p. 173.
† Nicholls' Leicestershire, vol. iii. p. 960.

Purbeck marble; so also is the first figure on the south side of the Round, whilst nearly all the others are of common stone. The tablet whereon it rests had been grooved round the edges and polished; three sides were perfect, but the fourth had decayed away to the extent of six or seven inches. The sides of the marble sarcophagus had also been carefully smoothed and polished. The same thing was not observable amongst the other sarcophagi and figures. It must, moreover, be mentioned, that the first figure on the south side had no coffin of any description under it. We may, therefore, reasonably conclude, that this figure is the monumental effigy of Geoffrey de Magnaville, earl of Essex. It represents an armed knight with his legs crossed,† in token that he had assumed the cross, and taken a vow to fight in defence of the Christian faith. His body is cased in chain mail, over which is worn a loose flowing garment confined to the waist by a girdle, his right arm is placed on his breast, and his left supports a long shield charged with rays on a diamond ground. On his right side hangs a ponderous sword of immense length, and his head, which rests on a stone cushion, is covered with an elegantly-shaped helmet.

Geoffrey de Magnaville, earl of Essex, to whose memory the above monument appears to have been erected, was one of the most violent of those "barons bold" who desolated England so fearfully during the reign of King Stephen. He was the son of that famous soldier, Geoffrey de Magnaville, who fought so valiantly at the battle of Hastings, and was endowed by the conqueror with one hundred and eighteen lordships in England. From his father William de Magnaville, and his mother Magaret, daughter and heiress of the great Eudo Dapifer, Sir Geoffrey inherited an immense estate in England and in Normandy. On the accession of King Stephen to the throne, he was made constable of the Tower, and created earl of Essex, and was sent by the king to the Isle of Ely to put down a rebellion which had been excited there by Baldwin de Rivers, and Nigel bishop of Ely.‡

In A.D. 1136, he founded the great abbey of Walden in Essex, which was consecrated by the bishops of London, Ely, and Norwich, in the presence of Sir Geoffrey, the lady Roisia his wife, and all his principal tenants.§ For some time after the commencment of the war between Stephen and the empress Matilda for the succession to the throne, he remained faithful

---

* " In portico ante ostium ecclesiæ occidentale." The word proticus, which means " a walking place environed with pillars," exactly corresponds with the external circular walk surrounding the round tower of the church.

† Some surprise has been expressed that the effigies of women should be found in this curious position. It must be recollected, that women frequently fought in the field during the Crusades, and were hightly applauded for so doing.

‡ Hoveden apud rer. Anglicar. Script. post Bedam, p. 488. Dugdale's Baronage, vol.i. p. 201. Lel. Coll. Vol. i. 864.

§ *Monast. Angl.*, vol. i. p. 444 to 464.

to the former, but after the fatal result of the bloody battle of Lincoln, in which King Stephen was taken prisoner, he, in common with most of the other barons, adhered to the party of Matilda; and that princess, fully sensible of his great power and commanding influence, left no means untried to attach him permanently to her interests. She confirmed him in his post of constable of the Tower; granted him the hereditary shrievalties of several counties, together with large estates and possessions both in England and in Normandy, and invested him with numerous and important privileges.* On the flight of the empress, however, and the discomfiture of her party, King Stephen was released from prison, and an apparent reconciliation took place between him and his powerful vassal the earl of Essex, but shortly afterward the king ventured upon the bold step of seizing and imprisoning the earl and his father-in-law, Aubrey de Vere, whilst they were unsuspectingly attending the court at Saint Alban's.

The earl of Essex was compelled to surrender the Tower of London, and several of his strong castles, as the price of his freedom;† but he was no sooner at liberty, than he collected together his vassals and adherents, and raised the standard of rebellion. He was joined by crowds of freebooters and needy adventurers, and soon found himself at the head of a powerful army. He laid waste the royal domains, pillaged the king's servants, and subsisted his followers upon plunder. He took and sacked the town of Cambridge, laid waste the surrounding country, and stormed several royal castles. He was afterwards compelled to retreat for a brief period into the fens before a superior force led against him by King Stephen in person.

The most frightful excesses are said to have been committed by this potent earl. He sent spies, we are told, to beg from door to door, and discover where rich men dwelt, that he might seize them at night in their beds, throw them into dungeons, and compel the payment of a heavy ransom for their liberty.‡ He got by water to Ramsey, and entering the abbey of St. Benedict at morning's dawn, surprised the monks asleep in their beds after the fatigue of nocturnal offices; he turned them out of their cells, filled the abbey with his soldiers, and made a fort of the church; he took away all the gold and silver vessels of the altar, the copes and vestments of the priests and singers ornamented with precious stones,

---

* *Dugd*. Bar., vol. i. p. 202. *Selden*, tit. hon. p. 647.

† *Triveti* annales apud Hall, p. 12, 13, ad ann. 1143. *Guill. Neubr*. Lib. i. cap. ii. p. 44. ad ann. 1143. Hoveden, p. 488, Hist. Minor. Matt. Par. in bib. Reg. apud S. Jacobum.

‡ *Henry Huntingdon*, lib. viii. Rer. Anglicar. Script. post Bedam, p. 393. *Chron. Gervasii,* apud script. X. col. R*adulph de Diceto*, ib. col. 508. Vir autem iste magnanimus, velut equus validus et infrænus, maneria, villas, cæteraque, proprietatem regiam contingents, invasit, igni combussit, &c. &c. MS. In Bibl. Arund., A. D. 1647, a. 43. cap. ix., now in the Library of the Royal Society. *Annales Dunstaple* apud Hearne, tom. i. p. 25.

and all the decorations of the church, and sold them for money to reward his soldiers.* The monkish historians of the period speak with horror of these sacrilegious excesses.

"He dared," says William, the monk of Newburgh, who lived in the reign of King Stephen, "to make that celebrated and holy place a robber's cave, and to turn the sanctuary of the Lord into an abode of the devil. He infested all the neighbouring provinces with frequent incursions, and at length, emboldened by constant success, he alarmed and harassed King Stephen himself by his daring attacks. He thus, indeed, raged madly, and it seemed as if the Lord slept and cared no longer for human affairs, or rather his own, that is to say, ecclesiastical affairs, so that the pious labourers in Christ's vineyard exclaimed, 'Arise, O God, maintain thine own cause . . . how long shall the adversary do this dishonour, how long shall the enemy blaspheme thy name?' But God, willing to make his power known, as the apostle saith, endured with much 'long-suffering the vessels of wrath fitted to destruction,' and at last smote his enemies in their hinder parts. It was discovered indeed, a short time before the destruction of this impious man, as we have learned from the true relation of many witnesses, that the walls of the church sweated pure blood,— a terrible manifestation, as it afterwards appeared, of the enormity of the crime, and of the speedy judgement of God upon the sinners."†

For this sacrilege and impiety Sir Geoffrey was excommunicated, but, deriding the spiritual thunders, he went and laid siege to the royal castle at Bur well. After a successful attack which brought him to the foot of the rampart, he took off his helmet, it being summer-time and the weather hot, that he might breathe more freely, when a foot soldier belonging to the garrison shot an arrow from a loophole in the castle wall, and gave him a slight wound on the head; "which slight wound," says our worthy monk of Newburgh, "although at first treated with derision, after a few days destroyed him, so that that most ferocious man, never having been

---

* Vaaa autem altaris aurea et argentea Deo sacrata, capaa etiam cantorum lapidibus preciosia ac opere mirifico contextas, casulaa cum albis et cæteris ecclesiastici decoris ornamentia rapuit, &c. MS. ut sup. Gest. reg. Steph. p. 693, 964.

† De vitâ sceleratâ et condigno interitu Gaufridi de Magnavilla.—*Guill. Neubr.* lib. i. cap. xi. p. 44 to 46. Henry of Huntingdon, who lived in King Stephen's reign, and kept up a correspondence with the abbot of Ramsay, thus speaks of this wonderful phenomenon, of which he declares himself an eye-witness. Dum autem ecclesia ilia pro castello teneretur, ebullivit sanguis a parietibus ecclesiæ; et claustri adjacentis, indignationem divinam manifestans; sceleratorum exterminationem denuntians, quod quidem multi viderant, *et ego ipse quidem meis oculis inspexi! Script. post Bedam.* lib. viii. p. 393, ed. 1601, Francfort. Hoveden, who wrote shortly after, has copied this account. Annales, ib. p. 488.

‡ *Guill Neubr,* ut supr. p. 45, 46. Chron. *Gervasii,* apud X. script, col. 1360. *Annal. S. Augustin.* Trivet ad ann. 1144, p. 14. *Chron. Brampton,* col. 1033. *Hoveden,* ut supr. p. 488.

absolved from the bond of the ecclesiastical curse, went to hell."‡

Peter de Langtoft thus speaks of these evil doings of the earl of Essex, in his curious poetic chronicle.

> "The abbay of Rameseie bi nyght he robbed it
> The tresore bare aweie with hand thei myght on hit.
> Abbot, and prior, and monk, thei did outchace,
> Of holy kirke a toure to theft thei mad it place.
> Roberd the Marmion, the same wayes did he,
> He robbed thorgh treson the kirk of Couentre.
> Here now of their schame, what chance befelle,
> The story sais the same soth as the gospelle:
> Geffrey of Maundeuile to fele wrouh ho wouh,*
> The deuelle gald him his while with an arrowe him slouh.
> The gode bishop of Chestre cursed this ilk Geffrey,
> The lif out of his estre in cursing went away.
> Arnulf his sonne was taken als thefe, and brouht in bond,
> Before the kyng forsaken, and exiled out of his lond."†

The monks of Walden tell us, that as the earl lay wounded on his sick couch, and felt the hand of death pressing heavy upon him, he bitterly repented of his evil deeds, and sought, but in vain, for ecclesiastical assistance. At last some Knights Templars came to him, and finding him humble and contrite, praying earnestly to God, and making what satisfaction he could for his past offences, they put on him the habit of their religion marked with the red cross. After he had expired, they carried the dead body with them to the Old Temple at London; but as the earl had died excommunicated, they durst not give him Christian burial in consecrated ground, and they accordingly soldered him up in lead, and hung him on a crooked tree in their orchard.‡ Some years afterwards, through the exertions and at the expense of William, whom the earl had made prior of Walden Abbey, his absolution was obtained from pope Alexander the Third, so that his body was permitted to be received amongst Christians, and the divine offices to be celebrated for him. The prior accordingly endeavoured to take down the corpse and carry it to Walden; but the Templars, being informed of his design, buried it in their own cemetery at the New Temple,* in the portico before the western door of the church.†

---

* Grew mad with much anger.

† Peter Langtoft's Chronicle, vol. i. 123, by Robert of Brunne, Translated from a MS. in the Inner Temple Library, Oxon. 1725.

‡ In pomoerio suo veteris, scilicet Templi apud London, canali inclusum plumbeo, in arbore torvâ suspenderant. *Ancient MS. De fundatione coenobii Sancti Jacobi de Waldena,* fol. 43, a. cap. ix. No. 51, in the Library of the Royal Society.

Pope Alexander, from whom the absolution was obtained, was elected to the pontifical chair in September, 1159, and died in 1181. It was this pontiff who, who by the bull *omne datum optimum*, promulgated in the year 1162, conceded to the Templars the privilege of having their own cemeteries free from the interference of the regular clergy. The land whereon the convent of the New Temple was erected, was purchased soon after the publication of the above bull, and a cemetery was doubtless consecrated there for the brethren long before the completion of the church. To this cemetery the body of the earl was removed after the absolution had been obtained, and when the church was consecrated by the patriarch, (A.D. 1185), it was finally buried in the portico before the west door.

The monks of Walden tell us that the above earl of Essex was a religious man, endowed with many virtues.‡ He was married to the famous Roisia de Vere, of the family of the earls of Oxford, who in her old age led an ascetic life, and constructed for herself an extraordinary subterranean cell or oratory, which was curiously discovered towards the close of the last century.§ He had issue by this illustrious lady four sons, Ernulph, Geoffrey, William, and Robert. Ernulph was exiled as the accomplice of the father in his evil deeds, and Geoffrey succeeded to the title and the estates.

The second of the cross-legged figures on the south side, in the Round of the Temple Church, is the monumental effigy of

WILLIAM MARSHALL, EARL OF PEMBROKE,

EARL MARSHALL, AND PROTECTOR OF ENGLAND, DURING the minority of King Henry the Third, and one of the greatest of the warriors and states-

---

* Cumque Prior ille, corpus defunctum deponere, et secum Waldenam transferre satageret, Templarii caute premeditati, statim illud tollentes, in cimiterio Novi Templi ignobili satis tradiderunt sepulturæ.—Ib.

† A.D. mclxiIII, sexto kal. Octobris, obiit Galfridus de Mandeuil, comes Essexiæ, fundator primus hujus monasterii de Walden, cujus corpus jacet Londoniis humatum, apud Temple-bar *in porticu ante ostium ecclesioe occidental.* MS. in the library of the Royal Society, marked No. 29, entitled *Liber de fundatione Sancti Jacobi Apostoli de Waldenâ.* Cotton, MS. Vesp. E. vi. fol. 25.

‡ Hoveden speaks of him as a man of the highest probity, but irreligious. Erat autem summæ probitatis, sed summæ in Deum obstinationis, magnæ in mundanis diligentiæ, magnæ in Deum negligentiæ. Hoveden ut supra.

§ It was a recess, hewn out of the chalk, of a bell shape and exactly circular, thirty feet high and seventy feet in diameter. The sides of this curious retreat were adorned with imagery in basso relievo of crucifixes, saints, martyrs, and historical pieces, which the pious and eccentric lady is supposed to have cut for her entertainment.—See the extraordinary account of the discovery, in 1742, of the Lady Roisia's Cave at Royston, published by Dr. Stukeley. Cambridge, 1795.

men who shine in English history. Matthew Paris describes his burial in the Temple Church in the year 1119, and in Camden's time, (A.D. 1586), the inscription upon his monument was legible. "In altero horum tumulo," says Camden, "literis fugien bus legi, *Comes Pembrochiæ*, et in latere, *Miles eram Martis, Mars multos vicerat armis.*"* Although no longer, ("the first of the cross-legged"), as described by Stow, A.D. 1598, yet tradition has always, since the days of Roger Gillingham, who moved these figures, pointed it out as "the monument, of the protector," and the lion rampant, still plainly visible upon the shield, was the armorial bearing of the Marshalls.

This interesting monumental effigy is carved in a common kind of stone, called by the masons fire-stone. It represents an armed warrior clothed from head to foot in chain mail; he is in the act of sheathing a sword which hangs on his left side; his legs are crossed, and his feet, which are armed with spurs, rest on a *lion couchant*. Over his armour is worn a loose garment, confined to the waist by a girdle, and from his left arm hangs suspended a shield, having a lion rampant engraved thereon. The greater part of the sword has been broken away and lost, which has given rise to the supposition that he is sheathing a dagger. The head is defended by a round helmet, and rests on a stone pillow.

The family of the Marshalls derived their name from the hereditary office of earl marshall, which they held under the crown.

The above William Marshall was the son and heir of John Marshall, earl of Strigul, and was the faithful and constant supporter of the royal house of Plantagenet. When the young Prince Henry, eldest son of King Henry the Second, was on his deathbed at the castle of Martel near Turenne, he gave to him, as his best friend, his cross to carry to Jerusalem.† On the return of William Marshall from the holy city, he was present at the coronation of Richard Cœur de Lion, and bore on that occasion the royal sceptre of gold surmounted by a cross.‡ King Richard the same year gave him in marriage Isabel de Clare, the only child and heiress of Richard de Clare, earl of Pembroke, surnamed Strongbow, and granted him with this illustrious lady the earldom of Pembroke.§ The year following (A.D. 1190) he became one of the sureties for the performance by King Richard of his part of the treaty entered into with the king of France for the accomplishment of the crusade to the Holy Land, and on the departure of King Richard for the far East he was appointed by that monarch one of the council for the government of the kingdom during his absence.*

---

* *Camden's Britannia, ed. 1600, p. 375.*

† Tradidit Willielmo Marescallo, familiari suo, crucem suam Jerosolymam deferendam. *Hoveden* ad ann. 1183, apud rer. Anglic. Script. post Bedam, p. 620.

‡ *Chron. Joan Brompton,* apud X. script. col. 1158. Hoveden, p. 655, 666.

§ Selden's Tit. of Honour, p. 677.

From the year 1189 to 1205 he was sheriff of Lincolnshire, and was after that sheriff of Sussex, and held that office during the whole of King Richard's reign. He attended Cœur de Lion in his expedition to Normandy, and on the death of that monarch by the hand of Bertram, the cross-bow-man, before the walls of Castle Ghaluz, he was sent over to England to keep the peace of the kingdom until the arrival of King John. In conjunction with Hubert, archbishop of Canterbury, he caused the freemen of England, both of the cities and boroughs, and most of the earls, barons, and free tenants, to swear fealty to John.†

On the arrival of the latter in England he was constituted sheriff of Gloucestershire and of Sussex, and was shortly afterwards sent into Normandy at the head of a large body of forces. He commanded in the famous battle fought A.D. 1202 before the fortress of Mirabel, in which the unfortunate Prince Arthur and his lovely sister Eleanor, "the pearl of Brittany," were taken prisoners, together with the earl of March, most of the nobility of Poictou and Anjou, and two hundred French knights, who were ignominiously put into fetters, and sent away in carts to Normandy. This battle was followed, as is well known, by the mysterious death of Prince Arthur, who is said to have been murdered by King John himself, whilst the beautiful Eleanor, nicknamed *La Bret*, who, after the death of her brother, was the next heiress to the crown of England, was confined in close custody in Bristol Castle, where she remained a prisoner for life. At the head of four thousand infantry and three thousand cavalry, the earl Marshall attempted to relieve the fortress of Chateau Gaillard, which was besieged by Philip king of France, but failed in consequence of the non-arrival of seventy flat-bottomed vessels, whose progress up the river Seine had been retarded by a strong contrary wind.‡ For his fidelity and services to the crown he was rewarded with numerous manors, lands, and castles, both in England and in Normandy, with the whole province of Leinster in Ireland, and he was made governor of the castles of Caermerden, Cardigan, and Coher.

In the year 1204 he was sent ambassador to Paris, and on his return he continued to be the constant and faithful attendant of the English monarch. He was one of the witnesses to the surrender by King John at Temple Ewell of his crown and kingdom to the pope,§ and when the barons' war broke out he was the constant mediator and negotiator between the king and his rebellious subjects, enjoying the confidence and respect of both parties. When the armed barons came to the Temple, where King John resided, to demand the liberties and laws of King Edward, he became

---

* *Hoveden*, p. 659, 660. *Radulf de Diceto*, apud X. script. p. 659.

† Matt. Par., p. 196. Hoveden, p. 792. Dugdale Baronage, tom. i. p. 601.

‡ Trivet, p. 144. Gul. Britt, lib. vii. Ann. Waverley, p. 168.

§ *Matt. Par.*, p. 237.

surety for the performance of the king's promise to satisfy their demands. He was afterwards deputed to inquire what these laws and liberties were, and after having received at Stamford the written demands of the barons, he urged the king to satisfy them. Failing in this, he returned to Stamford to explain the king's denial, and the barons' war then broke out. He afterwards accompanied King John to the Tower, and when the barons entered London he was sent to announce the submission of the king to their desires. Shortly afterwards he attended King John to Runnymede, in company with Brother Americ, the Master of the Temple, and at the earnest request of these two exalted personages, King John was at last induced to sign MAGNA CHARTA*.

On the death of that monarch, in the midst of a civil war and a foreign invasion, he assembled the loyal bishops and barons of the land at Gloucester, and by his eloquence, talents, and address, secured the throne for King John's son, the young Prince Henry.† The greater part of England was at that time in the possession of Prince Louis, the dauphin of France, who had landed with a French army at Sandwich, and was supported by the late king's rebellious barons in a claim to the throne. Pembroke was chosen guardian and protector of the young king and of the kingdom, and exerted himself with great zeal and success in driving out the French, and in bringing back the English to their ancient allegiance.‡ He offered pardon in the king's name to the disaffected barons for their past offences. He confirmed, in the name of the youthful sovereign, Magna Charta and the Charta ForestÆ; and as the great seal had been lost by King John, together with all his treasure, in the washes of Lincolnshire, the deeds of confirmation were sealed with the seal of the earl marshall change as marshall.§ He also extended the benefit of Magna Charta to Ireland, and commanded all the sheriffs to read it publicly at the county courts, and enforce its observance in every particular. Having thus exerted himself to remove the just complaints of the disaffected, he levied a considerable army, and having left the young king at Bristol, he proceeded to lay siege to the castle of Mountsorel in Leicestershire, which was in the possession of the French.

Prince Louis had, in the mean time, despatched an army of twenty

---

* *Matt. Par.*, p. 253—256, ad ann. 1215.

† See his eloquent address to the bishops and barons in behalf of the young king.— Hemingford, lib. iii. cap. 1. p. 562, apud Gale XV. script.

‡ Matt. Par., p. 289, ad ann. 1216. Acta Rymeri, tom. i. p. 216.

§ *Hemingford*, p. 565, 568. "These liberties, distinctly reduced to writing, we send to you our faithful subjects, sealded with the seal of our faithful William Marshall, earl of Pembroke, the guardian of us and our kingdom, because we have not as yet any seal." Acta *Rymeri*, tom. i. part 1. p. 146, ed. 1816. *Thomson*, on Magna Charta, p. 117, 130. All the charters and letters patent were sealed with the seal of the earl marshall, " Rectoris nostril et regni, eo quod *nondum sigillum habuimus*. Acta *Rymeri*, tom. i. 224, ed. 1704.

thousand men, officered by six hundred knights, from London against the northern counties. These mercenaries stormed various strong castles, despoiled the towns, villages, and religious houses, and laid waste the open country. The protector concentrated all his forces at Newarke, and on Whit-monday, A.D. 1217, he marched at their head, accompanied by his eldest son and the young king, to raise the siege of Lincoln Castle. On arriving at Stow he halted his army, and leaving the youthful monarch and the royal family at that place under the protection of a strong guard, he proceeded with the remainder of his forces to Lincoln. On Saturday in Whitsun week (A.D. 1217) he gained a complete victory over the disaffected English and their French allies, and gave a deathblow to the hopes and prospects of the dauphin. Four earls, eleven barons, and four hundred knights, were taken prisoners, besides common soldiers innumerable. The earl of Perch, a Frenchman, was slain whilst manfully defending himself in a churchyard, having previously had his horse killed under him. The rebel force lost all their baggage, provisions, treasure, and the spoil which they had accumulated from the plunder of the northern provinces, among which were many valuable gold and silver vessels torn from the churches and the monasteries.

As soon as the fate of the day was decided, the protector rode back to the young king at Stow, and was the first to communicate the happy intelligence of his victory.* He then marched upon London, where Prince Louis and his adherents had fortified themselves, and leaving a corps of observation in the neighbourhood of the metropolis, he proceeded to take possession of all the eastern counties. Having received intelligence of the concentration of a French fleet at Calais to make a descent upon the English coast, he armed the ships of the Cinque Ports, and, intercepting the French vessels, he gained a brilliant victory over a much superior naval force of the enemy.† By his valour and military talents he speedily reduced the French prince to the necessity of suing for peace.‡ On the 11th of September a personal interview took place between the latter and the protector at Staines near London, and it was agreed that the prince and all the French forces should immediately evacuate the country.

Having thus rescued England from the danger of a foreign yoke, and having established tranquillity throughout the country, and secured the young King Henry in the peaceable and undisputed possession of the throne, he died (A.D. 1219) at Caversham, leaving behind him, says Matthew Paris, such a reputation as few could compare with. His dead body was, in the first instance, conveyed to the abbey at Reading, where

---

* *Matt. Par.*, p. 292—296.

† Matthew Paris bears witness to the great superiority of the English sailors over the French even in those days.—Ibid., p. 298. *Trivet*, p. 167 — 169.

‡ Acta *Rymeri*, tom. i. p. 219, 221, 223.

it was received by the monks in solemn procession. It was placed in the choir of the church, and high mass was celebrated with vast pomp. On the following day it was brought to Westminster Abbey, where high mass was again performed; and from thence it was borne in state to the Temple Church, where it was solemnly interred on Ascension-day, A.D. 1219.* Matthew Paris tells us that the following epitaph was composed to the memory of the above distinguished nobleman:

"Sum quem Saturnum sibi sensit Hibernia, solem
Anglia, Mercurium Normannia, Gallia Martem."

For he was, says he, always the tamer of the mischievous Irish, the honour and glory of the English, the negotiator of Normandy, in which he transacted many affairs, and a warlike and invincible soldier in France.

The inscription upon his tomb was, in Camden's time, almost illegible, as before mentioned, and the only verse that could be read was,

"Miles eram Martis Mars multos vicerat armis."

All the historians of the period speak in the highest terms of the earl of Pembroke as a warrior† and a statesman, and concur in giving him a noble character. Shakspeare, consequently, in his play of King John, represents him as the eloquent intercessor in behalf of the unfortunate Prince Arthur.

Surrounded by the nobles, he thus addresses the King on his throne—

"PEMBROKE. I (as one that am the tongue of these,
To sound the purposes of all their hearts),
Both for myself and them, (but, chief of all,
Your safety, for the which myself and them
Bend their best studies), heartily request
The enfranchisement of Arthur; whose restraint
Doth move the murmuring lips of discontent
To break into this dangerous argument,—
If, what in rest you have, in right you hold,
Why then your feara, (which, as they say, attend
The steps of wrong), should move you to mew up
Your tender kinsman, and to choke his days
With barbarous ignorance, and deny his youth
The rich advantage of good exercise?
That the time's enemies may not have this
To grace occasions, let it be our suit

---

* *Dugd.* Baronage, tom. i. p. 602, A. D. 1219. Willielmus senior, mareschallus Regis et rector regni, diem clausit extremum, et Londini apud Novum Templum honorifice tumulatur, scilicet in ecclesia, in Ascensionis die videlicet xvii. Calendas Aprilis.—*Matt. Par.* p. 304. *Ann Dunstaple,* ad ann. 1219. *Ann. Waverley.*

† Miles strenuissimus et per universum orbem nominatissimus.—*Chron.* T. *Wikes* apud Gale, script. XV. p. 39.

That you have bid us ask his liberty;
Which for our goods we do no further ask,
Than whereupon our weal, on you depending.
Counts it your weal, he have his liberty."

Afterwards, when he is shown the dead body of the unhappy prince, he exclaims—

"O death, made proud with pure and princely beauty!
The earth had not a hole to hide this deed.

All murders past do stand excused in this:
And this, so sole, and so unmatchable,
Shall give a holiness, a purity,
To the yet unbegotten sin of times,
And prove a deadly bloodshed but a jest,
Exampled by this heinous spectacle."

This illustrious nobleman was a great benefactor to the Templars. He granted them the advowsons of the churches of Spenes, Castelan-Emby-an, together with eighty acres of land in Eschirmanhir.*

By the side of the earl of Pembroke, towards the northern windows of the Round of the Temple Church, reposes a youthful warrior, clothed in armour of chain mail; he has a long buckler on his left arm, and his hands are pressed together in supplication upon his breast. This is the monumental effigy of Robert Lord de Ros, and is the most elegant and interesting in appearance of all the cross-legged figures in the Temple Church. The head is uncovered, and the countenance, which is youth-ful, has a remarkably pleasing expression, and is graced with long and flowing locks of curling hair. On the left side of the figure is a ponderous sword, and the armour of the legs has a ridge or seam up the front, which is continued over the knee, and forms a kind of garter below the knee. The feet are trampling on a lion, and the legs are crossed in token that the warrior was one of those military enthusiasts who so strangely mingled religion and romance, "whose exploits form the connecting link between fact and fiction, between history and the fairy tale." It has generally been thought that this interesting figure is intended to represent a genuine Knight Templar clothed in the habit of his order, and the loose garment or surcoat thrown over the ring-armour, and confined to the waist by a girdle, has been described as "a flowing mantle with a kind of *cowl*." This supposed cowl is nothing more than a fold of the chain mail, which has been covered with a thick coating of paint. The mantle is the common surcoat worn by the secular warriors of the day, and is not the habit of the

* *Monast. Angl.*, p. 833, 834, 837, 843.

Temple. Moreover, the long curling hair manifests that the warrior whom it represents could not have been a Templar, as the brethren of the Temple were required to cut their hair close, and they wore long beards.

In an ancient genealogical account of the Ros family,* written at the commencement of the reign of Henry the Eighth, A.D. 1513, two centuries after the abolition of the Order of the Temple, it is stated that Robert Lord de Ros became a Templar, and was buried at London. The writer must have been mistakened, as that nobleman remained in possession of his estates up to the day of his death, and his eldest son, after his decease, had livery of his lands, and paid his fine to the king in the usual way, which would not have been the case if the Lord de Ros had entered into the Order of the Temple. He was doubtless an associate or honorary member of the fraternity, and the circumstance of his being buried in the Temple Church probably gave rise to the mistake. The shield of his monumental effigy is charged with three water bougets, the armorial ensigns of his family, similar to those observable in the north aisle of Westminster Abbey.

Robert Lord de Ros, in consequence of the death of his father in the prime of life, succeeded to his estates at the early age of thirteen, and in the second year of the reign of Richard Cœur de Lion, (A.D. 1190), he paid a fine of one thousand marks, (£666, 13s. 4d.), to the king for livery of his lands. In the eighth year of the same king, he was charged with the custody of *Hugh de Chaumont*, an illustrious French prisoner of war, and was commanded to keep him *safe as his own life*. He, however, devolved the duty upon his servant, William de Spiney, who, being bribed, suffered the Frenchman to escape from the Castle of Bonville, in consequence whereof the Lord de Ros was compelled by King Richard to pay eight hundred pounds, the ransom of the prisoner, and William de Spiney was executed.†

On the accession of King John to the throne, the Lord de Ros was in high favour at court, and received by grant from that monarch the barony of his ancestor, Walter l'Espec. He was sent into Scotland with letters of safe conduct to the king of Scots, to enable that monarch to proceed to England to do homage, and during his stay in Scotland he fell in love with Isabella, the beautiful daughter of the Scottish king, and demanded and obtained her hand in marriage. He attended her royal father on his journey into England to do homage to King John, and was present at the interview between the two monarchs on the hill near Lincoln, when the king of Scotland swore fealty on the cross of Hubert archbishop of Canterbury, in the presence of the nobility of both kingdoms, and a vast concourse of spectators.* From his sovereign the

---

* MS. Bib. Cotton.*Vitellius*, F. 4. *Monast. Angl.*, tom. i. p. 728, ed. 1655.

† *Matt. Par.*, p. 182. ad ann. 1196.

Lord de Ros obtained various privileges and immunities, and in the year 1213 he was made sheriff of Cumberland. He was at first faithful to King John, but, in common with the best and bravest of the nobles of the land, he afterwards shook off his allegiance, raised the standard of rebellion, and was amongst the foremost of those bold patriots who obtained Magna Charta. He was chosen one of the twenty-five conservators of the public liberties, and engaged to compel John to observe the great charter.† Upon the death of that monarch he was induced to adhere to the infant Prince Henry, through the influence and persuasions of the earl of Pembroke, the Protector,‡ and he received from the youthful monarch various marks of the royal favour. He died in the eleventh year of the reign of the young King Henry the Third, (A.D. 1227), and was buried in the Temple Church.§

The above Lord de Ros was a great benefactor to the Templars. He granted them the manor of Ribstane, and the advowson of the church, the ville of Walesford, and all his windmills at that place; the ville of Hulsyngore, with the wood and windmill there; also all his land at Cattail, and various tenements in Conyngstreate, York.**

Weever has evidently misapplied the inscription seen on the ancient monument of Brother Constance Hover, the visitor-general of the Order of the Temple, to the above nobleman.

As regards the remaining monumental effigies in the Temple Church, it appears utterly impossible at this distance of time to identify them, as there are no armorial bearings on their shields, or aught that can give us a clue to their history. There can be no doubt but that two of the figures are intended to represent William Marshall, junior, and Gilbert Marshall, both earls of Pembroke, and sons of the Protector. Matthew Paris tells us that these noblemen were buried by the side of their father in the Temple Church, and their identification would consequently have been easy but for the unfortunate removal of the figures from their original situations by the immortal *Roger Gillingham*.

Next to the Lord de Ros reposes a stern warrior, with both his arms crossed on his breast. He has a plain wreath around his head, and his shield, which has no armorial bearings, is slung on his left arm. By the side of this figure is a coaped stone, which formed the lid of an ancient sarcophagus. The ridges upon it represent a cross, the top of which terminates in a trefoil, whilst the foot rests on the head of a lamb. From the middle of the shaft of the cross issue two fleurets or leaves. As the

---

* *Hoveden* apud rer. Anglicar. script, post Bedam, p. 811.

† Matt. Par. p. 254, 262. Lel. Col. Vol. i. p. 362.

‡ Acta Rymeri, tom. i. p. 224. ad ann. 1217.

§ Dugd. Baronage, vol. i. p. 545, 546.

** Monast. Angl., vol. vi. part ii. p. 838, 842.

lamb was the emblem of the Order of the Temple, it is probable that the sarcophagus to which this coaped stone belonged, contained the dead body either of one of the Masters, or of one of the visitors-general of the Templars.

Of the figures in the northernmost group of monumental effigies in the Temple Church, only two are cross-legged. The first figure on the south side of the row, which is straight-legged, holds a drawn sword in its right hand pointed towards the ground; the feet are supported by a leopard, and the cushion under the head is adorned with sculptured foliage and flowers. The third figure has the sword suspended on the right side, and the hands are joined in a devotional attitude upon the breast. The fourth has a spirited appearance. It represents a cross-legged warrior in the act of drawing a sword, whilst he is at the same time trampling a dragon under his feet, It is emblematical of the religious soldier conquering the enemies of the Christian church. The next and last monumental effigy, which likewise has its legs crossed, is similar in dress and appearance to the others; the right arm reposes on the breast, and the left hand rests on the sword. These two last figures, which correspond in character, costume, and appearance, may perhaps be the monumental effigies of William and Gilbert Marshall, the two sons of the Protector.

William Marshall, commonly called the younger, was one of the bold and patriotic barons who compelled King John to sign Magna Charta. He was appointed one of the twenty-five conservators of the public liberties, and was one of the chief leaders and promoters of the barons' war, being a party to the covenant for holding the city and Tower of London.* On the death of King John, his father the Protector brought him over to the cause of the young King Henry, the rightful heir to the throne, whom he served with zeal and fidelity. He was a gallant soldier, and greatly distinguished himself in a campaign in Wales. He overthrew Prince Llewellyn in battle with the loss of eight thousand men, and laid waste the dominions of that prince with fire and sword.† For these services he had scutage of all his tenants in *twenty counties in England!* He was made governor of the castles of Cardigan and Carmarthen, and received various marks of royal favour. In the fourteenth year of the reign of King Henry the Third, he was made captain-general of the king's forces in Brittany, and, whilst absent in that country, a war broke out in Ireland, whereupon he was sent to that kingdom with a considerable army to restore tranquillity. He married Eleanor, the daughter of King John by the beautiful Isabella of Angoulême, and he was consequently the brother-in-law of the young King Henry the Third.* He died without issue, A.D. 1231, (16 Hen. III.), and on the 14th of April he was buried in the Temple Church at London,

---

* *Matt. Par.* p. 254, 256. Lel. col. vol. i. p. 841.
† *Matt. Par.* p. 317, ad ann. 1223.

by the side of his father the Protector. He was greatly beloved by King Henry the Third, who attended his funeral, and Matthew Paris tells us, that when the king saw the dead body covered with the mournful pall, he heaved a deep sigh, and was greatly affected.†

The manors, castles, estates, and possessions of this powerful noble-man in England, Wales, Ireland, and Normandy, were immense. He gave extensive forest lands to the monks of Tinterne in Wales; he founded the monastery of Friars preachers in Dublin, and to the Templars he gave the church of Westone with all its appurtenances, and granted and confirmed to them the borough of Baudac, the estate of Langenache, with various lands, windmills, and *villeins* of the soil.‡

GILBERT MARSHALL, EARL OF PEMBROKE, brother to the above, and third son of the Protector, succeeded to the earldom and the vast estates of his ancestors on the melancholy murder in Ireland of his gallant brother Richard, "the flower of the chivalry of that time," (A.D. 1234). The year after his accession to the title he married Margaret, the daughter of the king of Scotland, who is desribed by Matthew Paris as "a most elegant girl,"§ and received with her a splendid dowry. In the year 1236 he as-sumed the cross, and joined the king's brother, the earl of Cornwall, in the promotion of a Crusade to the Holy Land.

Matthew Paris gives a long account of an absurd quarrel which broke out between this earl of Pembroke and King Henry the Third, when the latter was eating his Christmas dinner at Winchester, in the year 1239.**

At a great meeting of Crusaders at Northampton, he took a solemn oath upon the high altar of the church of All Saints to proceed without delay to Palestine to fight against the enemies of the cross;†† but his intentions were frustrated by the hand of death. At a tournament held at Ware, A.D. 1241, he was thrown from his horse, and died a few hours afterwards at the monastery at Hertford. His entrails were buried in the church of the Virgin at that place, but his body was brought up to London, accompa-nied by all his family, and was interred in the Temple Church by the side of his father and eldest brother.*

---

* *Matt. Par.* p. 366. *Ann. Dunst.* p. 99. 134, 150.

† Eodem temppore, A.D. 1231, mense Aprili, Willielmus, Marescallus comes Pembrochiæ, in militia vir strenuous, in dolorem multorum, diem clausit extremum, et Londoniis apud Novum Templum sepultus est, juxta patrem suum, XVII calend. Maii. Rex autem qui eum indissolubiliter dilexit, cum hæc audivit, et cum vidisset, corpus defuncti pallâ coopertum, ex alto trahens suspiria, ait, Heu, heu, mihi ! nonne adhuc penitus vindicatus est sanguis beati Thomæ Martyris.—*Matt. Par.* p. 368.

‡ *Dugd.* Monast Angl. ut sup. p. 820.

§ Margaretam *pulleam elegantissimam* matrimonio sibi copulaverat.—*Matt. Par.*, p. 432, 404.

** *Matt. Par.* p. 483.

†† Ib. p. 431, 483, 516, 524.

The above Gilbert Marshall granted to the Templars the church of Weston, the borough of Baldok, lands and houses at Roydon, and the wood of Langnoke.†

All the five sons of the elder Marshall, the Protector, died without issue in the reign of Henry the Third, and the family became extinct. They followed one another to the grave in regular succession, so that each attained for a brief period to the dignity of the earldom, and to the hereditary office of EARL MARSHALL.

Matthew Paris accounts for the melancholy extinction of this noble and illustrious family in the following manner.

He tells us that the elder Marshall, the Protector, during a campaign in Ireland, seized the lands of the reverend bishop of Fernes, and kept possession of them in spite of a sentence of excommunication which was pronounced against him. After the Protector had gone the way of all flesh, and had been buried in the Temple Church, the reverend bishop came to London, and mentioned the circumstance to the king, telling him that the earl of Pembroke had certainly died excommunicated. The king was much troubled and alarmed at this intelligence, and besought the bishop to go to the earl's tomb and absolve him from the bond of excommunication, promising the bishop that he would endeavour to procure him ample satisfaction. So anxious, indeed, was King Henry for the safety of the soul of his quondam guardian, that he accompanied the bishop in person to the Temple Church; and Matthew Paris declares that the bishop, standing by the tomb in the presence of the king, and in the hearing of many bystanders, pronounced these words: "O William, who lyest here interred, and held fast by the chain of excommunication, if those lands which thou hast unjustly taken away from my church be rendered back to me by the king, or by your heir, or by any of your family, and if due satisfaction be made for the loss and injury I have sustained, I grant you absolution; but if not, I confirm my previous sentence, so that, enveloped in your sins, you stand for evermore condemned to hell!"

The restitution was never made, and the indignant bishop pronounced this further curse, in the words of the Psalmist: "His name shall be rooted out in one generation, and his sons shall be deprived of the blessing, INCREASE AND MULTIPLY; some of them shall die a miserable death; their inheritance shall be scattered; and this thou, O king, shall behold in thy lifetime, yea, in the days of thy flourishing youth." Matthew Paris dwells with great solemnity on the remarkable fulfilment of this dreadful prophecy, and declares that when the oblong portion of the Temple Church was consecrated, the body of the Protector was found entire, sewed up in a bull's hide, but in a state of putridity, and disgusting in appearance.*

* In crastino autem delatum est corpus ondinum, fratre ipsius prævio, cum tota sua familia comitante, juxta patrem suum et fratrem tumulandum. —Ib. p. 565. ad ann. 1241.

† *Dugd*. Monast. Angl., p. 833.

It will be observed that the dates of the burial of the above noble-man, as mentioned by Matthew Paris and other authorities, are as fol-low:—William Marshall the elder, A.D. 1219; Lord de Ros, A.D. 1227; William Marshall the younger, A.D. 1231; all before the consecration of the oblong portion of the church. Gilbert Marshall, on the other hand, was buried A.D. 1241, the year after that ceremony had taken place. Those, therefore, who suppose that the monumental effigies of the Mar-shall originally stood in the eastern part of the building, are mistaken.

Amongst the many distinguished persons interred in the Temple Church is WILLIAM PLANTAGENET, the fifth son of Henry the Third, who died A.D. 1256, under age.† The greatest desire was manifested by all classes of persons to be buried in the cemetery of the Templars.

King Henry the Third provided for his own interment in the Temple by a formal instrument couched in the following pious and reverential terms:

"To all faithful Christians to whom these presents shall come, Henry by the grace of God king of England, lord of Ireland, duke of Normandy and Aquitaine, and count of Anjou, salvation. Be it known to all of you, that we, being of sound mind and free judgment, and desiring with pious fore-thought to extend our regards beyond the passing events of this life, and to determine the place of our sepulture, have, on account of the love we bear to the Order and to the brethren of the chivalry of the Temple, given and granted, after this life's journey has drawn to a close, and we have gone the way of all flesh, our body to God and the blessed Virgin Mary, and to the house of the chivalry of the Temple at London, to be there buried, expecting and hoping that through our Lord and Saviour it will greatly contribute to the salvation of our soul ... We desire that our body, when we have departed this life, may be carried to the aforesaid house of the chivalry of the Temple, and be there decently buried as above men-tioned ... As witness the venerable father R., bishop of Hereford, &c. Given by the hand of the venerable father Edmund, bishop of Chichester, our chancellor, at Gloucester, the 27th of July, in the nineteenth year of our reign."*

Queen Eleanor also provided in a similar manner for her interment in the Temple Church, the formal instrument being expressed to be made

---

* Paucis ante evolutis annis, post mortem omnium suorum filiorum, videlicet, quando dedicata est ecclesia Novi Templi, inventum est corpus sæpedicti comitis quod erat insutum corio taurino, integrum, putridum tamen et prout videri potuit detestabile."— *Matt. Par.* p. 688. Surely this must be an interpolation by some wag. The last of the Pembrokes died A.D. 1245, whilst, according to Matthew Paris's own showing, the eastern part of the church was consecrated A.D. 1240, p. 526.

† *Mill's* Catalogues, p. 145. *Speed*, p. 551. *Sandford's* Genealogies, p. 92, 93, 2nd edition.

‡ Ex Registr. Hosp. S. Joh. Jerus. in Angliâ, in *Bib. Cotton*, fol. 25 a.

§ Ib

**Nicolas*, Testamenta Vetusta, p. 6.

with the consent and approbation of her lord, Henry the illustrious king of England, who had lent a willing ear to her prayers upon the subject. § These sepulchral arrangements, however, were afterwards altered, and the king by his will directed his body to be buried as follows: "I will that my body be buried in the church of the blessed Edward at Westminster, there being no impediment, having formerly appointed my body to be buried in the New Temple." **

CHAPTER XIII.

THE TEMPLE.

Antiquities in the Temple—The history of the place subsequent to the dissolution of the Order of the Knights Templars—The establishment of a society of lawyers in the Temple—The antiquity of this society—Its connexion with the ancient society of the Knights Templars—An order of knights and serving brethren established in the law—The degree of *frere serjen, or frater serviens,* borrowed from the ancient Templars—The modern Templars divide themselves into the two societies of the Inner and Middle Temple.

> "Those bricky towers,
> The which on Themrae's brode aged back do ride,
> Where now the studious lawyers have their bowers;
> There whilom wont the Templer Knights to bide,
> Till they decayed thro' pride."

THERE are but few remains of the ancient Knights Templars now existing in the Temple beyond the church. The present Inner Temple Hall was their ancient hall, but it has at different periods been so altered and re-paired as to have lost every trace and vestige of antiquity. In the year 1816 it was almost entirely rebuilt, and the following extract from "The Report and Observations of the Treasurer on the late Repairs of the Inner Temple Hall" may prove interesting, as showing the state of the edifice previous to that period.

"From the proportions, the state of decay, the materials of the eastern and southern walls, the buttresses of the southern front, the pointed form of the roof and arches, and the rude sculpture on the two doors of public entrance, the hall is evidently of very great antiquity . . . The northern wall appears to have been rebuilt, except at its two extremities, in modern times, but on the old foundations. ... The roof was found to be in a very decayed and precarious state; many timbers were totally rotten. It appeared to have undergone reparation at three separate periods of time, at each of which timber had been unnecessarily added, so as finally to accumulate a weight which had protruded the northern and southern walls. It became, therefore, indispensable to remove all the timber of the roof, and to replace it in a lighter form. On removing the old wainscoting of the western wall, a perpendicular crack of considerable height and width was discovered, which threatened at any moment the fall of that extremity of the building with its superincumbent roof . . . The turret of the clock and the southern front of the hall are only cased with stone; this was done in the year 1741, and very ill executed. The structure of the turret, composed of chalk, ragstone, and rubble, (the same material as the walls of the church), seems to be very ancient . . . The wooden cupola of the bell was so decayed as to let in the rain, and was obliged to be renewed in a form to agree with the other parts of the southern front.

"Notwithstanding the Gothic character of the building, in the year 1680, during the treasurership of Sir Thomas Robinson, prothonotary of C. B., a Grecian screen of the Doric order was erected, surmounted by lions' heads, cones, and other incongruous devices.

"In the year 1741, during the treasurership of John Blencowe, esq., low windows of Roman architecture were formed in the southern front.

"The dates of such innovations appear from inscriptions with the respective treasurers' names."

This ancient hall formed the far-famed refectory of the Knights Templars, and was the scene of their protid and sumptuous hospitality. Within its venerable walls they at different periods entertained King John, King Henry the Third, the haughty legates of Roman pontiffs, and the ambassadors of foreign powers. The old custom, alluded to by Matthew Paris,* of hanging around the wall the shields and armorial devices of the ancient knights, is still preserved, and each succeeding treasurer of the Temple still continues to hoist his coat of arms on the wall, as in the high and palmy days of the warlike monks of old.

At the west end of the hall are considerable remains of the ancient convent of the Knights Templars. A groined Gothic arch of the same style of architecture as the oldest part of the Temple Church forms the ceiling of the present buttery, and in the apartment beyond is a groined vaulted ceiling of great beauty. The ribs of the arches in both rooms are elegantly moulded, but are sadly disfigured with a thick coating of plaster and barbarous whitewash. In the cellars underneath these rooms are some old walls of immense thickness, the remains of an ancient window, a curious fireplace, and some elegant pointed Gothic arches corresponding with the ceilings above; but they are now, alas! shrouded in darkness, choked with modern brick partitions and staircases, and soiled with the damp and

* P. 899, 900.

dust of many centuries. These interesting remains form an upper and an under story, the floor of the upper story being on a level with the floor of the hall, and the floor of the under story on a level with the terrace on the south side thereof. They were formerly connected with the church by means of a covered way or cloister, which ran at right angles with them over the site of the present cloister-chambers, and commmunicated with the upper and under story of the chapel of St. Anne, which formerly stood on the south side of the church. By means of this corridor and chapel the brethren of the Temple had private access to the church for the performance of their strict religious duties, and of their secret ceremonies of admitting novices to the vows of the Order. In 9 Jac. I. A.D. 1612, some brick buildings three stories high were erected over this ancient cloister by Francis Tate, esq., and being burnt down a few years afterwards, the interesting covered way which connected the church with the ancient convent was involved in the general destruction, as appears from the following inscription upon the present buildings:

"Vetustissima Templariorum Porticu Igne Consumta, Anno 1678, Nova Hæc, sumptibus Medii Templi Extructa anno 1681 Gulielmo Whitelocke armigero, thesaurario.

"The very ancient portico of the Templars being consumed by fire in the year 1678, these new buildings were erected at the expense of the Middle Temple in the year 1681, William Whitlock, esq., being treasurer."

The cloisters of the Templars formed the medium of communication between the hall, the church, and the cells of the serving brethren of the Order.*

During the formation of the present new entrance into the Temple by the church, at the bottom of the Inner Temple-lane, a considerable portion of the brickwork of the old houses was pulled down, and an ancient wall of great thickness was disclosed. It was composed of chalk, rag-stone, and rubble, exactly resembling the walls of the church. It ran in a direction east and west, and appeared to have formed the extreme northern boundary of the old convent.

The site of the remaining buildings of the ancient Temple cannot now be determined with certainty.

The mansion-house, (Mansum Novi Templi), the residence of the Master and knights, who were lodged separately from the serving brethren and ate at a separate table, appears to have stood at the east end of the hall, on the site of the present library and apartments of the masters of the bench.

The proud and powerful Knights Templars were succeeded in the occupation of the Temple by a body of learned lawyers, who took possession of the old hall and the gloomy cells of the military monks, and converted

* Aute, p. 255.

the chief house of their order into the great and most ancient Common Law University of England.

For more than five centuries the retreats of the religious warriors have been devoted to "the studious and eloquent pleaders of causes," a new kind of Templars, who, as Fuller quaintly observes, now "defend one Christian from another as the old ones did Christians from Pagans." The modern Templars have been termed *milites justitiæ, or "soldiers of justice,"* for, as John of Salisbury, a writer of the twelfth century, saith, "neque reipublicse militant soli illi, qui galeis thoracisque muniti in hostes exercent tela quselibet, sed et patroni causarum, qui lapsa erigunt, fatigata reparant, nec minus provident humano generi, quam si laborantium vitam, spem, posterosque, armorum presidio, ab hostibus tueruntur." ("They do not alone fight for the state who, panoplied in helmets and breastplates, wield the sword and the dart against the enemy, for the pleaders of causes, who redress wrongs, who raise up the oppressed, do protect and provide for the human race as much as if they were to defend the lives, fortunes, and families of industrious citizens with the sword.")

> "Besides encounters at the bar
> Are braver now than those in war,
> In which the law does execution
> With leas disorder and confusion;
> Has more of honour in't, some hold,
> Not like the new way, but the old,
> When those the pen had drawn together
> Decided quarrels with the feather,
> And winged arrows killed as dead,
> And more than bullets now of lead:
> So all their combats now, as then,
> Are managed chiefly by the pen;
> That does the feat, with braver vigours,
> In words at length, as well as figures."

The settlement of the lawyers in the Temple was brought about in the following manner.

On the imprisonment of the Knights Templars, the chief house of the Order in London, in common with the other property of the military monks, was seized into the king's hands, and was committed to the care of James le Botiller and William de Basing, who, on the 9th of December, A.D. 1311, were commanded to hand it over to the sheriffs of London, to be taken charge of by them.* Two years afterwards the Temple was granted to that powerful nobleman, Aymer de Valence, earl of Pembroke, who had been one of the leaders of the baronial conspiracy against Piers Gavaston.† As Thomas earl of Lancaster, however, claimed the Temple by escheat as the immediate lord of the fee, the earl of Pembroke, on the

3rd of Oct., A.D. 1315, at the request of the king, and in consideration of other lands being granted to him by his sovereign, remised and released all his right and title therein to Lancaster.‡ This earl of Lancaster was cousin-german to the English monarch, and first prince of the blood; he was the most powerful and opulent subject of the kingdom, being possessed of no less than six earldoms, with a proportionable estate in land, and at the time that the Temple was added to his numerous other possessions he was at the head of the government, and ruled both the king and country as president of the council. In an ancient MS. account of the Temple, formerly belonging to lord Somers and afterwards to Nicholls, the celebrated antiquary, apparently written by a member of the Inner Temple, it is stated that the lawyers "made composition with the earl of Lancaster for a lodging in the Temple, and so came hither, and have continued here ever since." That this was the case appears highly probable from various circumstances presently noticed.

The earl of Lancaster held the Temple rather more than six years and a half.

When the king's attachment for Hugh le Despenser, another favourite, was declared, he raised the standard of rebellion. He marched with his forces against London, gave law to the king and parliament, and procured a sentence of attainder and perpetual exile against Hugh le Despenser. The fortune of war, however, soon turned against him. He was defeated, and conducted a prisoner to his own castle of Pontefract, where King Edward sat in judgment upon him, and sentenced him to be hung, drawn, and quartered, as a rebel and a traitor. The same day he was clothed in mean attire, was placed on a lean jade without a bridle, a hood was put on his head, and in this miserable condition he was led through the town of Pontefract to the place of execution, in front of his own castle.§

A few days afterwards, the king, whilst he yet tarried at Ponfract, granted the Temple to Aymer de Valence, earl of Pembroke, by a royal charter couched in the following terms:

"Edward by the grace of God, king, &c., to the archbishops, bishops, abbots, priors, earls, barons, justiciaries, &c &c. health. Know that on account of the good and laudable service which our beloved kinsman and faithful servant Aymer de Valence hath rendered and will continue to render to us, we have given and granted, and by our royal charter have confirmed to the said earl, the mansion-house and messuage called the

---

* *Joan Sarisburiensis.* Polycrat. lib. vi cap. 1.

† Acta *Rymeri*, tom. iii. p. 296, 297.

‡ Pat. 8. E. 2. m. 17. The Temple is described therein as "de feodo Thom æ Comitis Lancastriæ, et de honore Leicestrie."

§ Processus contra comitem Lancastriæ. Acta *Rymeri*, tom. iii. p. 936. *Lel.* coll. vol. i. p. 668. *La More, Wokingham.*

New Temple in the suburb of London, with the houses, rents, and all other things to the same mansion-house and messuage belonging, formerly the property of the Templars, and afterwards of Thomas earl of Lancaster, our enemy and rebel, and which, by the forfeiture of the same Thomas, have come into our hands by way of escheat, to be had and holden by the same Aymer and the heirs of his body lawfully begotten, of us and our heirs, and the other chief lords of the fee, by the same services as those formerly rendered; but if the said Aymer shall die without heirs of his body lawfully begotten, then the said mansion-house, messuage, &c. &c., shall revert to us and our heirs."*

Rather more than a year after the date of this grant, Aymer de Valence was murdered. He had accompanied Queen Isabella to the court of her father, the king of France, and was there slain (June 23rd, A.D. 1323) by one of the English fugitives of the Lancastrian faction, in revenge for the death of the earl of Lancaster, whose destruction he was believed to have compassed. His dead body was brought over to England, and buried in Westminster Abbey at the head of Edmund Crouchback, earl of Lancaster. He left no issue, and the Temple, consequently, once more reverted to the crown.†

It was now granted to Hugh le Despenser the younger, the king's favourite, at the very time that the act of parliament (17 Edward II.) was passed, conferring all the lands of the Templars upon the Hospitallers of St. John.‡ Hugh le Despenser, in common with the other barons, paid no attention to the parliament, and held the Temple till the day of his death, which happened soon after, for on the 24th of September, A.D. 1326, Queen Isabella landed in England with the remains of the Lancastrian faction; and after driving her own husband, Edward the Second, from the throne, she seized the favourite, and caused him instantly to be condemned to death. On St. Andrew's Eve he was led out to execution; they put on him his surcoat of arms reversed, a crown of nettles was placed on his head, and on his vestment they wrote six verses of the psalm, beginning, *Quid gloriaris in rnalitiâ.** After which he was hanged on a gallows eighty feet high, and was then beheaded, drawn, and quartered. His head was sent to London, and stuck upon the bridge; and of the four quarters of his body, one was sent to York, another to Bristol, another to Carlisle, and the fourth to Dover.†

Thus perished the last private possessor of the Temple at London.

The young prince, Edward the Third, now ascended the throne, leaving his parent, the dethroned Edward the Second, to the tender mercies of the gaolers of Berkeley Castle. He seized the Temple, as forfeited to him by

---

* Cart. 15. E. II. m. 21. Acta *Rymeri*, tom. iii. p. 940.

† *Dugd*, Baron., vol. i. p. 777, 778

‡ Rot. Escaet. l. E. III.

the attainder of Hugh le Despenser, and committed it to the keeping of the mayor of London, his escheator in the city. The mayor, as guardian of the Temple, took it into his head to close the gate leading to the waterside, which stood at the bottom of the present Middle Temple Lane, whereby the lawyers were much incommoded in their progress backwards and forwards from the Temple to Westminster. Complaints were made to the king on the subject, who, on the 2nd day of November, in the third year of his reign, wrote as follows to the mayor:

"The king to the mayor of London, his escheator‡ in the same city.

"Since we have been given to understand that there ought to be a free passage through the court of the New Temple at London to the river Thames, for our justices, clerks, and others, who may wish to pass by water to Westminster to transact their business, and that you keep the gate of the Temple shut by day, and so prevent those same justices, clerks of ours, and other persons, from passing through the midst of the said court to the waterside, whereby as well our own affairs as those of our people in general are oftentimes greatly hindered, we command you, that you keep the gates of the said Temple open by day, so that our justices and clerks, and other persons who wish to go by water to Westminster, may be able so to do by the way to which they have hitherto been accustomed.

"Witness ourself at Kenilworth, the 2nd day of November, and third year of our reign."§ The following year the king again wrote to the mayor, his escheator in the city of London, informing him that he had been given to understand that the bridge in the said court of the Temple, leading to the river, was so broken and decayed, that his clerks and law officers, and others, could no longer get across it, and were consequently prevented from passing by water to Westminster. "We therefore," he proceeds, "being desirous of providing such a remedy as we ought for this evil, command you to do whatever repairs are necessary to the said bridge, and to defray the cost thereof out of the proceeds of the lands and rents appertaining to the said Temple now in your custody; and when we shall have been informed of the things done in the matter, the expense shall be allowed you in your account of the same proceeds.

"Witness ourself at Westminster, the 15th day of January, and fourth year of our reign."*

Two years afterwards (6 E. III, A.D. 1333) the king committed the cus-

---

* *H. knyghton,* apud X.script. col. 2456.7 *Lel.* Itin. vol. vi. P 86. *Walsingham*, 106.

† Claus. 4. E. III. m. 9. Acta *Rymeri,* tom. iv. p. 461.

‡ There was in those days an *escheator* in each county, and in various large towns: it was the duty of this officer to seize into the king's hands all lands held in *capite* of the crown, on receiving a writ *De diem clausit extremum,* commanding him to assemble a jury to take inquisition of the value of the lands, as to who was the next heir of the deceased, the rents and services by which they were holden, &c. &c.

§ Claus 3. E. III. m. 6. d. Acta *Rymeri,* tom. iv. p. 406.

tody of the Temple to "his beloved clerk," William de Langford, "and farmed out the rents and proceeds thereof to him for the term of ten years, at a rent of 24*l.* per annum, the said William undertaking to keep all the houses and tenements in good order and repair, and so deliver them up at the end of the term."†

In the mean time, however, the pope, the bishops, and the Hospitallers had been vigorously exerting themselves to obtain a transfer of the property, late belonging to the Templars, to the Order of the Hospital of Saint John. The Hospitallers petitioned the king, setting forth that the church, the cloisters, and other places within the Temple, were consecrated and dedicated to the service of God, that they had been unjustly occupied and de-tained from them by Hugh le Despenser the younger, and, through his attainder, had lately come into the king's hands, and they besought the king to deliver up to them possession thereof. King Edward accordingly commanded the mayor of London, his escheator in that city, to take inquisition concerning the premises.

From this inquisition, and the return thereof, it appears that many of the founders of the Temple Church, and many of the brethren of the Order of Knights Templars, then lay buried in the church and cemetery of the Temple; that the bishop of Ely had his lodging in the Temple, known by the name of the bishop of Ely's chamber; that there was a chapel dedicated to St. Thomas-à-Becket, which extended from the door of the Temple Hall as far as the ancient gate of the Temple; also a cloister which began at the bishop of Ely's chamber, and ran in an *easterly* direction; and that there was a wall which ran in a northerly direction as far as the said king's highway; that in the front part of the cemetery towards the north, bordering on the king's highway, were thirteen houses formerly erected, with the assent and permission of the Master and brethren of the Temple, by Roger Blom, a messenger of the Temple, for the purpose of holding the lights and ornaments of the church; that the land whereon these houses were built, the cemetery, the church, and all the space inclosed between St. Thomas's chapel, the church, the cloisters, and the wall running in a northerly direction, and all the buildings erected thereon, together with the hall, cloisters, and St. Thomas's chapel, were sanctified places dedicated to God; that Hugh le Despenser occupied and detained them unjustly, and that through his attainder and forfeiture, and not otherwise, they came into the king's hands.*

After the return of this inquisition, the said sanctified places were assigned to the prior and brethren of the Hospital of Saint John; and the king, on the 11th of January, in the tenth year of his reign, A.D. 1337, directed his writ to the barons of the Exchequer, commanding them to

---

* Claus. 4. E. III. m. 7. Acta *Rymeri*, tom. iv. p. 464.

† Pat.6. E. III. p. 2. m. 22. in original, apud Rolls Garden ex parte Remembr. Thesaur.

take inquisition of the value of the said sanctified places, so given up to the Hospitallers, and of the residue of the Temple, and certify the same under their seals to the king, in order that a reasonable abatement might be made in William de Langford's rent. From the inquiry made in pursuance of this writ before John de Shorditch, a baron of the Exchequer, it further appears that on the said residue of the Temple upon the land then remaining in the custody of William de Langford, and withinside the great gate of the Temple, were another hall† and four chambers connected therewith, a kitchen, a garden, a stable, and a chamber beyond the great gate; also eight shops, seven of which stood in Fleet Street, and the eighth in the suburb of London, without the bar of the New Temple; that the annual value of these shops varied from ten to thirteen, fifteen, and sixteen shillings; that the fruit out of the garden of the Temple sold for sixty shillings per annum in the gross; that seven out of the thirteen houses erected by Roger Blom were each of the annual value of eleven shillings; and that the eighth, situated beyond the gate of entrance to the church, was worth four marks per annum. It appears, moreover, that the total annual revenue of the Temple then amounted to 73*l*. 6*s*. II*d*., equal to about 1,000*l*. of our present money, and that William de Langford was abated 12*l*. 4*s*. 2*d*. of his said rent.‡

Three years after the taking of this inquisition, and in the thirteenth year of his reign, A.D. 1340, King Edward the Third in consideration of the sum of one hundred pounds, which the prior of the Hospital promised to pay him towards the expense of his expedition into France, granted to the said prior all the residue of the Temple then remaining in the kings hands, to hold, together with the cemetery, cloisters, and the other sanctified places, to the said prior and his brethren, and their successors, of the king and his heirs, for charitable purposes, for ever.* From the above grant it appears that the porter of the Temple received sixty shillings and ten pence per annum, and twopence a day wages, which were to be paid him by the Hospitallers.

At this period Philip Thane was prior of the Hospital; and he appears to have exerted himself to impart to the celebration of divine service in the Temple Church, the dignity and the splendour it possessed in the

---

* Rot. Escaet. 10. E. 3. 66. Claus 11 E. 3. p. 1. m. 10.

† Sunt etiam ibidem claustrum, capella Sancti Thomse, et quædam platea terra eidem capellæ annexata, cum *una aula* et camera supra edificata, qua sunt loca sancta, et Deo dedicata, et dictæ ecclesæ annexata, et eidem Priori per idem breve liberata . . . . Item dicunt, quod præter ista, sunt ibidem in custodia Wilielmi de Langford infra Magnam Portam dicti Novi Templi, *extra metas et disjunctiones prcedictas,* una *aula* et quatuor camera, una coquina, unum gardinum, unum Btabulum, et una camera ultra Magnam Portam praedictam, &c.

‡ In memorandis Scacc. inter recorda de Termino Sancti Hilarii, 11. E. 3. in officio Remembratoris Thessaurarii.

time of the Templars. He, with the unanimous consent and approbation of the whole chapter of the Hospital, granted to Brother Hugh de Lichefeld, priest, and to his successors, guardians of the Temple Church, towards the improvement of the lights and the celebration of divine service therein, all the land called Ficketzfeld, and the garden called Cotterell Garden;† and two years afterwards he made a further grant, to the said Hugh and his successors, of a thousand fagots a year to be cut of the wood of Lilleston, and carried to the New Temple to keep up the fire in the said church.‡

King Edward the Third, in the thirty-fifth year of his reign, A.D. 1362, notwithstanding the grant of the Temple to the Hospitallers, exercised the right of appointing to the porter's office and by his letters patent he promoted Roger Small to that post for the term of his life, in return for the good service rendered him by the said Roger Small.§

It is at this period that the first distinct mention of a society of lawyers in the Temple occurs.

The poet Chaucer, who was born at the close of the reign of Edward the Second, A.D. 1327, and was in high favour at court in the reign of Edward the Third, thus speaks of the MANCIPLE, or the purveyor of provisions of the lawyers in the Temple:

> "A gentil Manciple was there of the TEMPLE,
> Of whom achatours mighten take ensemple,
> For to ben wise in bying of vitaille.
> For whether that he paid or toke by taille,
> Algate he waited so in his achate,
> That he was aye before in good estate.
> Now is not that of God a Ml fayre grace,
> That swiche a lewed mannes wit shal pace,
> The wisdome of an hepe of lerned men?"
> "Of maisters had he mo than thries ten,
> THAT WERE OF LAWS EXPERT AND CURIOUS:
> Of which there was a dosein in that hous
> Worthy to ben stewardes of rent and lond
> Of any lord that is in Englelond,
> To maken him live by his propre good,
> In honour detteles, but if he were wood,

---

* Pat. 12. E. 3. p. 2. m. 22. *Dugd.* Monasticon, vol. vii. p. 810, 811.

† Ex registr. Sancti Johannis Jerus. Fol. 141.a. *Dugd.* Monast., tom. vi. Part 2, p. 832.

‡ Ibid. ad ann. 1341.

§ Rex omnibus ad quos &c. salutem. Sciatis quod de gratiâ nostrâ speciali, et pro bono servitio quod Rogerus Small nobis impendit et impendat in futuro, concessimus ei officium *Janitoris Novi Templi* London Habend. &c. pro vitâ suâ &c. pertinend. &c. omnia vada et feoda &c. eodem modo qualia Robertus Petyt defunct. Qui officium illud ex concessione domini Edwardi nuper regis Angliæ patris nostri habuit ... Teste meipso apud Westm. 5 die Aprilis, anno regni nostri 35. Pat. 35. E. 3. p. 2. m. 33.

Or live as scarsly, as him list desire;
And able for to helpen all a shire,
In any cas that mighte fallen or happe;
And yet this manciple sette hir aller cappe."*

It appears, therefore, that the lawyers in the Temple, in the reign of Edward the Third, had their purveyor of provisions as at this day, and were consequently then keeping commons, or dining together in hall.

In the fourth year of the reign of Richard the Second, A.D. 1381, a still more distinct notice occurs of the Temple, as the residence of the *learners* and the *learned* in the law.

We are told in an ancient chronicle, written in Norman French, formerly belonging to the abbey of St. Mary's at York, that the rebels under Wat Tyler went to the Temple and pulled down the houses, and entered the church and took all the books and the rolls of remembrances which were in the chests of the learners of the law in the Temple, and placed them under the large chimney and burnt them. ("Les rebels alleront a le Temple et jetteront les measons a la terre et avegheront tighles, issint que ils fairont coverture en mal array; et alleront en l'esglise, et pristeront touts les liveres et rolles de remembrances, que furont en leur huches deins le Temple de Apprentices de la Ley; et porteront en le haut chimene et les arderont."†) And Walsingham, who wrote in the reign of Henry the Sixth, about fifty years after the occurrence of these events, tells us that after the rebels, under Wat Tyler and Jack Straw, had burnt the Savoy, the noble palace of John of Gaunt, duke of Lancaster, they pulled down the place called Temple Barr, where the apprentices or learners of the highest branch of the profession of the law dwelt, on account of the spite they bore to Robert Hales, Master of the Hospital of Saint John of Jerusalem, and burnt many deeds which the lawyers there had in their custody. ("Quibus perpetratis, satis malitiose etiam locum qui vocatur Temple Barre, in quo *apprenticii juris* morabantur *nobiliores,* diruerunt, ob ram quam conceperant contra Robertum de Hales Magistrum Hospitalis Sancti Johannis Jerusalem, ubi plura munimenta, quæ Juridici in custodiâ habuerunt, igne consumpta sunt.")*

In a subsequent passage, however, he gives us a better clue to the attack upon the Temple, and the burning of the deeds and writings, for he tells us that it was the intention of the rebels to decapitate all the lawyers, for they thought that by destroying them they could put an end to the law, and so be enabled to order matters according to their own will and pleasure. ("Ad decollandum omnes juridicos, escaetores, et universos qui

---

* Prologue to the Canterbury Tales. The wages of the Manciples of the Temple, temp. Hen. VIII. were xxxvis. Viiid. per annum. Bib. *Cotton.* Vitellius, c. 9, f. 320, a.

† Annal. Olim-Sanctæ Manse Ebor.

vel in lege docti fuere, vel cum jure ratione officii communicavere. Men-
te nempe conceperant, doctis in lege necatis, universa juxta communis
plebis scitum de cætero ordinare, et nullam omnino legem fore futuram,
vel si futura foret, esse pro suorum arbitrio statuenda.")

It is evident that the lawyers were the immediate successors of the
Knights Templars in the occupation of the Temple, as the lessees of the
earl of Lancaster.

Whilst the Templars were pining in captivity in the dungeons of London and of York, King Edward the Second paid to their servants and
retainers the pensions they had previously received from the treasury
of the Temple, on condition that they continued to perform the services
and duties they had rendered to their ancient masters. On the 26th of
November, A.D. 1311, he granted to Robert Styfford, clerk, for his maintenance in the house of the Temple at London, two deniers a day, and five
shillings a year for necessaries, provided he did service in the church;
and when unable to do so, he was to receive only his food and lodging.
Geoffrey Talaver was to receive, in the same house of the Temple, three
deniers a day for his sustenance, and twenty shillings a year for necessaries, during the remainder of his life; also one denier a day for the support of his boy, and five shillings a year for his wages. Geoffrey
de Cave, clerk, and John de Shelton, were also, each of them, to receive
from the same house, for their good services, an annual pension of forty
shillings for the term of their lives.† Some of these retainers, in addition
to their various stipends, were to have a gown of the class of free-serving
brethren of the Order of the Temple‡ each year; one old garment out of
the stock of old garments belonging to the brethren;§ one mark a year
for their shoes, &c.; their sons also received so much *per diem*, on condition that they did the daily work of the house. These retainers were of the
class of free servants of office; they held their posts for life, and not being
members of the Order of the Temple, they were not included in the general proscription of the fraternity. In return for the provision made them
by the king, they were to continue to do their customary work as long as
they were able.

Now it is worthy of remark, that many of the rules, customs, and
usages of the society of Knights Templars are to this day observed in
the Temple, naturally leading us to conclude that these domestics and

---

* *Walsing.* 4 Ric. 2. ad ann. 1381. Hist. p. 249, ed. 1603.

† Rot. claus 5. E. 2. m. 19. Acta *Rymeri*, tom. iii. p. 292, 293,294.

‡ Unam robam per annum de secta liberorum rvientium, et quinque solid« per annum, et
deserviat quamdiu potent loco liberi mentis in domo prtedictâ. Ib. m. 2. Acta *Rymeri*, tom.
iii. p. 331, 332.

§ Quolibet anno ad Natale Domini unum vetus indumentum de veteribus indumentis
fratrum, et quolibet die 2 denarios pro yictu garcionis sui, et 5 solidos per annum per
stipendiis ejusdem garcionis, sed idem garcio deserviet in domo illâ. Ib.

retainers of the ancient brotherhood became connected with the legal society formed therein, and transferred their services to that learned body.

From the time of Chaucer to the present day, the lawyers have dined together in the ancient hall, as the military monks did before them; and the rule of their order requiring "two and two to eat together," and "all the fragments to be given in brotherly charity to the domestics," is observed to this day, and has been in force from time immemorial. The attendants at table, moreover, are still called *paniers*, as in the days of the Knights Templars.* The leading punishments of the Temple, too, remain the same as in the olden time. The ancient Templar, for example, for a light fault, was "withdrawn from the companionship of his fellows," and not allowed "to eat with them at the same table,"† and the modern Templar, for impropriety of conduct, is "expelled the hall" and "put out of commons." The brethren of the ancient fraternity were, for grave offences, in addition to the above punishment, deprived of their lodgings,‡ and were compelled to sleep with the beasts in the open court; and the members of the modern fellowship have in bygone times, as a mode of punishment, been temporarily deprived of their chambers in the Temple for misconduct, and padlocks have been put upon the doors. The Master and Chapter of the Temple, in the time of the Knights Templars, exercised the power of imprisonment and expulsion from the fellowship, and the same punishments have been freely used down to a recent period by the Masters of the Bench of the modern societies. Until of late years, too, the modern Templars have had their readers, officers of great dignity, whose duty it has been to read and expound law in the hall, at and after meals, in the same way as the readers of the Knights Templars read and expounded religion.

There has also been, in connexion with the modern fellowship, a class of *associates* similar to the associates of the ancient Templars.* These were illustrious persons who paid large sums of money, and made presents of plate, to be admitted to the fellowship of the Masters of the Bench; they were allowed to dine at the Bench table, to be as it were honorary members of the society, but were freed from the ordinary exercises and regulations of the house, and had at the same time no voice in the government thereof.

The conversion of the chief house of the most holy order of the Temple

---

* Thomas of Wothrope, at the trial of the Templars in England, was unable to give an account of the reception of some brethren into the Order, quia erat *panetarius* et vacabat circa suum officium. *Concil. Mag. Brit.*, tom. ii. p. 355. Tunc panetarius mittat comiti duos panes atque vini sextarium... Ita appellabant officialem domesticum, qui mensæ panem, mappas et manutergia subministrabat. *Ducange, Gloss.* Verb. Panetarius.

† *Regula Templariorum*, cap. lxvii. ante p. 25.

‡ *Concil. Mag. Brit,* tom. ii. p. 371 to 373, ante, p. 235.

of Solomon in England into a law university, was brought about in the following manner.

Both before, and for a very considerable period after, the Norman conquest, the study of the law was confined to the ecclesiastics, who engrossed all the learning and knowledge of the age.† In the reign of King Stephen, the foreign clergy who had flocked over after the conquest, attempted to introduce the ancient civil law of Rome into this country, as calculated to promote the power and advantage of their order, but were resolutely resisted by the king and the barons, who clung to their old customs and usages. The new law, however, was introduced into all the ecclesiastical courts, and the clergy began to abandon the municipal tribunals, and discontinue the study of the common law. Early in the reign of Henry the Third, episcopal constitutions were published by the bishop of Salisbury, forbidding clerks and priests to practise as advocates in the common law courts. (*Nec advocati sint clerici vel sacerdotes in foro sœculari, nisi vel proprias causas vel miserabilium personarum prosequantur.‡*) Towards the close of the same reign, (A.D. 1254), Pope Innocent IV. forbade the reading of the common law by the clergy in the English universities and seminaries of learning, because its decrees were not founded on the *imperial constitutions,* but merely on the *customs of the laity.§*

As the common law consequently gradually ceased to be studied and taught by the clergy, who were the great depositaries of legal learning, as of all other knowledge in those days, it became necessary to educate and train up a body of laymen to transact the judicial business of the country; and Edward the First, who, from his many legal reforms and improvements, has been styled "the English Justinian," made the practice of the common law a distinct profession.

In ancient times the Court of *Common Pleas* had the exclusive administration of the *common law*, and settled and decided all the disputes which arose between *subject* and *subject*; and in the twentieth year of the reign of Edward the First, (A.D. 1292), the privilege of pleading causes in this court was confined to a certain number of learned persons appointed by authority. By an order in council, the king commanded John de Metingham, chief justice of the Court of Common Pleas, and the rest of his fel-

---

* *Dugd. Orig.* Jurid., p. 212.

† Nullus clericus nisi causidicus. Will. Malm., lib. Iv. f. 69. *Radulph de Diceto,* apud Hist. Angl. Script. Antiq., lib. vii. col. 606, from whom it appears that the chief justitiary and justices itinerant were all *priests.*

‡ *Spelm.* Concil., tom. ii. ad ann. 1217.

§ Innocentius, &c. ... Præterea cum in Angliæ, Scotiæ, Walliæ regnis, causæ laicorum non imperatoriis legibus, sed laicorum consuetudinibus decidantur, fratrum nostrorum, et aliorum religiosorum consilio et rogatu, statuimus quod in prædictis regnis *leges sœeulares* de cætero non legantur. *Matt. Par.,* p. 883, ad ann. 1254, et in additamentis, p. 191.

low justices, that they, according to their discretions, should provide and ordain from every county a certain number of attorneys and apprentices of the law, of the best and most apt for their learning and skill, to do service to his court and people, and those so chosen should follow his court and transact the affairs therein, and *no others*; the king and his council deeming the number of fourscore to be sufficient for that employment; but it was left to the discretion of the said justices to add to that number, or to diminish it, as they should think fit.*

At this period the Court of Common Pleas had been fixed at Westminster, which brought together the professors of the common law at London; and about the period of the dissolution of the Order of the Temple, a society appears to have been in progress of formation, under the sanction of the judges, for the education of a body of learned secular lawyers to attend upon that court. The deserted convent of the Knights Templars, seated in the suburb of London, away from the noise and bustle of the city, and presenting a ready and easy access by water to Westminster, was a desirable retreat for the learned members of this infant legal society; and we accordingly find, that very soon after the dissolution of the religio-military order of Knights Templars, the professors of the common law of England mustered in considerable strength in the Temple.

In the sixth year of the reign of Edward the Third, (A.D. 1333), when the lawyers had just established themselves in the convent of the Temple, and had engrafted upon the old stock of Knights Templars their infant society for the study of the practice of the common law, the judges of the Court of Common Pleas were made knights,† being the earliest instance on record of the grant of the honour of knighthood for services purely civil, and the professors of the common law, who had the exclusive privilege of practising in that court, assumed the title or degree of freres serjens or fratres servientes, so that knights and serving-brethren, similar to those of the ancient order of the Temple, were most curiously revived and introduced into the profession of the law.

It is true that the word *serviens, serjen,* or *serjeant,* was applied to the professors of the law long before the reign of Edward the Third, but not to denote a *privileged brotherhood.* It was applied to lawyers in common with all persons who did any description of work for another, from the *serviens domini regis aa legem,* who prosecuted the pleas of the crown in the county court, to the *serviens or serjen* who walked with his cane before the concubine of the Patriarch in the streets of Jerusalem.* The priest who worked for the Lord was called *serjens de Dieu,* and the lover who

---

* Et quod ipsi quos ad hoc elegerint, curiam sequantur, et se de negotiis in eadem curia intromittant, et *alii non.* Et videtur regi et ejus concilio, quod septies vigenti sufficere poterint, &c.—*Rolls of Parl.* 20. E. 1. vol. i. p. 84, No. 22.

† *Dugd.* Orig. Jurid., cap. xxxix. p. 102.

served the lady of his affections *serjens d'amour.** It was in the Order of the Temple that the word *freres serjens* or *fratres servientes* signified an honorary title or degree, and denoted a powerful privileged class of men. The *fratres servientes armigeri or freres serjens des armes,* of the chivalry of the Temple, were of the rank of gentlemen. They united in their own persons the monastic and the military character, they were allotted one horse each, they wore the red cross of the Order of the Temple on their breasts,† they participated in all the privileges of the brotherhood, and were eligible to the dignity of Preceptor. Large sums of money were frequently given by seculars who had not been advanced to the honour of knight- hood, to be admitted amongst this highly-esteemed order of men.

The *freres serjens* of the Temple wore linen *coifs,* and red caps close over them.‡ At the ceremony of their admission into the fraternity, the Master of the Temple placed the coif upon their heads, and threw over their shoulders the white mantle of the Temple; he then caused them to sit down on the ground, and gave them a solemn admonition concerning the duties and responsibilities of their profession.§ They were warned that they must enter upon a new life, that they must keep themselves fair and free from stain, like the white garment that had been thrown around them, which was the emblem of purity and innocence; that they must render complete and perfect obedience to their superiors; that they must protect the weak, succour the needy, reverence old men, and do good to the poor.

The knights and serjeants of the common law, on the other hand, have ever constituted a privileged *fraternity*, and always address one another by the endearing term *brother*. The religious character of the ancient ceremony of admission into this legal brotherhood, which took place in church, and its striking similarity to the ancient mode of reception into the fraternity of the Temple, are curious and remarkable.

"Capitalis Justitiarius," says an ancient MS. account of the creation of seijeants-at-law in the reign of Henry the Seventh, "monstrabat eis plura bona exempla de eorum prædecessoribus, et tunc posuit les *coyfes** super eorum capitibus, et induebat eos singulariter de capital de skarletto, et sic creati fuerunt *servientes ad legem.*" In his admonitory exhortation, the chief justice displays to them the moral and religious duties of their profession. "Ambulate in vocatione in quâ vocati estis. ... Disce cultum

---

* Ante, p. 118. Mace-bearers, bell-ringers, thief-takers, gaolers, bailiffs, public executioners, and all persons who performed a specific task for another, were called servientes, serjens, or serjeants.—*Ducange Gloss. Pasquier's* Researches, liv. Viii. cap. 19.

† Will. *Tyr.*, lib. i. p. 50, lib. xii. P. 814.

‡ *Dugd.* Hist. Warwickshire, p. 704.

§ Et tunc Magister Templi dedit sibi mantellum, et imposuit pileum capiti suo, et tunc fecit eum sedere ad terrain, injungens sibi, &c.—*Acta contra Templarios. Concil. Mag. Brit.*, tom. ii. p. 380. See also p. 335.

Dei, *reverentiam superioris (!), misericordiam pauperi."* He tells them the coif is sicut vestis Candida et immaculata, the emblem of purity and virtue, and he commences a portion of his discourse in the scriptural language used by the popes in the famous bull conceding to the Templars their vast spiritual and temporal privileges, *"Omne datum optimum et omne donum perfectum desursum est descendens a patre luminum &c. &c. !*†

The *freres serjens* of the Temple were strictly enjoined to "eat their bread in silence," and "place a watch upon their mouths," and the *freres serjens* of the law, we are told, after their admission, did "dyne together with sober countenance and lytel communycacion."

The common-law lawyers, after their location in the Temple, continued rapidly to increase, and between the reigns of Richard the Second and Henry the Sixth, they divided themselves into two bodies. "In the raigne of King Henry the Sixth," says the MS. account of the Temple, written 9 Charles the First, "they were soe multiplied and grown into soe great a bulke as could not conveniently be regulated into one society, nor indeed was the old hall capable of containing so great a number, whereupon they were forced to divide themselves. A new hall was then erected which is now the Junior Temple Hall, whereunto divers of those who before took their repast and diet in the old hall resorted, and in process of time became a distinct and divided society."

From the inquisition taken 10. E.III. A.D. 1337, it appears that in the time of the Knights Templars there were *two halls* in the Temple, so that it is not likely that a fresh one was built. One of these halls, the present Inner Temple Hall, had been assigned, the year previous to the taking of that inquisition, to the prior and brethren of the Hospital of Saint John, together with the church, cloisters, &c., as before mentioned, whilst the other hall remained in the hands of the crown, and was not granted to the Hospitallers until 13 E. III. A.D. 1340. It was probably soon after this period that the Hospitallers conceded the use of *both halls* to the profes-

---

* It has been supposed that the coif was first introduced by the clerical practitioners of the common law to hide the *tonsure* of those priests who practised in the Court of Common Pleas, notwithstanding the ecclesiastical prohibition. This was not the case.

The early portraits of our judges exhibit them with a coif of very much larger dimensions than the coifs now worn by the serjeants-at-law, very much larger than would be necessary to hide the *mere clerical tonsure*. A covering for that purpose indeed would be absurd. The ancient coifs of the serjeants-at-law were small linen or silk caps fitting close to the top of the head. This peculiar covering is worn universally in the East, where the people shave their heads and cut their hair close. It was imported into Europe by the Knights Templars, and became a distinguishing badge of their order. From the *freres serjens* of the Temple it passed to the *freres serjens* of the law.

† Ex cod. MS. apud sub-thesaurarium Hosp. Medii Templi, f. 4. a. Dugd. Orig. Jurid. cap. 43, 46.

sors of the law, and these last, from dining apart and being attached to different halls, at last separated into two societies, as at present.

"Although there be two several societies, yet in sundry places they are promiscuously lodged together without any metes or bounds to distinguish them, and the ground rooms in some places belong to the new house, and the upper rooms to the old one, a manifest argument that both made at first but one house, nor did they either before or after this division claim by several leases, but by one entire grant. And as they took their diet apart, so likewise were they stationed apart in the church, viz. those of the Middle Temple on the left hand side as you go therein, and those of the old house on the right hand side, and so it remains between them at this day."*

Burton, the antiquary, who wrote in the reign of Queen Elizabeth, speaks of this "old house" (the Inner Temple) as "the mother and most ancient of all the other houses of courts, to which," says he, "I must acknowledge all due respect, being a fellow thereof, admitted into the same society on the 20th of May, 1593."† The two societies of the Temple are of *equal antiquity*; the members in the first instance dined together in one or other of the ancient halls of the Templars as it suited their convenience and inclination; and to this day, in memory of the old custom, the benchers or ancients of the one society dine once every year in the hall of the other society. The period of the division has been generally referred to the commencement of the reign of Henry the Sixth, as at the close of that long reign the present *four* Inns of Court were all in existence, and then contained about two thousand students. The Court of King's Bench, the Court of Exchequer, and the Court of Chancery, had then encroached upon the jurisdiction of the Common Pleas, and had taken cognizance of civil causes between subject and subject, which were formerly decided in that court alone.‡ The legal business of the country had consequently greatly increased, the profession of the law became highly honourable, and the gentry and the nobility considered the study of it a necessary part of education.

Sir John Fortescue, who was chief justice of the King's Bench during half the reign of Henry the Sixth, in his famous discourse *de laudibus legum Angliæ*, tells us that in his time the annual expenses of each law-

---

* MS. in Bib. Int. Temp. No. 17. fo. 408.

† *Burton's* Leicestershire, p. 235.

‡ After the courts of King's Bench and Exchequer had by a fiction of law drawn to themselves a vast portion of the civil business originally transacted in the Common Pleas alone, the degree of serjeant-at-law, with its exclusive privilege of practising in the last-named court, was not sought after as before. The advocates or barristers of the Kingl Bench and Exchequer were, consequently, at different times, commanded by writ to take upon them the degree of the *coif*, and transfer their practice to the Common Pleas.

student amounted to more than 28*l*., (equal to about 460*l*. of our present money), that all the students of the law were gentlemen by birth and fortune, and had great regard for their character and honour; that in each Inn of Court there was an academy or *gymnasium*, where singing, music, and dancing, and a variety of accomplishments, were taught. Law was studied at stated periods, and on festival days: after the offices of the church were over, the students employed themselves in the study of history, and in reading the Holy Scriptures. Everything good and virtuous was there taught, vice was discouraged and banished, so that knights, barons, and the, greatest of the nobility of the kingdom, placed their sons in the Temple and the other Inns of Court; and not so much, he tells us, to make the law their study, or to enable them to live by the profession, as to form their manners and to preserve them from the contagion of vice. "Quarrelling, insubordination, and murmuring, are unheard of; if a student dishonours himself, he is expelled the society; a punishment whieh is dreaded more than imprisonment and irons, for he who has been driven from one society is never admitted into any of the others; whence it happens, that there is a constant harmony amongst them, the greatest friendship, and a general freedom of conversation."

The two societies of the Temple are now distinguished by the several denominations of the Inner and the Middle Temple, names that appear to have been adopted with reference to a part of the ancient Temple, which, in common with other property of the Knights Templars, never came into the hands of the Hospitallers. After the lawyers of the Temple had separated into two bodies and occupied distinct portions of ground, this part came to be known by the name of the outward Temple, as being the farthest away from the city, and is thus referred to in a manuscript in the British Museum, written in the reign of James the First. "A third part, called *outward Temple,* was procured by one Dr. Stapleton, bishop of Exeter, in the days of King Edward the Second, for a residing mansion-house for him and his successors, bishops of that see. It was called Exeter Inn until the reign of the late Queen Mary, when the lord Paget, her principal secretary of state, obtained the said third part, called Exeter-house, to him and his heirs, and did re-edify the same. After whom the said third part of the Templar's house came to Thomas late duke of Norfolk, and was by him conveyed to Sir Robert Dudley, knight, earl of Leicester, who bequeathed the same to Sir Robert Dudley, knight, his son, and lastly, by purchase, came to Robert late earl of Essex, who died in the reign of the late Queen Elizabeth, and is still called Essex-house."*

When the lawyers came into the Temple, they found engraved upon the ancient buildings the armorial bearings of the Knights Templars, which were, on a shield argent, a plain cross gules, and (*brochant sur le tout*) the holy lamb bearing the banner of the Order, surmounted by a red cross. These arms remained the emblem of the Temple until the fifth year of the reign of Queen Elizabeth, when unfortunately the society of the Inner Temple, yielding to the advice and persuasion of Master Gerard Leigh, a member of the College of Heralds, abandoned the ancient and honourable device of the Knights Templars, and assumed in its place a galloping winged horse called a Pegasus, or, as it has been explained to us, "a horse striking the earth with its hoof, or *Pegasus luna on a field argent!*" Master Gerard Leigh, we are told, "emblazoned them with precious stones and planets, and by these strange arms he intended to signify that the knowledge acquired at the learned seminary of the Inner Temple would raise the professors of the law to the highest honours, adding, by way of motto, *volat ad œthera virtus*, and he intended to allude to what are esteemed the more liberal sciences, by giving them Pegasus forming the fountain of Hippocrene, by striking his hoof against the rock, as a proper emblem of lawyers becoming poets, as Chaucer and Gower, who were both of the Temple!"

The society of the Middle Temple, with better taste, still preserves, in that part of the Temple over which its sway extends, the widely-renowned and time-honoured badge of the ancient order of the Temple.

The assumption of the prancing winged horse by the one society, and the retention of the lamb by the other, have given rise to the following witty lines—

> "As thro' the Templars' courts you go,
>   The lamb and horse displayed,
> The emblematic figures show
>   The merits of their trade.
>
> That clients may infer from hence
>   How just is their profession;
> The lamb denotes their INNOCENCE,
>   The horse their EXPEDITION.
>
> Oh, happy Britain! happy isle!
>   Let foreign nations say,
> Here you get justice without guile,
>   And law without delay."

> **ANSWER.**
>
> "Unhappy man! those courts forego,
>   Nor trust Buch cunning elves,
> The artful emblems only show
>   Their *clients*, not *themselves*.
>
> These all are tricks,

---

* *Malcom.* Lond. Rediviv., vol. ii. p. 282.

These all are shams,
   With which they mean to cheat ye,
But have a care, for you're the LAMBS,
   And they the wolves that eat ye.

Nor let the plea of no delay
   To these their courts misguide ye,
For you're the prancing horse; and they
   The jockeys that would ride you"

CHAPTER XIV.

THE TEMPLE.

The Temple Garden—The erection of new buildings in the Temple—The dissolution of the Order of the Hospital of Saint John—The law societies become leasees of the crown—The erection of the magnificent Middle Temple Hall— The conversion of the old hall into chambers—The grant of the inheritance of the Temple to the two law societies—Their magnificent present to his Majesty—Their ancient orders and customs, and ancient hospitality—Their grand entertainments—Reader's feasts—Grand Christmasses and Revels—The fox-hunt in the hall—The dispute with the Lord Mayor—The quarrel with the *custos* of the Temple Church.

> "PLANTAGENET. Great lords and gentlemen, what means this silence?
>   Dare no man answer in a case of truth?
> SUFFOLK...   Within the TEMPLE HALL we were too loud:
>   The GARDEN here is more convenient."

SHAKSPEARE makes the Temple Garden, which is to this day celebrated for the beauty and profusion of its flowers, the scene of the choice of the white and red roses, as the badges of the rival houses of York and Lancaster. Richard Plantagenet and the earl of Somerset retire with their followers from the hall into the garden, where Plantagenet thus addresses the silent and hesitating bystanders:

> "Since you are tongue-ty'd, and so loath to speak,
> In dumb significants proclaim your thoughts:
> Let him, that is a true-born gentleman,
> And stands upon the honour of his birth,
> If he suppose that I have pleaded truth,
> From off this brier pluck a white rose with me.
>   *Somerset.* Let him that is no coward, nor no flatterer,
> But dare maintain the party of the truth,
> Pluck a red rose from off this thorn with me.
>   *Warwick.* I love no colours; and, without all colour

Of base insinuating flattery,
I pluck this white rose with Plantagenet.
    Suffolk. I pluck this red rose with young Somerset,
And say withal I think he held the right.
    Vernon. Then for the truth and plainness of the case,
I pluck this pale and maiden blossom here,
Giving my verdict on the white rose side.
    Somerset. ... Come on, who else?
    Lawyer. Unless my study and my books be false,
The argument you held was wrong in you;
In sign whereof I pluck a white rose too.   [To Somerset.
    Warwick. ... This brawl to-day,
Grown to this faction in the Temple Garden,
Shall send, between the red rose and the white,
A thousand souls to death and deadly night."

In the Cotton Library is a manuscript written at the commencement of the reign of Henry the Eighth, entitled "A description of the Form and Manner, how, and by what Orders and Customs the State of the Fellow-shyppe of the Myddil Temple is maintained, and what ways they have to attaine unto Learning."* It contains a great deal of curious information concerning the government of the house, the readings, mot-yngs, boltings, and other exercises formerly performed for the advancement of learning, and of the different degrees of benchers, readers, cupboard-men, inner-barristers, utter-barristers, and students, together with "the chardges for their mete and drynke by the yeare, and the manner of the dyet, and the stipende of their officers." The writer tells us that it was the duty of the "Tresorer to gather of certen of the fellowship a tribute yerely of iiis. *iiid.* a piece, and to pay out of it the rent due to my lord of Saint John's for the house that they dwell in."

"Item; they have no place to walk in, and talk and confer their learnings, but in the church; which place all the terme times hath in it no more of quietnesse than the perwyse of Pawles, by occasion of the confluence and concourse of such as be suters in the lawe." The conferences between lawyers and clients in the Temple Church are thus alluded to by Butler:

"Retain all aorta of witnesses
That ply in the Temple under trees,
Or walk the Round with knights of the posts,
About the cross-legged knights their hosts."

"Item; they have every day three masses said one after the other, and the first masse doth begin at seaven of the clock, or thereabouts. On festivall days they have mattens and masse solemnly sung; and during the

---

* MS. *Bib. Cotton.* Vitellius, c, 9, fol. 320, a.

matyns singing they have three masses said."*

At the commencement of the reign of Henry VIII. a wall was built between the Temple Garden and the river; the Inner Temple Hall was "seeled," various new chambers were erected, and the societies expended sums of money, and acted as if they were absolute proprietors of the Temple, rather than as lessees of the Hospitallers of Saint John.

In 32 Hen. VIII. was passed the act of parliament dissolving the Order of the Hospital, and vesting all the property of the brethren in the crown, saving the rights and interests of lessees, and others who held under them.

The two law societies consequently now held of the crown.

In 5 Eliz. the present spacious and magnificent Middle Temple Hall, one of the most elegant and beautiful structures in the kingdom, was commenced, (the old hall being converted into chambers;) and in the reigns both of Mary and Elizabeth, various buildings and sets of chambers were erected in the Inner and Middle Temple, at the expense of the Benchers and members of the two societies. All this was done in full reliance upon the justice and honour of the crown. In the reign of James I., however, some Scotchman attempted to obtain from his majesty a grant of the fee-simple or inheritance of the Temple, which being brought to the knowledge of the two societies, they forthwith made "humble suit" to the king, and obtained a grant of the property to themselves. By letters patent, bearing date at Westminster the 13th of August, in the sixth year of his reign, A.D. 1609, King James granted the Temple to the Benchers of the two societies, their heirs and assigns for ever, for the lodging, reception, and education of the professors and students of the laws of England, the said Benchers yielding and paying to the said king, his heirs, and successors, ten pounds yearly for the mansion called the Inner Temple, and ten pounds yearly for the Middle Temple.†

In grateful acknowledgment of this donation, the two societies caused to be made, at their mutual cost, "a stately cup of pure gold, weighinge two hundred ounces and an halfe, of the value of one thousand markes, or thereabouts, the which in all humbleness was presented to his excellent majestie att the court att Whitehall, in the said sixth year of his majestie's raigne over the realme of England, for a new yeare's gifte, by the hands of the said sir Henry Mountague, afterwards baron Mountague, viscount Mandevil, the earl of Manchester, Richard Daston, esq., and other eminent persons of both those honourable societies, the which it pleased his majesty most gratiously to accept and receiue . . . Upon one side of this cup is curiously engraven the proporcion of a church or temple beautified, with turrets and pinnacles, and on the other side is figured an altar, whereon is a representation of a holy fire, the flames propper, and over

---

* MS. *Bib. Cotton*, c. 9, fol. 320, a.

† *Hargrave*, MS. No. 19, 81. f. 5. fol. 46.

the flames these words engraven, *Nil nisi vobis.* The cover of this rich cup of gold is in the upper parte thereof adorned with a fabrick fashioned like a pyramid, whereon standeth the statue of a military person leaning, with the left hand upon a Roman-fashioned shield or target, the which cup his excellent majestie, whilst he lived, esteemed for one of his roialest and richest jewells."*

Some of the ancient orders and regulations for the government of the two societies are not unworthy of attention.

From the record of a parliament holden in the Inner Temple on the 15th of November, 3 and 4 Ph. and Mary, A.D. 1558, it appears that eight gentlemen of the house, in the previous reading vocation, "were *committed to the Fleete* for wilfull demenoure and disobedience to *the Bench*, and were worthyly expulsed the fellowshyppe of the house, since which tyme, upon their humble suite and submission unto the said Benchers of the said house, it is agreed that they shall be readmitted into the fellowshyppe, and into commons again, without payeing any ffine."†Amongst the ancient customs and usages derived from the Knights Templars, which were for a lengthened period religiously preserved and kept up in the Temple, was the oriental fashion of long beards. In the reign of Philip and Mary, at the personal request of the queen, attempts were made to do away with this time-honoured custom, and to limit the length of a lawyer's beard.

On the 22nd of June, 3 and 4 Philip and Mary, A.D. 1557, it was ordered that none of the companies of the Inner and Middle Temple, under the degree of a knight being in commons, should wear their beards above three weeks growing, upon pain of XLs., and so double for every week after monition. They were, moreover, required to lay aside their arms, and it was ordered "that none of the companies, when they be in commons, shall wear Spanish cloak, sword and buckler, or rapier, or gownes and hats, or gownes girded with a dagger;" also, "that "none of the companions, except Knights or Benchers, should thenceforth wear in their doublets or hoses any light colours, except scarlet and crimson; or wear any upper velvet cap, or any scarf, or wings on their gownes, white jerkyns, buskins or *velvet shoes,* double cuffs on their shirts, feathers or ribbens on their caps! That no attorney should be admitted into either of the houses, and that, in all admissions from thenceforth, it should be an implied condition, that if the party admitted "should practyse any attorneyship," he was *ipso facto* dismissed.*

In 1 Jac. I., it was ordered, in obedience to the commands of the king,

---

* MS. in Bib. In. Temp., No. 19, fol.

† In. Temp. Ad. Parliament, ibm. XV. die Novembris Anno Philippi et Mariæ tertio et quarto, coram Johe Baker Milite, Nicho Hare Milite, Thoma Whyte Milite, et al. MS. Bib. In. Tem. Div. p, shelf 5, vol. xvii. Fol. 393.

that no one should be admitted a member of either society who was not *a gentleman by descent*—that none of the gentlemen should come into the hall "in cloaks, boots, spurs, swords, or daggers;" and it was publicly declared that their "yellow bands, and ear toyes, and short cloaks, and weapons," were "much disliked and forbidden."

In A.D. 1623, King James recommended the ancient way of wearing caps to be carefully observed; and the king was pleased to take notice of the good order of the house of the Inner Temple in that particular. His majesty was further pleased to recommend that boots should be laid aside as ill befitting gownsmen; "for boots and spurs," says his majesty, "are the badges rather of roarers than of civil men, who should use them only when they ride. Therefore we have made example in our own court, that no boots shall come into our presence."

The modern Templars for a long period fully maintained the ancient character and reputation of the Temple for sumptuous and magnificent hospitality, although the venison from the royal forests, and the wine from the king's cellars,† no longer made its periodical appearance within the walls of the old convent. Sir John Fortescue alludes to the revels and pastimes of the Temple in the reign of Henry VI., and several ancient writers speak of the grand Christmasses, the readers' feasts, the masques, and the sumptuous entertainments afforded to foreign ambassadors, and even to royalty itself. Various dramatic shows were got up upon these occasions, and the leading characters who figured at them were the *"Marshall of the Knights Templars!"* the constable marshall, the master of the games, the lieutenant of the Tower, the ranger of the forest, the lord of misrule, the king of Cockneys, and Jack Straw!

The Constable Marshall came into the hall on banqueting days "fairly mounted on his mule," clothed in complete armour, with a nest of feathers of all colours upon his helm, and a gilt poleaxe in his hand. He was attended by halberdiers, and preceded by drums and fifes, and by sixteen trumpeters, and devised some sport "for passing away the afternoon."

The Master of the Game, and the Ranger of the Forest, were apparelled in green velvet and green satin, and had hunting horns about their necks, with which they marched round about the fire, "blowing three blasts of venery."

The most remarkable of all the entertainments was *the hunt in the hall,* when the huntsman came in with his winding horn, dragging in with him a cat, a fox, a purse-net, and nine or ten couple of hounds! The cat and the fox were both tied to the end of a staff, and were turned loose into the hall; they were hunted with the dogs amid the blowing of hunting horns, and were killed under the grate!!

---

* Ex registr. In. Temp., f. 112, 119, b. Med. Temp., f. 24, a. *Dugd.,* Orig. Jurid., p. 310, 311.
† Ante, p. 180.

The quantity of venison consumed on these festive occasions particularly at the readers' feasts, was enormous. In the reign of Queen Mary, it was ordered by the benchers of the Middle Temple, that no reader should spend less than fifteen bucks in the hall, and this number was generally greatly exceeded: "there be few summer readers," we are informed in an old MS. account of the readers' feasts, "who, in half the time that heretofore a reading was wont to continue, spent so little as threescore bucks, besides red deer; some have spent fourscore, some a hundred ..."* The lawyers in that golden age breakfasted on "brawn and malmsey," and supped on "venison pasties and roasted hens!" Among the viands at dinner were "faire and large bores' heads served upon silver platters, with minstralsye, roasted swans, bustards, herns, bitterns, turkey chicks, curlews, godwits, &c. &c."

The following observations concerning the Temple, and a grand entertainment there, in the reign of Queen Mary, will be read with interest. "Arriuing in the faire river of Thames, I landed within halfe a leage from the city of London, which was, as I coniecture in December last. And drawing neere the citie, sodenly hard the shot of double cannons, in so great a number, and so terrible, that it darkened the whole aire, wherewith, although I was in my native countrie, yet stoode I amazed, not knowing what it ment. Thus, as I abode in despaire either to returne or to continue my former purpose, I chaunced to see comming towardes me an honest citizen, clothed in long garment, keping the highway, seming to walke for his recreation, which prognosticated rather peace than perill Of whom I demaunded the cause of this great shot, who frendly answered,' It is the warning shot to th' officers of the Constable Marshall of the Inner Temple to prepare to dinner! Why, said I, is he of that estate, that seeketh not other meanes to warn his officers, then with such terrible shot in so peaceable a countrey? Marry, saith he, he vttereth himselfe the better to be that officer whose name he beareth. I then demanded what prouince did he gouerne that needeth such an officer. Hee answered me, the prouince was not great in quantitie, but ancient in true nobilitie; a place, said he, priuileged by the most excellent princess, the high gouernour of the whole land, wherein are store of gentilmen of the whole realme, that repaire thither to learne to rule, and obey by laws, to yeelde their fleece to their prince and common weale, as also to vse all other exercises of bodie and minde whereunto nature most aptly serueth to adorne by speaking, countenance, gesture, and vse of apparel, the person of a gentleman; whereby amitie is obtained and continued, that gentilmen of al countries in theire young yeares, norished together in one place, with such comely order and daily conference, are knit by continual acquaintance in such vnitie of mindes and manners, as lightly neuer after

* *Dugd.* Orig. Jurid. p. 316. *Herbert* Antiq., p. 223 to 272.

is seuered, then which is nothing more profitable to the commonweale.

"And after he had told me thus much of honor of the place, I commended in mine own conceit the pollicie of the gouernour, which seemed to vtter in itselfe the foundation of a good commonweale. For that the best of their people from tender yeares trayned vp in precepts of justice, it could not chose but yeelde forth a profitable people to a wise commonweale. Wherefore I determined with myselfe to make proofe of that I heard by reporte.

"The next day I thought for my pastime to walke to this Temple, and entering in at the gates, I found the building nothing costly; but many comly gentlemen of face aud person, and thereto very courteous, saw I passe too and fro. Passing forward, I entered into a church of auncient building, wherein were many monumentes of noble personnages armed in knighteley habite, with their cotes depainted in auncient shieldes, whereat I took pleasure to behold . . . . .

"Anon we heard the noise of drum and fyfe. What meaneth this drumme? said I. Quod he, this is to warn gentlemen of the household to repaire to the dresser; wherefore come on with me, and yee shall stand where ye may best see the hall serued; and so from thence brought me into a long gallerie that stretcheth itselfe alongest the hall, neere the prince's table, where I saw the prince set, a man of tall personage, of mannelye countenance, somewhat browne of visage, strongelie featured, and thereto comelie proportioned. At the neather end of the same table were placed the ambassadors of diuers princes. Before him stood the caruer, seruer, and cup-bearer, with great number of gentlemen wayters attending his person. The lordes steward, treasorer, with diuers honorable personages, were placed at aside-table neere adjoyning the prince on the right hand, and at another table on the left side were placed the treasorer of the household, secretarie, the prince's serjeant of law, the four masters of the reaulles, the king of armes, the deane of the chapell, and diuers gentlemen pentioners to furnish the same. At another table, on the other side, were set the maister of the game, and his chiefe ranger, maisters of household, clerkes of the greene cloth and checke, with diuers other strangers to furnish the same. On the other side, againste them, began the table of the lieutenant of the Tower, accompanied with diuers captaines of footbandes and shot. At the neather ende of the hall, began the table of the high butler and panter, clerkes of the kitchen, maister cooke of the priue kitchen, furnished throughout with the souldiours and guard of the prince . . .

"The prince was serued with tender meates, sweet fruites, and daintie delicates, confectioned with curious cookerie, as it seemed woonder a word to serue the prouision. And at euerie course, the trompettes blew the courageous blaste of deadlye warre, with noise of drum and fyfe, with the sweet harmony of viollens, shakbuts, recorders, and cornettes, with other instruments of musicke, as it seemed Apolloe's harpe had tewned their stroke."

After dinner, prizes were prepared for "tilt and turney, and such knighteley pastime, and for their solace they masked with bewtie's dames with such heauenly armonie as if Apollo and Orpheus had shewed their cunning."[*]

Masques, revels, plays, and eating and drinking, seem to have been as much attended to in the Temple in those days as the grave study of the law. Sir Christopher Hatton, a member of the Inner Temple, gained the favour of Queen Elizabeth, for his grace and activity in a masque which was acted before her majesty. He was made vice-chamberlain, and afterwards lord chancellor![†] In A.D. 1568, the tragedy of Tancred and Gismund, the joint production of five students of the Inner Temple, was acted at the Temple before Queen Elizabeth and her court.[‡]

On the marriage of the Lady Elizabeth, daughter of King James I., to Prince Frederick, the elector palatine, (Feb. 14th, A.D. 1613), a masque was performed at court by the gentlemen of the Temple, and shortly after, twenty Templars were appointed barristers there in honour of Prince Charles, who had lately become prince of Wales, "the chardges thereof being defrayed by a contribution of xxxs. from each bencher, xvs. from euery barister of seauen years' standing, and xs. a peice from all other gentlemen in commons."[§]

Of all the pageants prepared for the entertainment of the sovereigns of England, the most famous one was that splendid masque, which cost upwards of £20,000, presented by the Templars, in conjunction with the members of Lincoln's Inn and Gray's Inn, to King Charles I., and his young queen, Henrietta of France. Whitelock, in his Memorials, gives a minute and most animated account of this masque, which will be read with interest, as affording a characteristic and admirable exhibition of the manners of the age.

The procession from the Temple to the palace of Whitehall was the most magnificent that had ever been seen in London. "One hundred gentlemen in very rich clothes, with scarce anything to be seen on them but gold and silver lace, were mounted on the best horses and the best furniture that the king's stable and the stables of all the noblemen in town could afford." Each gentleman had a page and two lacqueys in livery waiting by his horse's side. The lacqueys carried torches, and the page his master's cloak. "The richness of their apparel and furniture glittering by the light of innumerable torches, the motion

---

[*] *Leigh's* Armorie, fol. 119. ed. 1576.

[†] *Naunton's* Fragmenta Regalia, p. 248.

[‡] *Chalmer's* Diet. Biograph., vol. xvii. p. 227.

[§] *Dugd.* Orig. Jurid., p. 150. Ex registro Hosp. In. Temp. f. 123.

and stirring of their mettled horses, and the many and gay liveries of their servants, but especially the personal beauty and gallantry of the handsome young gentlemen, made the most glorious and splendid show that ever was beheld in England."

These gallant Templars were accompanied by the finest band of picked musicians that London could afford, and were followed by the *antimasque* of beggars and cripples, who were mounted on "the poorest, leanest jades that could be gotten out of the dirtcarts." The habits and dresses of these cripples were most ingeniously arranged, and as the "gallant Inns of Court men" had their music, so also had the beggars and cripples. It consisted of *keys, tongs, and gridirons,* "snapping and yet playing in concert before them." After the beggars' antimasque came a band of pipes, whistles, and instruments, sounding notes like those of birds, of all sorts, in excellent harmony; and these ushered in *"the antimasque of birds,"* which consisted of an owl in an ivy bush, with innumerable other birds in a cluster about the owl, gazing upon her. "These were little boys put into covers of the shape of those birds, rarely fitted, and sitting on small horses with footmen going by them with torches in their hands, and there were some besides to look unto the children, and these were very pleasant to the beholders." Then came a wild, harsh band of northern music, bagpipes, horns, &c., followed by the *"antimasque of projectors"* who were in turn succeeded by a string of chariots drawn by four horses a breast, filled with "gods and goddesses," and preceded by heathen priests. Then followed the chariots of the grand masquers drawn by four horses abreast.

The chariots of the Inner and Middle Temple were silver and blue. The horses were covered to their heels with cloth of tissue, and their heads were adorned with huge plumes of blue and white feathers. "The torches and flaming flamboys borne by the side of each chariot made it seem lightsom as at noonday . . . It was, indeed, a glorious spectacle."

Whitelock gives a most animated description of the scene in the banqueting-room. "It was so crowded," says he, "with fair ladies glittering with their rich cloaths and richer jewels, and with lords and gentlemen of great quality, that there was scarce room for the king and queen to enter in." The young queen danced with the masquers herself, and judged them "as good dancers as ever she saw!" The great ladies of the court, too, were "very free and easy and civil in dancing with all the masquers as they were taken out by them."

Queen Henrietta was so delighted with the masque, "the dances, speeches, musick, and singing," that she desired to see the whole thing *acted over again!* whereupon the lord mayor invited their majesties and all the Inns of Court men into the city, and entertained them with great state and magnificence at Merchant Taylor's Hall.*

Many of the Templars who were the foremost in these festive scenes afterwards took up arms against their sovereign. Whitelock himself commanded a body of horse, and fought several sanguinary engagements with the royalist forces.

The year after the restoration, Sir Heneage Finch, afterwards earl of Nottingham, kept his readers' feast in the great hall of the Inner Temple with extraordinary splendour. The entertainments lasted from the 4th to the 17th of August.

At the first day's dinner were several of the nobility of the kingdom and privy councillors, with divers others of his friends; at the second were the lord mayor, aldermen, and principal citizens of London; to the third, which was two days after the former, came the whole college of physicians, who all appeared in their caps and gowns; at the fourth were all the judges, advocates, and doctors of the civil law, and all the society of Doctors'Commons; at the fifth were entertained the archbishops, bishops, and chief of the clergy; and on the 15th of August his majesty King Charles the Second came from Whitehall in his state barge, and dined with the reader and the whole society in the hall. His majesty was accompanied by the duke of York, and attended by the lord chancellor, lord treasurer, lord privy seal, the dukes of Buckingham, Richmond, and Ormond; the lord chamberlain, the earls of Ossory, Bristol, Berks, Portland, Strafford, Anglesy, Essex, Bath, and Carlisle; the lords Wentworth, Cornbury, De la Warre, Gerard of Brandon, Berkley of Stratton and Cornwallis, the comptroller and vice-chamberlain of his majesties's household; Sir William Morice, one of his principal secretaries of state; the earl of Middleton, lord commissioner of Scotland, the earl of Glencairne, lord chancellor of Scotland, the earls of Lauderdale and Newburgh, and others the commissioners of that kingdom, and the earl of Kildare and others, commissioners of Ireland.

An entrance was made from the river through the wall into the Temple Garden, and his majesty was received on his landing from the barge by the reader and the lord chief justice of the Common Pleas, whilst the path from the garden to the hall was lined with the readers' servants in scarlet cloaks and white tabba doublets, and above them were ranged the benchers, barristers, and students of the society, "the loud musick playing from the time that his majesty landed till he entered the hall, where he was received with xx. violins." Dinner was brought up by fifty of the young gentlemen of the society in their gowns, "who gave their attendance all dinner-while, none other appearing in the hall but themselves."

On the 3rd of November following, his royal highness the duke of York, the duke of Buckingham, the earl of Dorset, and Sir William Morrice, secretary of state, were admitted members of the society of the Inner

---

* *Whitelock's* Memorials, p. 18—22. Ed. 1732.

Temple, the duke of York being called to the bar and bench.*

In 8 Car. II., A.D. 1668, Sir William Turner, lord mayor of London, came to the readers' feast in the Inner Temple with his sword and mace and external emblems of civic authority, which was considered to be an affront to the society, and the lord mayor was consequently very roughly handled by some of the junior members of the Temple. His worship complained to the king, and the matter was inquired into by the council, as appears from the following proceedings:

"At the Courte att Whitehall, the 7th April, 1669,

"Present the king's most excellent majestie."

H. R. H. the duke of York.	Lord bishop of London.
Lord Keeper.	Lord Arlington.
Duke of Ormonde.	Lord Newport.
Lord Chamberlaine.	Mr. Treasurer.
Earle of Bridgewater.	Mr. Vice-chamberlaine.
Earle of Bath.	Mr. Secretary Trevor.
Earle of Craven.	Mr. Chancellor of the Dutchy.
Earle of Middleton.	Mr. John Duncombe.

"Whereas, it was ordered the 31st of March last, that the complaints of the lord maior of the city of London concerneing personall indignities offered to his lordshippe and his officers when he was lately invited to dine with the reader of the Inner Temple, should this day have a further hearing, and that Mr. Hodges, Mr. Wyn, and Mr. Mundy, gentlemen of the Inner Temple, against whome particular complaint was made, sshould appeare att the board, when accordingly, they attendinge, and both parties being called in and heard by their counsell learned, and affidavits haveing been read against the said three persons, accuseing them to have beene the principall actors in that disorder, to which they haveing made their defence, and haveing presented severall affidavits to justifie their carriage that day, though they could not extenuate the faults of others who in the tumult affronted the lord maior and his officers; and the officers of the lord maior, who was alleaged to have beene abused in the tumult, did not charge it upon anie of their particular persons; upon consideration whereof it appeareing to his majestie that the matter dependinge very much upon the right and priviledge of beareing up the lord maior's sword within the Temple, which by order of this board of the 24th of March last is left to be decided by due proceedings of lawe in the courts of Westminster Hall; his majestie therefore thought fitt to suspend the declaration of his pleasure thereupon until the said right and priviledge shall accordinglie be determined att lawe."

On the 4th of November, 14 Car. II., his highness Rupert prince palatine, Thomas earl of Cleveland, Jocelyn lord Percy, John lord Berkeley of Stratton, with Henry and Bernard Howard of Norfolk, were admitted

---

* *Dugd.* Orig. p. 157. *Biog.* Brit. vol. xiv. p. 305.

members of the fellowship of the Inner Temple.*

We must now close our remarks on the Temple, with a short account of the quarrel with Dr. Micklethwaite, the custos or guardian of the Temple Church.

After the Hospitallers had been put into possession of the Temple by King Edward the Third, the prior and chapter of that order, appointed to the ancient and honourable post of custos, and the priest who occupied that office, had his diet in one or other of the halls of the two law societies, in the same way as the guardian priest of the Order of the Temple formerly had his diet in the hall of the ancient Knights Templars. He took his place, as did also the chaplains, by virtue of the appointment of the prior and chapter of the Hospital, without admission, institution or induction, for the Hospitallers were clothed with the privileges, as well as with the property, of the Knights Templars, and were exempt from episcopal jurisdiction. The custos had, as before mentioned, by grant from the prior and chapter of the Order of St. John, one thousand faggots a year to keep up the fire in the church, and the rents of Ficketzfeld and Cotterell Garden to be employed in improving the lights and providing for the due celebration of divine service. From two to three chaplains were also provided by the Hospitallers, and nearly the same ecclesiastical establishment appears to have been maintained by them, as was formerly kept up in the Temple by the Knights Templars. In 21 Hen. VII. these priests had divers lodgings in the Temple, on the east side of the churchyard, part of which were let out to the students of the two societies.

By sections 9 and 10 of the act 32 Hen. VIII., dissolving the Order of the Hospital of St. John, it is provided that William Ermsted, clerk, the custos or guardian of the Temple Church, who is there styled "Master of the Temple," and Walter Limseie and John Winter, chaplains, should receive and enjoy, during their lives, all such mansion-houses, stipends, and wages, and all other profits of money, in as large or ample a manner as they then lawfully had the same, the said Master and chaplains of the Temple doing their duties and services there, as they had previously been accustomed to do, and letters patent confirming them in their offices and pensions were to be made out and passed under the great seal. This appellation of "Master of the Temple," which anciently denoted the superior of the proud and powerful order of Knights Templars in England, the counsellor of kings and princes, and the leader of armies, was incorrectly applied to the mere custos or guardian of the Temple Church. The act makes no provision for the successors of the custos and chaplains, and Edward the Sixth consequently, after the decease of William Ermsted, conveyed the lodgings, previously appropriated to the officiating ministers, to a Mr. Keilway and his heirs, after which the custos and clergymen

* *Dugd.* Orig. p. 158.

had no longer of right any lodgings at all in the Temple.*

From the period of the dissolution of the Order of Saint John, down to the present time, the custos, or, as he is now incorrectly styled, "the Master of the Temple," has been appointed by letters patent from the crown, and takes his place as in the olden time, without the ceremony of admission, institution, or induction. These letters patent are couched in very general and extensive terms, and give the custos or Master many things to which he is justly entitled, as against the crown, but no longer obtains, and profess to give him many other things which the crown had no power whatever to grant. He is appointed, for instance, "to rule, govern, and superintend the house of the New Temple;" but the crown had no power whatever to make him governor thereof, the government having always been in the hands of the Masters of the bench of the two societies, who succeeded to the authority of the Master and chapter of the Knights Templars. In these letters patent the Temple is described as a rectory, which it never had been, nor anything like it. They profess to give to the custos "all and all manner of tythes," but there were no tythes to give, the Temple having been specially exempted from tythe as a religious house by numerous papal bulls. The letters patent give the custos all the revenues and profits of money which the custodes had at any time previously enjoyed by virtue of their office, but these revenues were dissipated by the crown, and the property formerly granted by the prior and chapter of Saint John, and by pious persons in the time of the Templars, for the maintenance of the priests and the celebration of divine service in the Temple Church was handed over to strangers, and the custos was thrown by the crown for support upon the voluntary contributions of the two societies. He received, indeed, a miserable pittance of 37l 6s. 8d. per annum from the exchequer, but for this he was to find at his own expense a minister to serve the church, and also a clerk or sexton !

As the crown retained in its own hands the appointment of the custos and all the ancient revenues of the Temple Church, it ought to have provided for the support of the officiating ministers, as did the Hospitallers of Saint John.

"The chardges of the fellowshyppe," says the MS. account of the Temple written in the reign of Hen. VIII., "towards the salary or mete and drink of the priests, is none; for they are found by my lord of Saint John's, and they that are of the fellowshyppe of the house are chardged with nothing to the priests, saving that they have eighteen offring days in the yeare, so that the chardge of each of them is xviiid."*

In the reign of James the First, the custos, Dr. Micklethwaite's, put forward certain unheard-of claims and pretensions, which led to a rupture between him and the two societies. The Masters of the bench of the soci-

* *Harleian* MS., No. 830

ety of the Inner Temple, taking umbrage at his proceedings, deprived the doctor of his place at the dinnertableland "willed him to forbear the hall till he was sent for." In 8 Car. I., A.D. 1633, the doctor presented a petition to the king, in which he claims precedence within the Temple "according to auncient custome, he being master of the house," and complains that "his place in the hall is denyed him and his dyett, which place the Master of the Temple hath ever had both before the profession of the lawe kept in the Temple and ever since, whensoever he came into the hall. That tythes are not payde him, whereas by pattent he is to have omnes et omnimodas deci-mas. ... That they denye all ecclesiastical jurisdiction to the Master of the Temple, who is appointedby the king's majesty master and warden of the house ad reyendum, gubernandum, et officiendum dornum et ecclesiam," &c. The doctor goes into a long list of grievances showing the little authority that he possessed in the Temple, that he was not summoned to the deliberations of the houses, and he complains that "they will give him no consideración in the Inner House for his supernumerarie sermons in the forenoon, nor for his sermons in the afternoon," and that the officers of the Inner Temple are commanded to disrespect the Master of the Temple when he comes to the hall."

The short answer to the doctor's complaint is, that the custos of the church never had any of the things which the doctor claimed to be entitled to, and it was not in the power of the crown to give them to him.

The ancient custos being, as before mentioned, a priest of the Order of the Temple, and afterwards of the Order of the Hospital, was a perfect slave to his temporal superiors, and could be deprived of his post, be condemned to a diet of bread and water, and be perpetually imprisoned, without appeal to any power, civil or ecclesiastical, unless he could cause his complaints to be brought to the ear of the pope. Dr. Micklethwaite quite misunderstood his position in the Temple, and it was well for him that the masters of the benches no longer exercised the despotic power of the ancient master and chapter, or he would certainly have been condemned to the penitential cell in the church, and would not have been the first custos placed in that unenviable retreat.*

The petition was referred to the lords of the council, and afterwards to Noy, the attorney-general, and in the mean time the doctor locked up the church and took away the keys. The societies ordered fresh keys to be made, and the church to be set open. Noy, to settle all differences, appointed to meet the contending parties in the church, and then alluding to the pretensions of the doctor, he declared that if he were visitor he would proceed against him *tanquam elatus et superbus.*

In the end the doctor got nothing by his petition.

In the time of the Commonwealth, after Dr. Micklethwaite's death, Oli-

* MS. Bib. *Cotton.* Vitellius, c. 9. fol. 320 a.

ver Cromwell sent to inquire into the duties and emoluments of the post of "Master of the Temple," as appears from the following letter:

"From his highness I was commanded to speake with you for resolution and satisfaction in theise following particulers—

"1. Whether the Master of the Temple be to be putt in him by way of presentation, or how?

"2. Whether he be bound to attend and preach among them in terme times and out of terme?

"3. Or if out of terme an assistant must be provided? then, whether at the charge of the Master, or how otherwise?

"4. Whether publique prayer in the chapell be allwayes performable by the Master himselfe in terme times? And whether in time of vacation it be constantly expected from himselfe or his assistant.

"5. What the certain revenue of the Master is, and how it arises?

"6. Sir, the gentleman his highness intends to make Master is. Mr. Resburne of Oundle, a most worthy and learned man, pastor of the church there, whereof I myselfe am an unworthy member.

"7. The church would be willing (for publique good) to spare him in terme times, but will not part with him altogether. And in some of the particulers aforementioned Mr. R. is very desirous to be satisfyd; his highness chiefly in the first.

"8. I begg of you to leave a briefe answer to the said partienlars, and I shall call on your servant for it.

"For the honourable Henry Scobell, esq., theise."†

During the late repair of the Temple Church, A.D. 1830, the workmen discovered an ancient seal of the Order of the Hospital, which was carried away, and appears to have got into the hands of strangers. On one side of it is represented the holy sepulchre of Jerusalem, with the Saviour in his tomb. At his head is an elevated cross, and above is a tabernacle or chapel, from the roof of which depend two incense pots. Around the seal is the inscription, "Fr—— Berengarii Custos Pauperum Hospitalis Jherusalem." On the reverse a holy man is represented on his knees in the attitude of prayer before a patriarchal cross, on either side of which are the letters Alpha and Omega. Under the first letter is a star.

These particulars have been furnished me by Mr. Savage, the architect.

THE END.

* See the examination of Brother Radulph de Barton, priest of the Order of the Temple, and custos of the Temple Church, before the papal inquisitors at London.—*Concil Mag. Brit.*, tom. ii. p. 335, 338, ante, p. 221, 222.

† *Peck*, Desiderata Curiosa, lib. xiii. p. 504, 505. Ed. 1779.